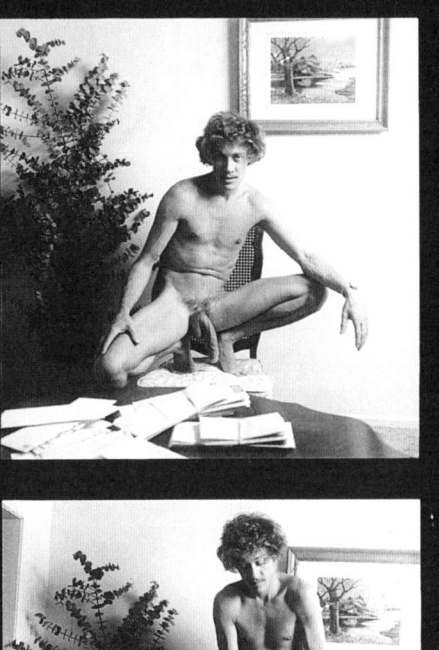

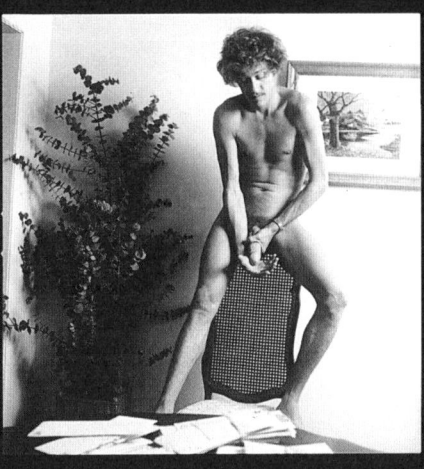
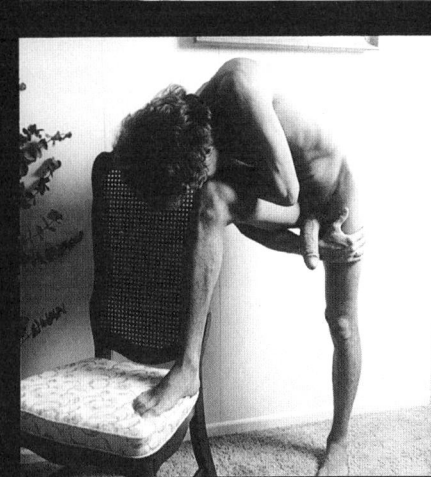
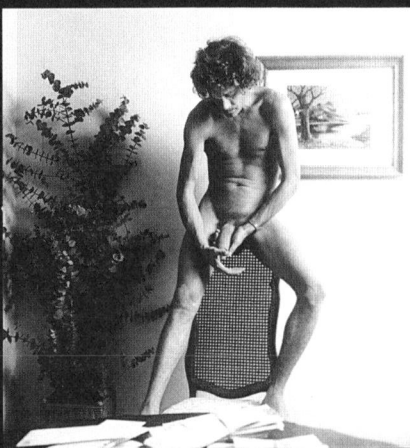
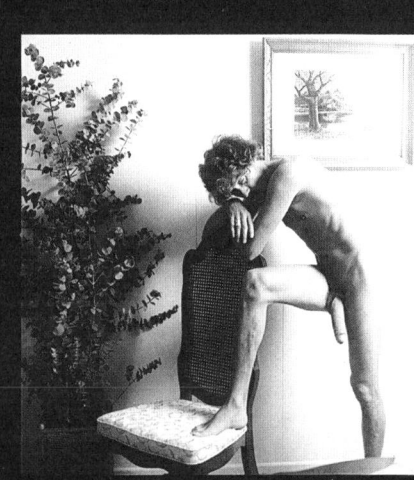

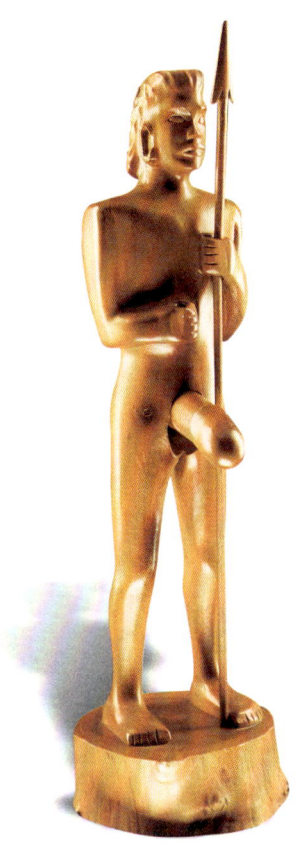

"Surely the book all other
books have been leading up to
since Gutenberg invented
the printing press."
— *GSCENE*, LONDON

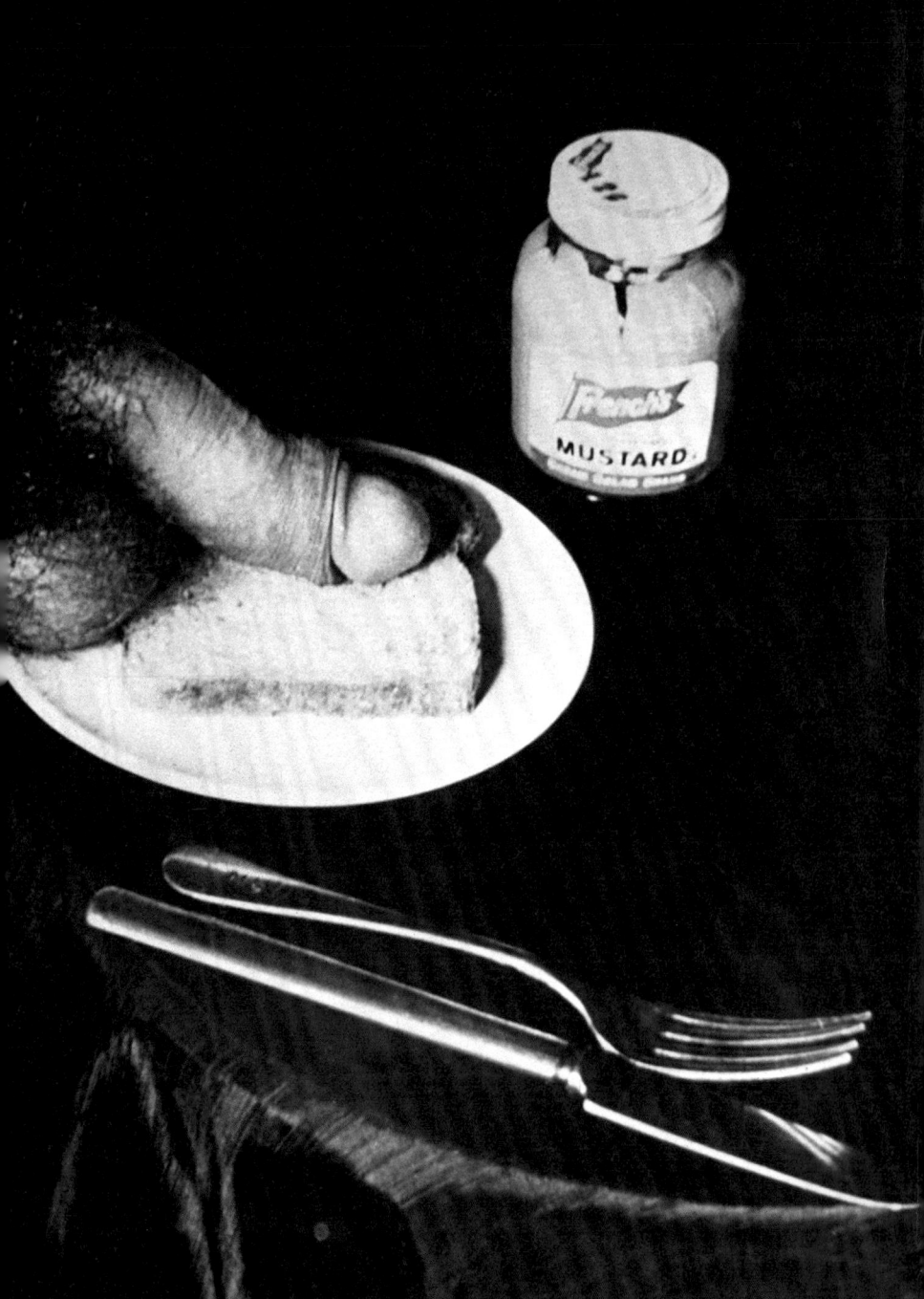

DIAN HANSON

THE LITTLE
Big Penis
BOOK

The Compact Age
of Rigid Tools

TASCHEN

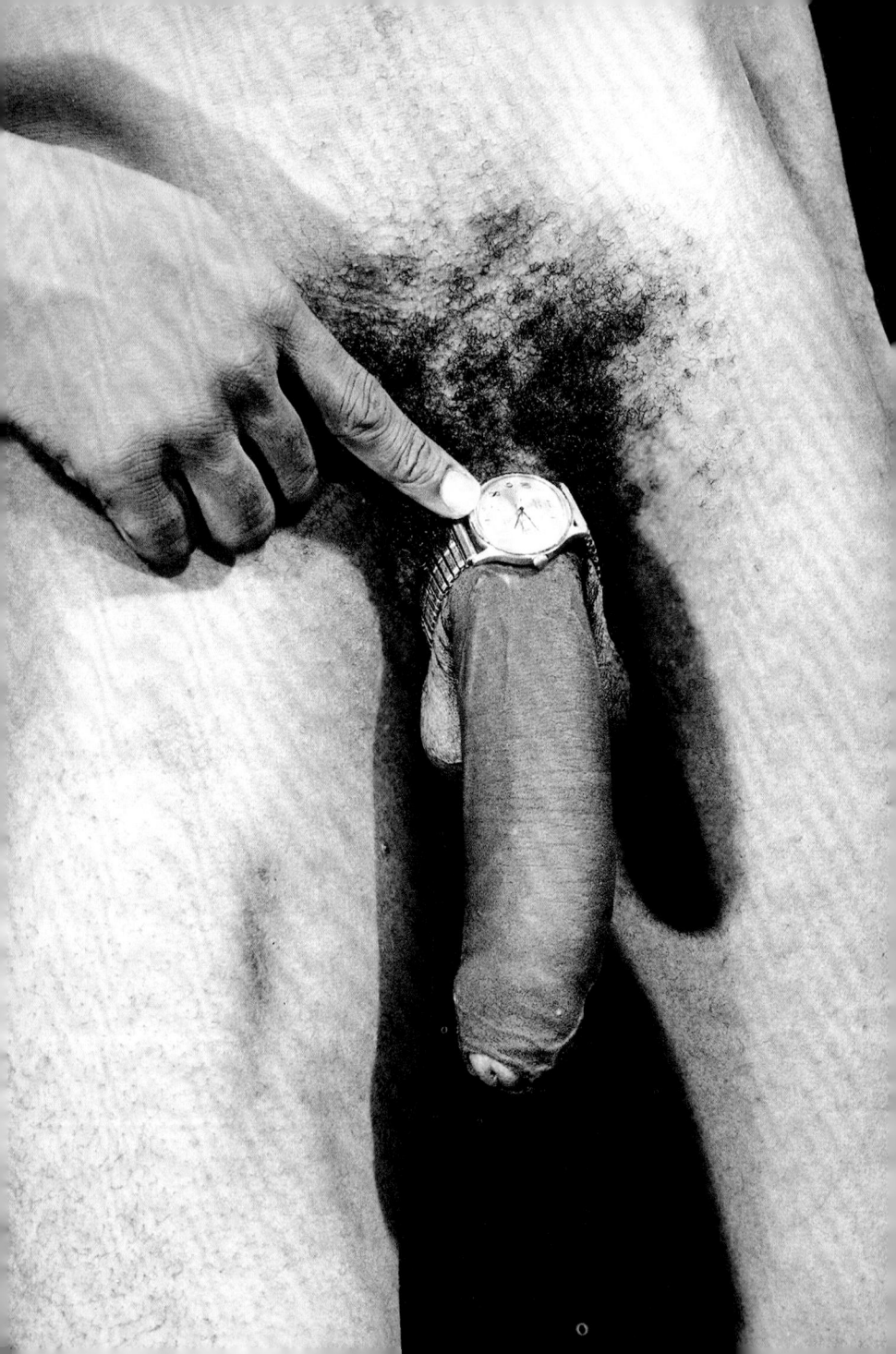

OK, SIZE DOESN'T REALLY MATTER.
A caring, sensitive lover can satisfy his partner with a penis of any size and can certainly satisfy himself. A big penis doesn't make a man more of a man, just as a small penis doesn't make him any less.

Penis Time

BY DIAN HANSON

No racial or ethnic group is uniformly large and no group is uniformly small. Women, we are constantly assured, care nothing about penis size. Men may be more candid, but there are also male fans of the small penis, either as a symbol of youth or for its amazing ability to make one's own penis look larger.

All that out of the way, who can deny the allure of a big dick? Flaccid or erect, it is esthetically stunning — commanding every onlooker to consider capacity and consequence. Many viewing the photos for this book blurted out, "I wouldn't let that near me!" As if anyone were offering. Everyone takes the big penis personally, as an object of fear, arousal, and endless fascination, that last derived from the Latin *fascinum*, meaning both *phallus* and *magical spirit*. Big shoulders, big lapels, and big hair may come and go, but the big penis never goes out of fashion.

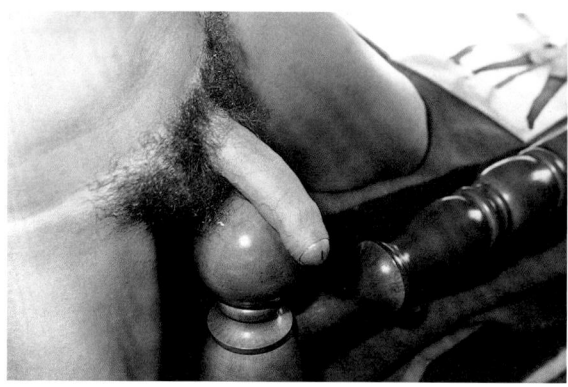

In photography, however, female nudes have always been more common than male, and the blame rests largely on the penis. This graphic and all too obvious sex organ may fascinate, but it also offends delicate temperaments, ruins the graceful flowing lines of the body, and has long marked the dividing line between art and obscenity.

The German "body culture" movement of the early 20th century helped to legitimize the penis in photography. You weren't a nudist without exposed genitals, so the early naturist magazines were penis friendly. Nudist philosophy also glorified the robust, unspoiled peasant, who became a popular subject for photographers. German cousins Wilhelm von Gloeden and Guglielmo Pluschow found their noble peasants in Italy, earning surprising acclaim back in Berlin for their homoerotic photos of young Sicilians.

Under the Weimar regime Germany continued its acceptance of male nudity, which was portrayed in dozens of body-culture magazines, many with overt gay themes. This unequalled tolerance was due largely to Magnus Hirschfeld's Wissenschaftlich-humanitäre Komitee (Scientific-Humanitarian Committee), publishers of the world's first gay rights magazine in 1899. Not all citizens shared Hirschfeld's progressive views, however. On May 10, 1933, following Adolf Hitler's appointment as chancellor, students burned the contents of Hirschfeld's Berlin library, destroying 40 years of research and 10,000 books and magazines. Following the book burning German nudist magazines were returned to a purely health and fitness theme, still filled with heroically naked men, but with no hint of sexuality.

The first bodybuilding magazines were launched at about the same time as the nudist titles. Bernarr Macfadden's *Physical Culture*, also founded in 1899, was the raciest of the early muscle mags, but while Macfadden enjoyed parading across its pages in a leopard loincloth, he railed against homosexuality as the depth of moral decay. Other bodybuilders were less conflicted. Tony Sansone, the premier muscleman of the 1930s, posed for highly erotic photos by Edwin F. Townsend to support himself through

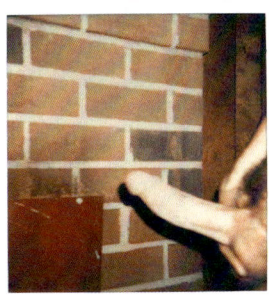

the Depression, then married and opened a string of gyms in New York City. The basic narcissism of bodybuilders benefited a broad range of photographers in the following decades. While George Platt Lynes, Cecil Beaton, Herbert List, and George Hoyningen-Huene won acceptance for "physique" nudes in the art world, the average beefcake fan found satisfaction in fitness magazines.

Bob Hoffman's *Strength & Health* debuted in 1932. Though Hoffman was as macho as Macfadden, telling *Fortune* magazine in 1947 that his strength required two girlfriends, his magazine showed a bit less homophobia. Up front were the articles on weight routines, illustrated by photos of oiled, near-naked young men, while in the back pages were ads for photos you wouldn't find in the local art gallery.

Athletic Model Guild, Warner Studios, Al Urban, Bruce of Los Angeles, Lon of New York — their ads in *Strength & Health* promised "handsome young men" in "artistic poses" full of "drama, form, and tension." The intended audience had no trouble understanding the code. Neither

did the US Postal Service, which bullied the magazine into removing the physique photography ads in 1950. This so displeased Bob Mizer at Athletic Model Guild that he launched his own magazine the following year.

Physique Pictorial was not openly gay and initially included no nudity, but neither did it contain articles on barbell routines. Its contents were simply photos and artwork of handsome young men in brief posing straps smiling provocatively at the viewer. It was a bold move in conservative post-war America, but because Mizer kept the penises carefully covered he managed to stay in business and inspire a host of imitators.

By the late '50s physique titles selling alongside the muscle magazines included *Trim Studio Quarterly*, *Tomorrow's Man*, *Vim*, and Joe Weider's *Adonis*, *Demi-Gods*, *The Young Physique*, and *Body Beautiful*. There were still no penises, but it was perfectly clear that these magazines were for the pleasure of gay men, and this pissed off the postal authorities.

The post office has served as America's censor since 1873, when the government gave anti-obscenity crusader Anthony

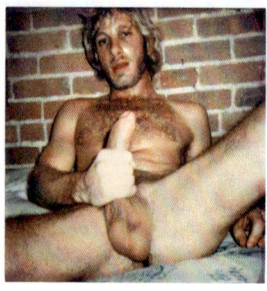

Comstock control of the mail. Under the Comstock laws it remains illegal to send anything "obscene, lewd, or lascivious" through the mails, with the interpretation of obscenity left to postal authorities. The U.S. Postal Service won many obscenity convictions through the years, but in 1960 it went after the wrong deviant.

Herman Lynn Womack was the 300-pound albino publisher of *Grecian Guild Pictorial*, *MANual*, and *Trim* physique magazines. When he was convicted of obscenity for publishing photos of bare buttocks in *MANual* he avoided prison by claiming insanity, based on the American Psychiatric Association's definition of homosexuality as a mental illness. The court gave him 18 months in St. Elizabeth's Hospital for the Insane, where he continued to run his magazines from a private room and plot his attack on the postal service.

In the case known as *MANual v. Day*, Womack sued U.S. Postmaster General J. Edward Day for return of his mailing rights. He lost in federal District Court and Court of Appeals, but succeeded in getting his case tried before the U.S. Supreme Court. On June 25, 1962, Womack won a reversal of his obscenity conviction — the first ever against the post office. More significantly, the precedent set by *MANual v. Day* prohibited courts from judging photos of men by different criteria than photos of women, even if those photos appealed to so-called "deviant" tastes. From that day on it was only a matter of time before the penis escaped the posing strap.

It took a few more years, many more court cases, the sexual revolution, and the introduction of the adult bookstore to accomplish it, but in 1968 penises first appeared in frankly sexual U.S. magazines, albeit veiled under sheer fabric. The next year, following Stonewall and formation of the Gay Liberation Front, the penis went totally bare. In 1970 full erections could be found in the adult bookstores and by 1975 naked men were right out on the newsstand.

Predictably, this sudden freedom brought a flood of explicit new magazines, dooming the physique titles and

"Big shoulders, big lapels, and big hair may come and go, but the big penis never goes out of fashion."

most of their creators. New photographers emerged, mostly untrained young men with fantasies, cameras, and the nerve to approach prospective models in the street, as there were no talent agencies for beefcake. Young hustlers were a staple, found on Market Street in San Francisco and along Selma Avenue in Hollywood: $15 or $20 would get a man to pose, $15 more would buy sex, for those who were interested. Tricking with models was common in the '70s, sometimes with dire consequences. Photographers were beaten, robbed, and even killed by men paid to pose for them — dangers unknown in the cheesecake world — and yet they continued, intoxicated with sudden independence, drunk on sexual autonomy, the lure of the next hot model, and the fascination of the phallus.

For this book I've chosen to concentrate on photographers active during this first exhilarating burst of freedom, spanning the period from 1968 through the early '90s. Their studio names are well known to many who came of age in the post-physique magazine era. Just as Womack's

modest bodybuilders helped the previous generation discover its true self, photos of exuberantly naked hustlers by AMG, Colt, Falcon, Old Reliable, Sierra Domino, and others showed young men of the '70s and '80s that somewhere there were men just like them.

Except with very, very large penises.

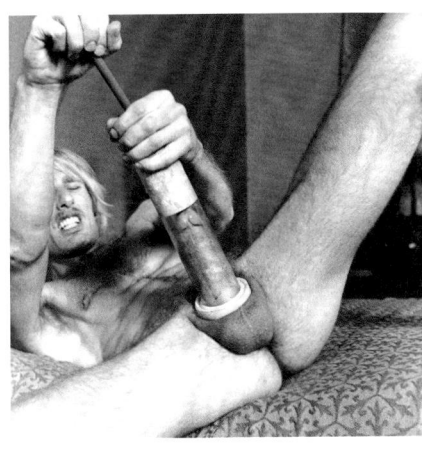

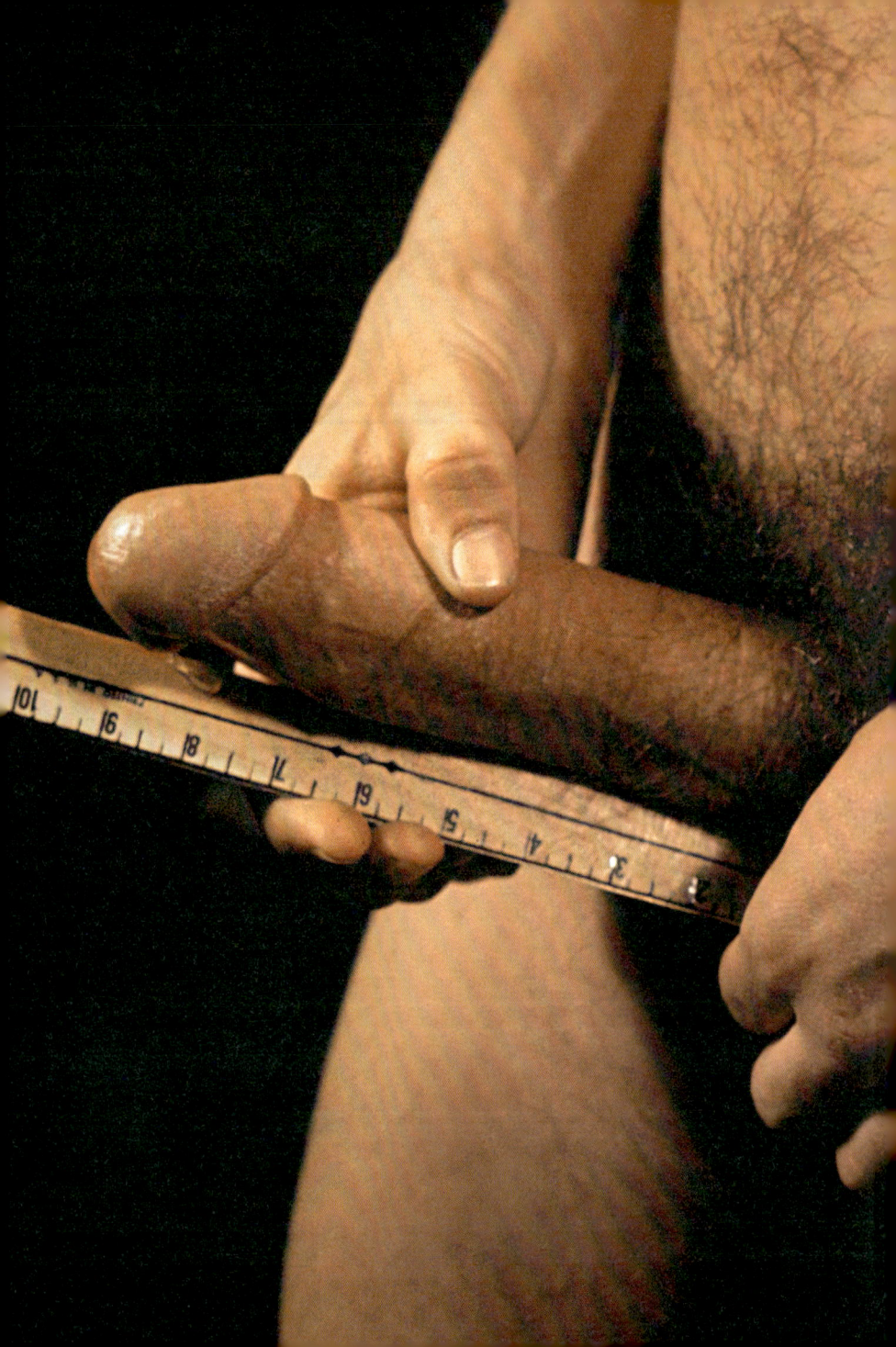

NA GUT, ES KOMMT NICHT WIRKLICH AUF DIE GRÖSSE AN.
Ein zärtlicher, einfühlsamer Liebhaber kann seinem
Partner oder seiner Partnerin – und erst recht sich
selbst – immer Genuss und Befriedigung verschaffen,
egal wie groß sein Penis ist.

Penispause

VON DIAN HANSON

Ein großer Schwanz macht einen Mann nicht zu einem besseren Mann und ein kleiner nicht zu einem geringeren. Es gibt auch keine ethnische Gruppe, in der alle Männer besonders groß oder klein bestückt sind. Frauen, so wird uns permanent versichert, sei die Penisgröße ohnehin egal. Männer mögen da etwas aufrichtiger sein, doch es gibt auch unter Männern Fans kleiner Penisse, sei es, weil sie so knabenhaft wirken, oder weil sie den eigenen Schwanz größer erscheinen lassen.

Doch wer will die Anziehungskraft eines großen Schwanzes ernsthaft leugnen? Ob schlaff oder erigiert, ein großer Penis ist ein atemberaubender Anblick und zwingt jeden Betrachter, sich Gedanken über sein Leistungsvermögen und seine Wirkung zu machen – oder was am Ende dabei rauskommt. So mancher, der die Bilder für diesen Band vorab betrachtete, rief erschrocken aus: „Mein Gott, so was würd ich niemals an mich ranlassen!" Große Penisse nimmt jeder persönlich, ob angstbesetzt oder als Objekt der

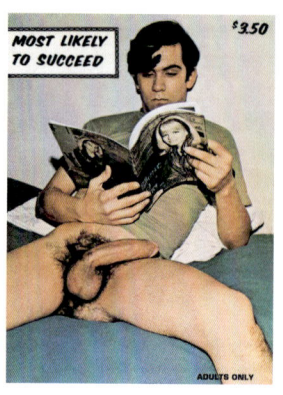

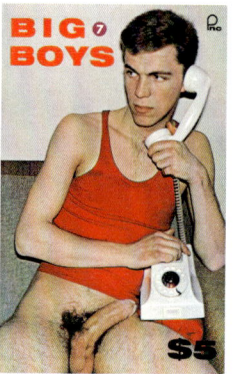

Begierde und grenzenlosen Faszination. Letzteres leitet sich übrigens vom lateinischen *fascinum* her, was sowohl „Phallus" wie „behexend" bedeutet.

In der Fotografie waren nackte Frauen seit jeher ein wesentlich häufigerer Anblick als nackte Männer, was vor allem am Penis liegt. So faszinierend dieses Geschlechtsorgan auch sein mag, es sticht doch so aggressiv ins Auge, dass es sensiblere Gemüter verschreckt und die sanft fließenden Konturen des menschlichen Körpers stört. Über lange Zeit markierte das männliche Glied in der Fotografie die Grenzlinie zwischen Kunst und Pornografie.

Erst die deutsche FKK-Bewegung zu Beginn des 20. Jahrhunderts befreite den Penis aus diesem Schattendasein. Wenn man nicht gänzlich alles zeige, was man hatte, war man auch kein echter Nudist, daher zeigten sich die frühen FKK-Magazine durchwegs penisfreundlich. Zugleich glorifizierte die Freikörperkultur den robusten, unverdorbenen Körper des einfachen Burschen vom Land. Die deutschen Vettern Wilhelm von Gloeden und

Wilhelm Plüschow etwa fanden ihre edlen Wilden in Italien und ernteten für ihre homoerotischen Fotos junger Sizilianer in Berlin einen überraschend großen Beifall.

Die tolerante Haltung der Weimarer Republik zum Männerakt schlug sich in zahllosen FKK-Magazinen nieder, von denen viele unverhohlen an eine schwule Leserschaft adressiert waren. Diese bis dato beispiellose Toleranz ist zum großen Teil Magnus Hirschfeld und seinem Wissenschaftlich-humanitären Komitee zu verdanken, das bereits 1899 die erste Zeitschrift für Schwulenrechte publizierte. Diese progressive Geisteshaltung fand mit der Machtergreifung Adolf Hitlers 1933 jäh ein Ende. Am 10. Mai 1933 verbrannten fanatisierte Schüler und Studenten in Berlin auch Hirschfelds gesamtes Archiv mit rund 10.000 Büchern und Zeitschriften und vernichteten die Früchte von 40 Jahren Forschungsarbeit. Nach der Bücherverbrennung wurden auch die FKK-Magazine gleichgeschaltet und widmeten sich nur noch Themen der Leibeszucht und Volksgesundheit; nackte

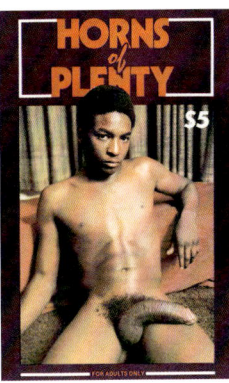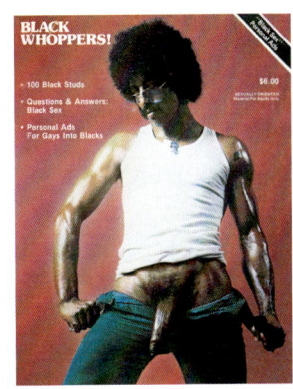

Männer sah man zwar immer noch, aber nun in heroischen Posen und ohne jede Andeutung der sexuellen Natur.

Die ersten Bodybuilding-Magazine tauchten ungefähr zur gleichen Zeit auf wie die Nudistentitel. Bernarr Macfaddens *Physical Culture*, ebenfalls 1899 ins Leben gerufen, war das gewagteste dieser frühen Blätter, doch obwohl Macfadden sich gerne im Lendenschurz aus Leopardenfell in Szene und ins Heft setzte, zog er doch zugleich gegen die Homosexualität als Abgrund moralischer Verkommenheit vom Leder. Andere Bodybuilder waren da weniger engstirnig. Tony Sansone, der angesagteste Muskelmann der 1930er, ließ sich von Edwin F. Townsend in überaus erotischen Posen ablichten, um gut durch die Zeit der Wirtschaftskrise zu kommen, heiratete dann und eröffnete in New York eine Kette von Sportstudios. Der vielen Bodybuildern eigene Narzissmus kam in den folgenden Jahrzehnten einer breiten Palette von Fotografen zugute. Während Männer wie George Platt Lynes, Cecil Beaton, Herbert List oder George

Hoyningen-Huene für ihre „Physique"-Akte in der Kunstszene Anerkennung fanden, hielt sich der durchschnittliche Fan leicht bekleideten Männerfleisches an die Bodybuilding-Magazine.

Bob Hoffmans *Strength & Health* erschien erstmals 1932. Obwohl Hoffman nicht weniger machohaft war als Macfadden und dem Magazin *Fortune* 1942 verriet, dass er zwei Freundinnen für seine Manneskraft benötige, zeigte sich sein Blatt doch nicht ganz so homophob. Während sich die Artikel, illustriert mit Fotos eingeölter, fast nackter junger Männer, ganz dem Kraftsport widmeten, wurden hinten im Anzeigenteil Fotos angeboten, die man wohl kaum in einer Kunstgalerie fand.

Die Anzeigen von Athletic Model Guild, Warner Studios, Al Urban, Bruce of Los Angeles oder Lon of New York in *Strength & Health* versprachen „knackige junge Burschen" in „künstlerischen Posen" voller „Dynamik, Ausdruck und Spannung". Das angesprochene Publikum hatte keine Schwierigkeiten, diesen Code zu entschlüsseln. Der US Postal Service, die

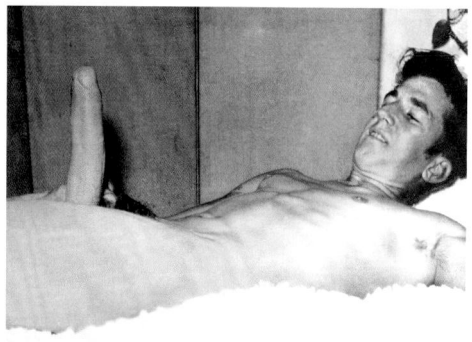

oberste Zensurbehörde des Landes, allerdings auch nicht. Sie zwang das Magazin in den 1950er-Jahren, den Abdruck solcher Anzeigen einzustellen. Das ärgerte Bob Mizer von der Athletic Model Guild so sehr, dass er ein Jahr später sein eigenes Magazin an den Start brachte.

Physique Pictorial war nicht offen schwul und präsentierte anfangs auch keine Nacktheit, aber es brachte auch keine Artikel über den Kraftsport. Es zeigte einfach Fotos von jungen Männern in knappen Posing-Straps, die provokant in die Kamera grinsten. Das war ein wagemutiger Schritt im konservativen Amerika der Nachkriegszeit. Da Mizer aber sorgsam darauf achtete, dass der Penis stets bedeckt war, hielt er sich am Markt und inspirierte zahllose Nachahmer.

Ende der 1950er-Jahre erschienen neben den Bodybuilding-Magazinen Titel wie *Trim Studio Quarterly*, *Tomorrow's Man*, *Vim* und Joe Weiders *Adonis*, *Demi-Gods*, *The Young Physique* und *Body Beautiful*, die zwar allesamt noch keine Schwänze zeigten, aber eindeutig an Schwule adressiert waren, was die Postbehörden alarmierte.

Die Post fungierte seit 1873 als Zensurbehörde, als die US-Regierung Anthony Comstock, dem notorischen Anstoßnehmer und Kreuzritter gegen die Lust, die Gewalt über das Postwesen gab. Comstock setzte durch, dass der Postversand von allem, was „obszön, anstößig oder schlüpfrig" war, verboten wurde, wobei es der Post überlassen blieb, wie diese Begriffe zu definieren waren. Über Jahrzehnte hinweg erwirkte der US Postal Service zahllose Verurteilungen wegen der Verbreitung von Pornografie, doch 1960 legte er sich mit dem Falschen an.

Herman Lynn Womack, ein 136 Kilogramm schwerer Albino, brachte die „Physique"-Titel *Grecian Guild Pictorial*, *MANual* und *Trim* heraus. Als er wegen Pornografie verurteilt werden sollte, weil er in *MANual* nackte Männerhintern abgedruckt hatte, entging er der Haftstrafe, indem er auf geistige Unzurechnungsfähigkeit plädierte. Dabei konnte er sich auf die American Psychiatrist Association berufen, die Homosexualität zu einer Geisteskrankheit erklärt hatte. Das Gericht verurteilte ihn zu 18 Monaten in

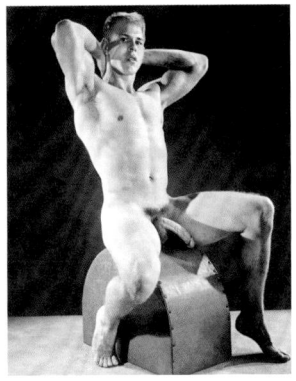

der Nervenklinik St. Elizabeth's Hospital. Von dort aus verlegte er weiter seine Magazine und plante seinen Rachefeldzug gegen die Post.

In dem als *MANual v. Day* bekannten Prozess klagte Womack gegen den US Postmaster General J. Edward Day, um seine Hefte wieder mit der Post verschicken zu dürfen. Nach zwei Niederlagen in unteren Instanzen brachte er seinen Fall vor den US Supreme Court. Am 25. Juni 1962 wurde das Urteil gegen ihn aufgehoben – es war das erste Mal, dass die Post in einem derartigen Verfahren unterlag. Der Präzedenzfall *MANual v. Day* hinderte Gerichte von nun an daran, Aktbilder von Männern anders zu bewerten als Aktbilder von Frauen, auch wenn diese Fotos auf sogenannte abartige Vorlieben verwiesen. Von nun an war es nur noch eine Frage der Zeit, bis die Schwänze den Posing-Straps entschlüpfen würden.

Es waren noch einige Jahre, eine Reihe von Gerichtsverfahren, die sexuelle Revolution und die Erfindung des Sexshops vonnöten, um dieses Ziel zu erreichen, doch 1968 waren erstmals Penisse in amerikanischen Sex-Magazinen zu sehen, wenngleich noch unter hauchdünnen Textilien verborgen. Ein Jahr darauf, nach Stonewall und der Gründung der Gay Liberation Front, fiel auch dieser letzte Schleier. 1970 konnte man in Sexshops schon volle Erektionen bewundern, und 1975 eroberte der nackte Mann schließlich sogar den Zeitungskiosk um die Ecke.

Die plötzliche Freiheit brachte eine Fülle einschlägiger neuer Publikationen hervor, die für die traditionellen „Physique"-Titel und ihre Verleger das Aus bedeuteten. Neue Fotografen erschienen auf der Szene, vorwiegend junge Männer ohne fotografische Vorkenntnisse, dafür aber bewaffnet mit einer Kamera, Fantasie und dem Mumm, potenzielle Modelle auf der Straße anzusprechen, denn Modell-Agenturen für Beefcake gab es nicht. Junge Stricher stellten das Gros der Modelle. Sie fanden sich auf der Market Street in San Francisco oder an der Selma Avenue in Hollywood; für 15 bis 20 Dollar ließen sie sich fotografieren, für weitere 15 Dollar flachlegen. Sex mit Modellen war in den 1970er-Jahren gang und gäbe, oftmals mit

„Ob schlaff oder erigiert, ein großer Penis ist ein atemberaubender Anblick."

bitteren Konsequenzen. Fotografen wurden zusammengeschlagen, ausgeraubt und einige gar ermordet, Gefahren, die in der Welt des Cheesecake, der Arbeit mit weiblichen Modellen, unbekannt waren. Dennoch machte die Mehrzahl weiter, berauscht von der plötzlichen Unabhängigkeit, der sexuellen Freizügigkeit, den Lockungen des nächsten Modells und der Faszination des Phallus.

Für dieses Buch habe ich mich auf Fotografen konzentriert, die in dieser ersten rauschhaften Phase neu gewonnener Freiheit aktiv waren, in dem Zeitraum zwischen 1968 bis Anfang der 1990er-Jahre. Ob AMG, Colt, Falcon, Old Reliable oder etwa Sierra Domino, die Namen ihrer Studios haben für viele, die in der Ära nach den klassischen „Physique"-Titeln großgeworden sind, einen magischen Klang. So wie Womacks sittsame Muckimänner dereinst der Generation davor geholfen hatten, ihr wahres Selbst zu entdecken, zeigten nun gut bestückte Stricher jungen Männern der 1970er- und 1980er-Jahre, dass es da draußen Männer genau wie sie gab – allerdings mit sehr, sehr großen Schwänzen.

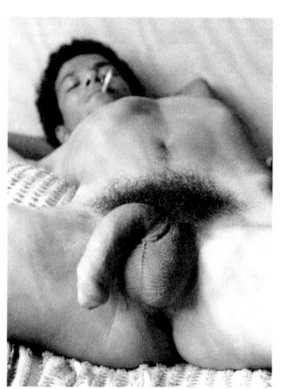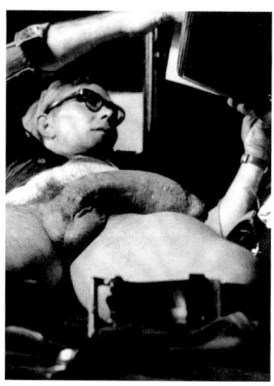

FAR LEFT AND LEFT Unknown models, circa 1968. The Magazine Archives, SF.

OPPOSITE Unknown penis impresses its partner, circa 1975.

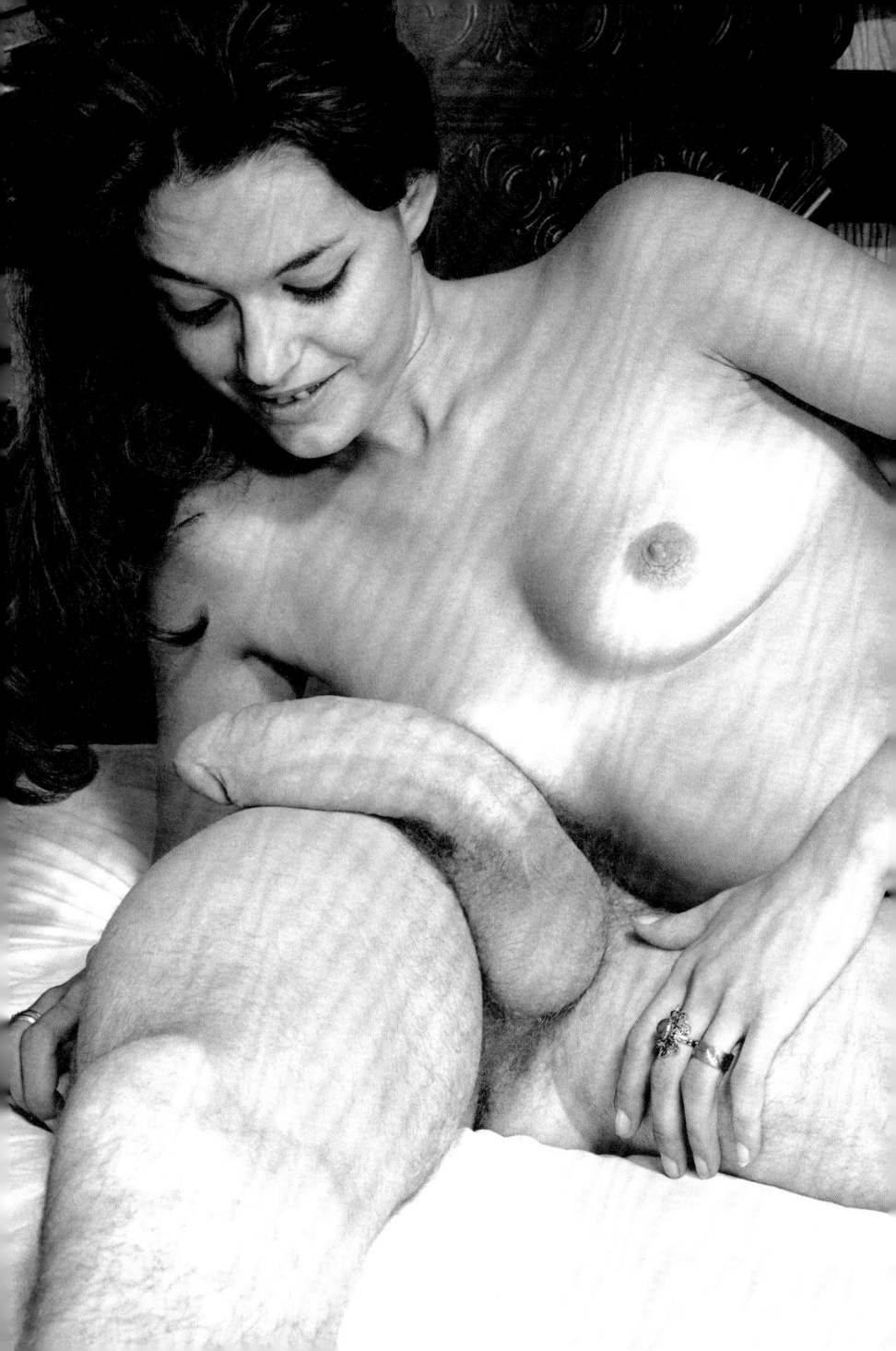

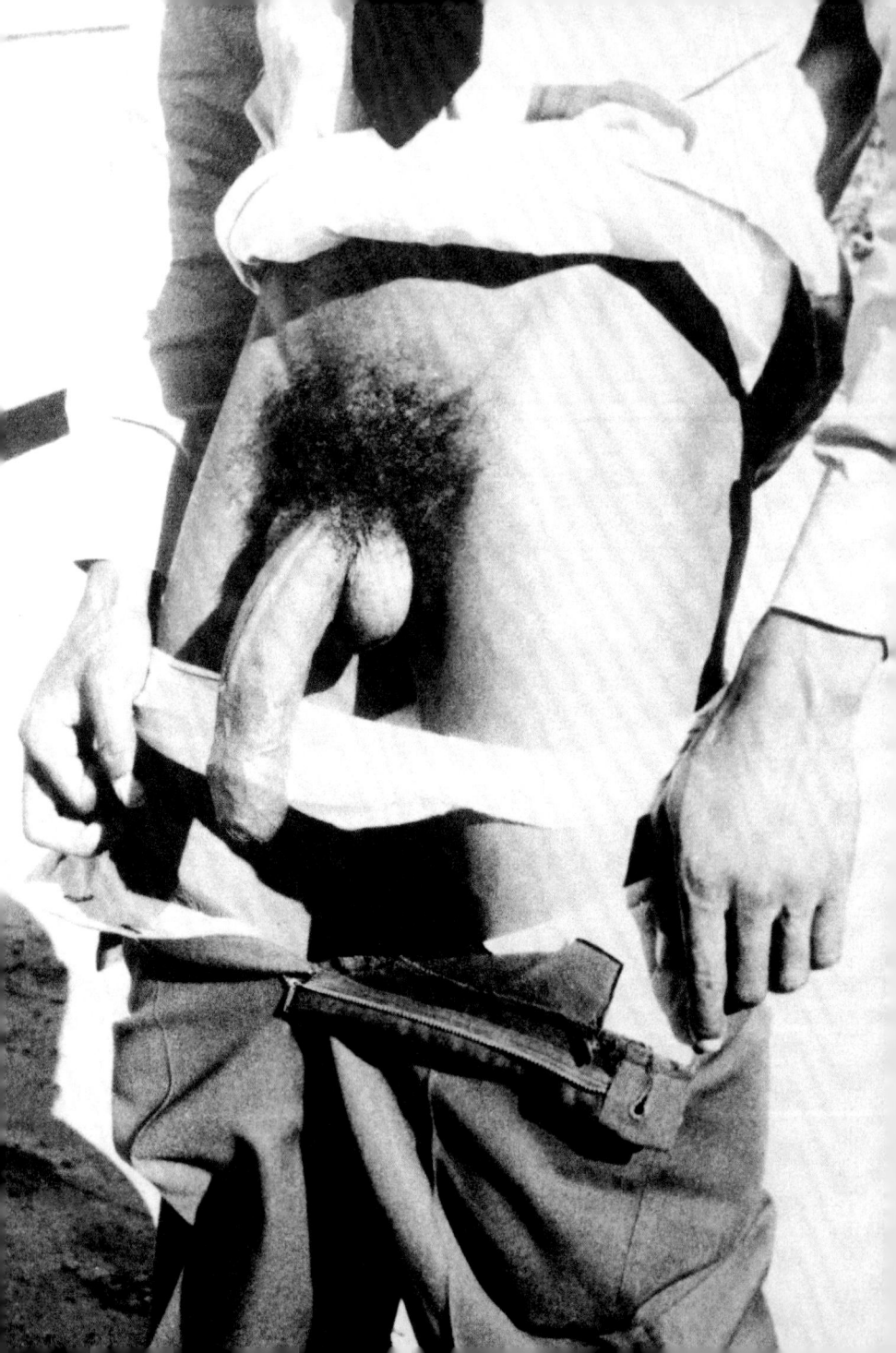

BON D'ACCORD, LA TAILLE COMPTE.
Un amant tendre et attentionné saura satisfaire son
ou sa partenaire (et *a fortiori* se satisfaire) quelle
que soit la taille de son pénis. Un homme ne l'est pas
davantage parce qu'il a une grosse verge, et il ne l'est
pas moins parce qu'il en a une petite.

Pause Pénis

PAR DIAN HANSON

Aucun groupe ethnique n'est spécialisé dans les gros calibres, aucun dans les petits. Pour les femmes, nous assure-t-on, la taille du pénis n'a pas d'importance. Quant aux hommes, peut-être plus francs sur la question, certains apprécient les sexes de dimensions modestes, soit parce qu'ils rappellent la jeunesse, soit parce que le leur paraît plus gros en comparaison.

Une fois cela mis de côté, peut-on vraiment nier l'attrait qu'exerce une grosse bite ? Flasque ou dure, elle est d'un esthétisme saisissant, et engage chaque personne qui la regarde à imaginer ses compétences et capacités. Le gros pénis ne laisse personne indifférent, qu'il provoque appréhension, excitation ou fascination — terme dérivé du latin *fascinum*, signifiant à la fois « phallus » et « esprit magique ». Les épaulettes, les revers larges et les cheveux longs, ça va et ça vient, mais les gros pénis, eux, ne passent jamais de mode.

En photographie, cependant, les nus féminins ont toujours été plus prisés que les masculins, en grande partie à cause

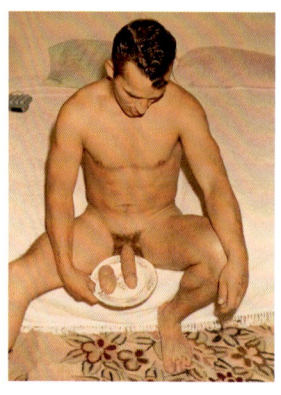

du pénis. Cet organe sexuel proéminent, indécent, provocant peut fasciner, mais il choque aussi les tempéraments délicats ; il casse la fluidité des lignes corporelles et marque souvent la frontière entre art et obscénité.

Dans les années 1920, le mouvement allemand de la Culture du corps libre a participé à la légitimation du pénis en photographie. Impossible d'être nudiste sans exposer ses parties génitales, si bien que tous les magazines naturistes de la première heure n'hésitaient pas à en montrer. La philosophie nudiste glorifiait le paysan rustique et robuste, qui devint un sujet traditionnel pour les photographes. Les cousins allemands Wilhelm von Gloeden et Guglielmo Plüschow allaient trouver leurs modèles en Italie, et leurs photos homoérotiques de jeunes Siciliens remportèrent un succès surprenant à Berlin.

L'acceptation de la nudité masculine se poursuivit sous la République de Weimar, pendant laquelle parurent des dizaines de magazines nudistes traitant souvent de thèmes ouvertement homosexuels.

Cette tolérance inégalée était en grande partie l'œuvre du Comité scientifique humanitaire de Magnus Hirschfeld (Wissenschaftlich-humanitäres Komitee), qui publia le tout premier magazine de défense des droits des homosexuels en 1899. Tous les citoyens allemands ne partageaient bien sûr pas les opinions progressistes de Hirschfeld. Le 10 mai 1933, après l'avènement d'Adolf Hitler au poste de chancelier, des étudiants mirent le feu à la bibliothèque berlinoise de Hirschfeld, réduisant ainsi en cendres quarante années de recherches et 10 000 livres et magazines. Après cet autodafé, les magazines nudistes allemands revinrent à un contenu tourné vers le culte du corps, toujours illustré de photos d'hommes nus et héroïques, mais sans une once de sexualité.

Les premiers magazines de culturisme furent lancés à peu près au même moment que les publications nudistes. *Physical Culture* de Bernarr Macfadden, également fondé en 1899, était le plus corsé de ces titres, mais si Macfadden aimait parader dans les pages de son

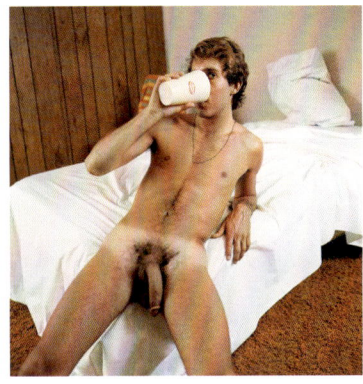 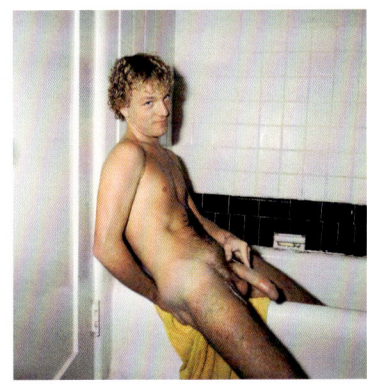

magazine simplement vêtu d'un pagne léopard, il clamait aussi que l'homosexualité était la pire des déviances morales. D'autres culturistes avaient moins d'états d'âme. Ainsi Tony Sansone, premier Monsieur Muscle des années 1930, posa sous l'objectif d'Edwin F. Townsend pour des photos hautement érotiques afin de survivre à la Grande Dépression, avant de se marier et d'ouvrir une série de salles de sport à New York. Le narcissisme fondamental des culturistes servit un large éventail de photographes au cours des décennies suivantes. Tandis que George Platt Lynes, Cecil Beaton, Herbert List et George Hoyningen-Huene gagnaient la reconnaissance du milieu artistique grâce à leurs nus « physiques », les magazines culturistes offraient toute satisfaction à l'amateur lambda de beaux paquets.

Le magazine *Strength & Health* de Bob Hoffman parut en 1932. Même si Hoffman était aussi macho que Macfadden – en 1947, il déclara au magazine *Fortune* qu'il lui fallait deux petites amies pour satisfaire sa virilité –, son titre était un peu moins homophobe. Les premières pages fournissaient des conseils pour se façonner un corps d'Apollon, illustrés par des photos de jeunes garçons huilés et quasi nus, et les dernières étaient remplies de petites annonces permettant de se procurer des photos que les galeries d'art locales n'exposaient pas.

Les annonces publiées dans *Strength & Health* par l'Athletic Model Guild, les studios Warner, Al Urban, Bruce de Los Angeles ou Lon de New York promettaient aux lecteurs « de beaux jeunes gens » dans des « poses artistiques » où se mêlaient « spectaculaire, forme et tension ». Les lecteurs ciblés n'avaient aucun mal à décoder le message… et les services postaux américains non plus, qui forcèrent le magazine à supprimer les annonces pour photos culturistes en 1950. Cette censure fâcha tant Bob Mizer, de l'Athletic Model Guild, qu'il lança son propre magazine l'année suivante.

Physique Pictorial n'était pas ouvertement gay et n'exposait au départ aucune nudité, mais il ne proposait pas non plus d'articles sur les exercices d'haltères. Son contenu se résumait à des photos

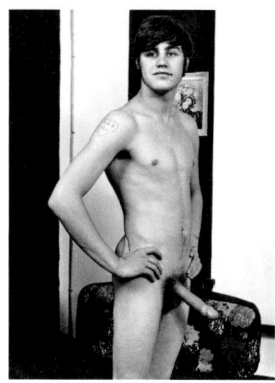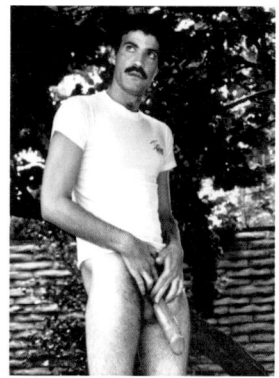

et œuvres picturales représentant de « beaux jeunes gens » au sourire aguicheur. La démarche était osée dans l'Amérique conservatrice de l'après-guerre, mais comme Mizer veillait à couvrir les verges, il parvint à faire durer son titre et en inspira pléthore d'autres.

À la fin des années 1950, plusieurs publications dédiées au corps paraissaient aux côtés des magazines culturistes, parmi lesquelles *Trim Studio Quarterly*, *Tomorrow's Man*, *Vim*, *l'Adonis* de Joe Weider, *Demi-Gods*, *The Young Physique* et *Body Beautiful*. Les pénis étaient toujours cachés, mais ces titres étaient clairement destinés à assouvir les désirs des hommes homosexuels, ce qui ne manqua pas d'agacer à nouveau les services postaux.

L'autorité postale servait de censeur aux États-Unis depuis 1873, date à laquelle le gouvernement confia le contrôle du courrier à Anthony Comstock, pourfendeur d'obscénité devant l'Éternel. La loi Comstock interdit ainsi l'envoi par la poste de tout objet « obscène, lubrique ou lascif », les services postaux ayant toute

latitude pour juger ce qui l'était ou pas. L'US Postal Service a remporté beaucoup de procès pour atteinte aux bonnes mœurs au fil des années, mais en 1960, il s'est attaqué au mauvais débauché.

Herman Lynn Womack, albinos de 136 kg, était le directeur des magazines *Grecian Guild Pictorial*, *MANual* et *Trim*. Lorsqu'il fut inculpé pour avoir publié des photos de fesses nues dans *MANual*, il évita la prison en plaidant la folie, basant sa défense sur la définition de l'homosexualité comme maladie mentale par l'Association américaine de psychiatrie. Le tribunal le condamna à dix-huit mois d'internement à l'hôpital psychiatrique St. Elizabeth. À l'abri dans sa chambre individuelle, il continua à diriger ses magazines, et fomenta sa vengeance contre la Poste américaine.

Ce fut l'affaire *MANual* contre Day : Womack poursuivit l'inspecteur général des Postes J. Edward Day pour exiger le respect de ses droits en tant qu'usager des services postaux. Il perdit devant le tribunal fédéral, puis en appel, mais réussit à présenter son cas devant la Cour

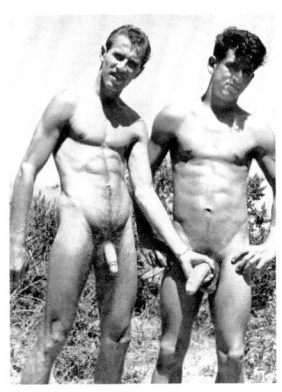

suprême. Le 25 juin 1962, Womack eut la joie de voir sa condamnation annulée – un premier revers historique pour la Poste américaine qui fit jurisprudence et interdit dès lors aux tribunaux de s'appuyer sur des critères différents pour juger les photos d'hommes et de femmes, même si ces photos satisfaisaient des penchants considérés comme déviants. La libération du pénis n'était plus qu'une question de temps.

Pour y parvenir, il fallut encore quelques années et bien d'autres avancées judiciaires, puis la révolution sexuelle et l'apparition des librairies pour adultes, mais en 1968 les premiers pénis s'exhibèrent dans des magazines américains à la thématique sexuelle assumée, bien qu'encore voilés par des tissus d'une finesse suggestive. L'année suivante, après les émeutes de Stonewall et la formation du Gay Liberation Front, le pénis se dénuda enfin. En 1970 les premières érections firent leur apparition dans les librairies spécialisées et en 1975 les hommes nus avaient atteint les têtes de gondole.

Cette liberté soudaine provoqua bien sûr une déferlante de magazines érotiques qui envoyèrent aux oubliettes les magazines culturistes à la papa et la plupart de leurs créateurs. De nouveaux photographes émergèrent, le plus souvent des jeunes gens inexpérimentés mais dotés d'une imagination fertile, d'appareils photo, et de l'aplomb nécessaire pour aborder des modèles potentiels dans la rue, puisqu'il n'existait pas alors d'agence spécialisée dans les beaux paquets. Les petits gigolos foisonnaient sur Market Street, à San Francisco, et le long de Selma Avenue, à Hollywood, qui acceptaient de poser pour 15 ou 20 dollars et couchaient pour 15 de plus. Le mélange des genres était fréquent à l'époque, ce qui avait parfois des conséquences terribles. Les photographes se faisaient tabasser, dépouiller et parfois tuer par des hommes qu'ils avaient payés pour poser – ce n'est pas dans le milieu de la pin-up que cela arriverait – et pourtant ils continuaient leur quête dangereuse, intoxiqués par leur indépendance, accros à l'autonomie sexuelle, à la traque

« **Les épaulettes, les revers larges et les cheveux longs, ça va et ça vient, mais les gros pénis, eux, ne passent jamais de mode.** »

du prochain modèle bandant, à la fascination du phallus.

Pour ce livre, j'ai choisi de me concentrer sur les photographes actifs pendant cette explosion exaltante de liberté, entre 1968 et le début des années 1990. Leurs noms d'artistes sont connus de ceux qui ont atteint l'âge adulte après l'avènement des magazines dits « de charme ». Tout comme les innocents culturistes de Womack ont aidé la génération précédente à découvrir son identité réelle, les photos de jeunes prostitués prises par AMG, Colt, Falcon, Old Reliable, Sierra Domino et d'autres ont montré aux jeunes garçons des années 1970 et 1980 qu'il existait, quelque part, des hommes comme eux.

À part qu'eux avaient des pénis très, très gros.

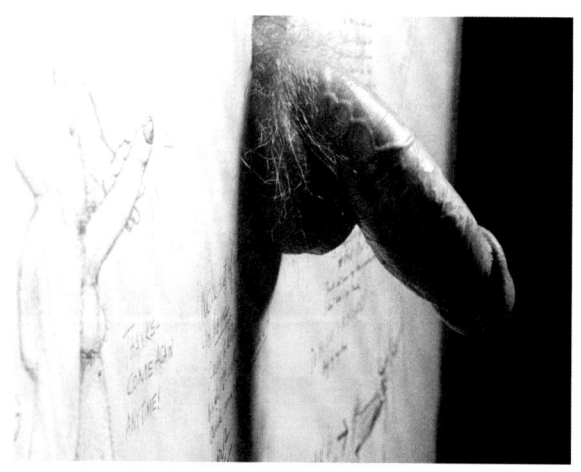

LEFT The glory hole, which allowed people to enjoy truly anonymous sex, was an institution of the 1970s. The Magazine Archives, SF.

OPPOSITE A large perfect penis in its natural state, circa 1970. The Magazine Archives, SF.

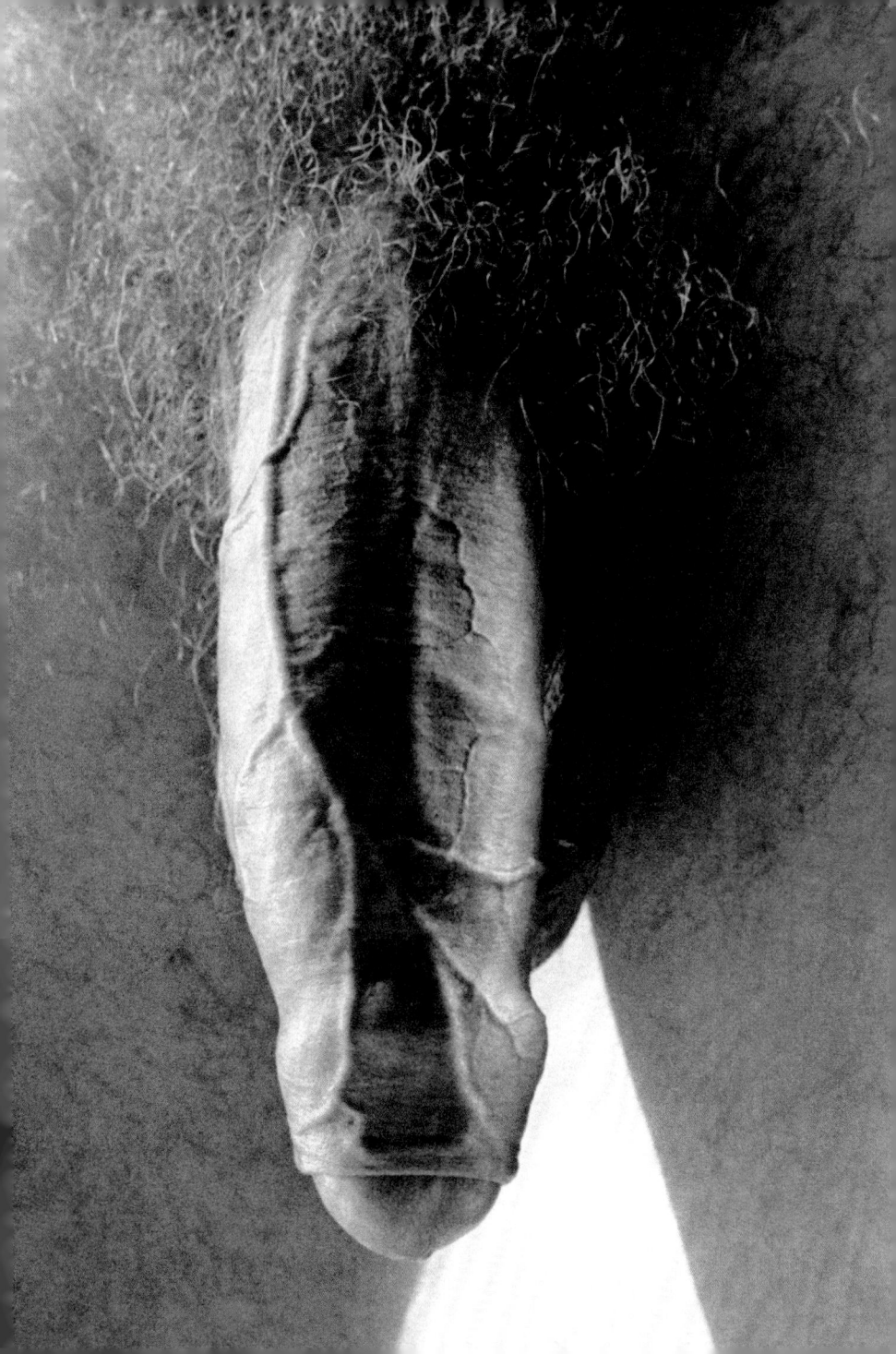

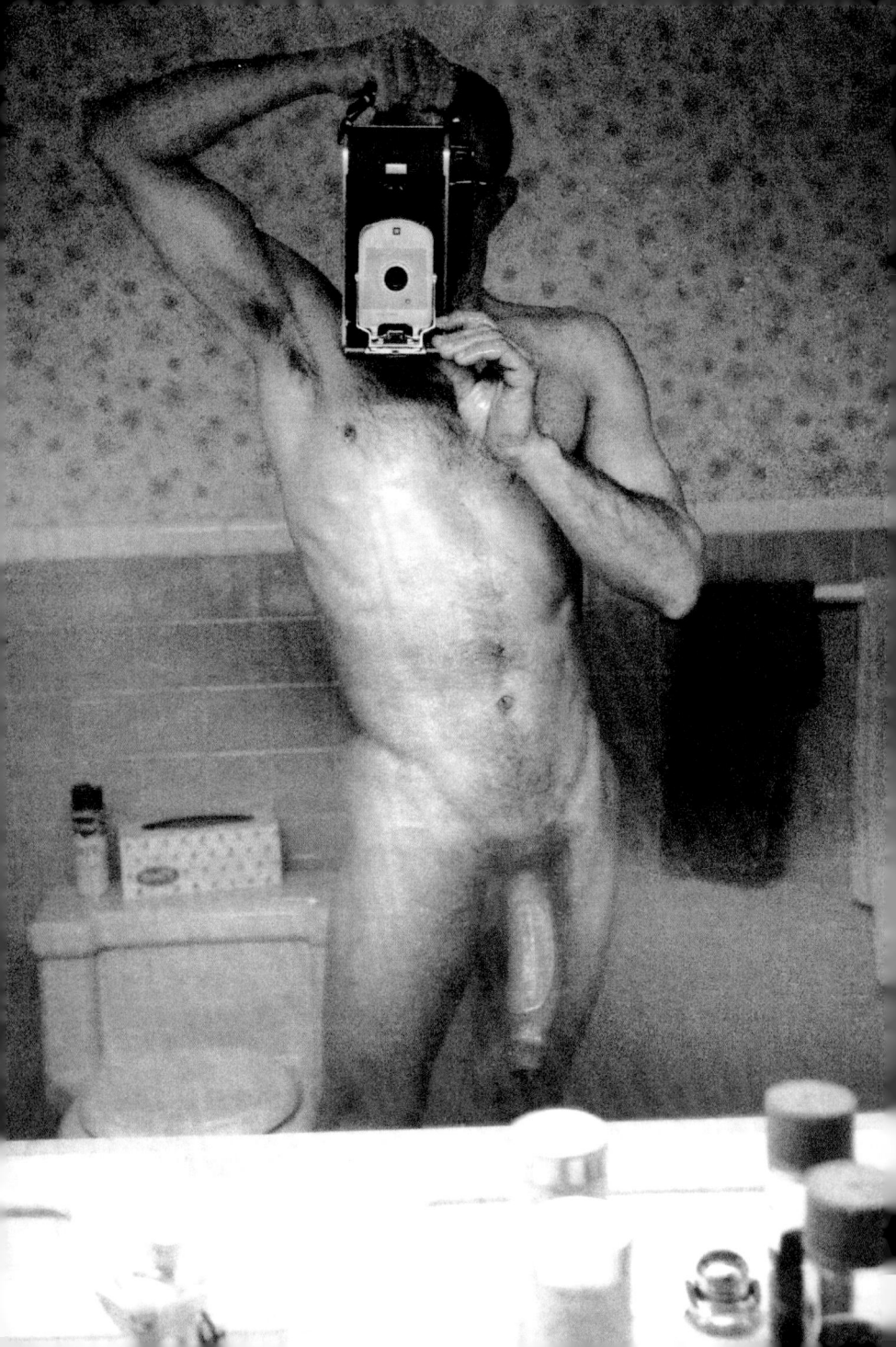

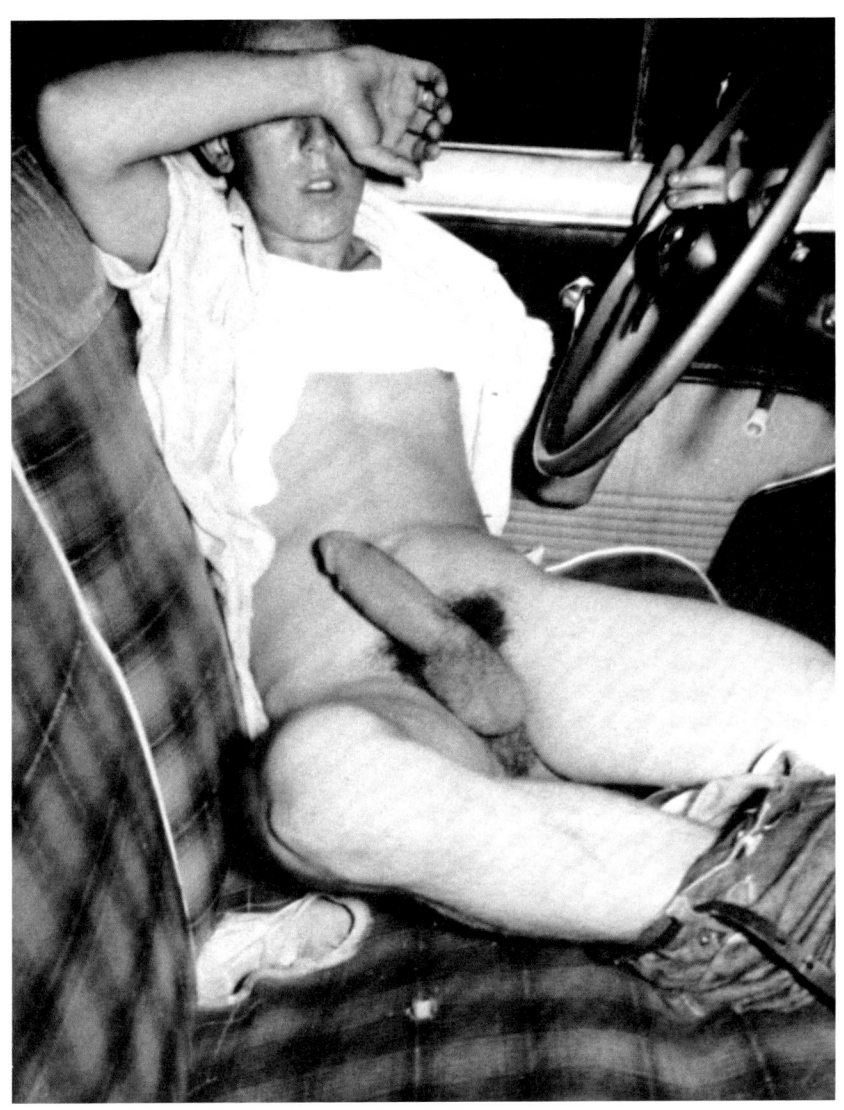

OPPOSITE AND ABOVE **Unknown**

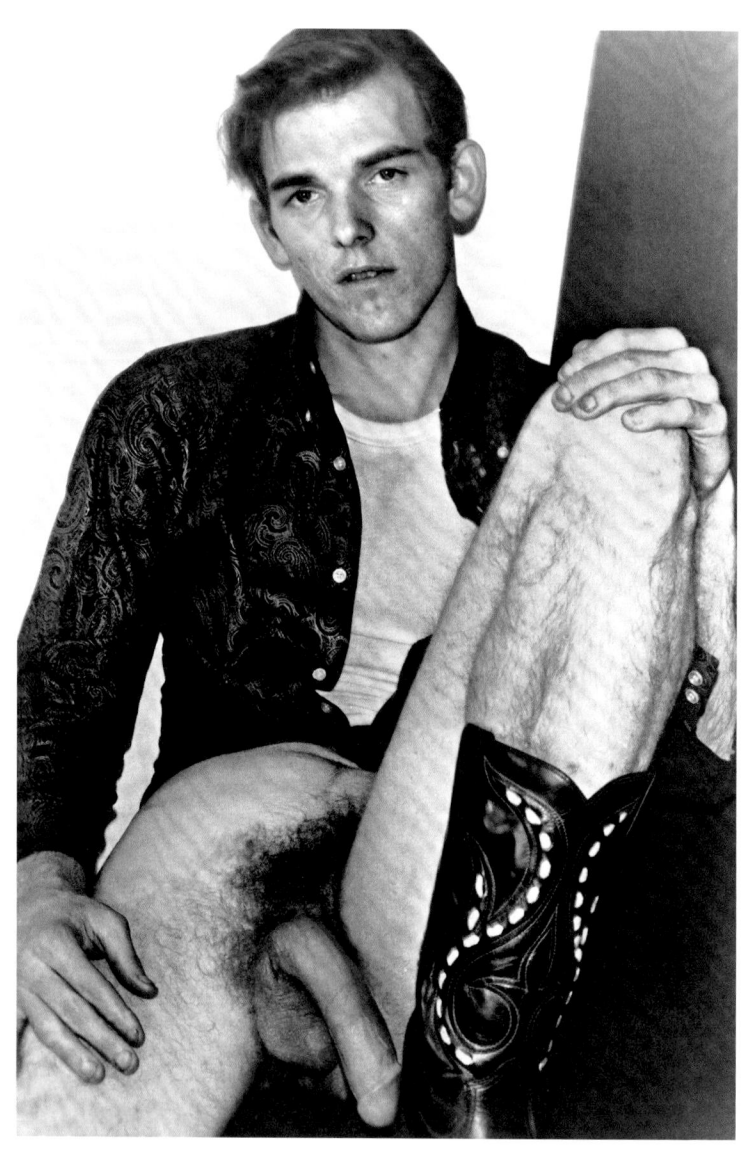

ABOVE AND OPPOSITE **Unknown**

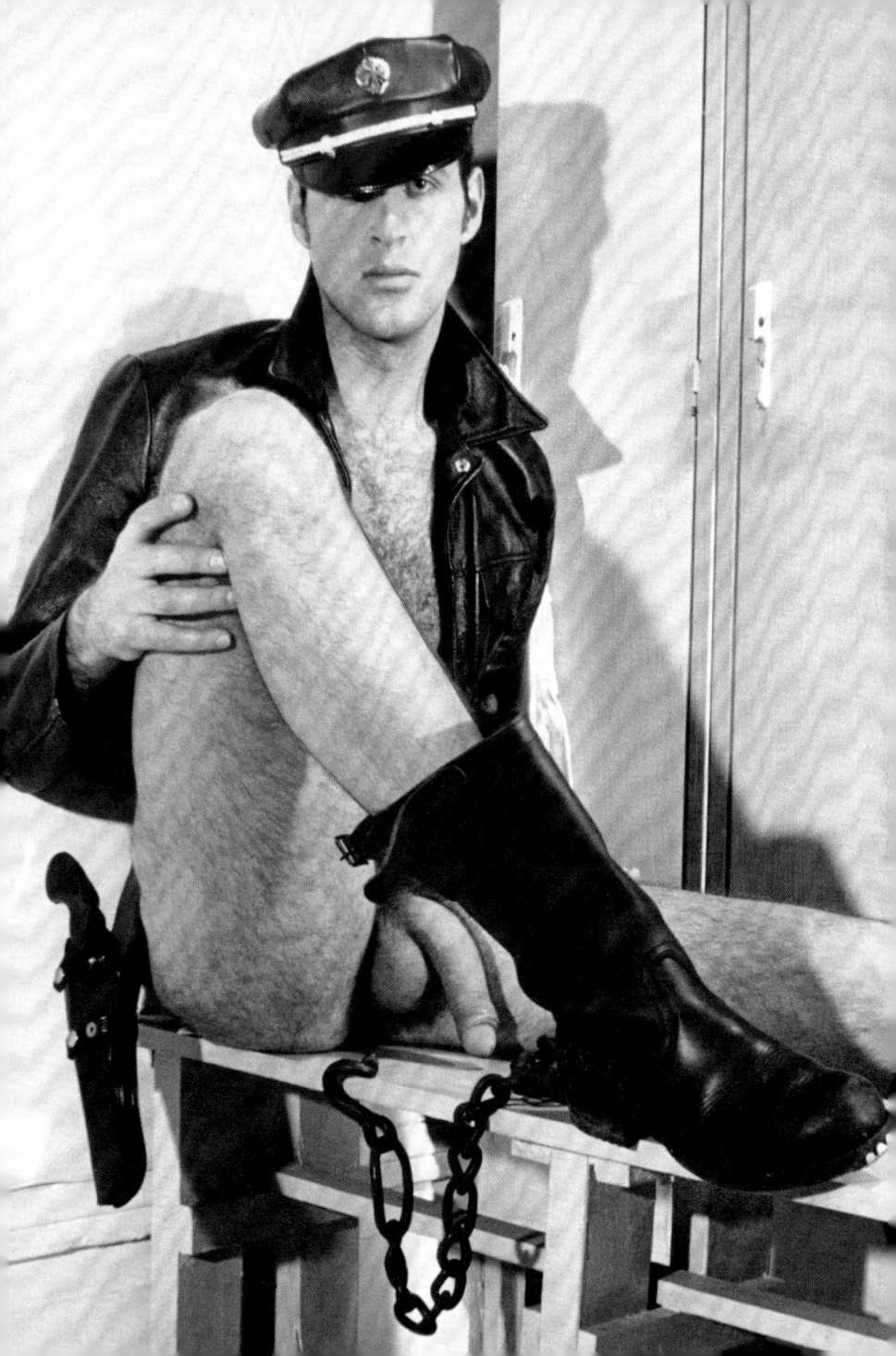

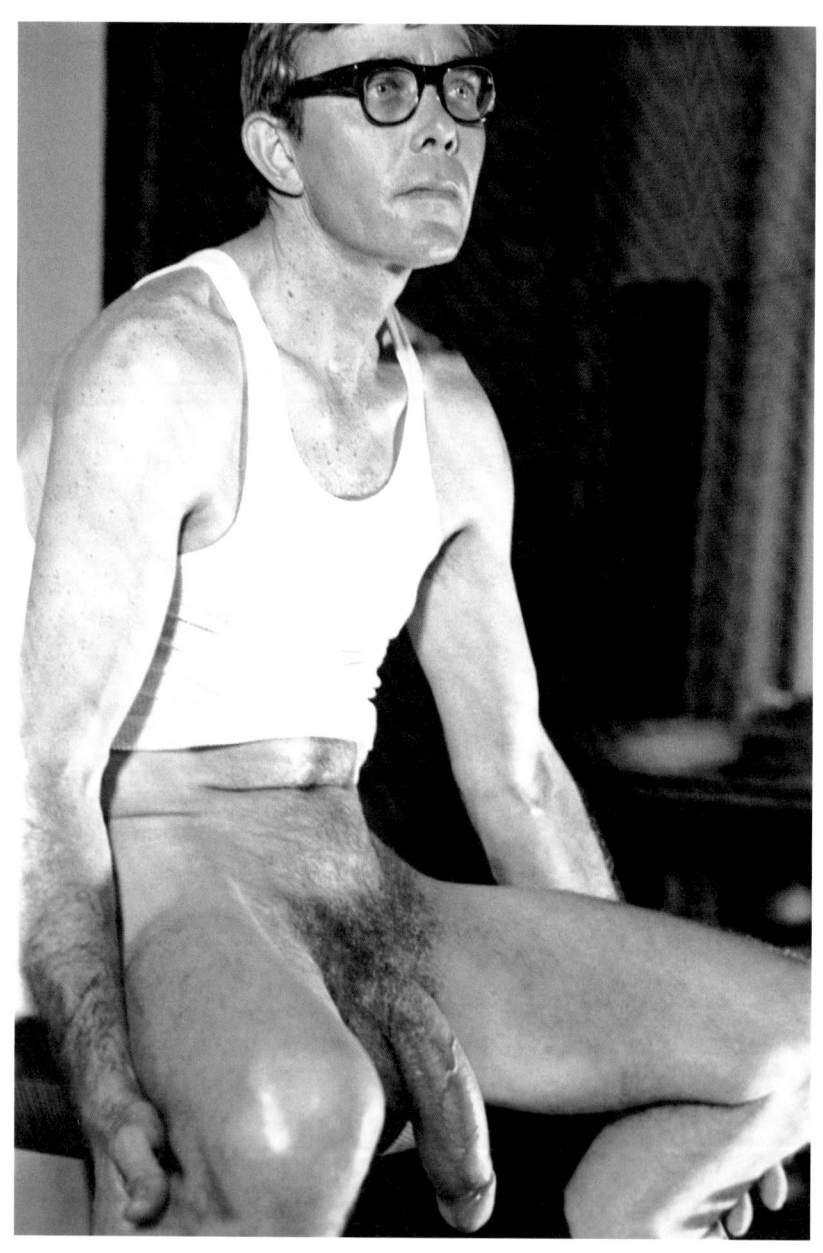

ABOVE AND OPPOSITE **Unknown**

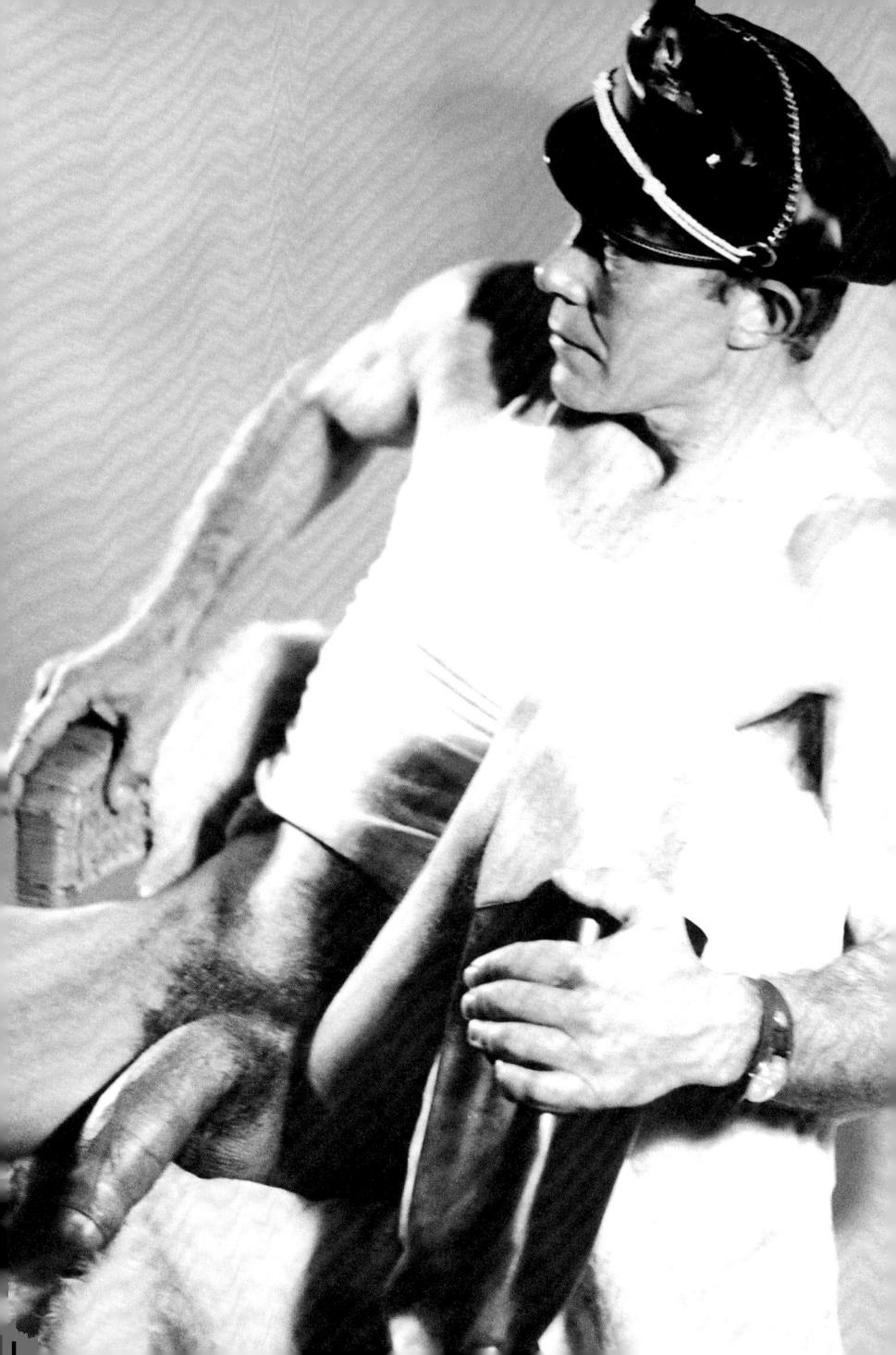

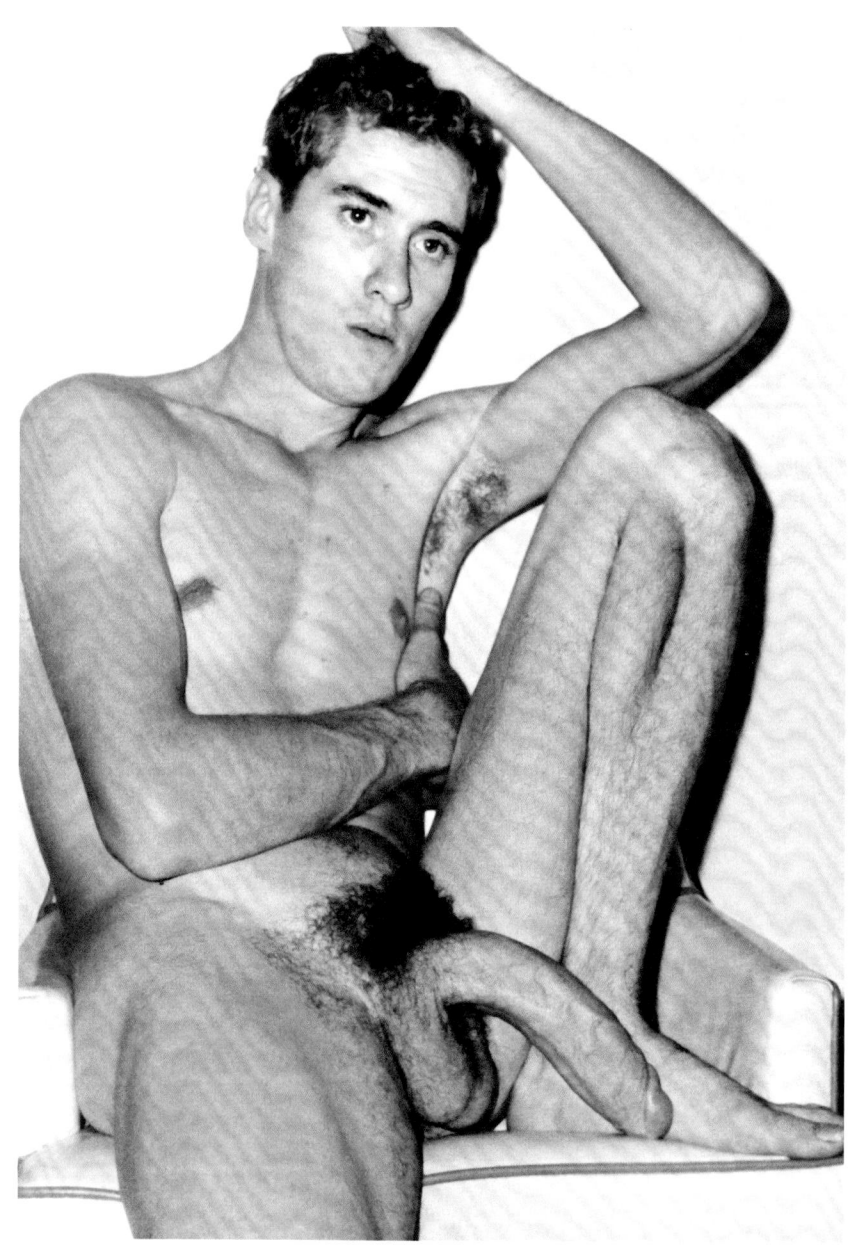

ABOVE AND OPPOSITE **John Holmes**   PAGES 34-35 **Dickie Doolittle**

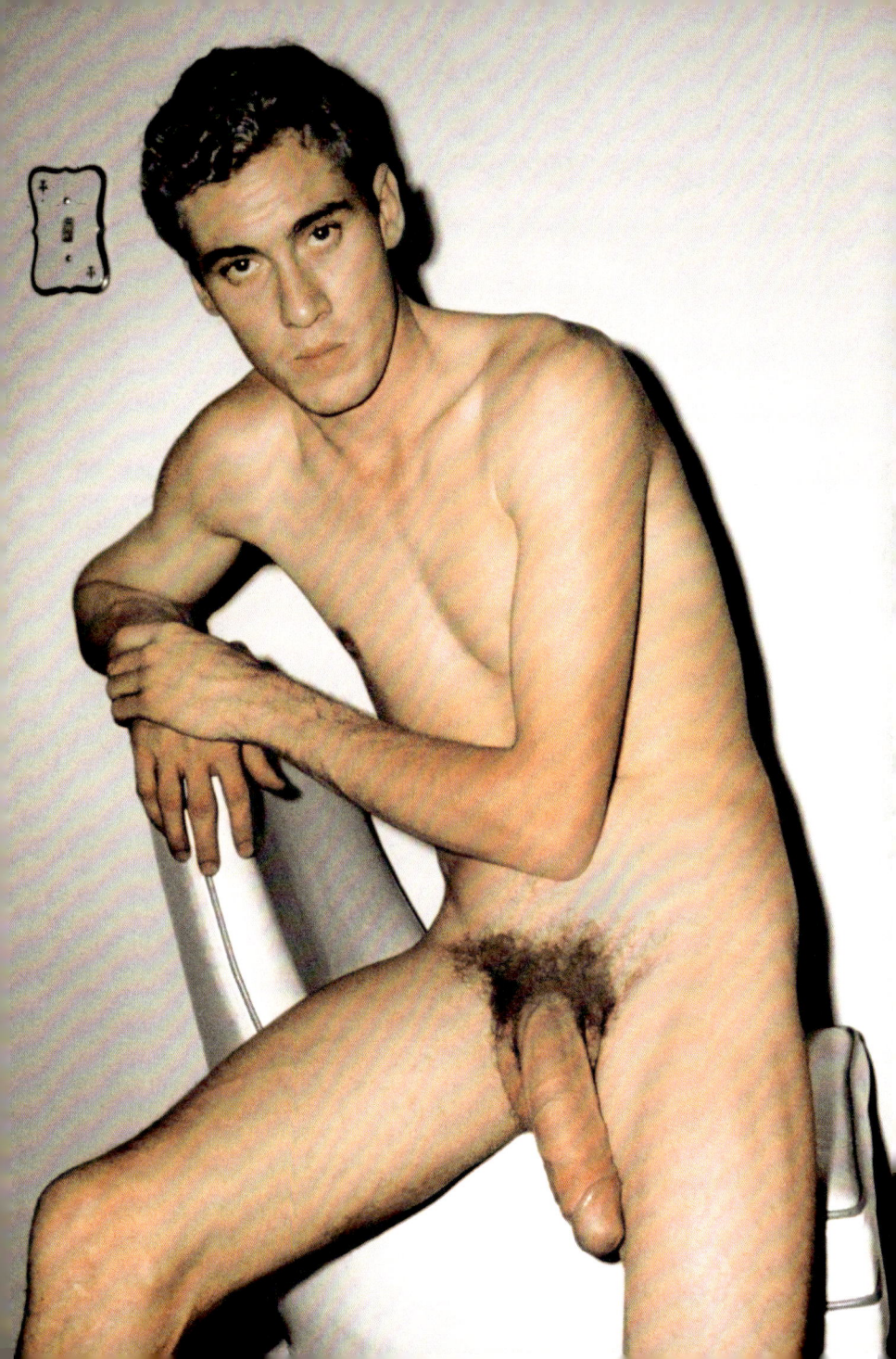

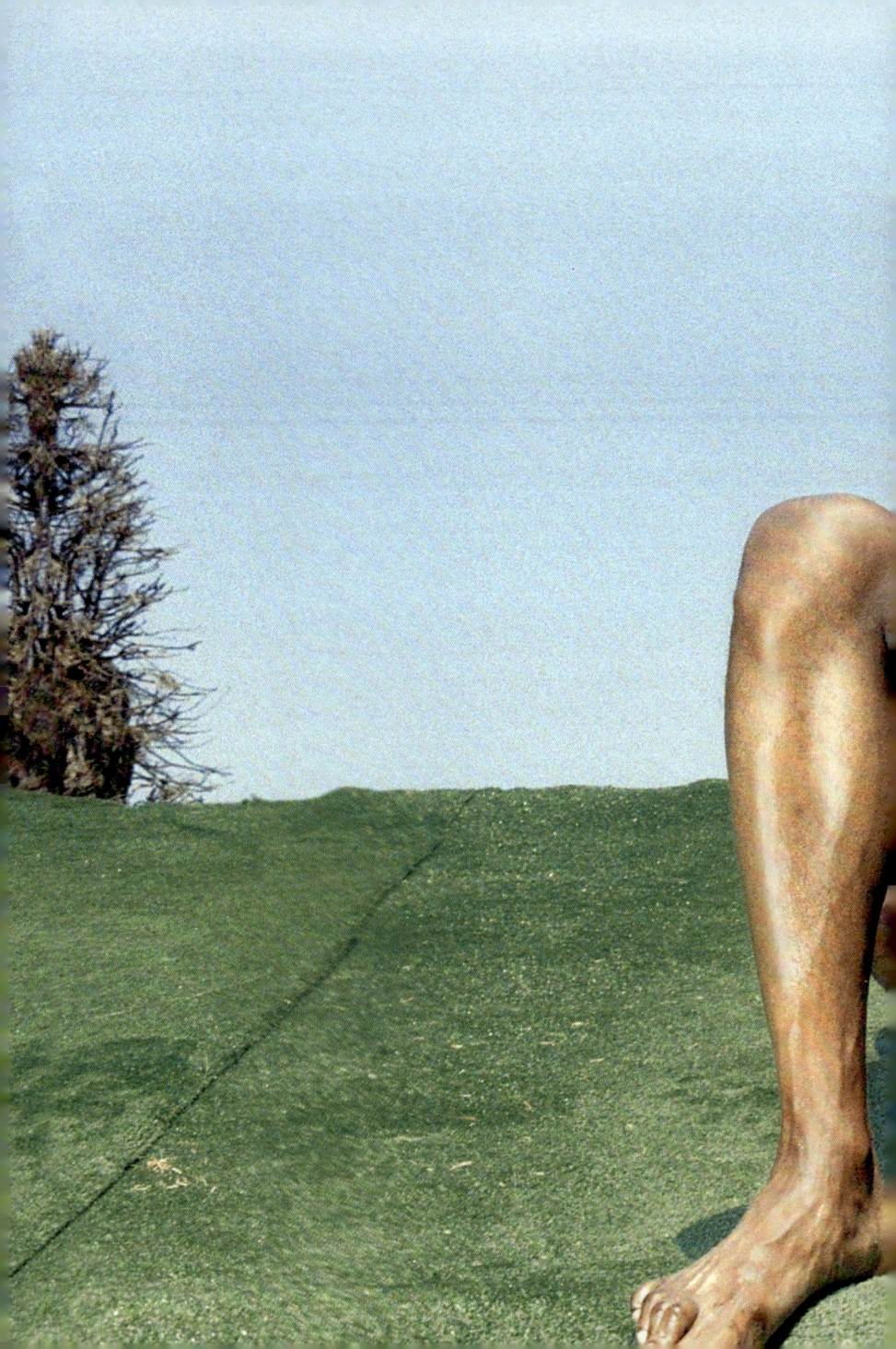

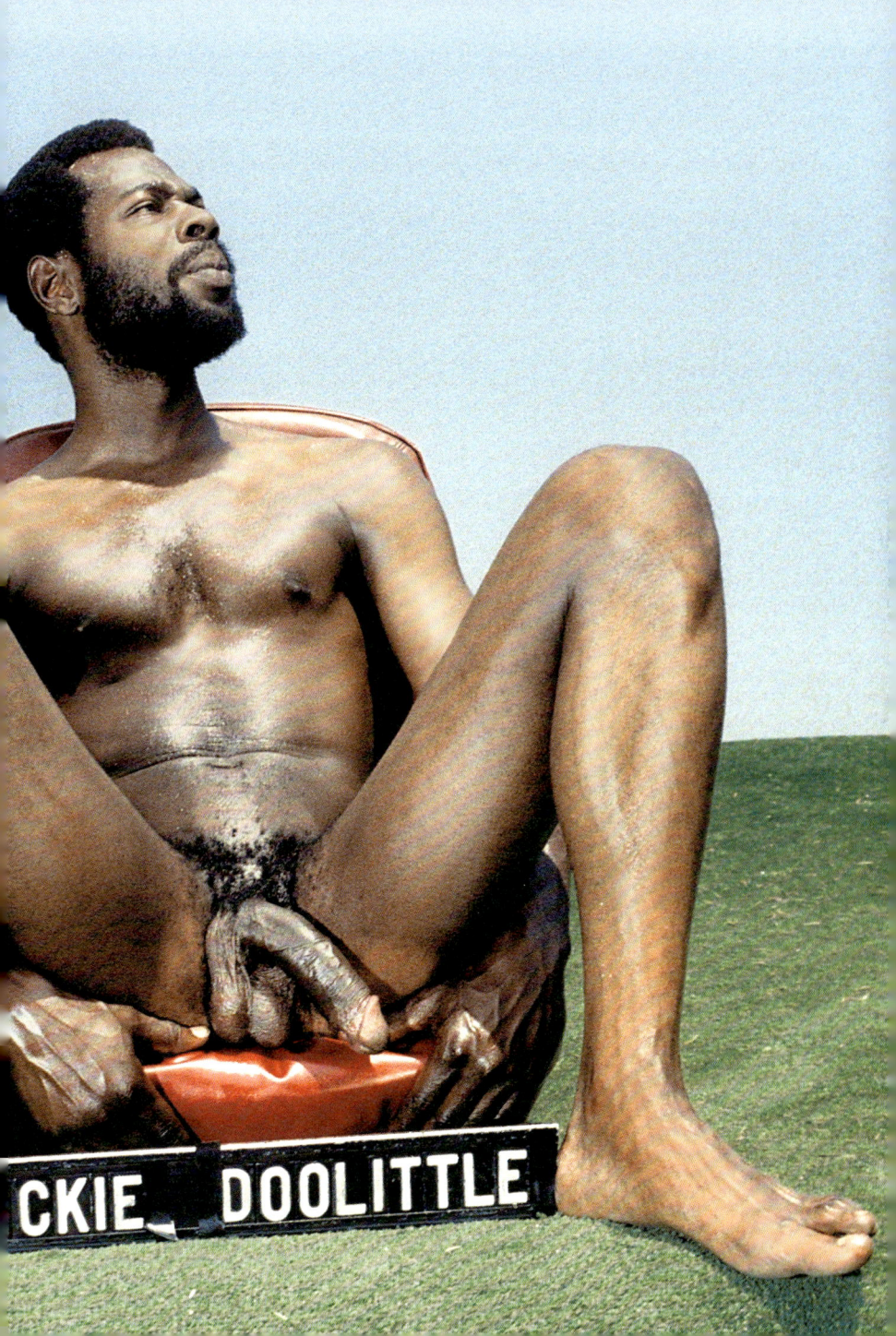

CKIE DOOLITTLE

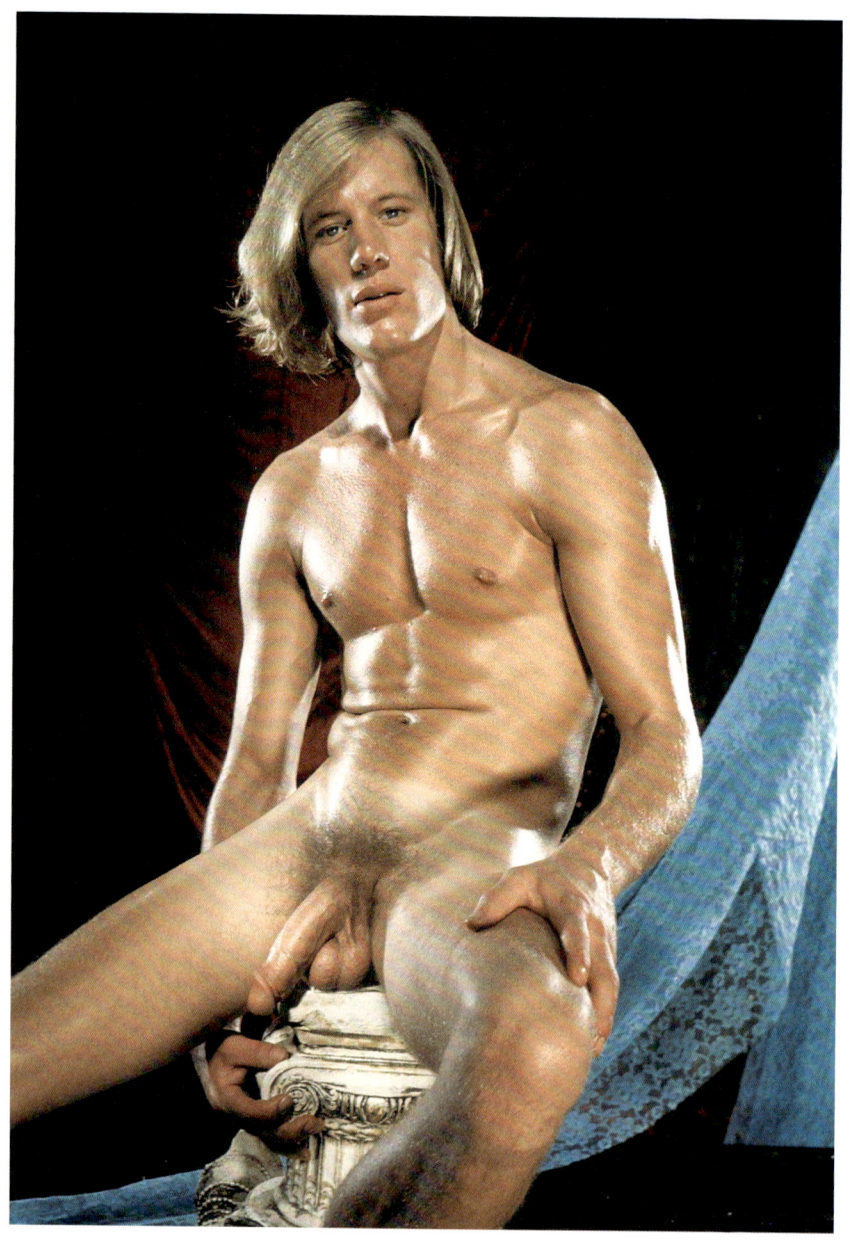

Ronald Sprague

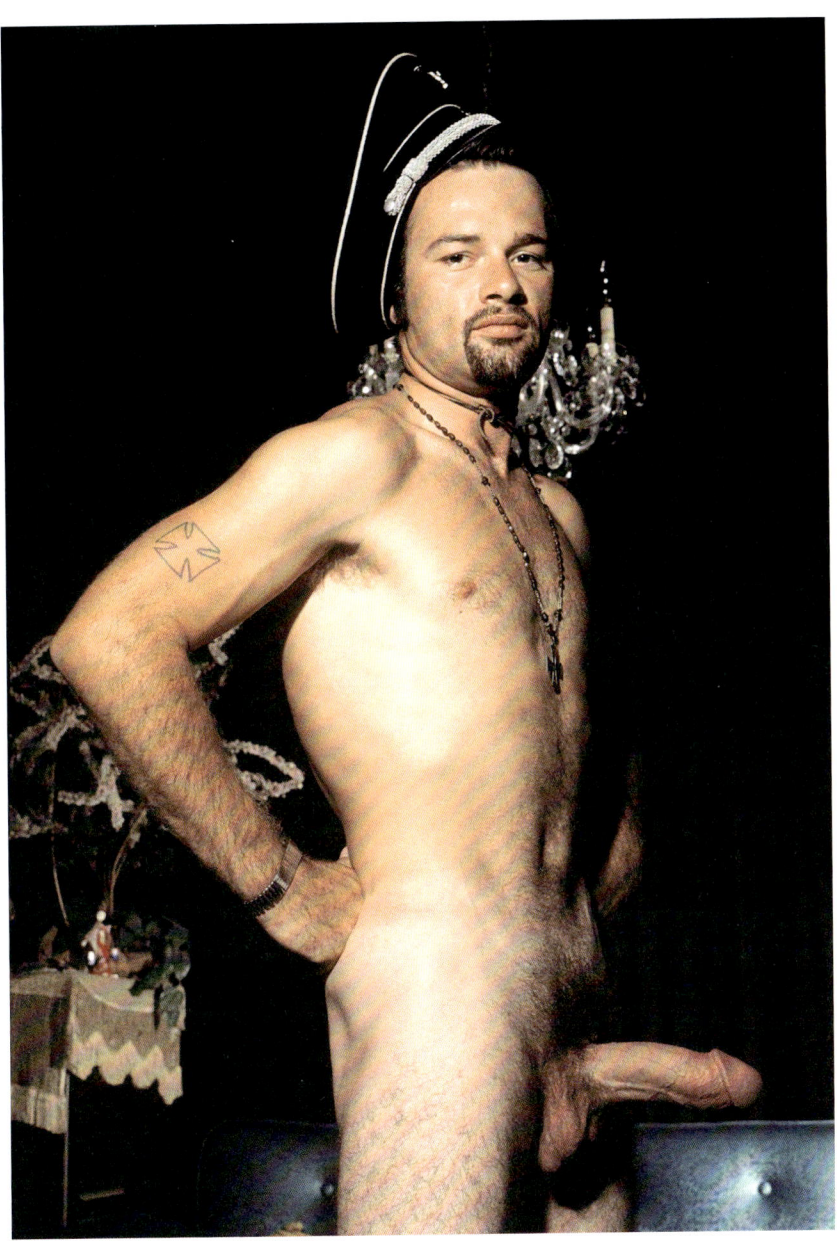

ABOVE **Chris Hansen**   PAGES 38-39 **Mark Hamilton**

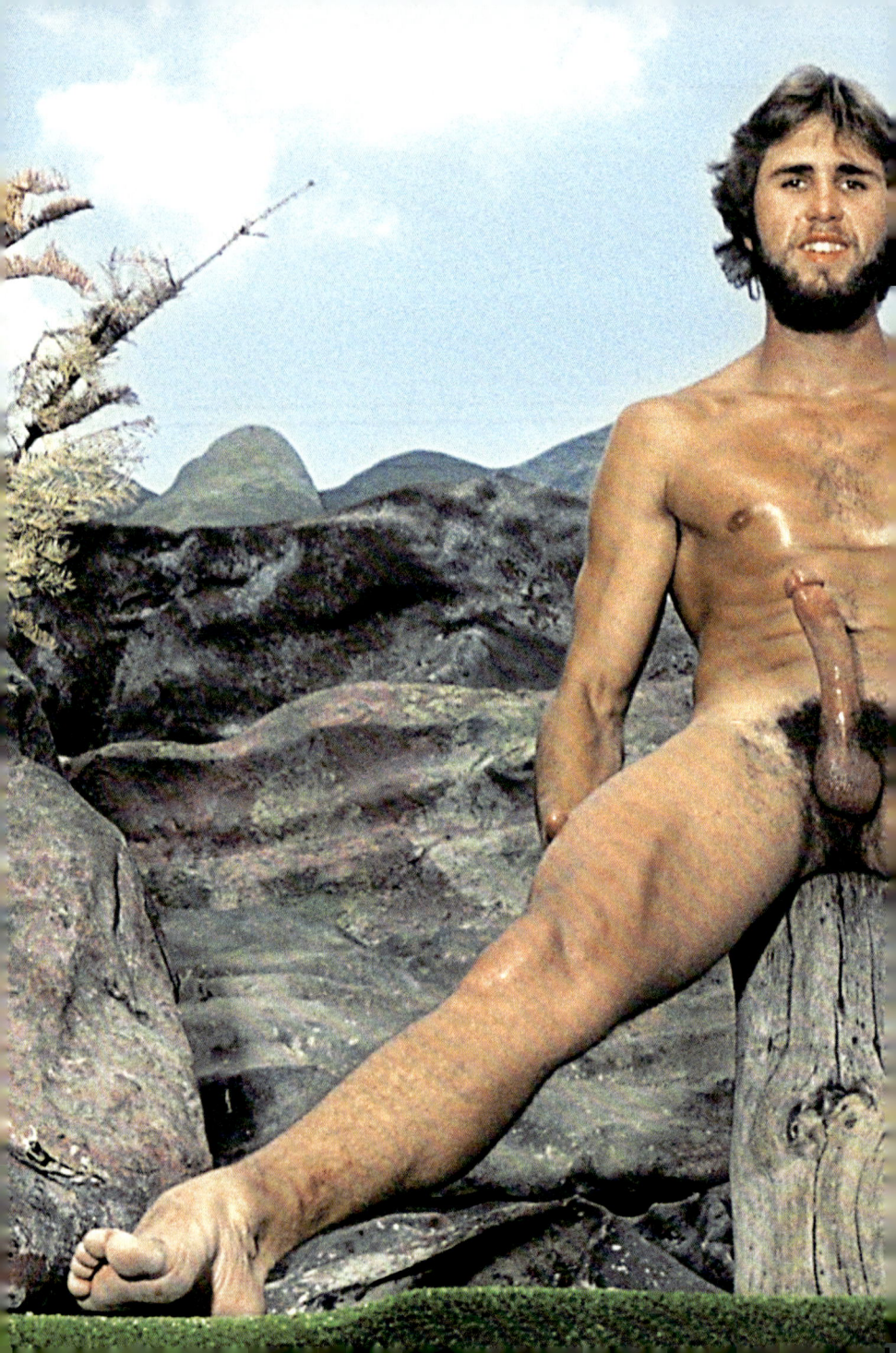

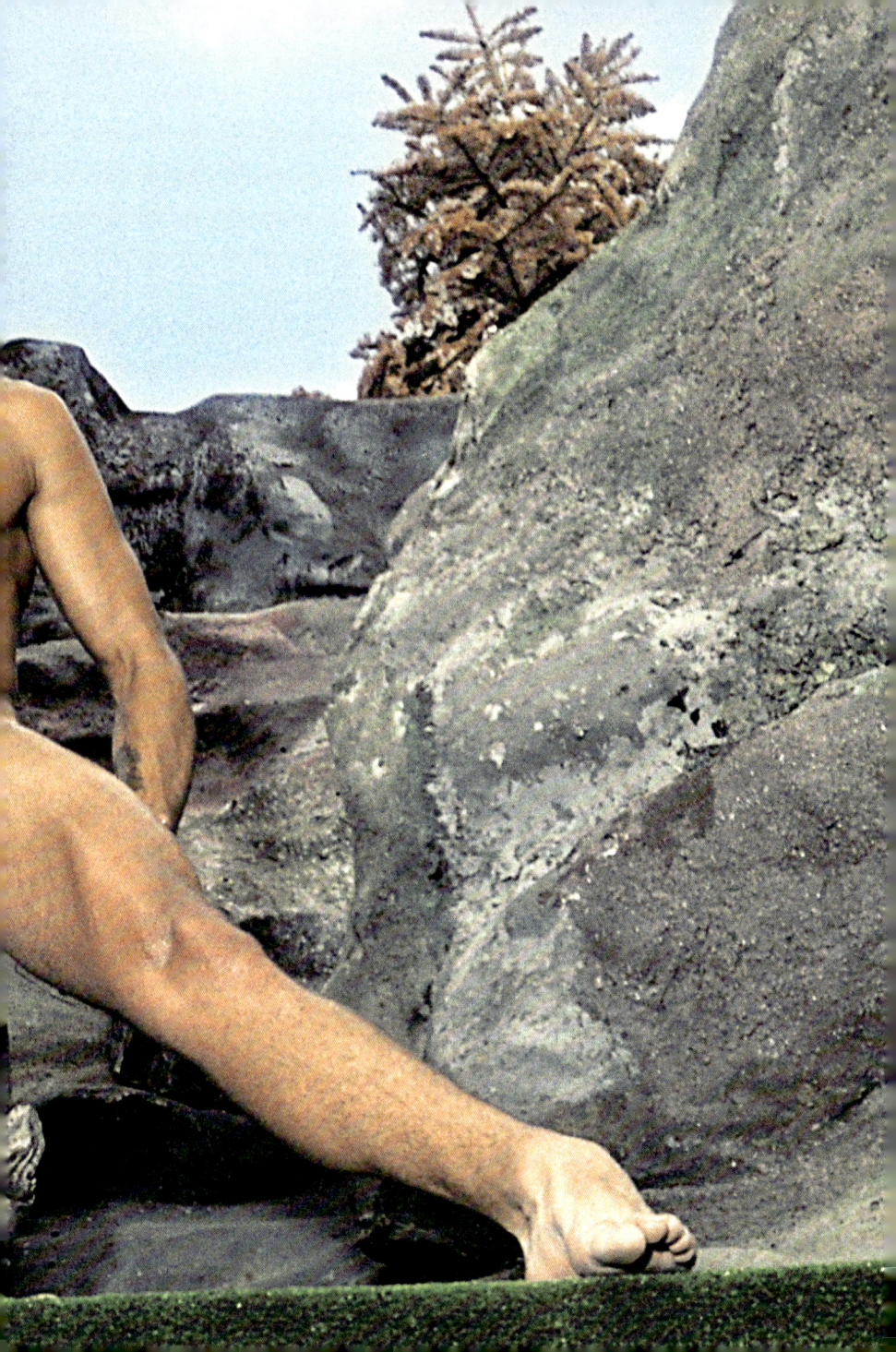

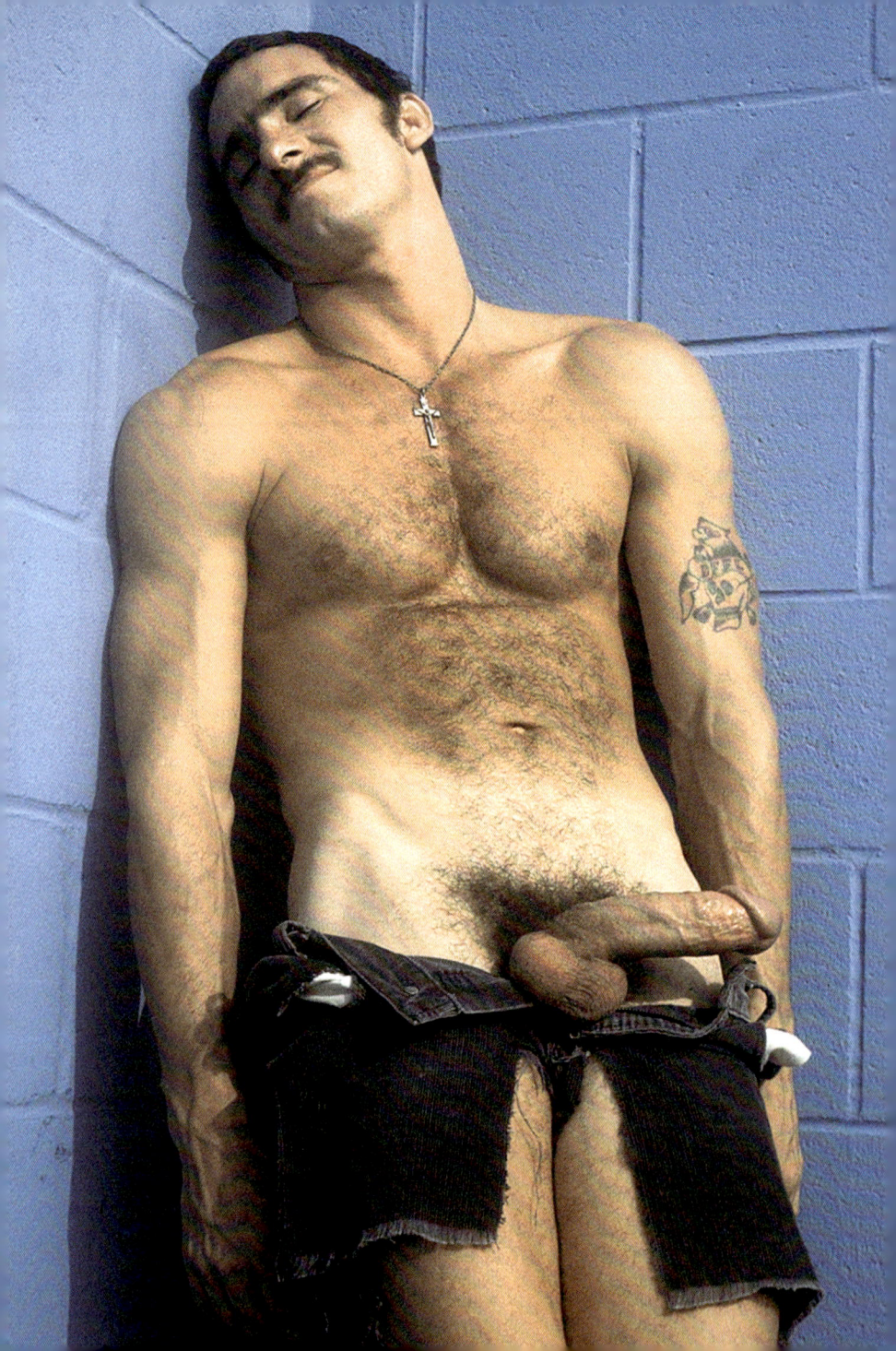

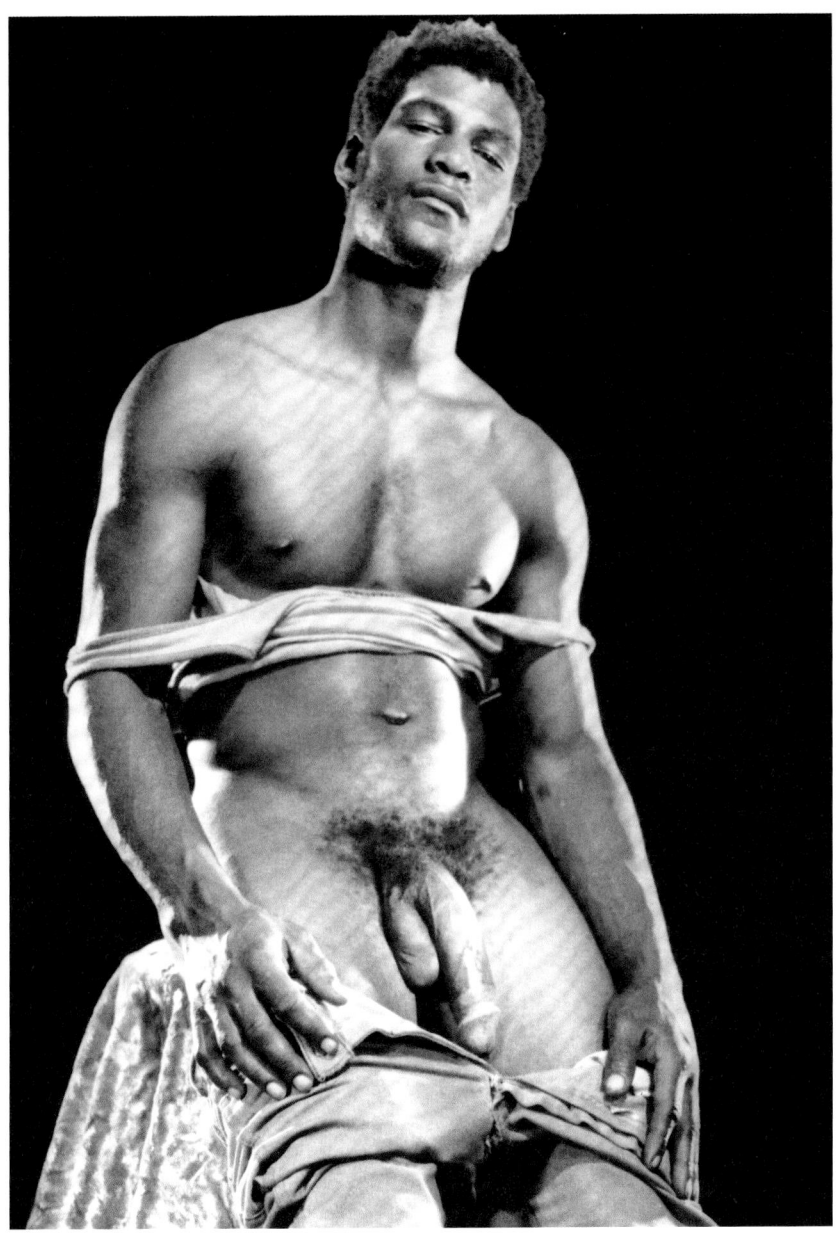

OPPOSITE **Tico Patterson**   ABOVE **Gerald Oglesby**   PAGES 42-43 **James Sheppard**

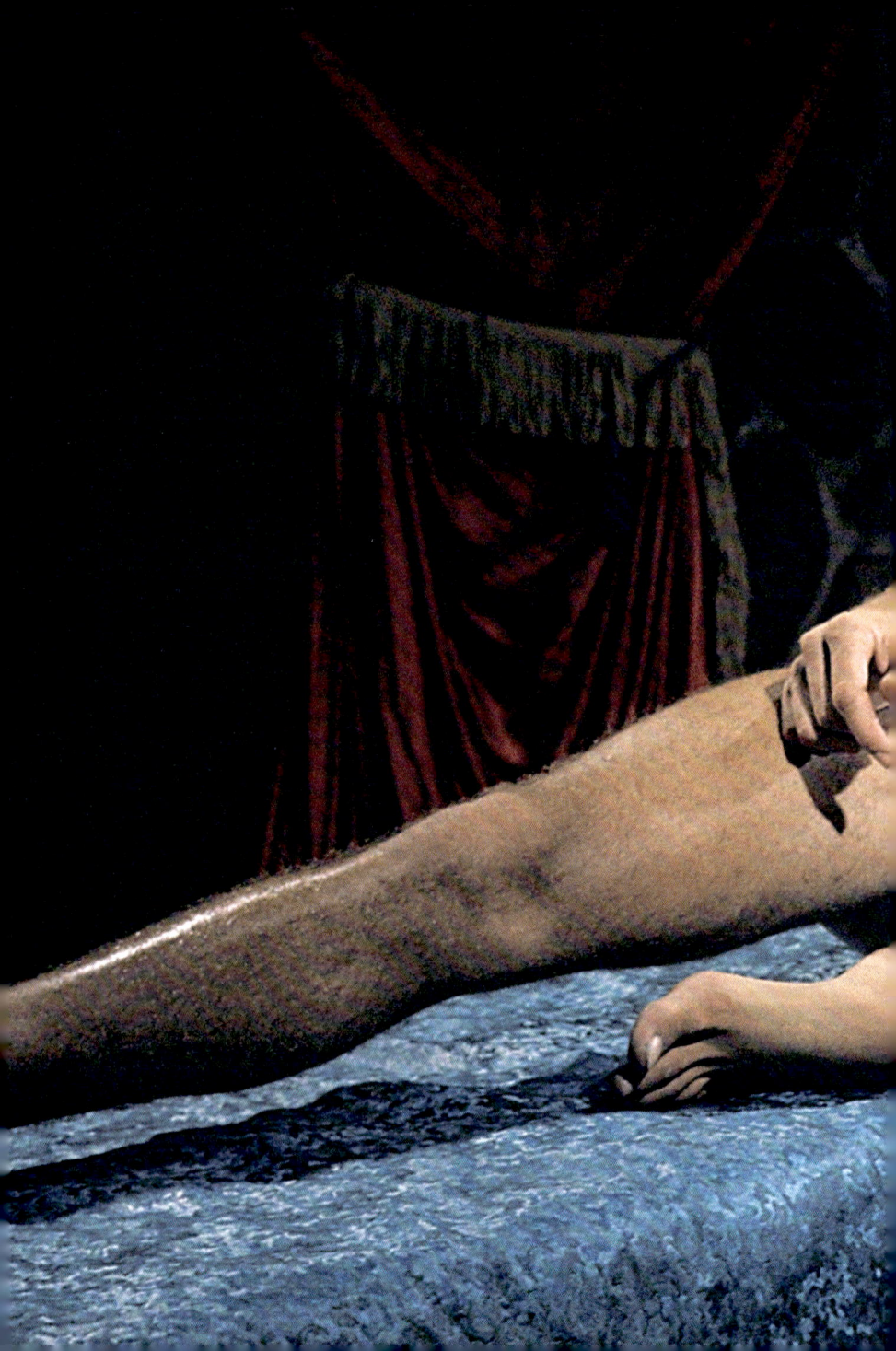

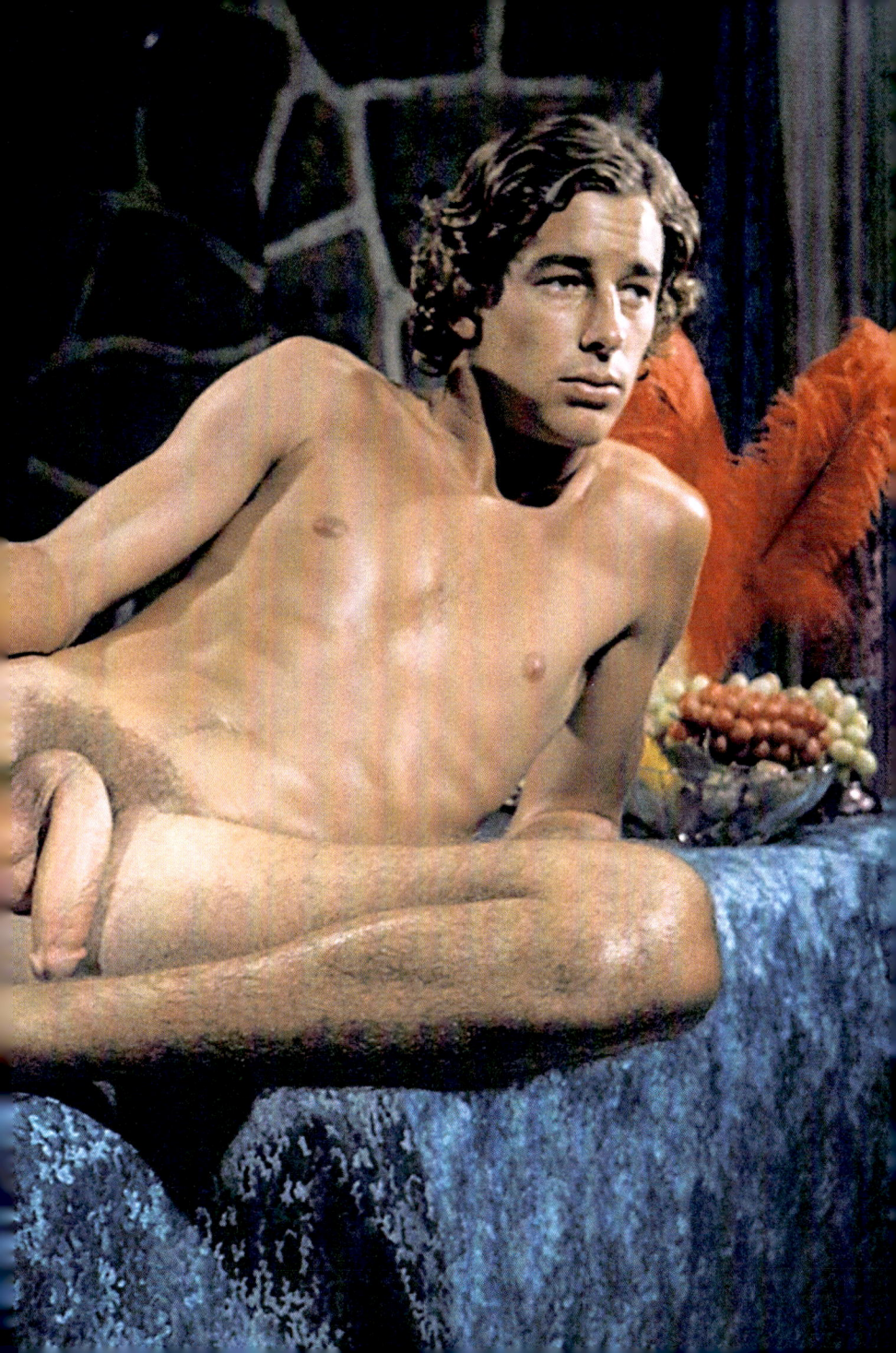

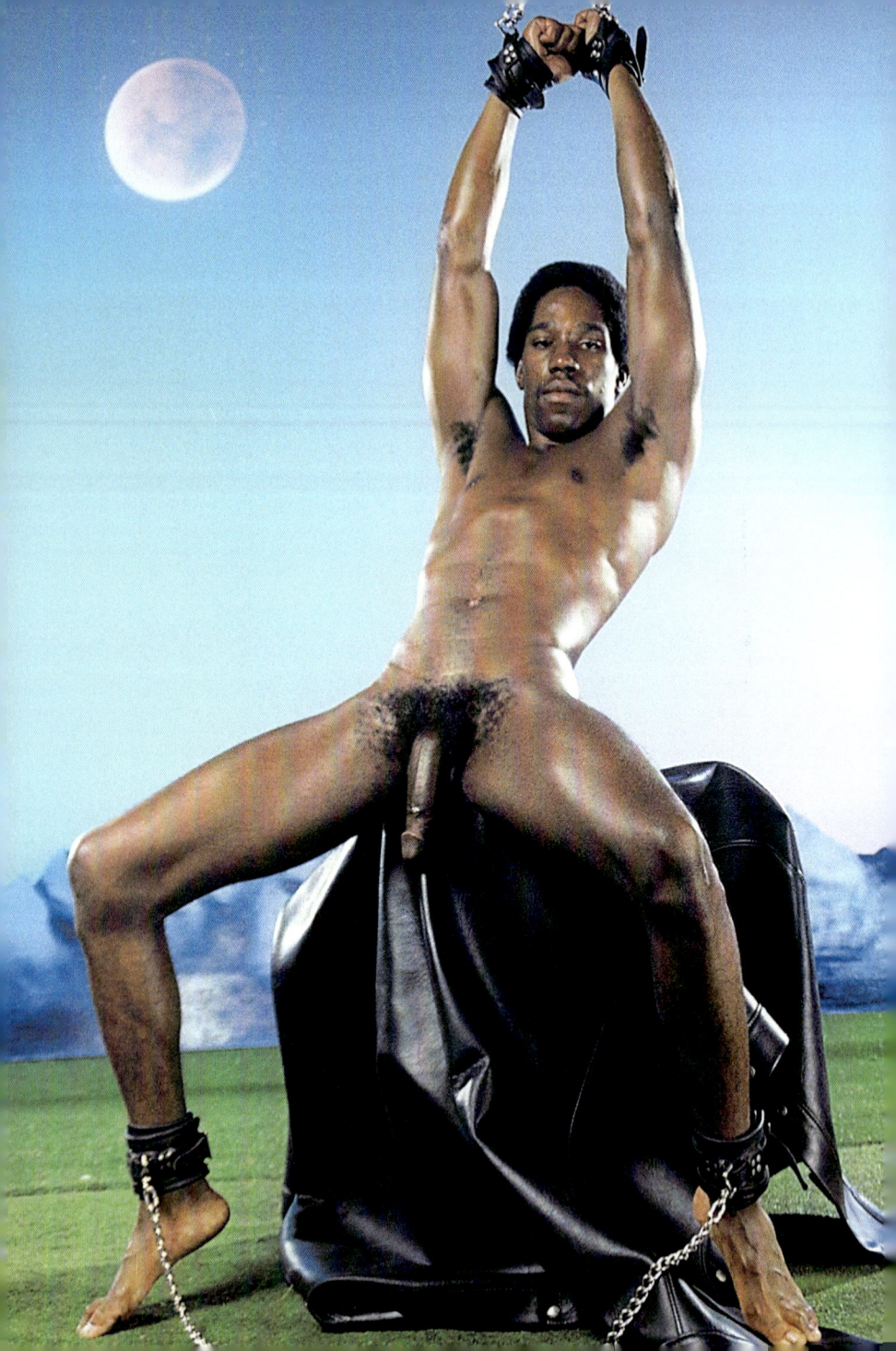

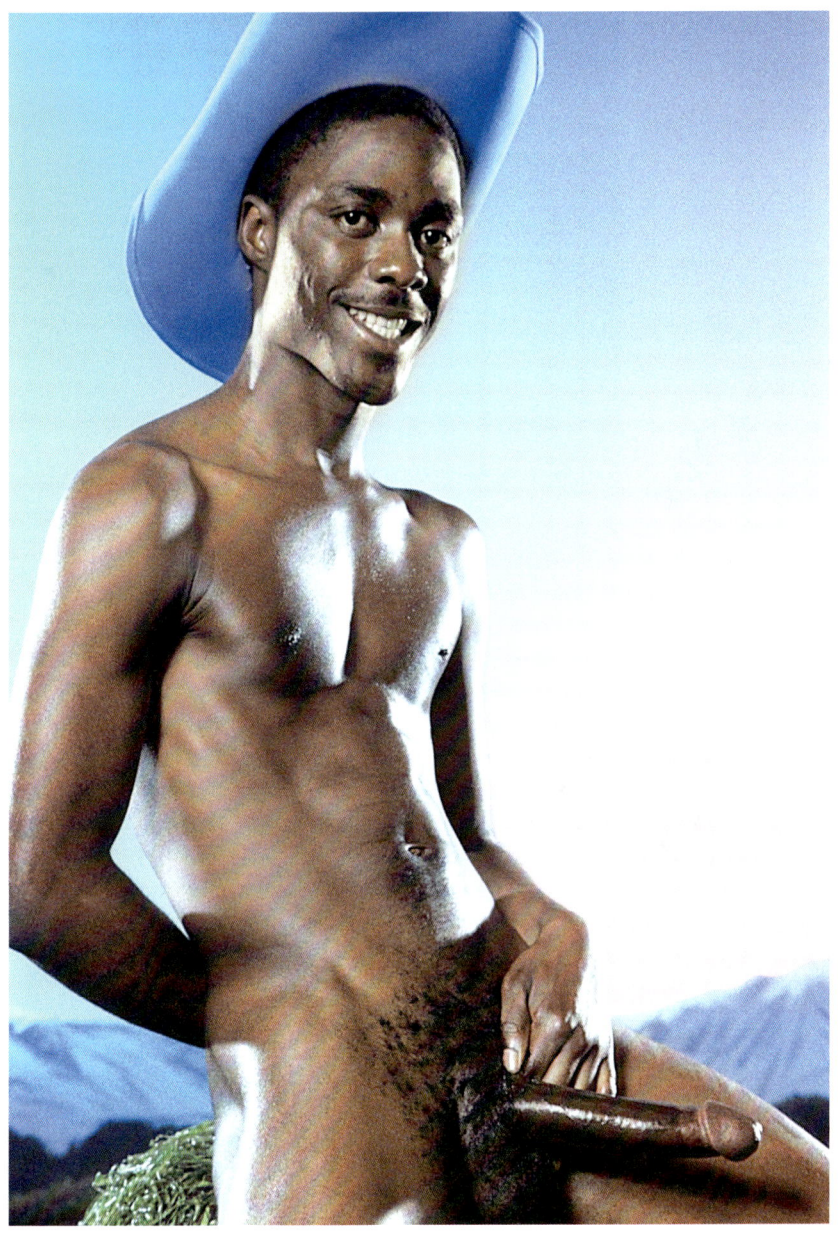

OPPOSITE **T. J. Swann**   ABOVE **Paul George**   PAGES 46-47 **Barry Hoffman**

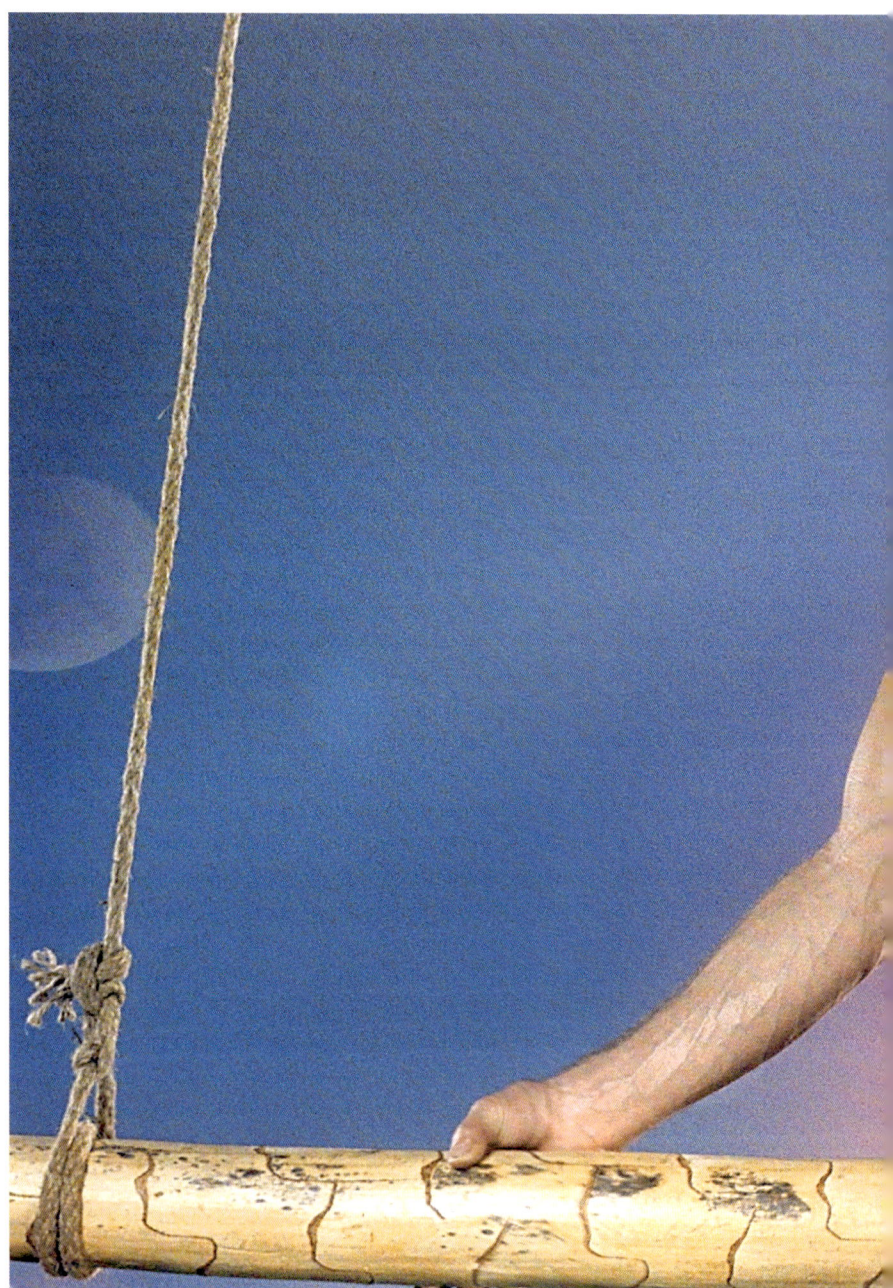

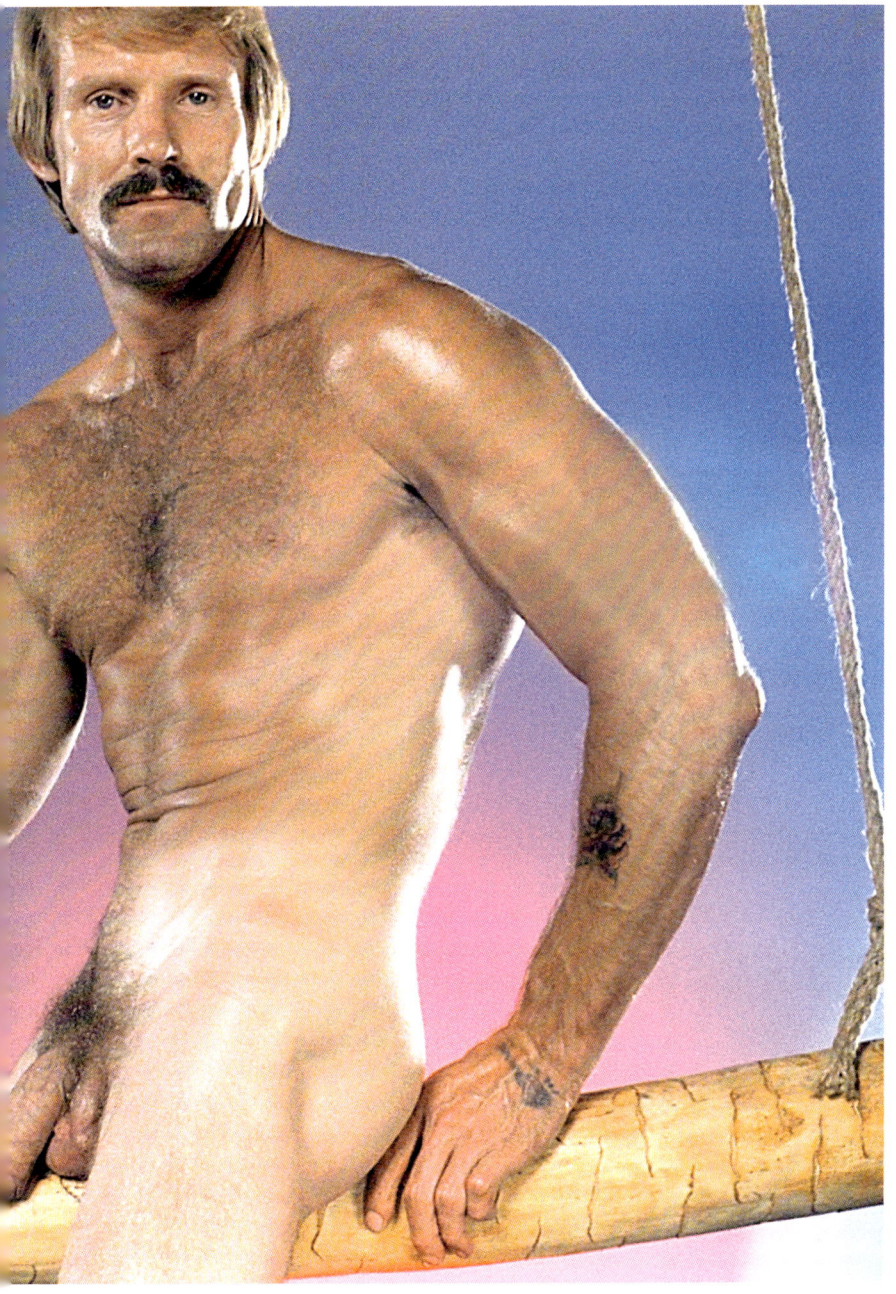

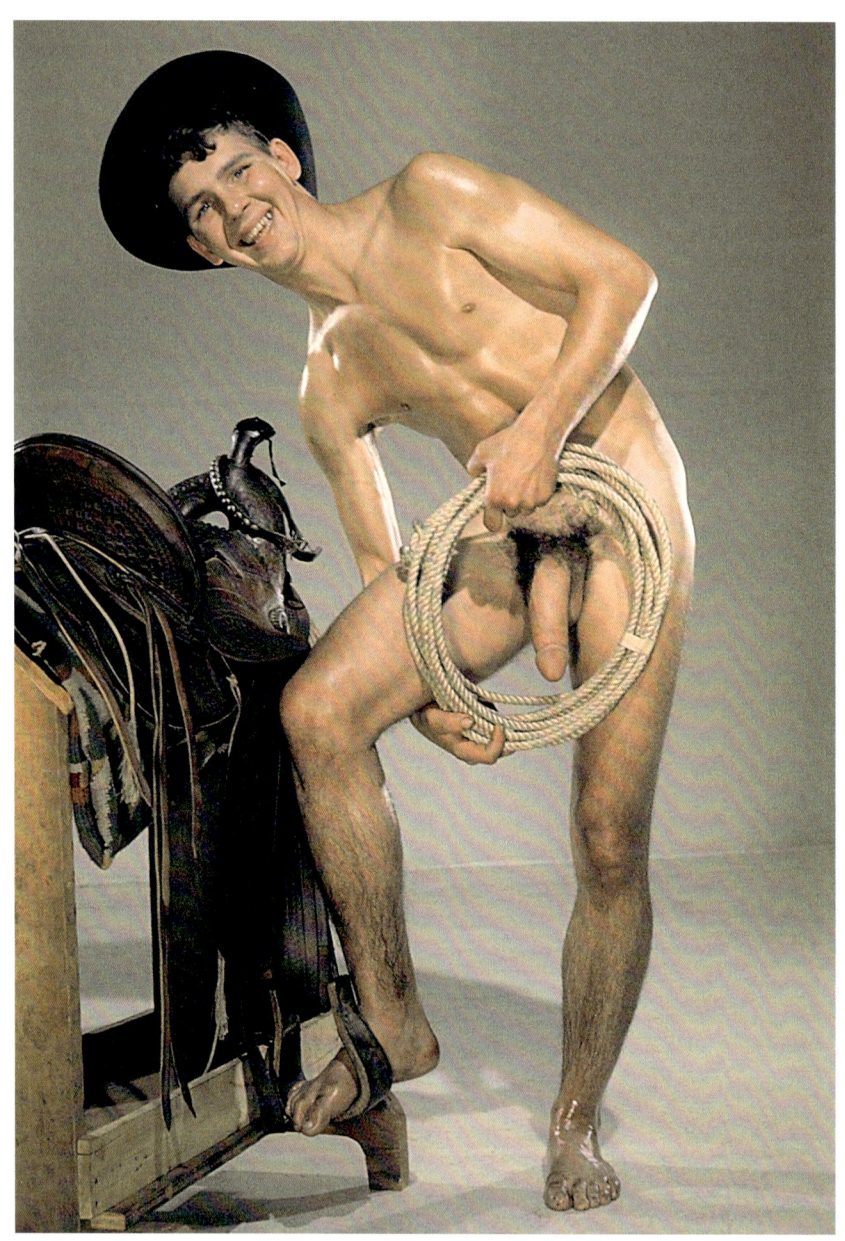

ABOVE AND OPPOSITE **Bob Moore**

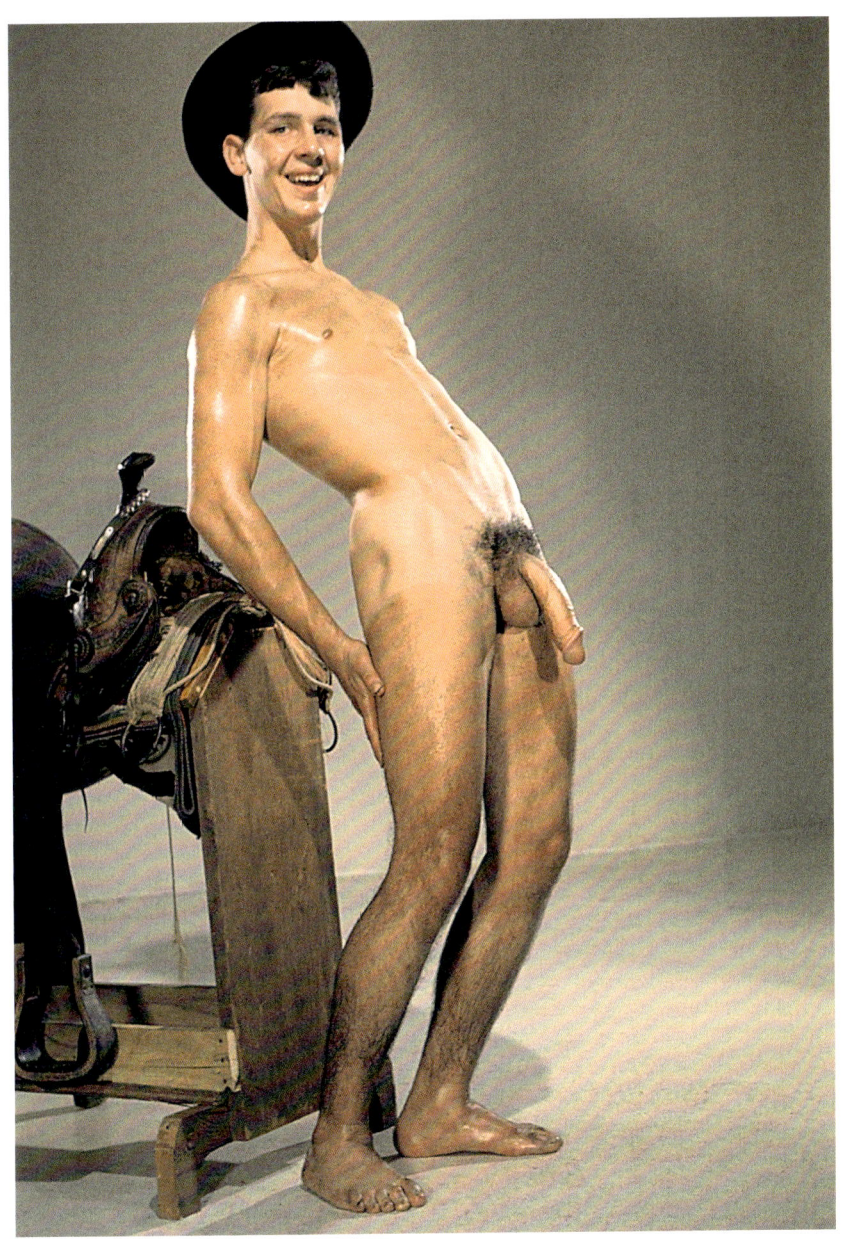

PAGES 50-51 **Tyrone Jones**

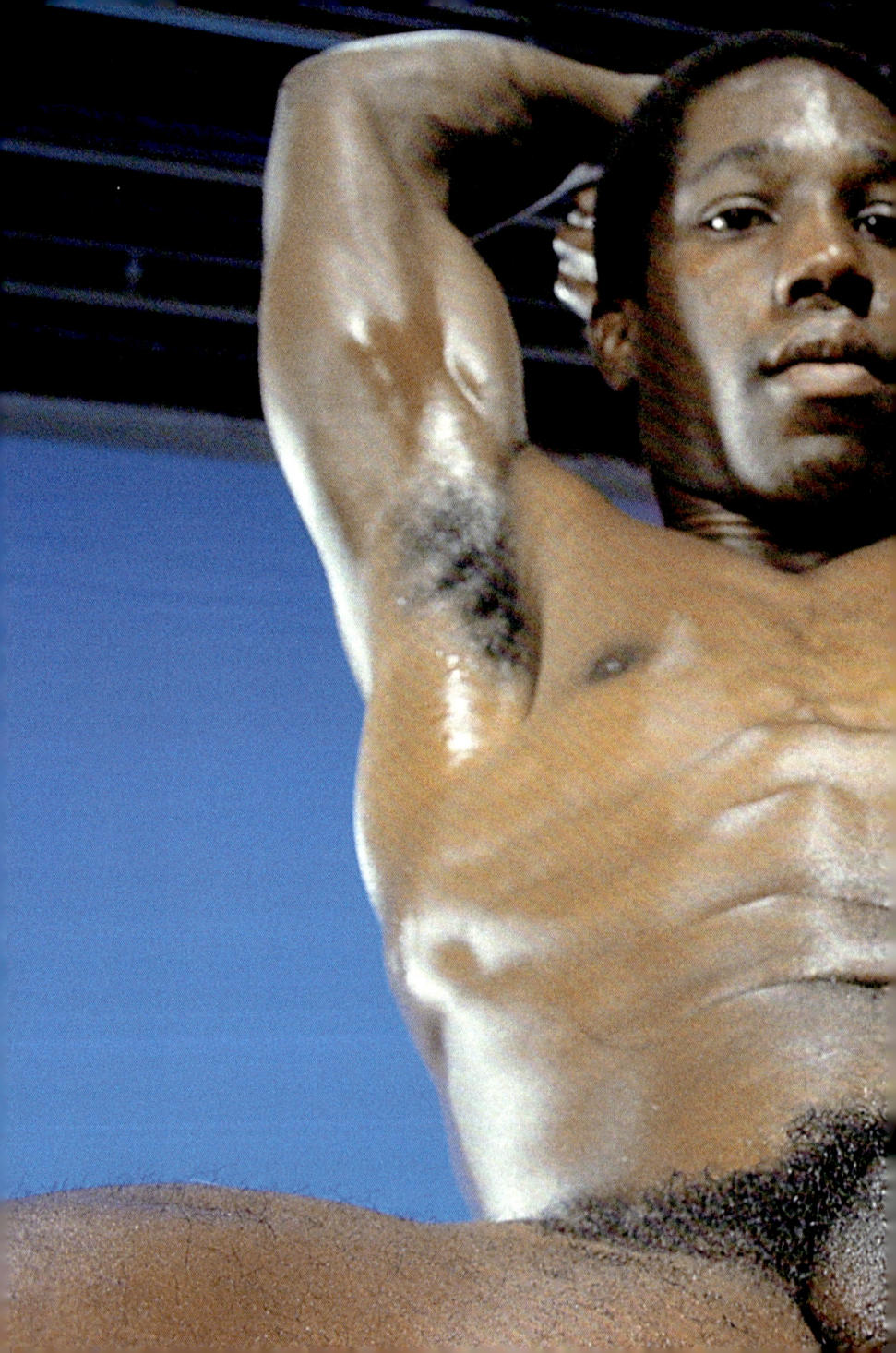

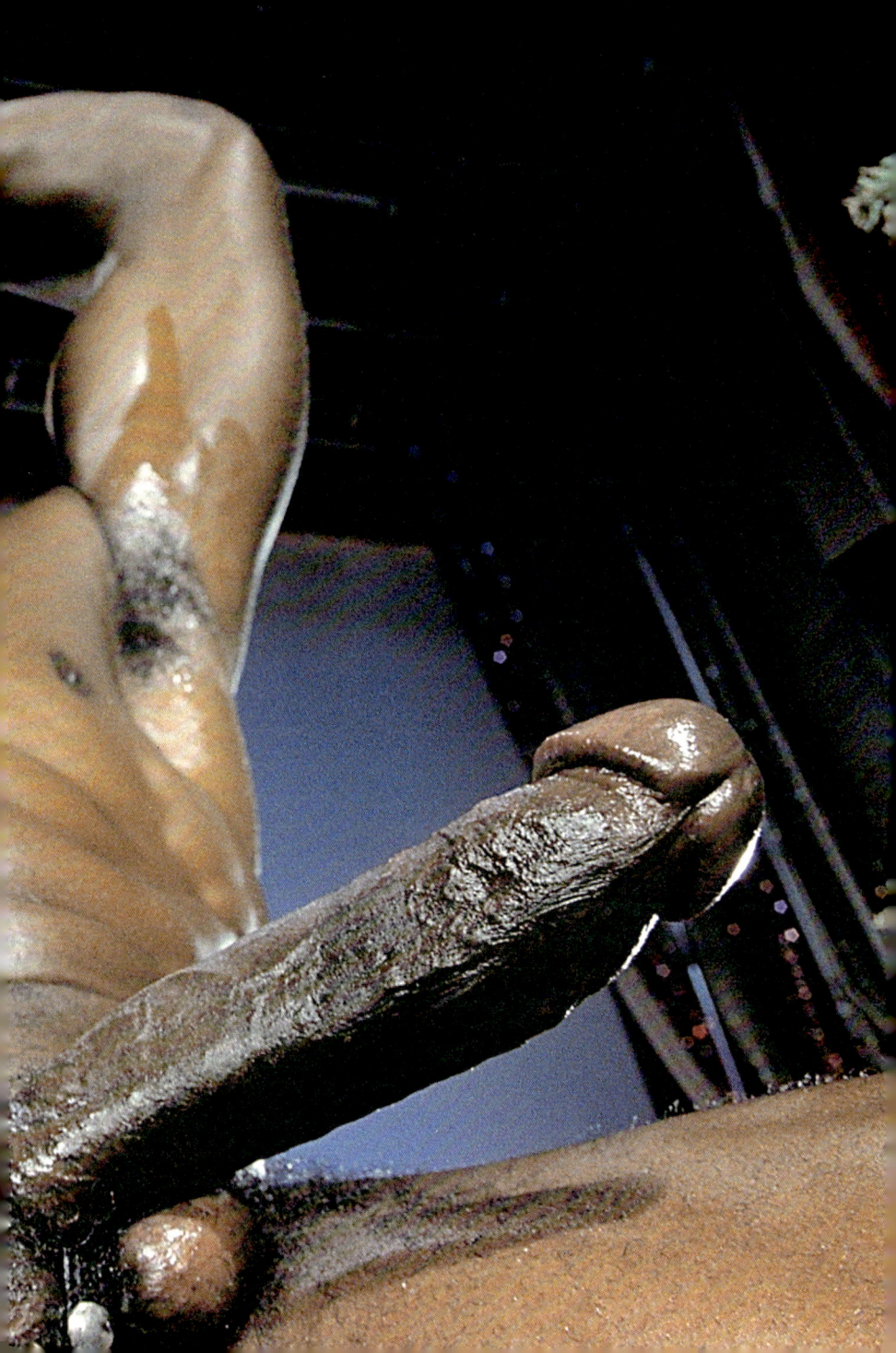

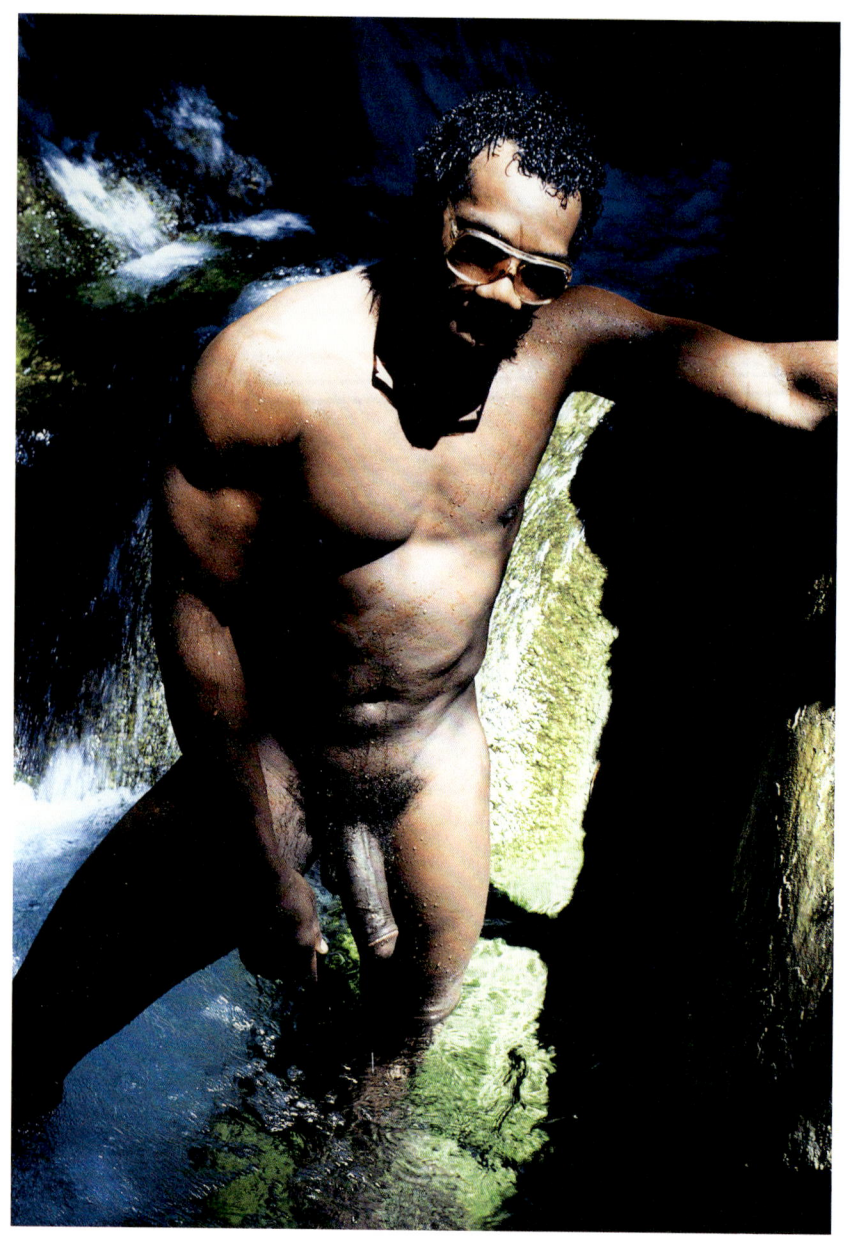

ABOVE **Sonje**   OPPOSITE **F. Lorenzo**   PAGE 54 **Cueler**

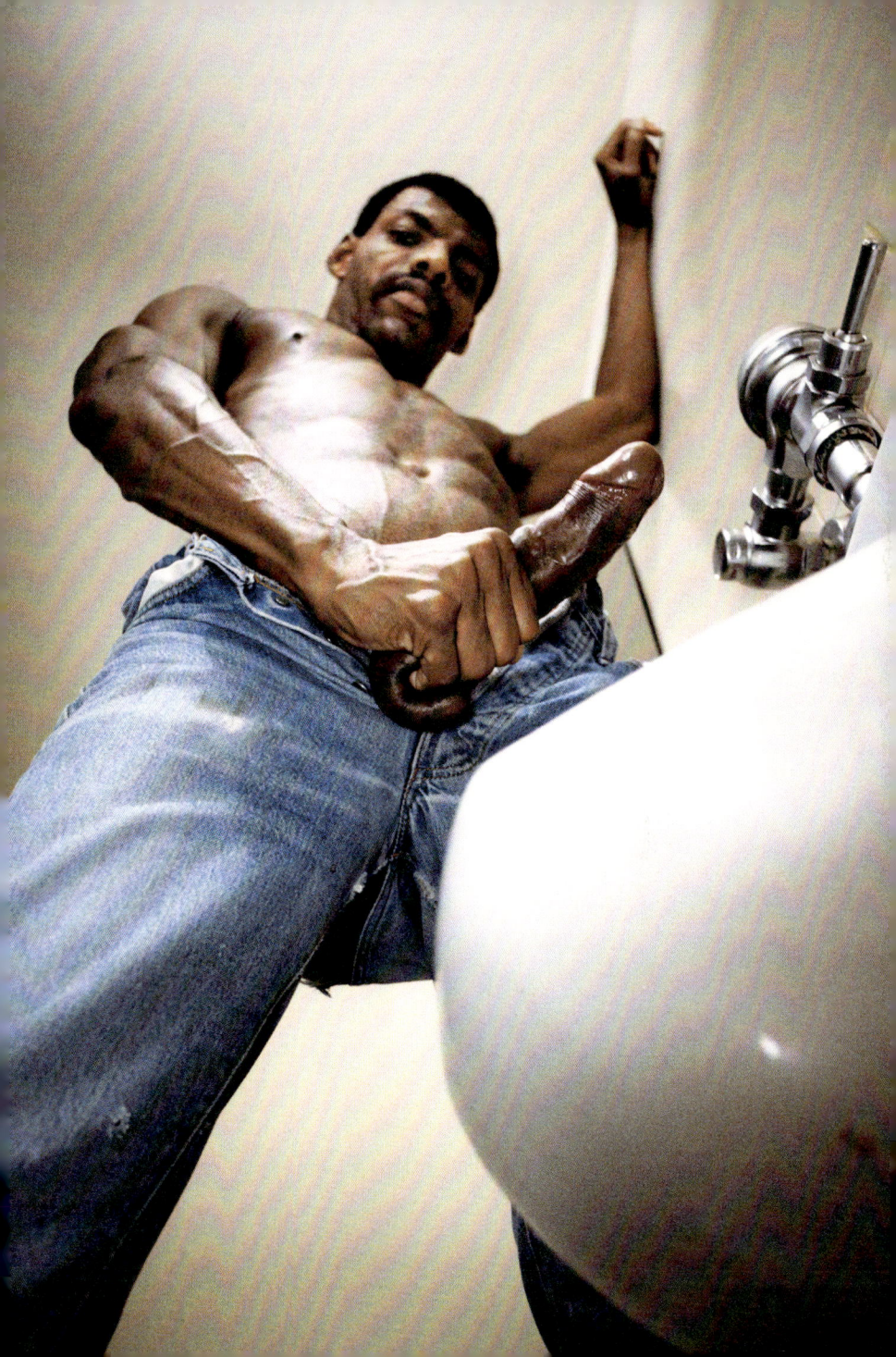

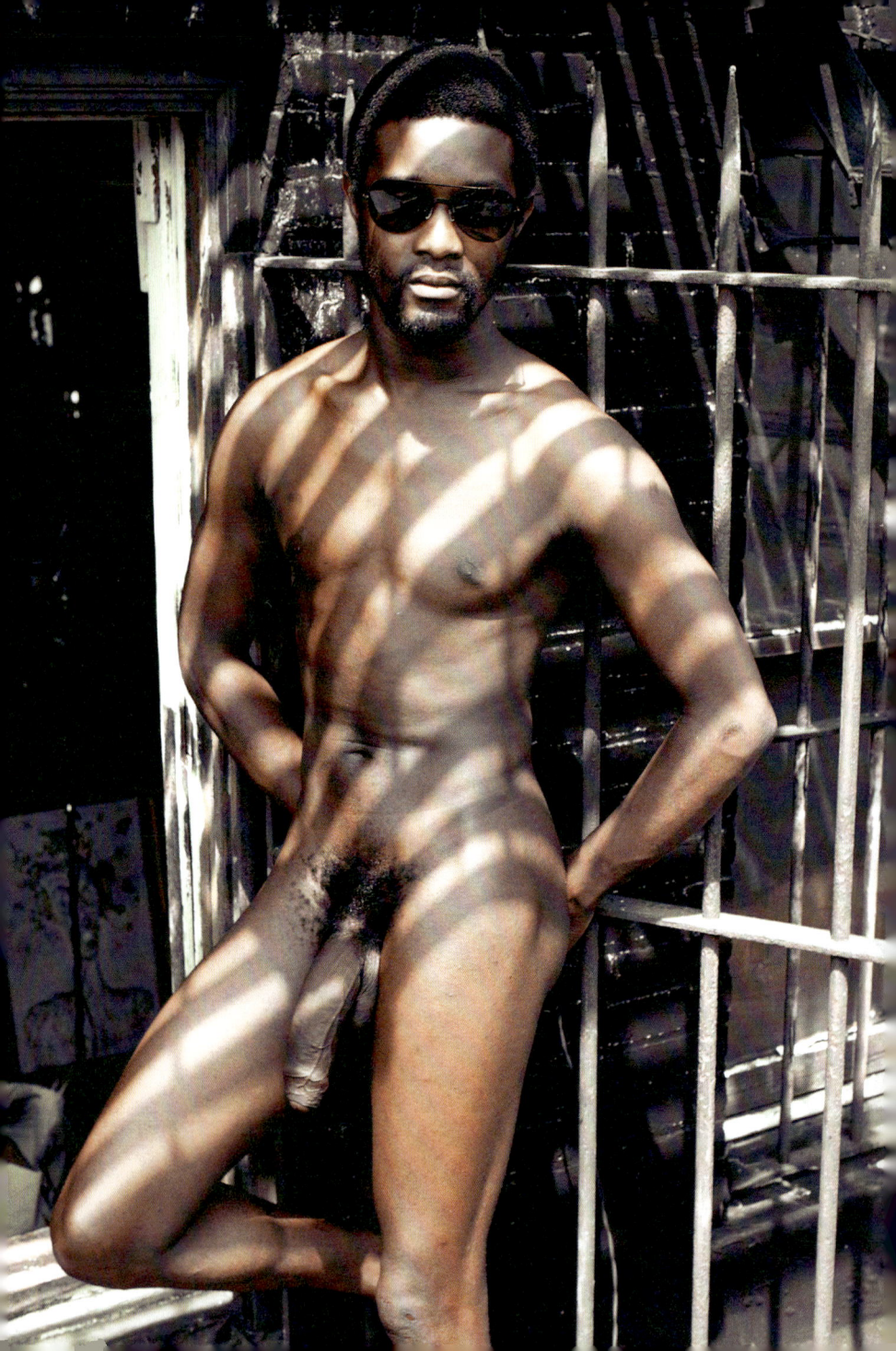

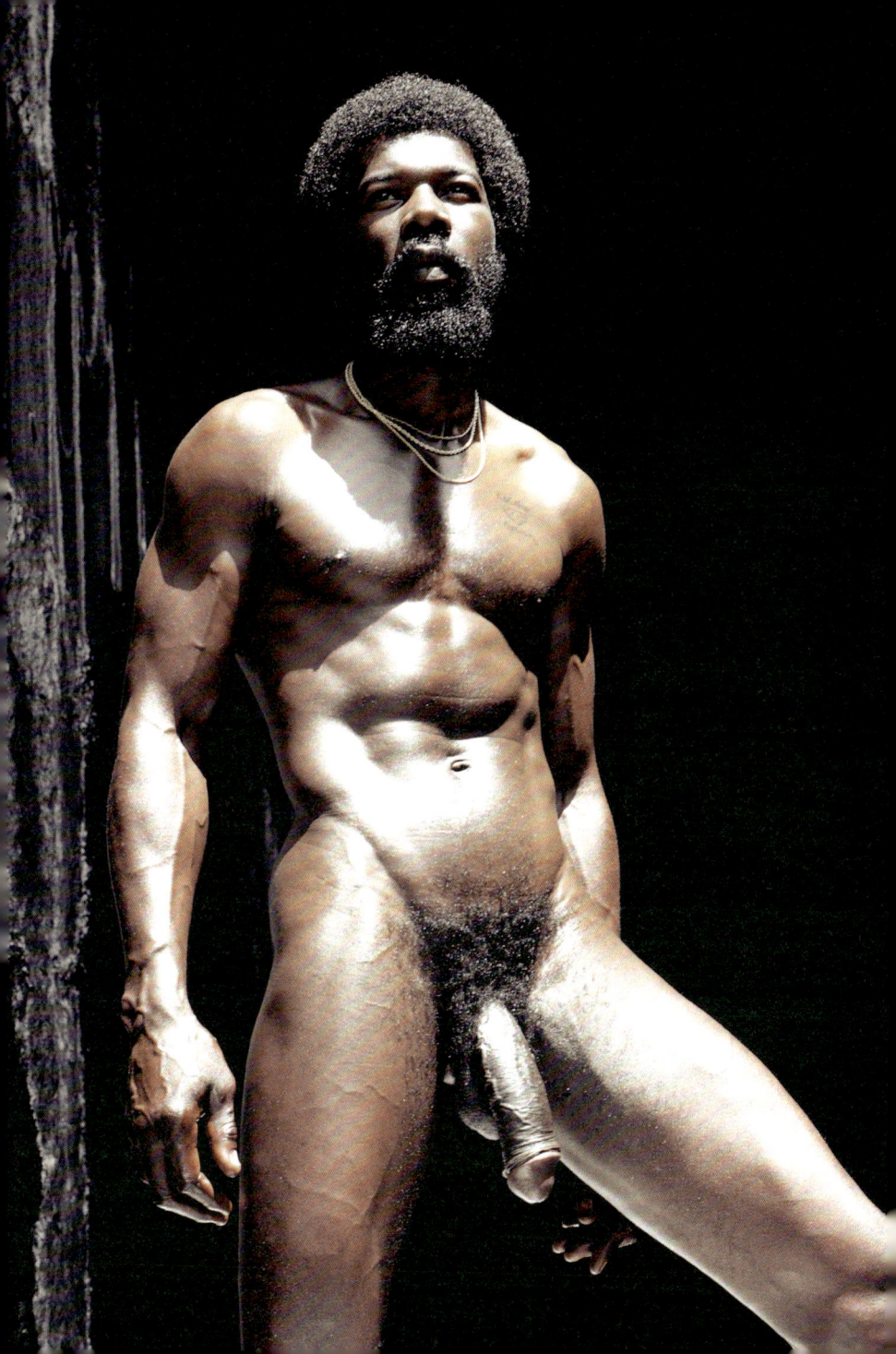

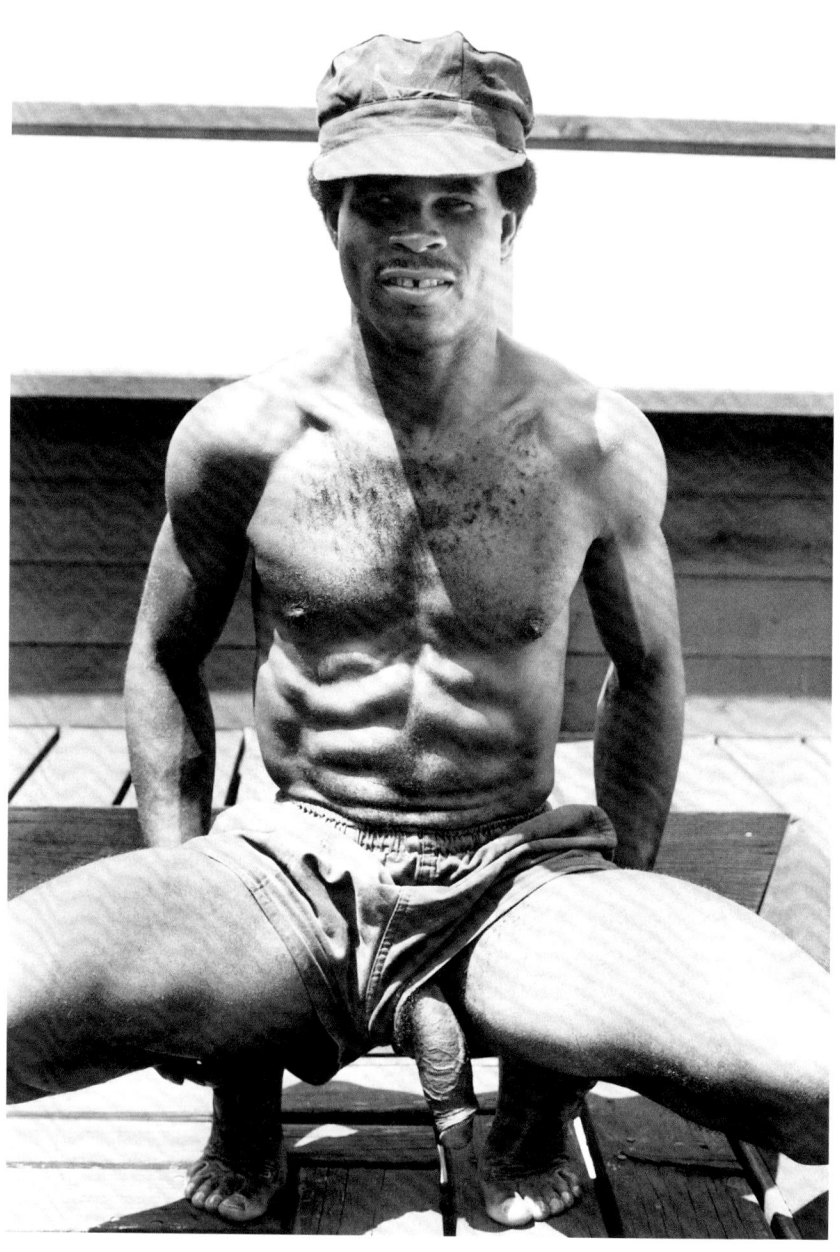

PAGE 55 **Bernard**   ABOVE **J. Smith-Cousins**   OPPOSITE **Austin**

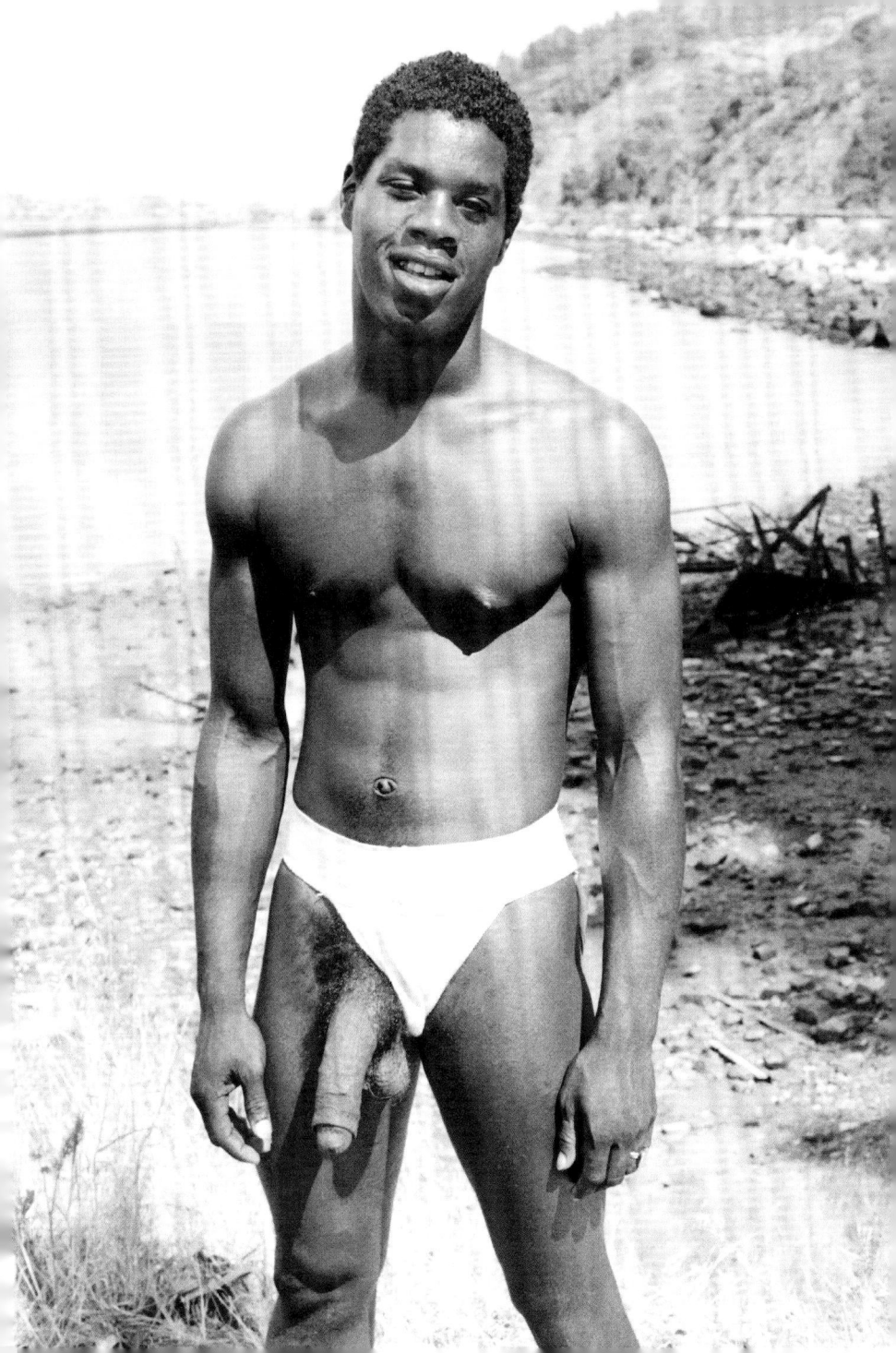

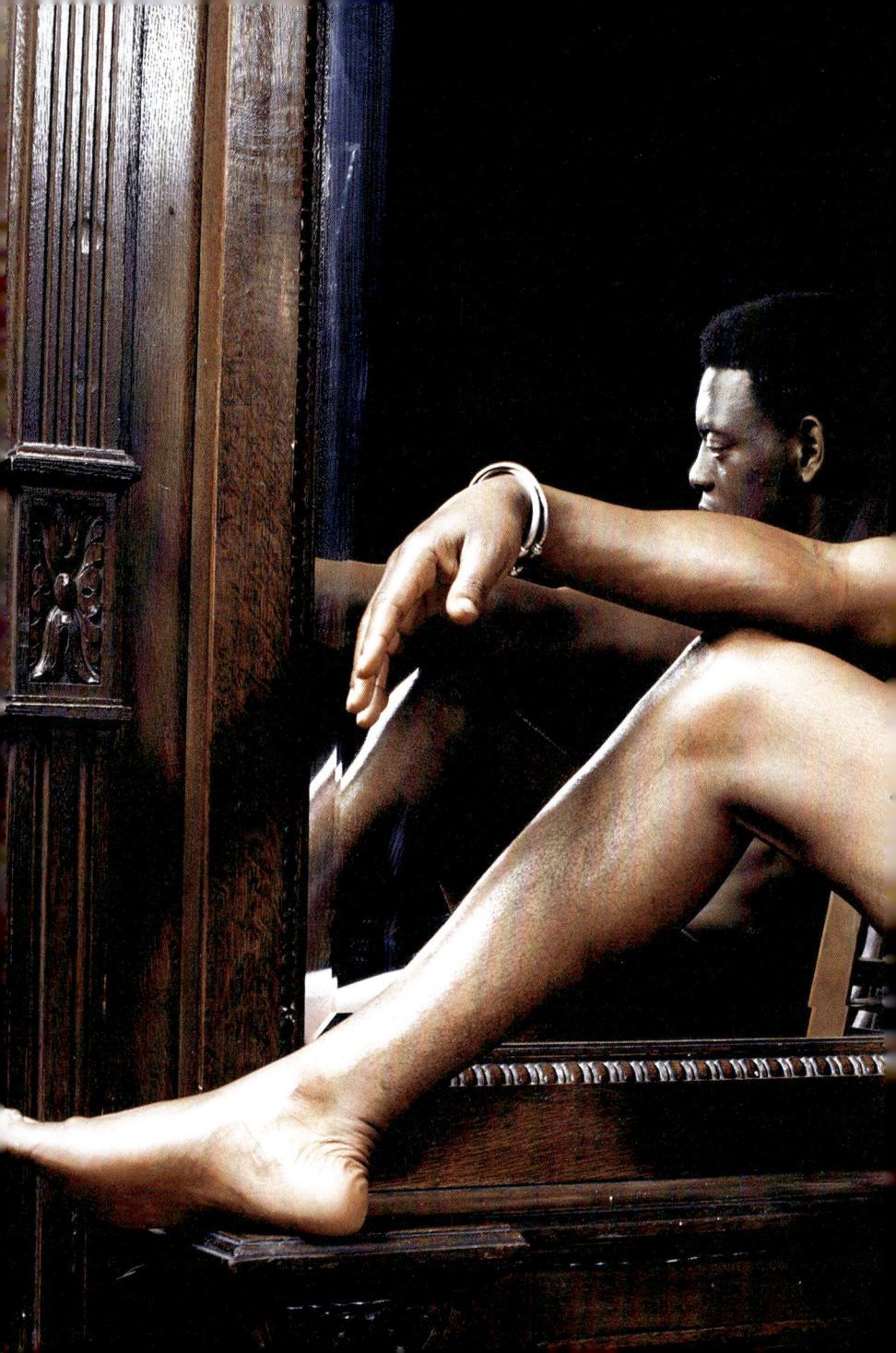

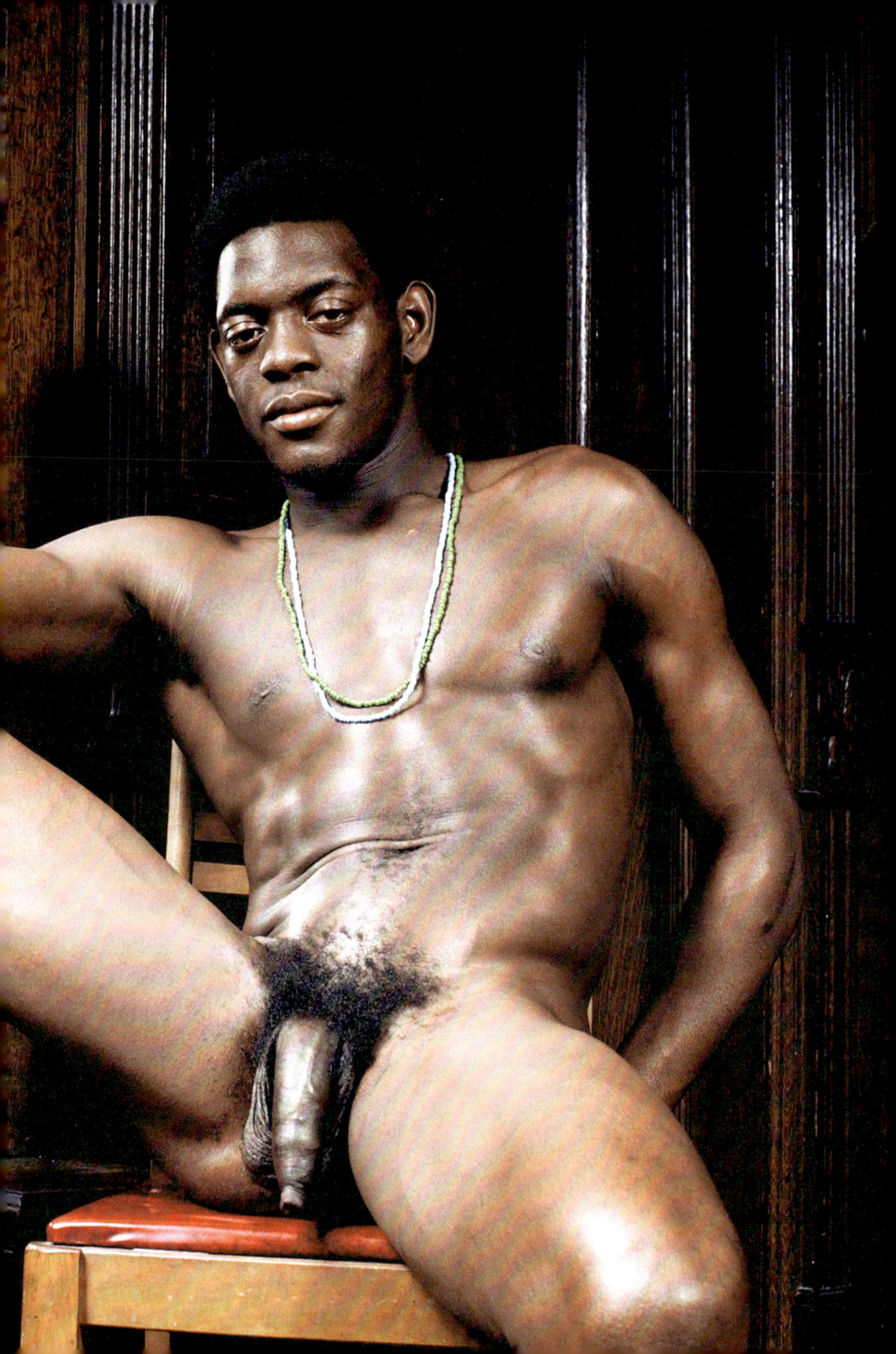

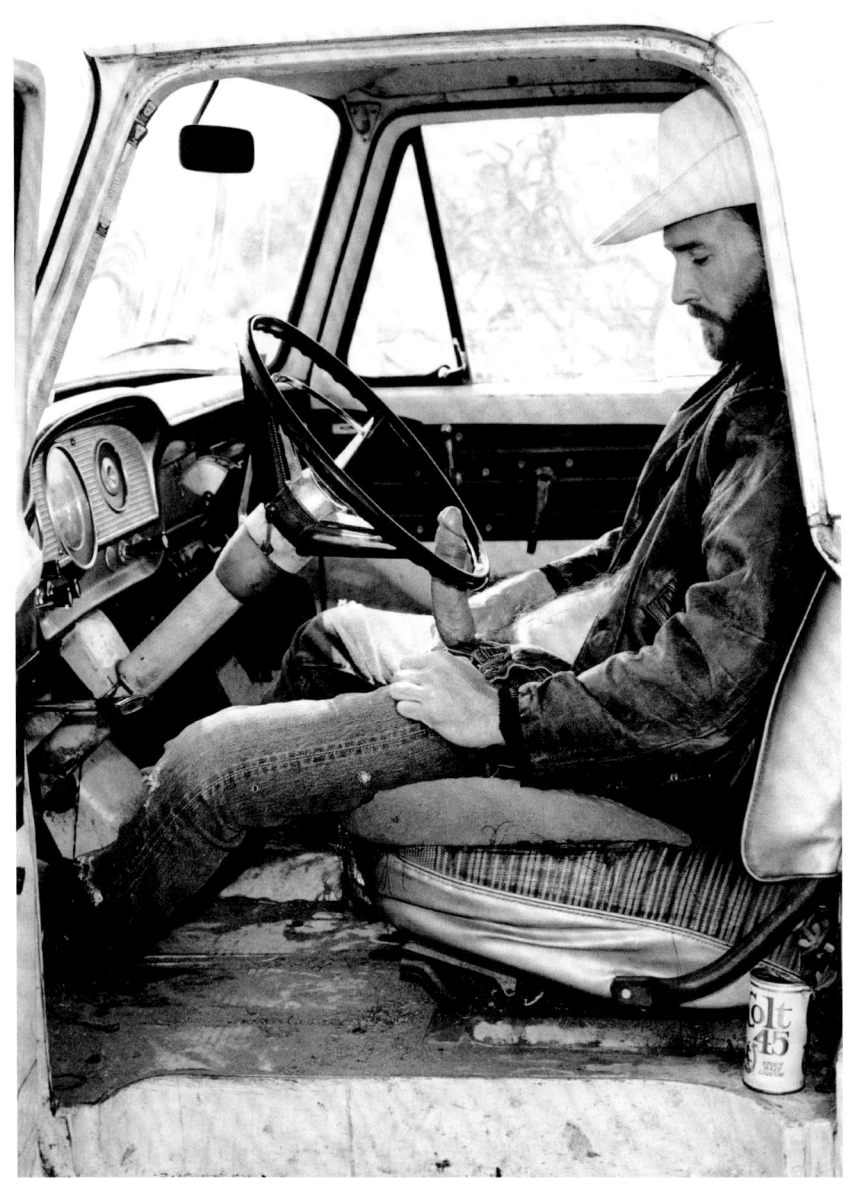

PAGES 58-59 **Youngblood**   ABOVE **Ken Orsino**   OPPOSITE **Toby**

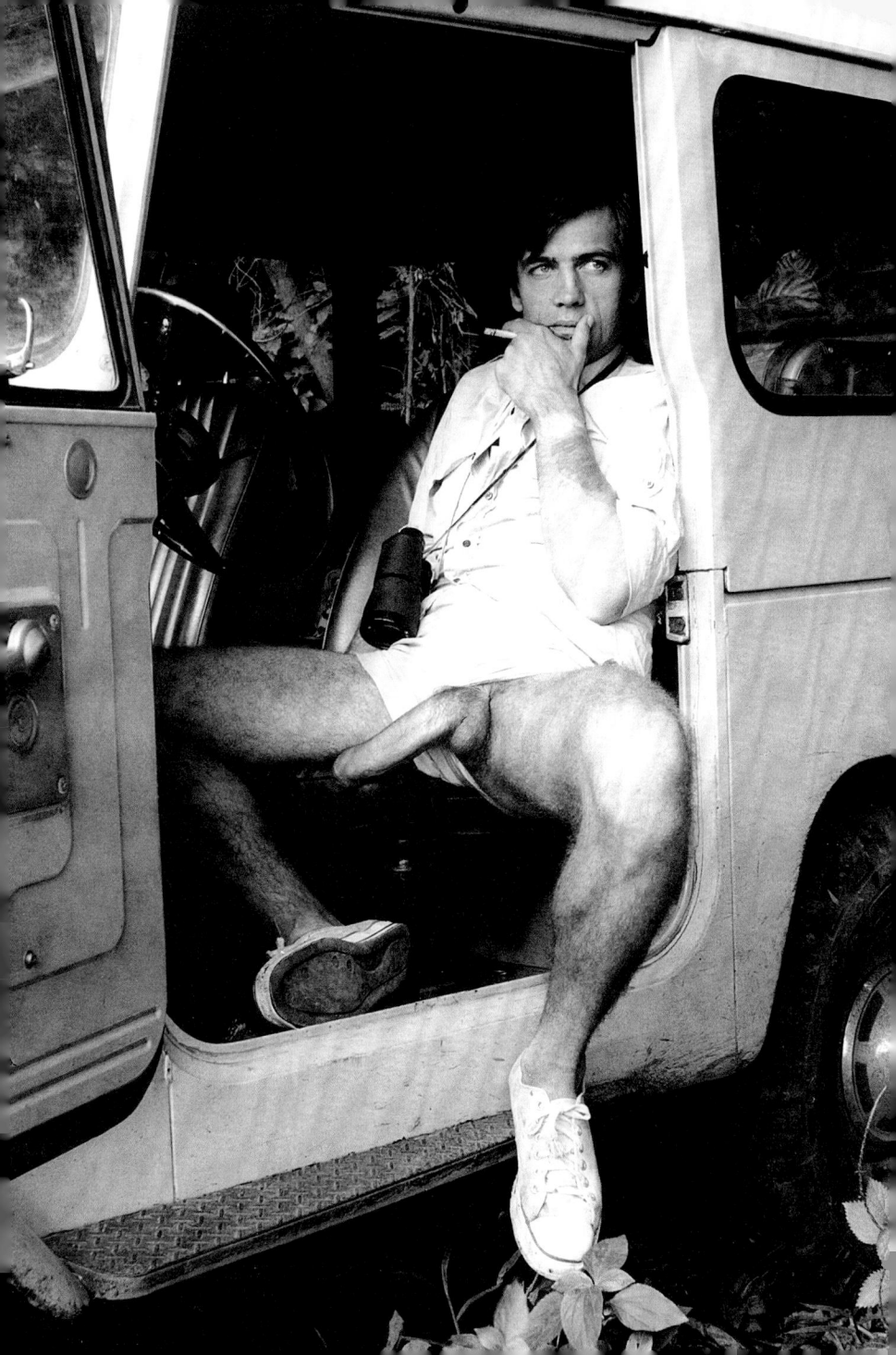

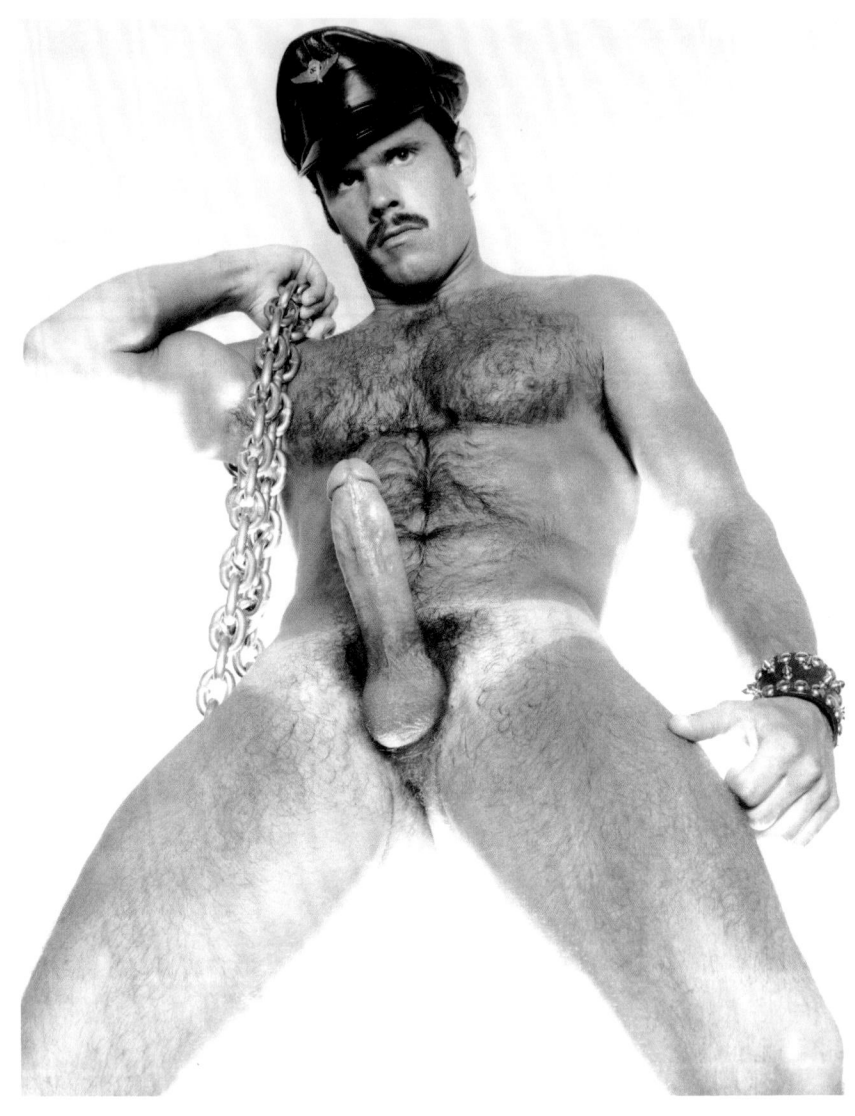

Peter Stride

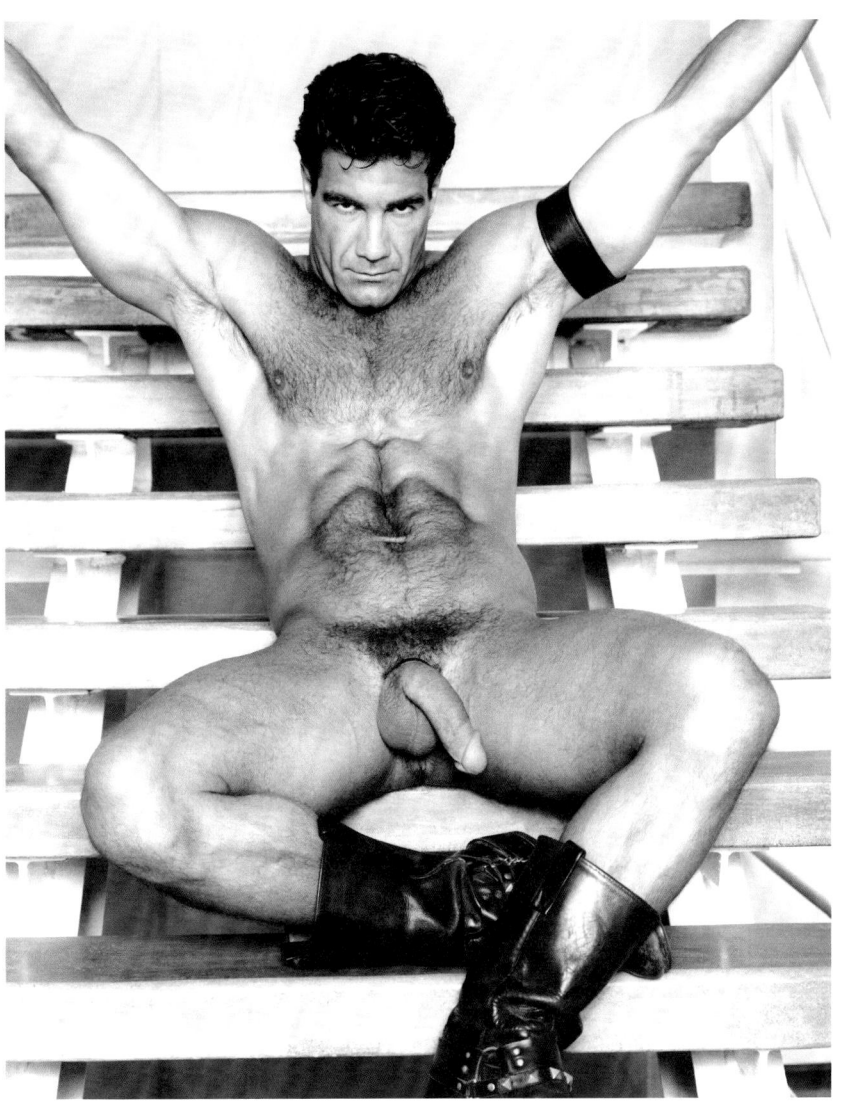

Tony Ganz

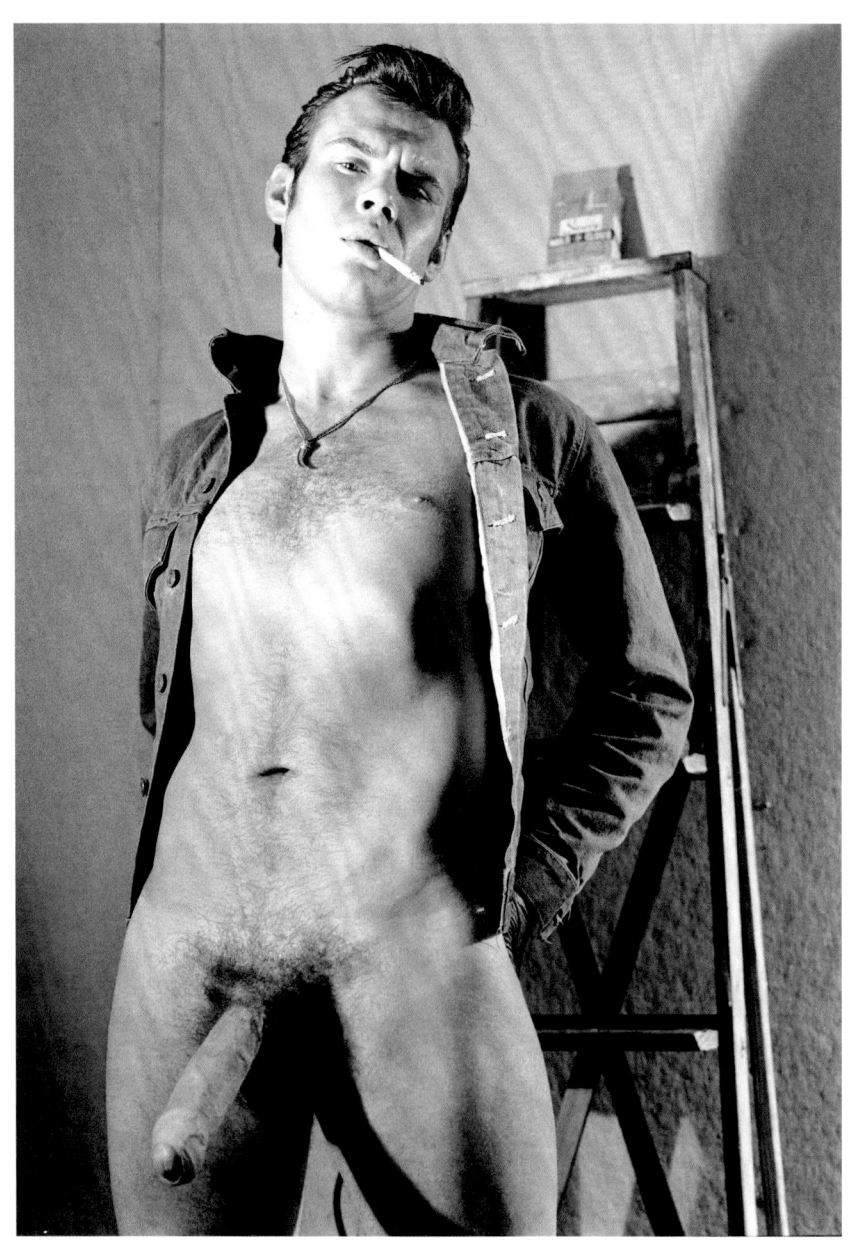

ABOVE **Duke** OPPOSITE **Glenn Steers**

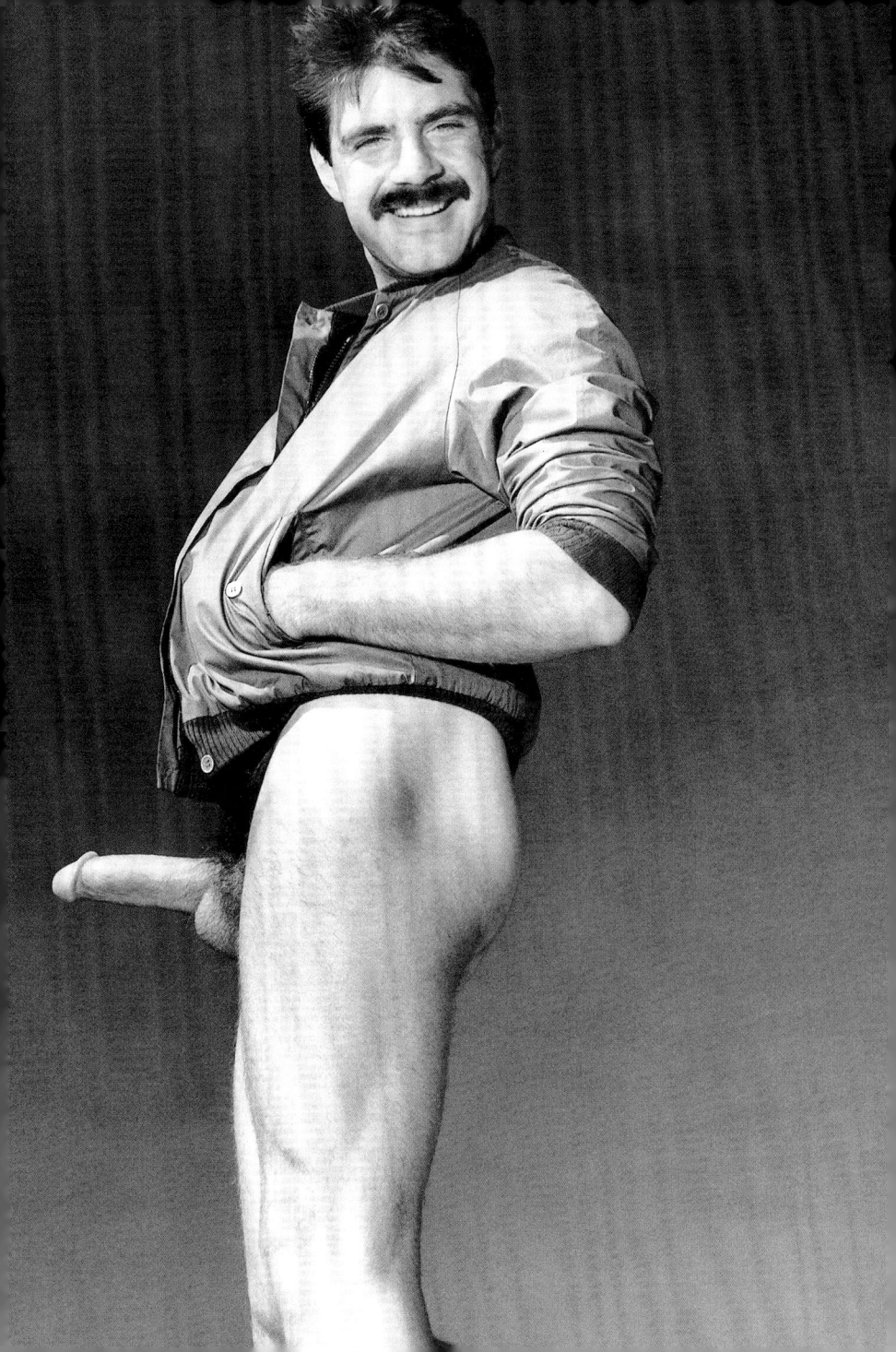

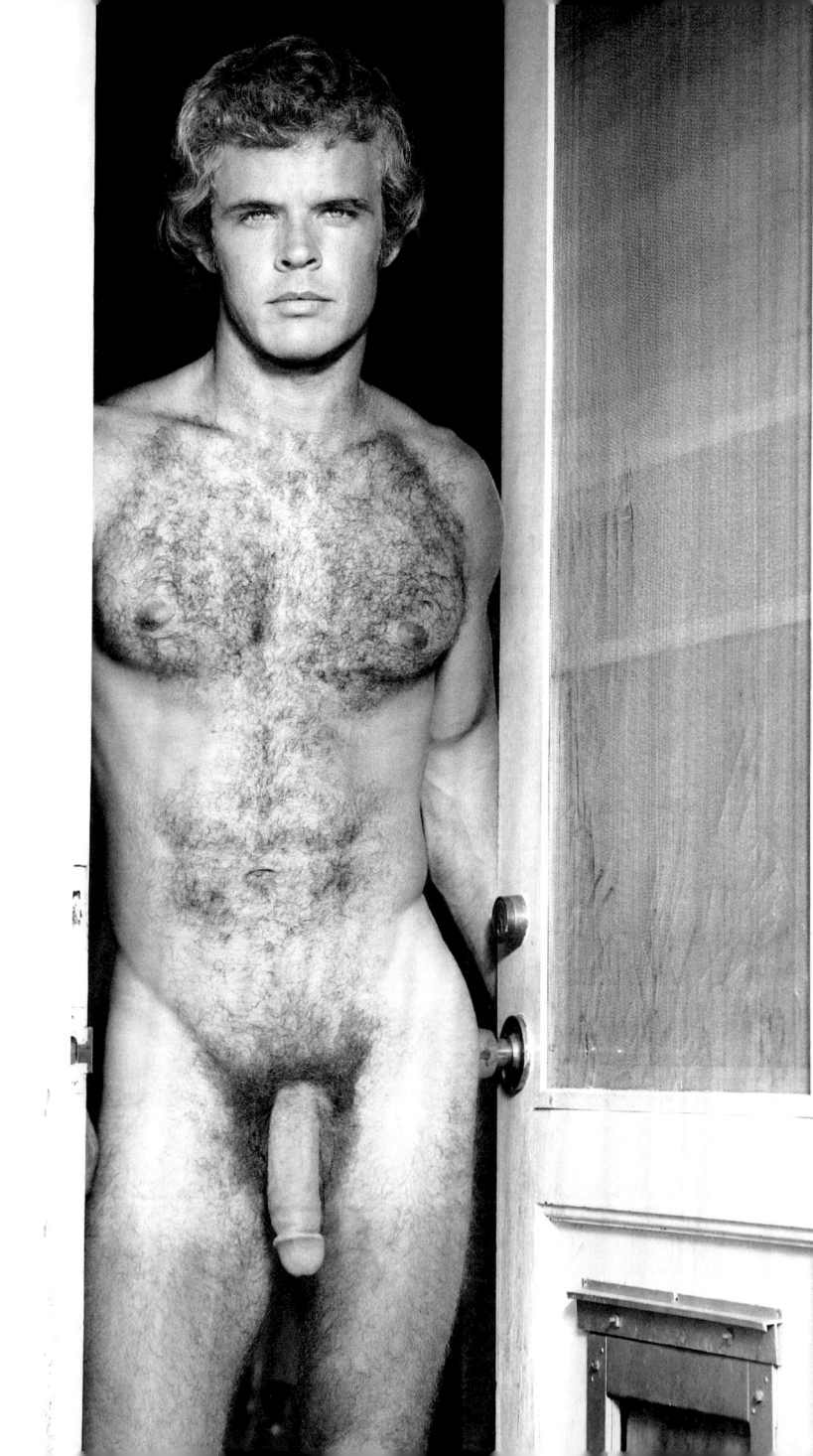

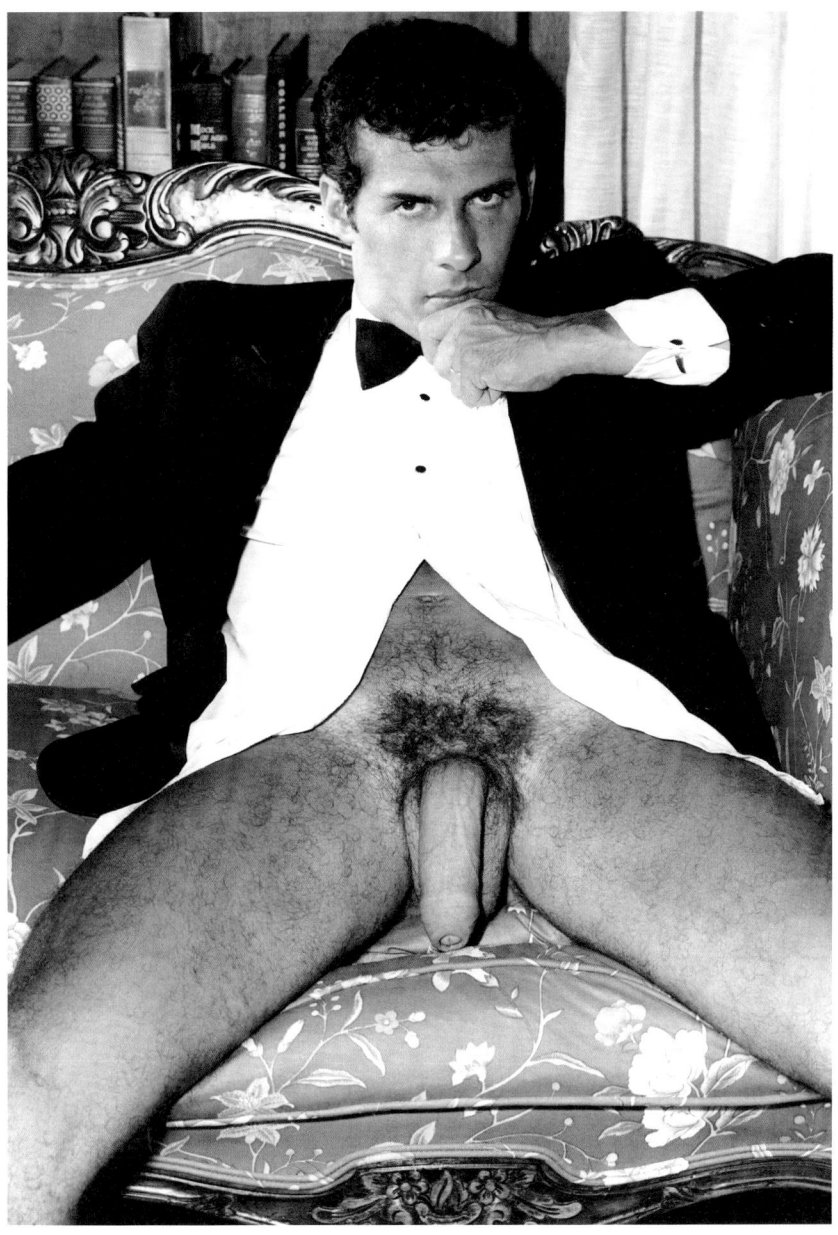

OPPOSITE **Richard Gunning**   ABOVE **Rocco Rizzoli**

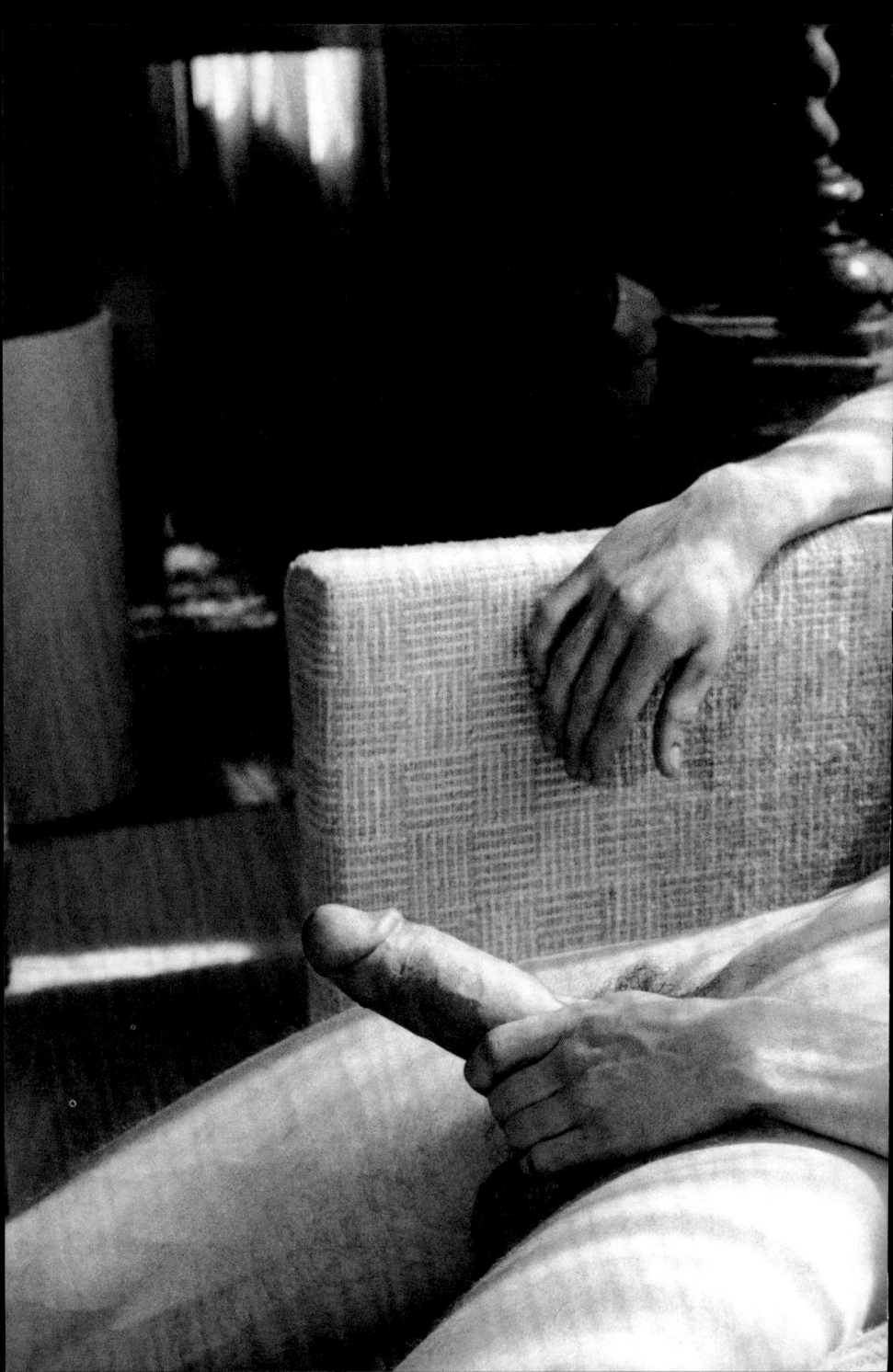

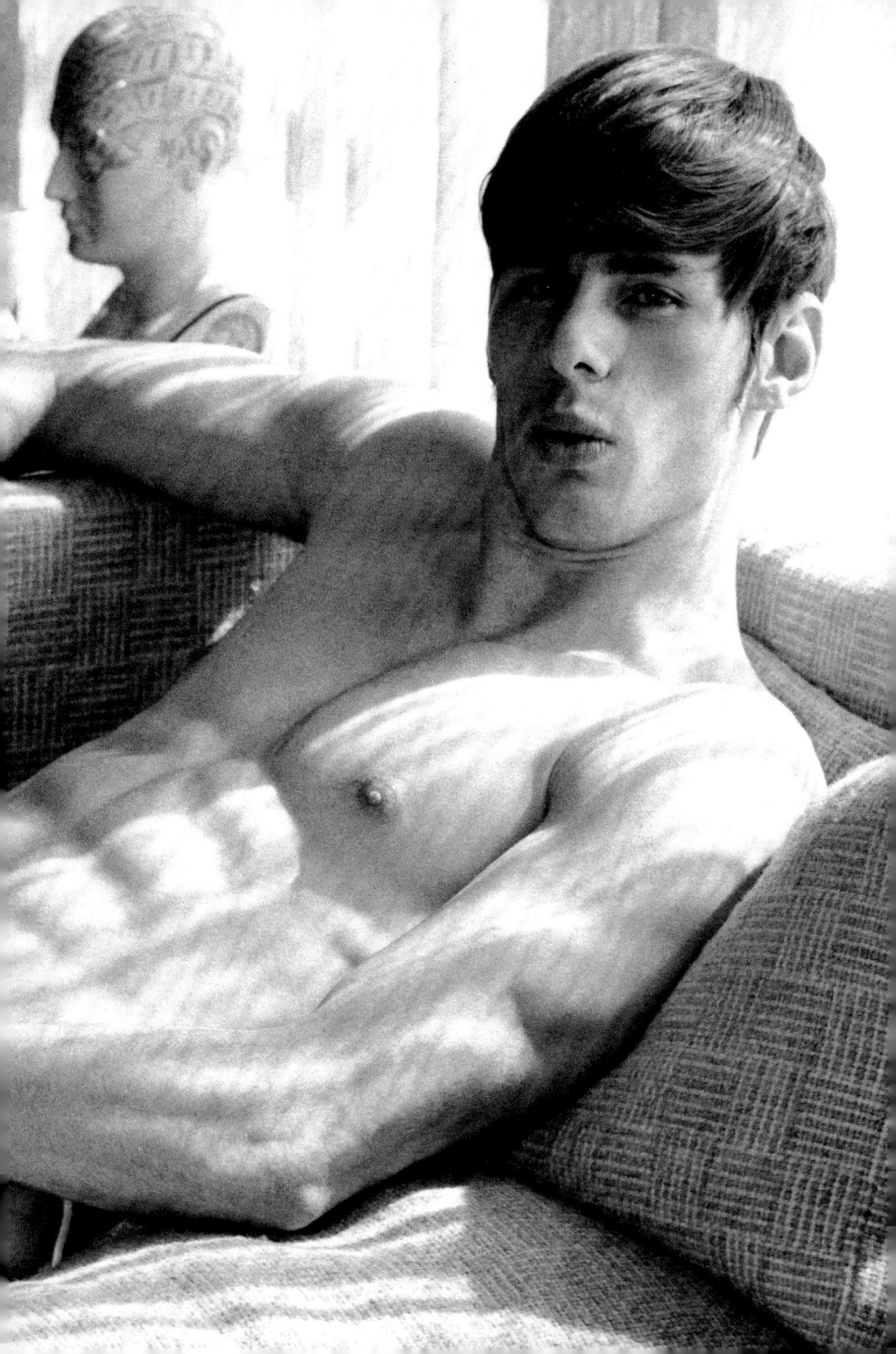

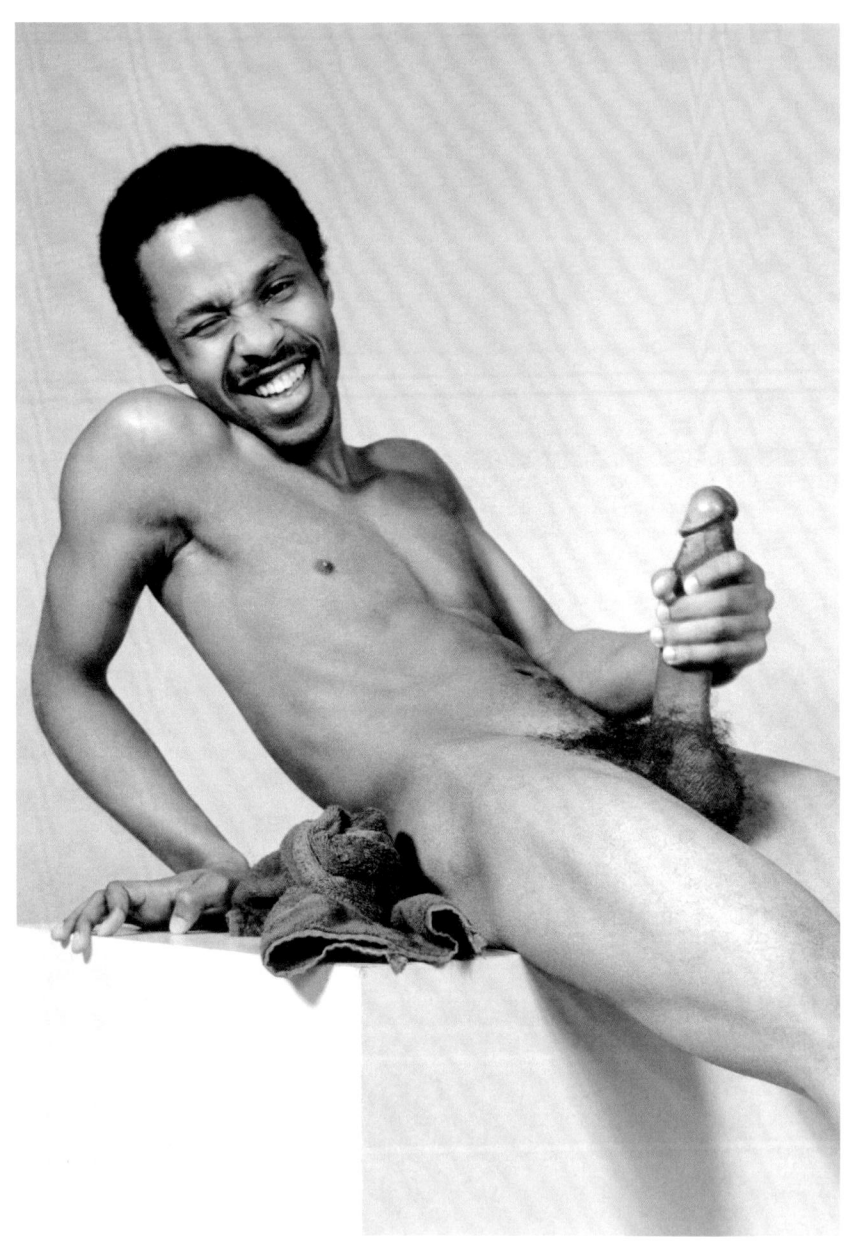

PAGES 68-69 **Billy**   ABOVE **Daniel**

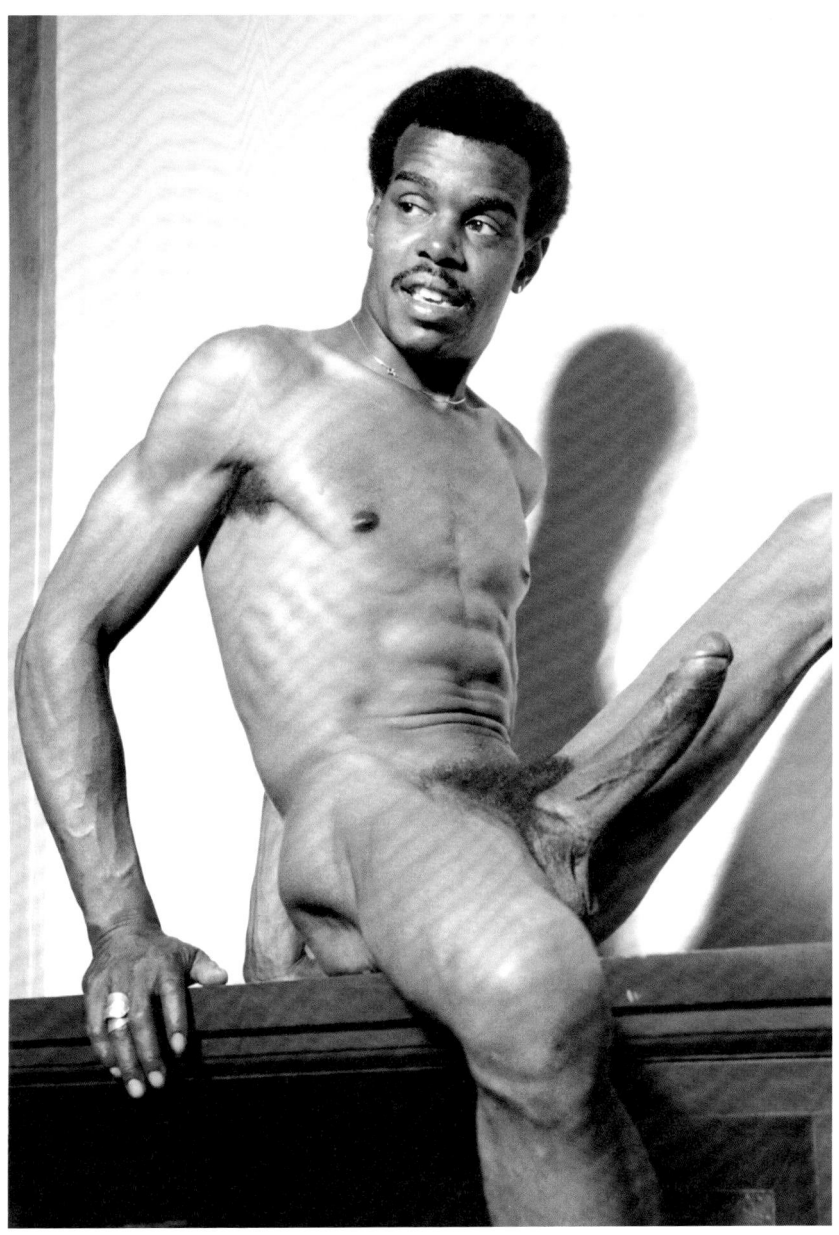

Dynamite

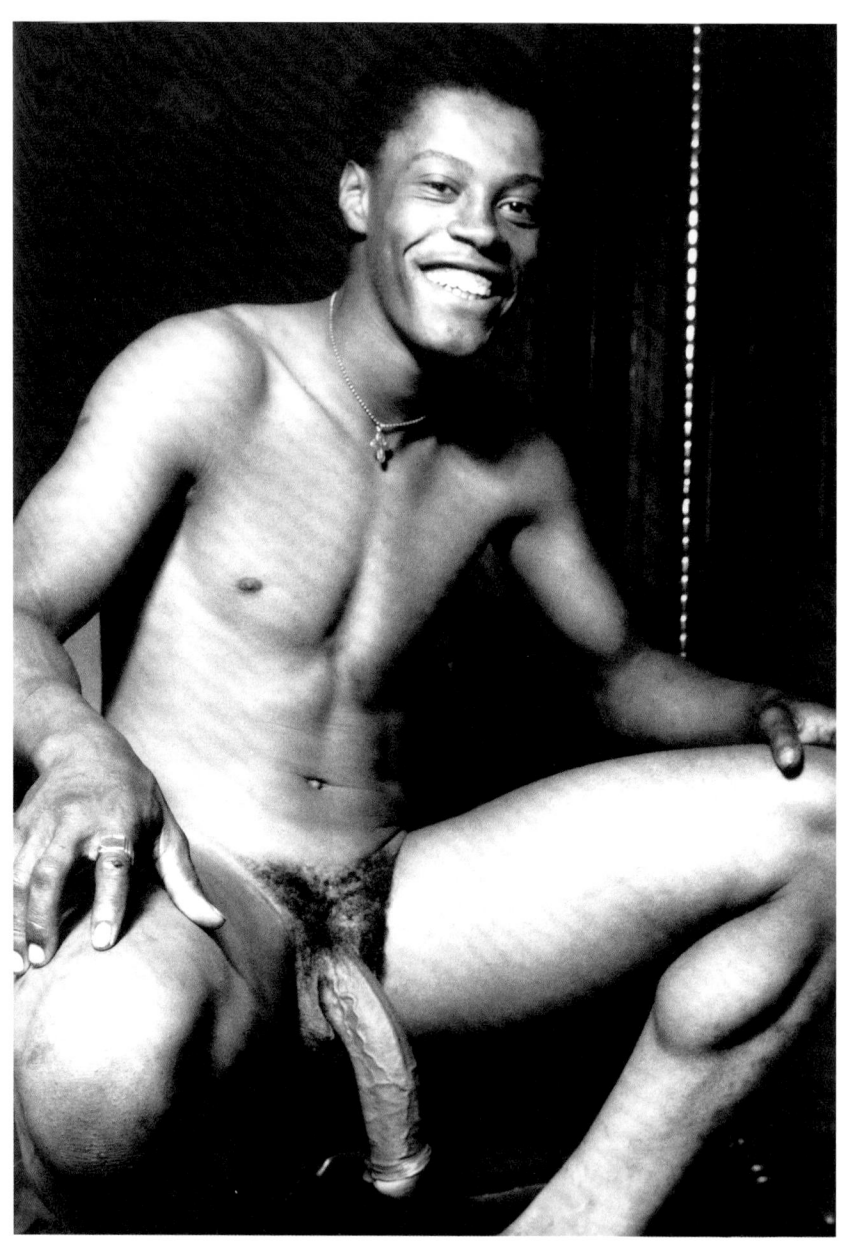

ABOVE **Sputnik** OPPOSITE **Cowboy**

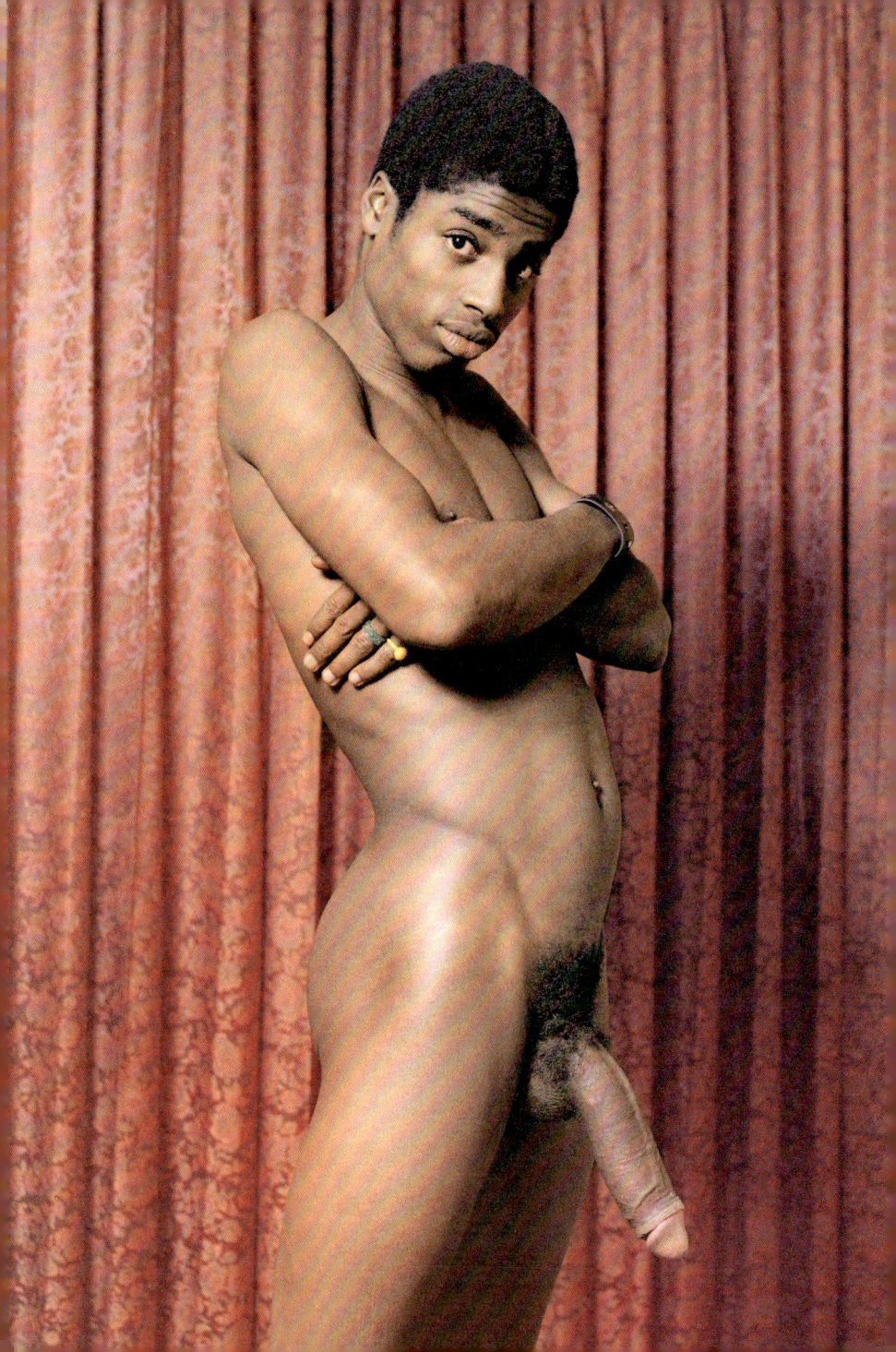

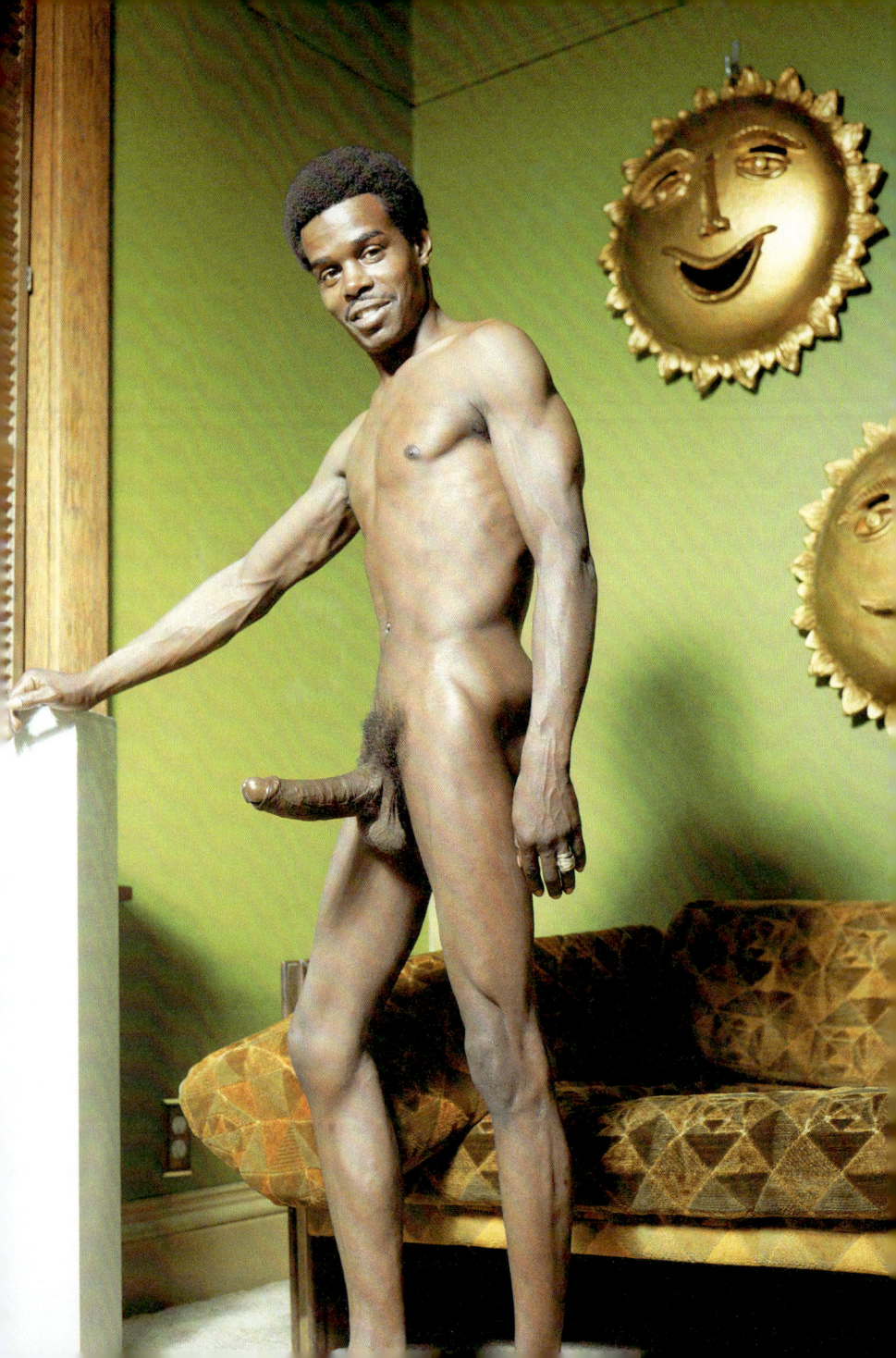

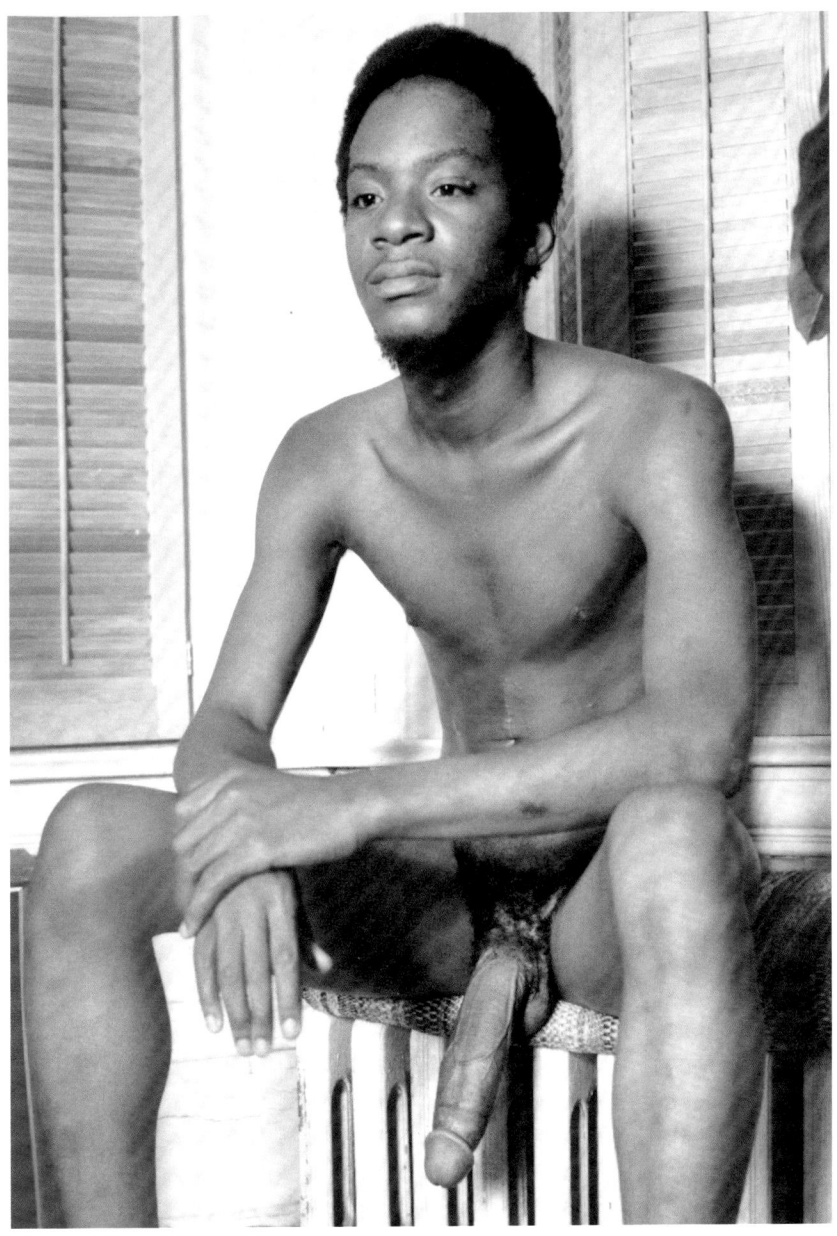

OPPOSITE **Dynamite**   ABOVE **Outlaw**   PAGES 76-77 **Mark**

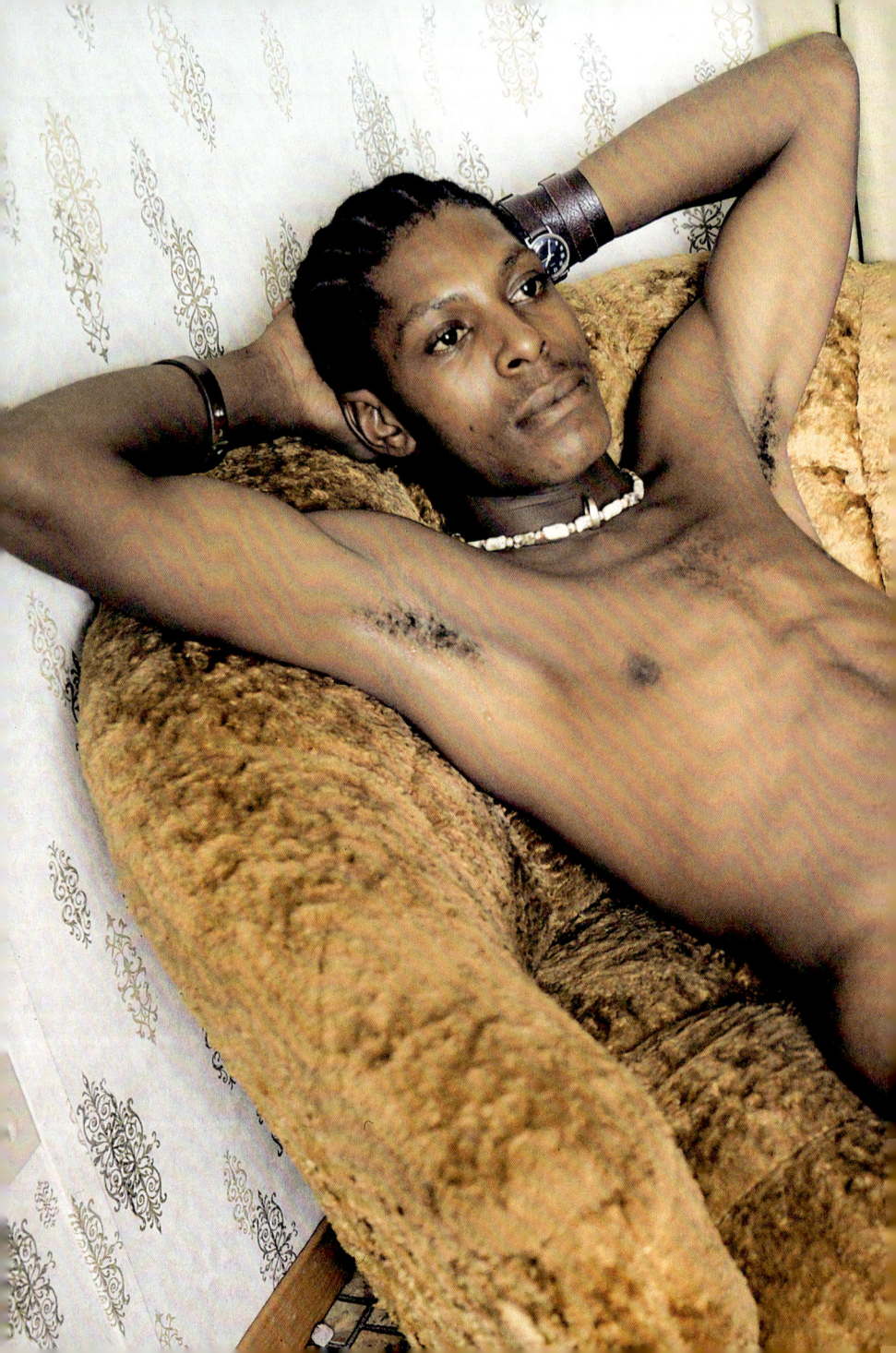

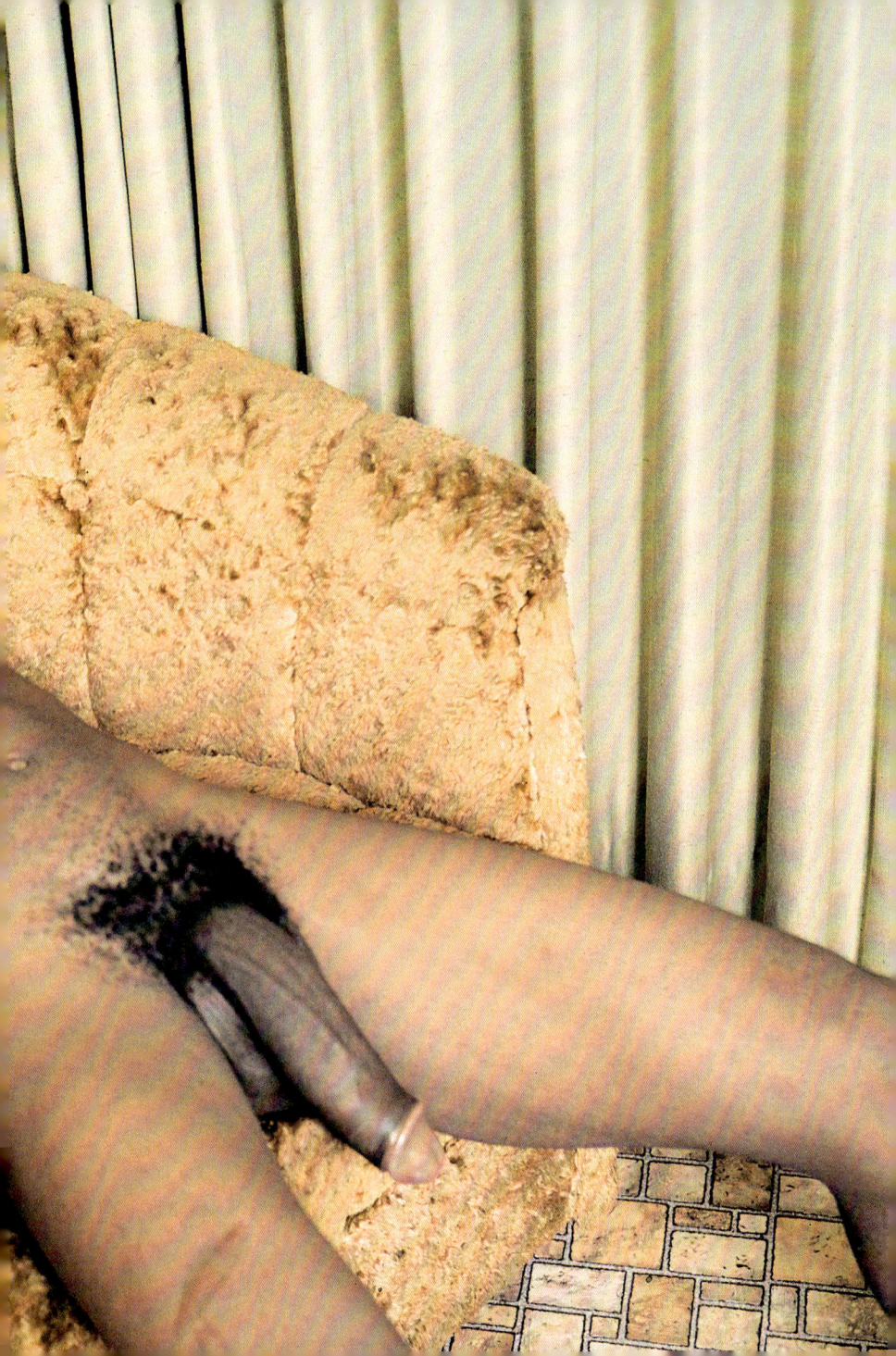

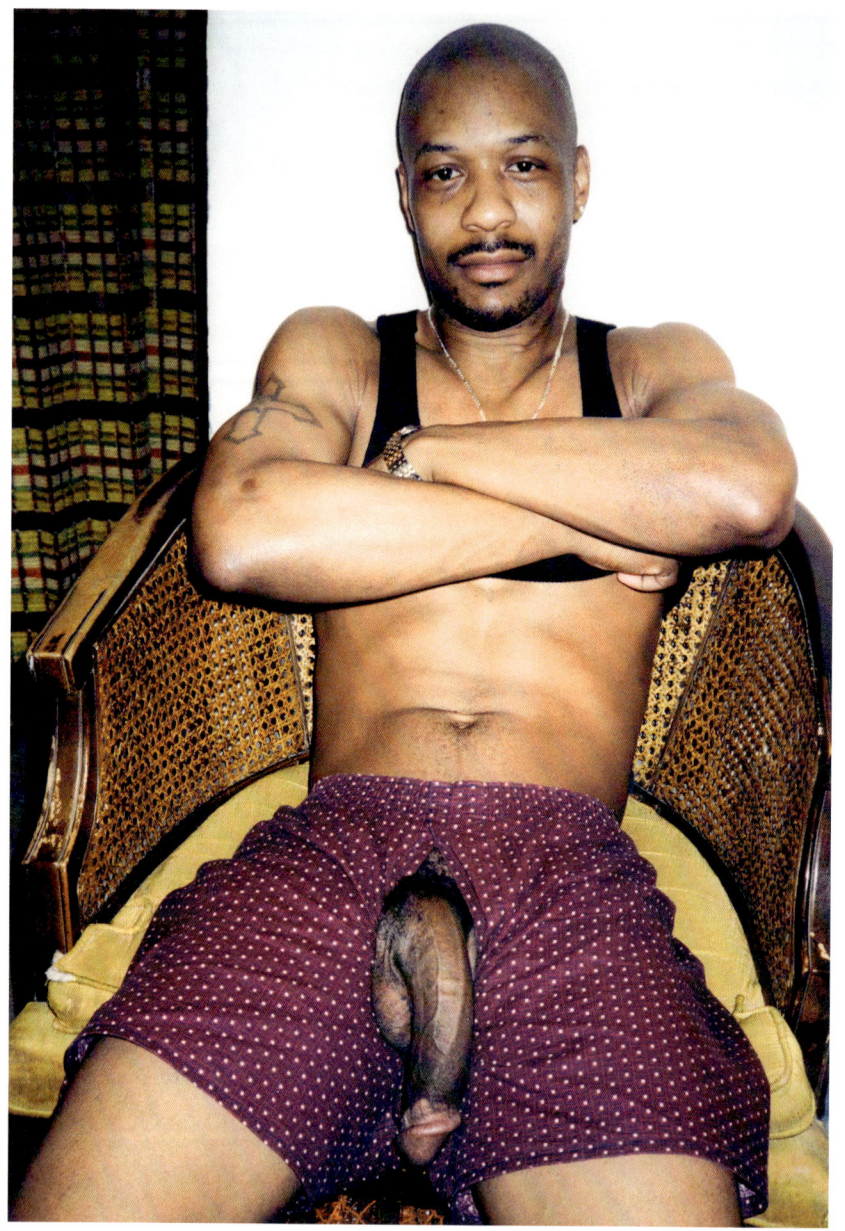

Paris

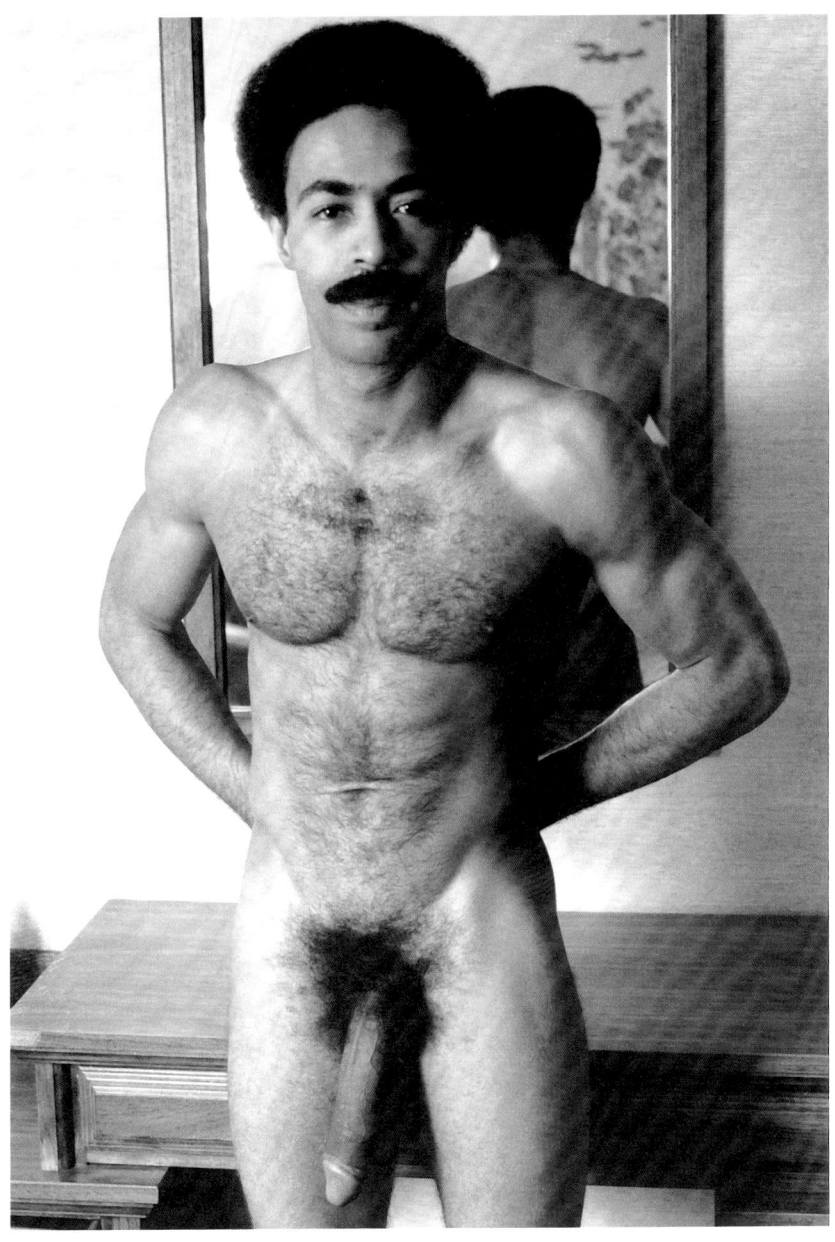

Reefer

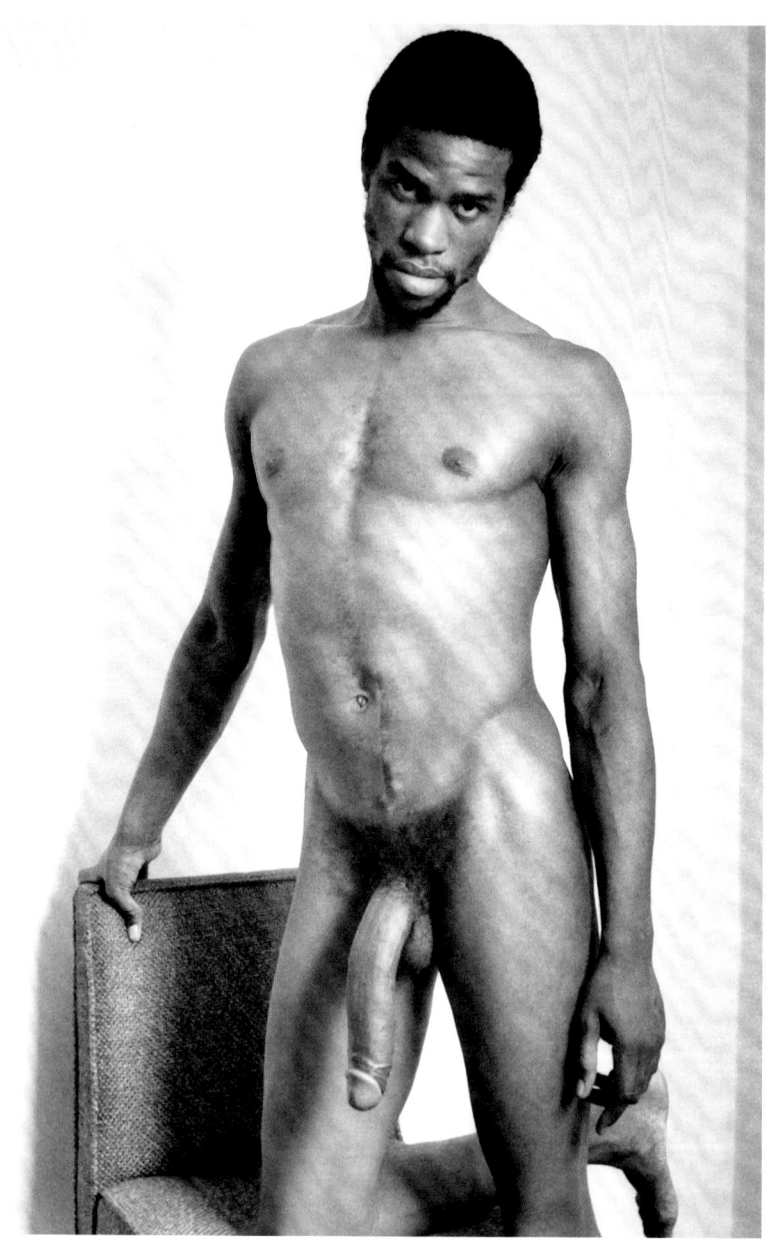

ABOVE **Gus**   OPPOSITE **Stan**   PAGES 82-83 **Dixon**

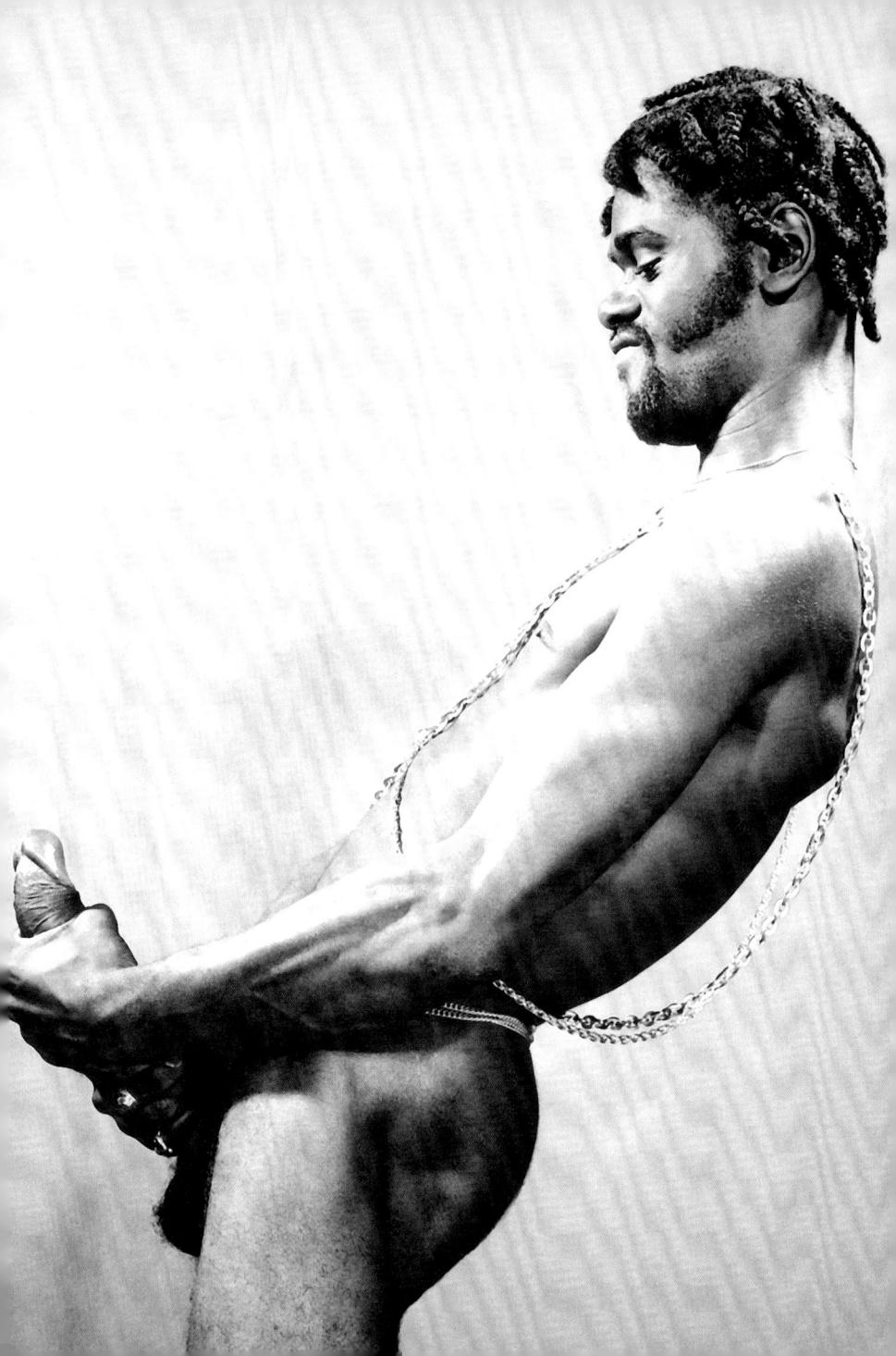

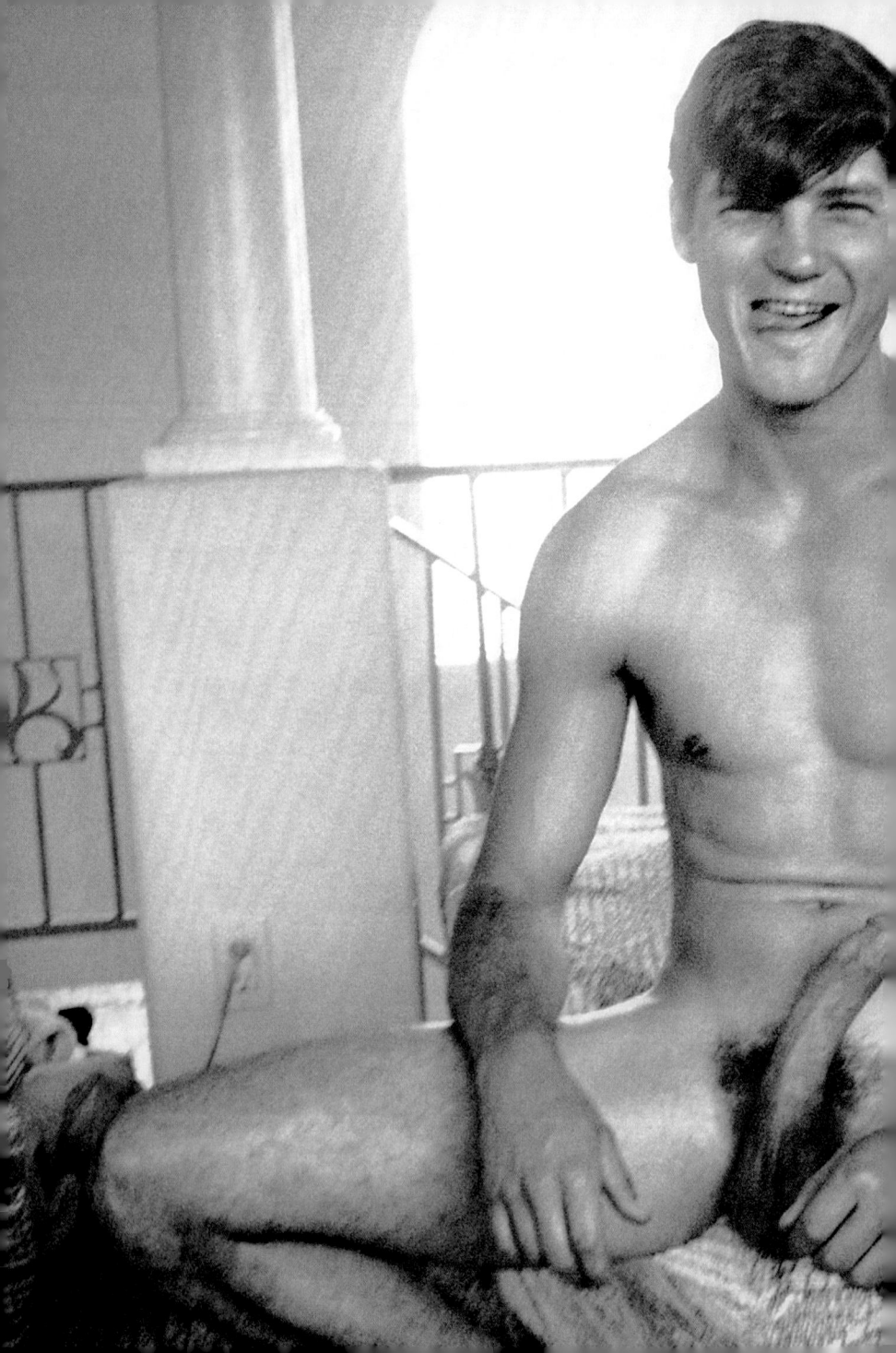

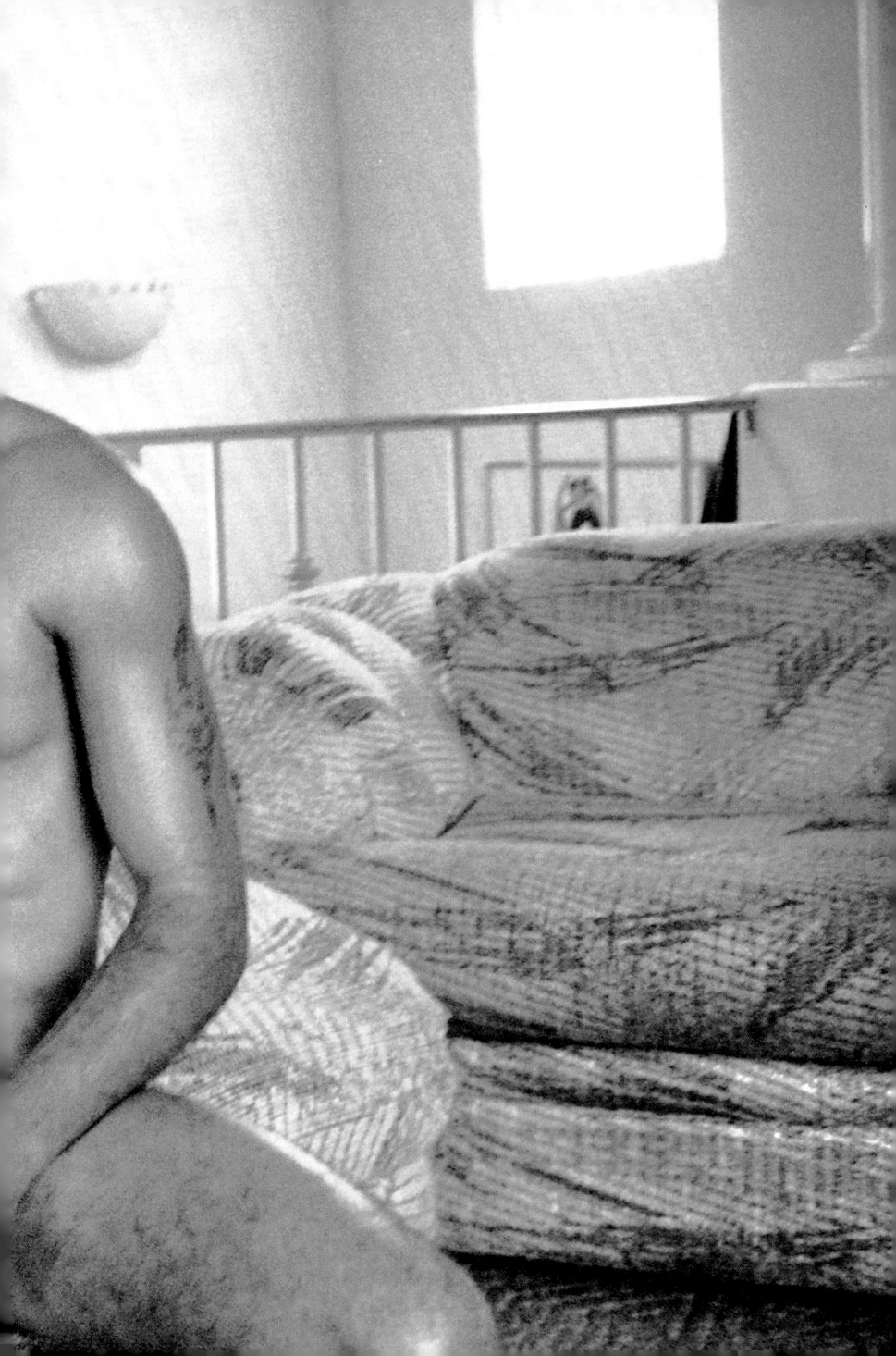

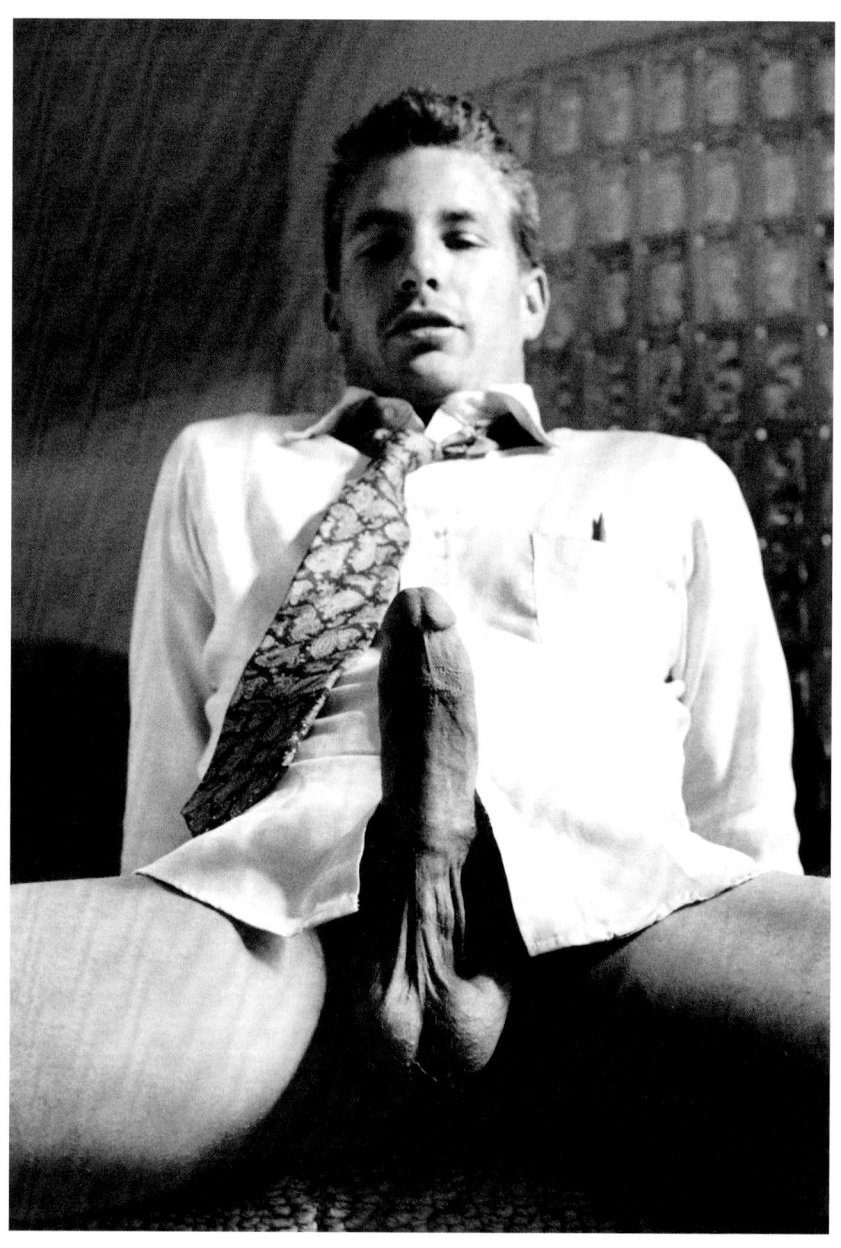

ABOVE **Springer** OPPOSITE **Steve Cougar** PAGES 86-87 **Ricky**

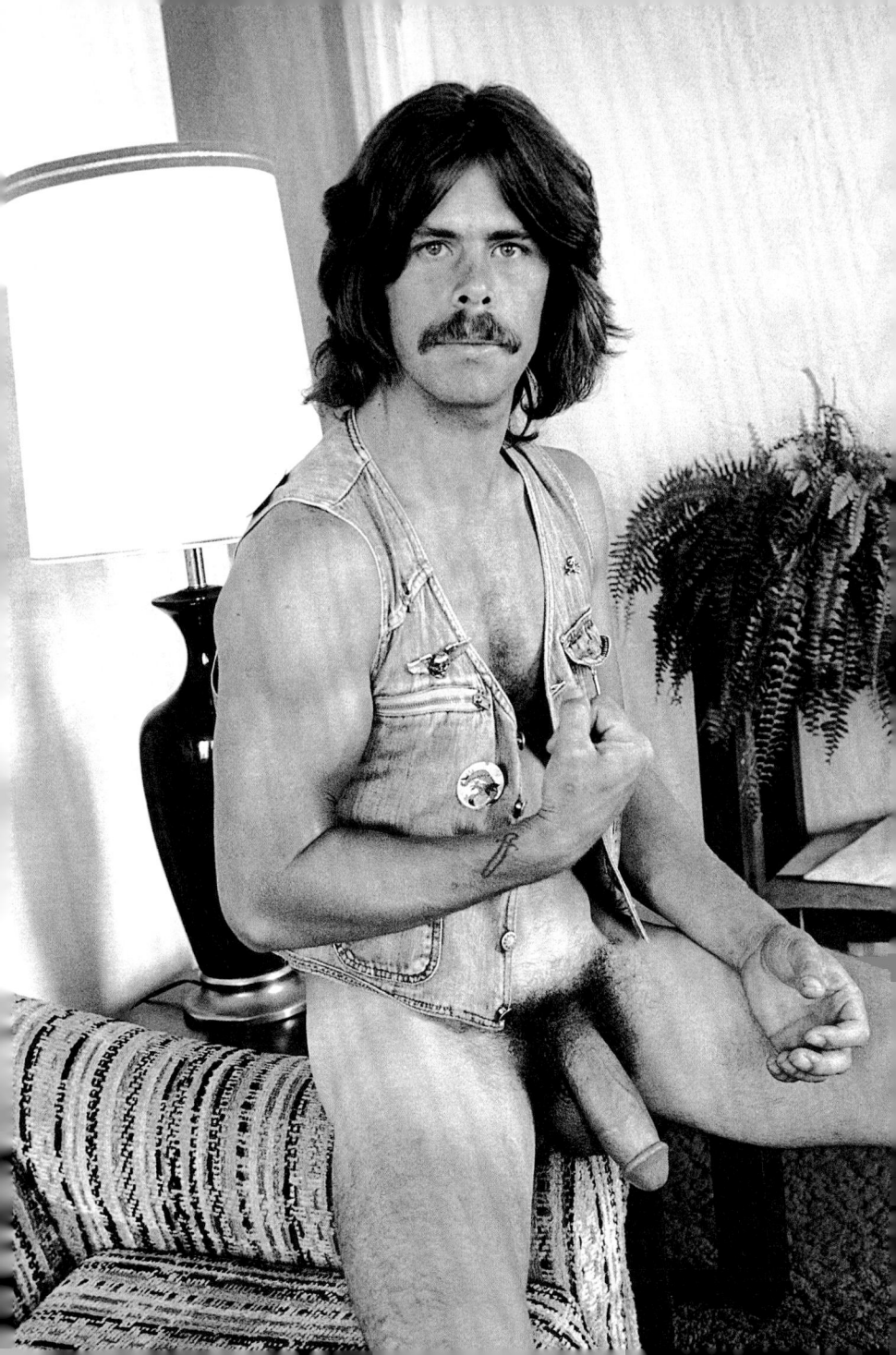

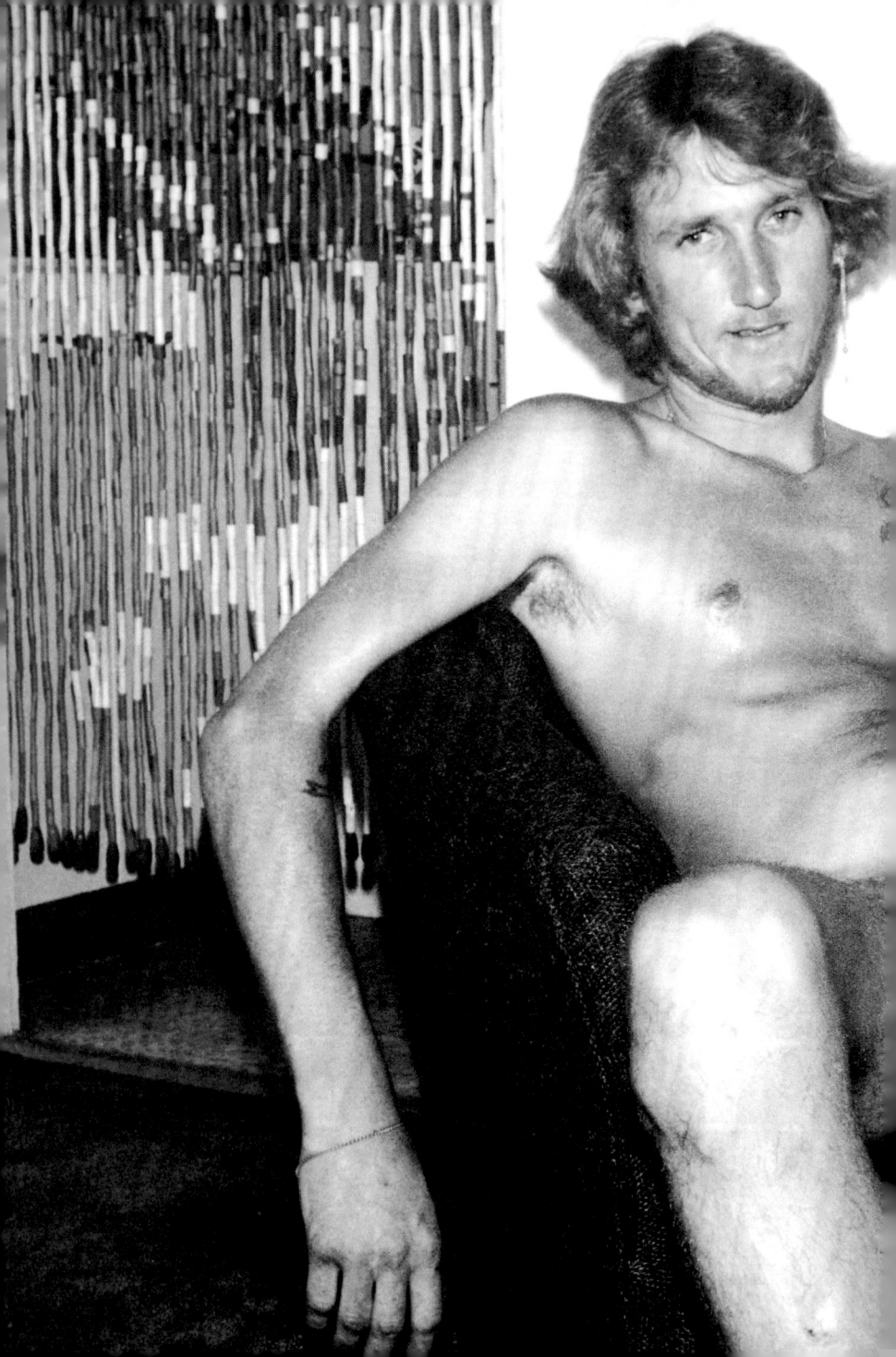

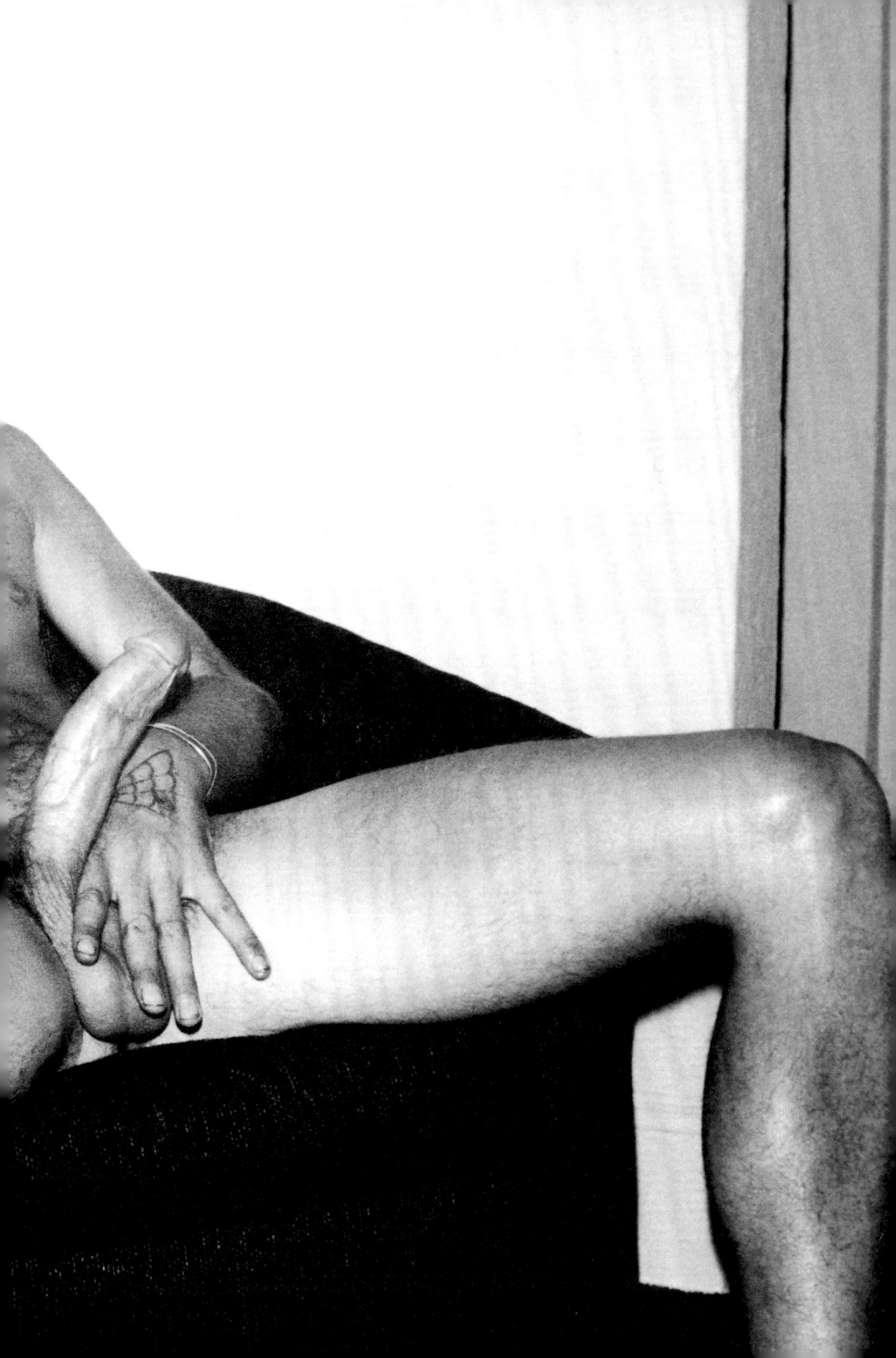

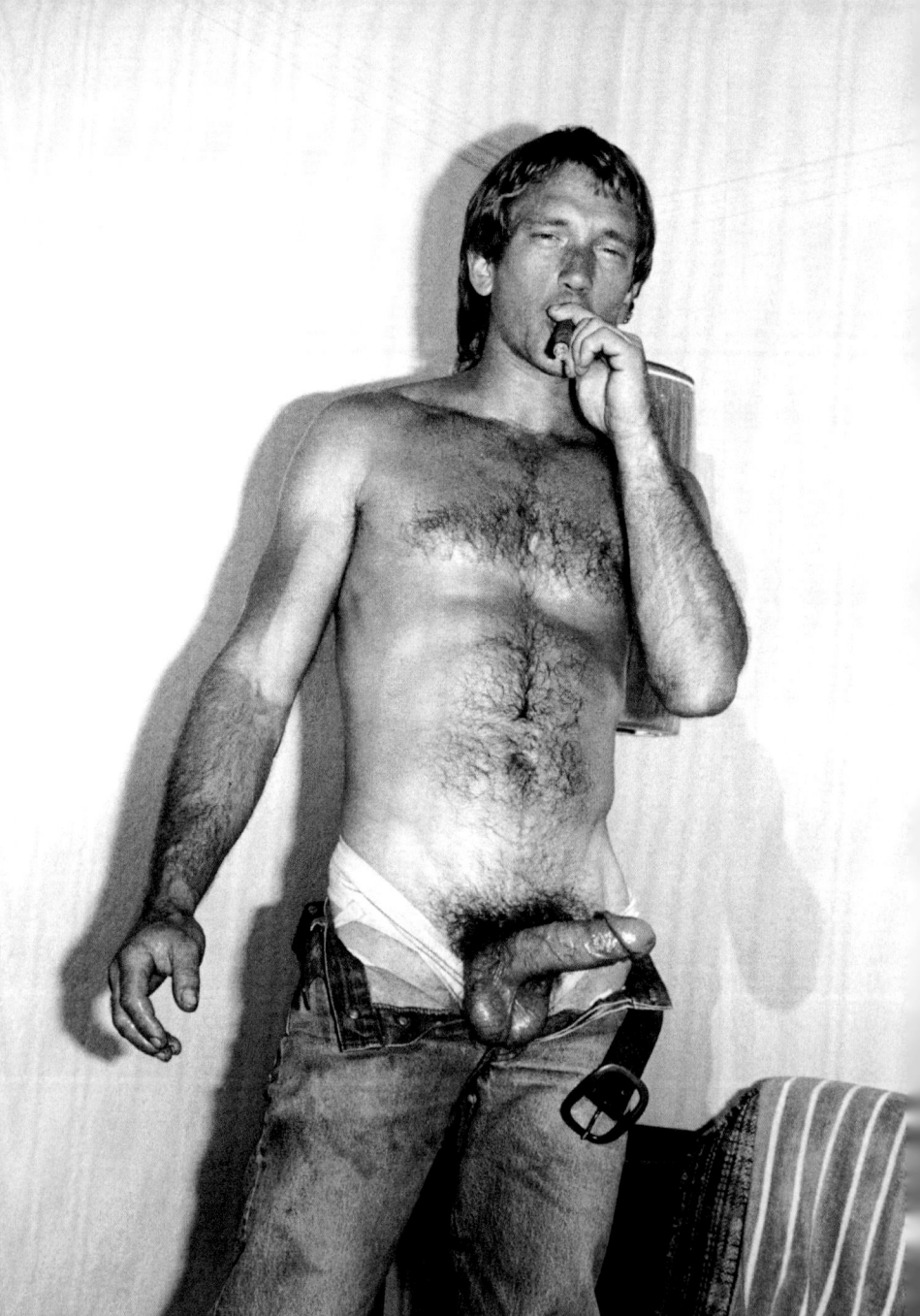

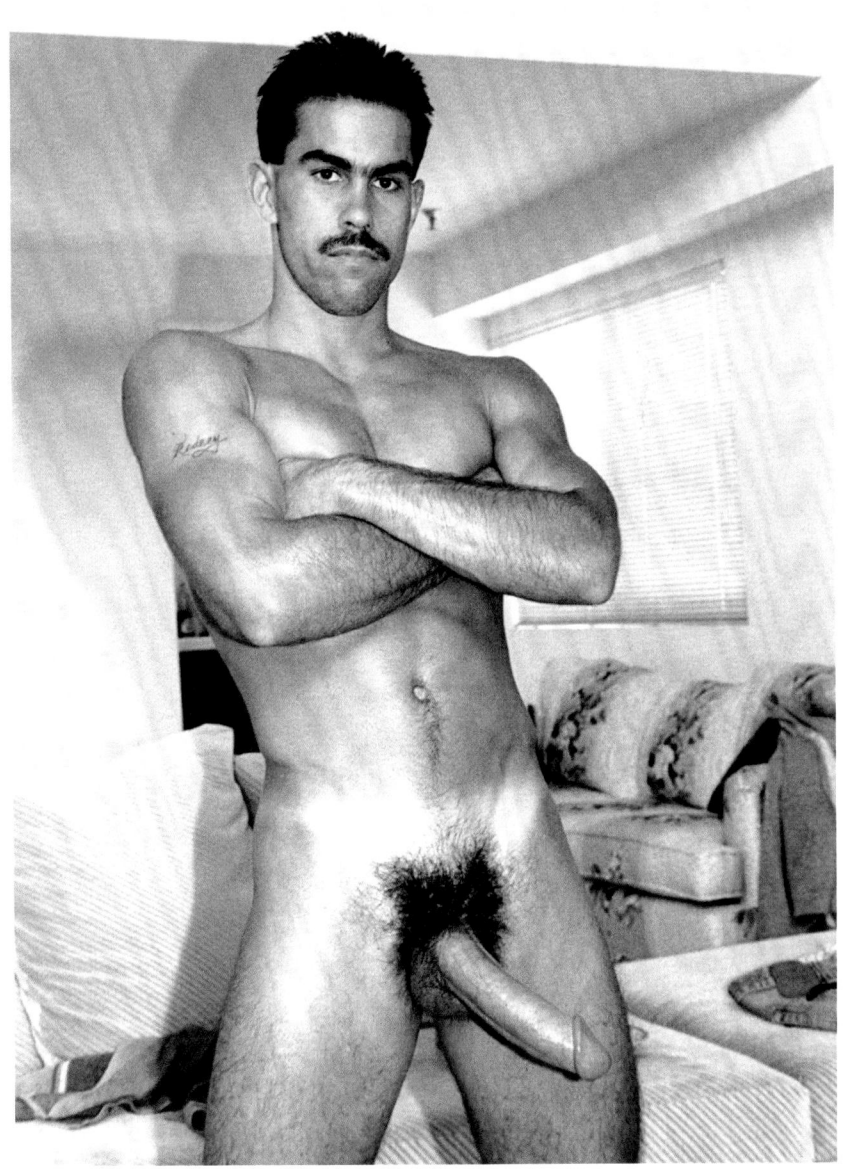

OPPOSITE **Bill Morgan**　ABOVE **Rod**　PAGES 90-91 **Lee**

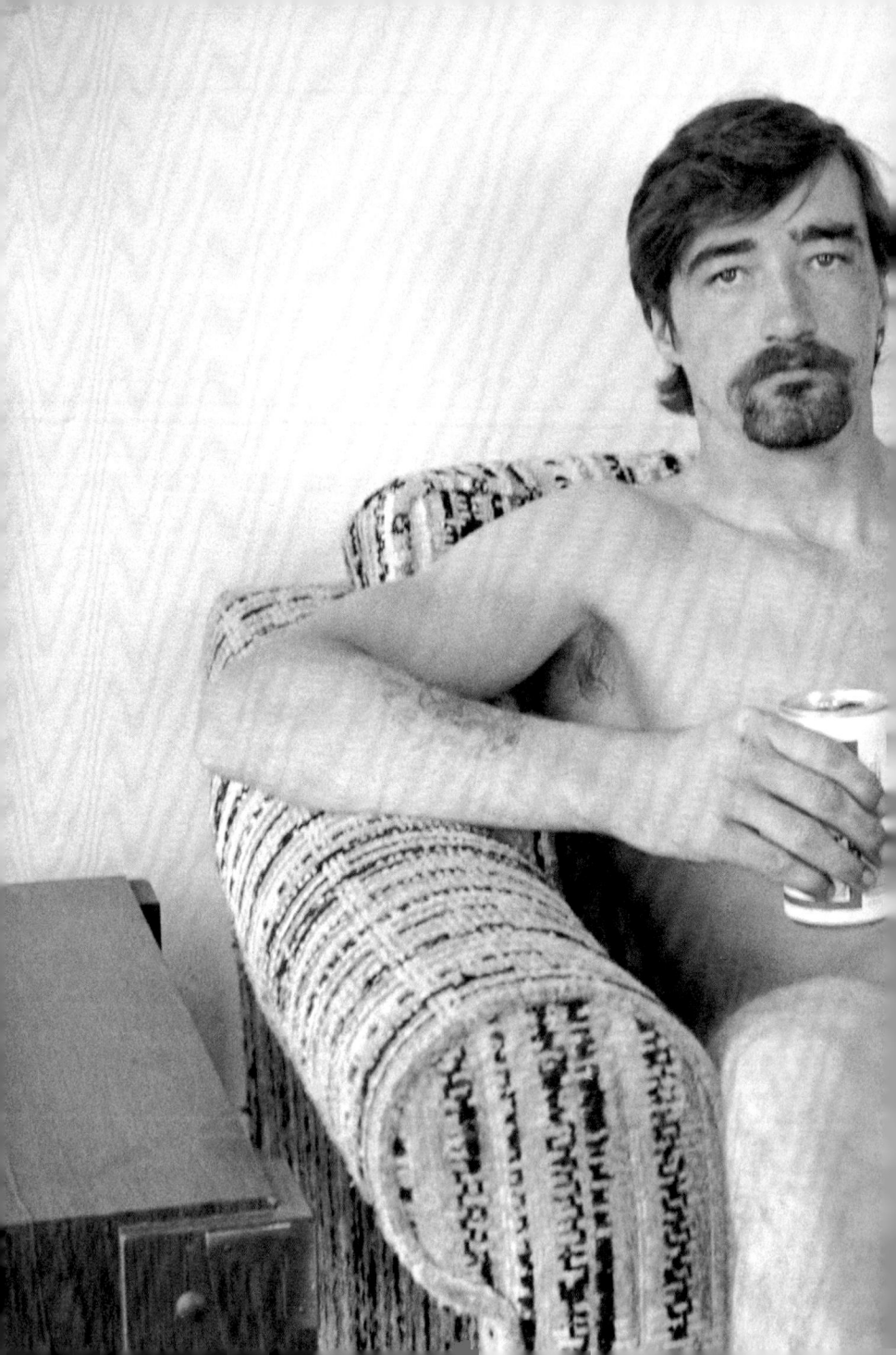

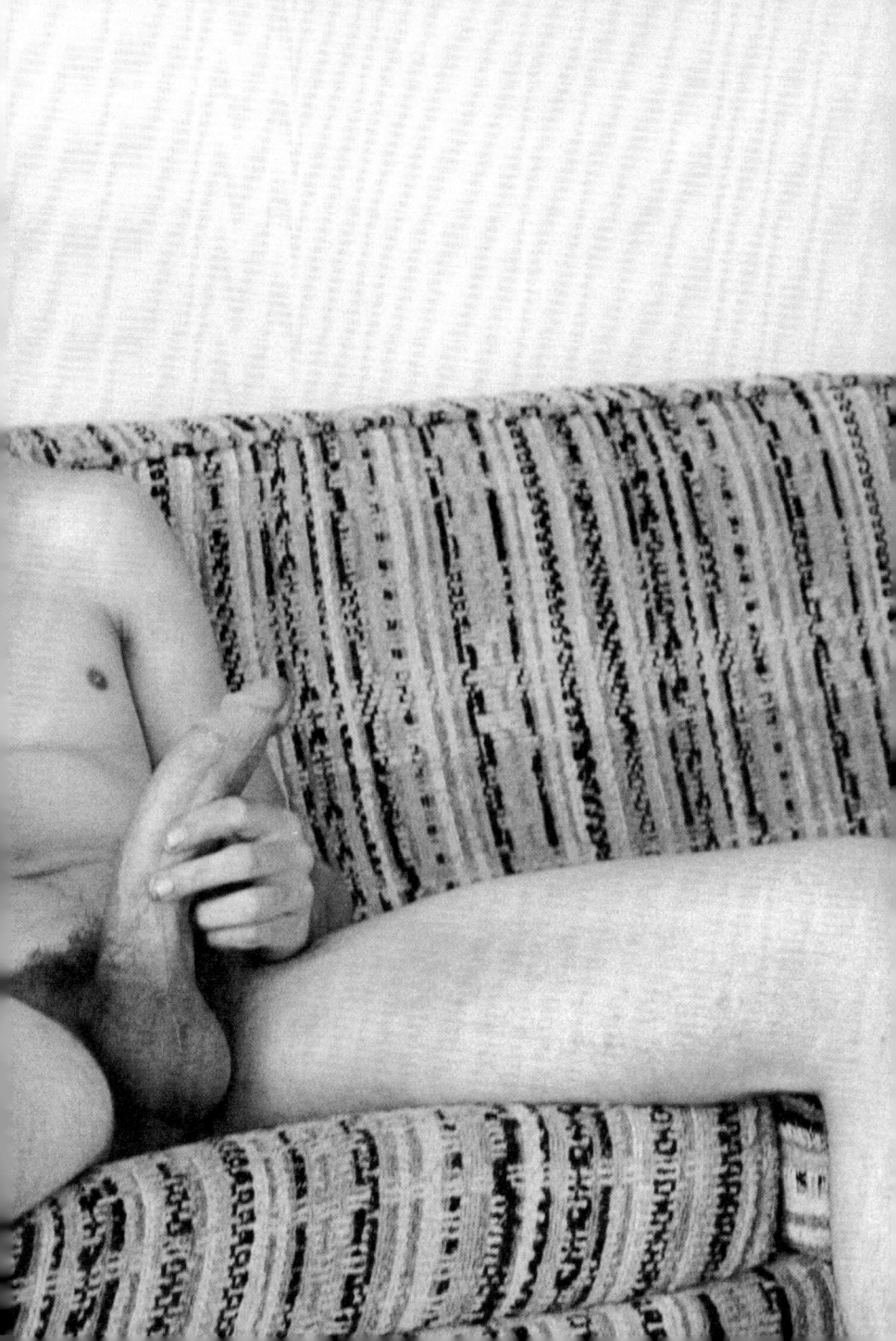

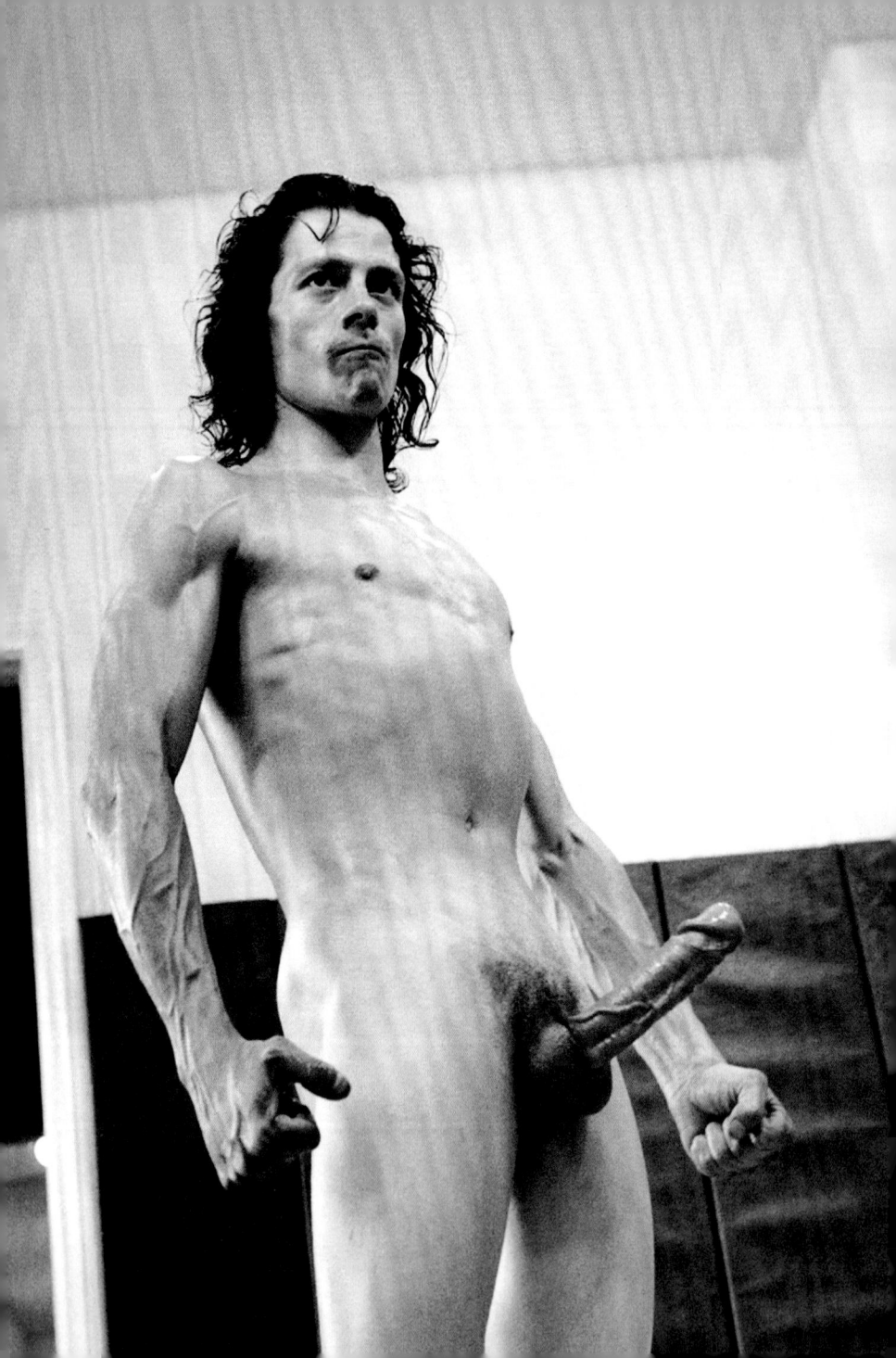

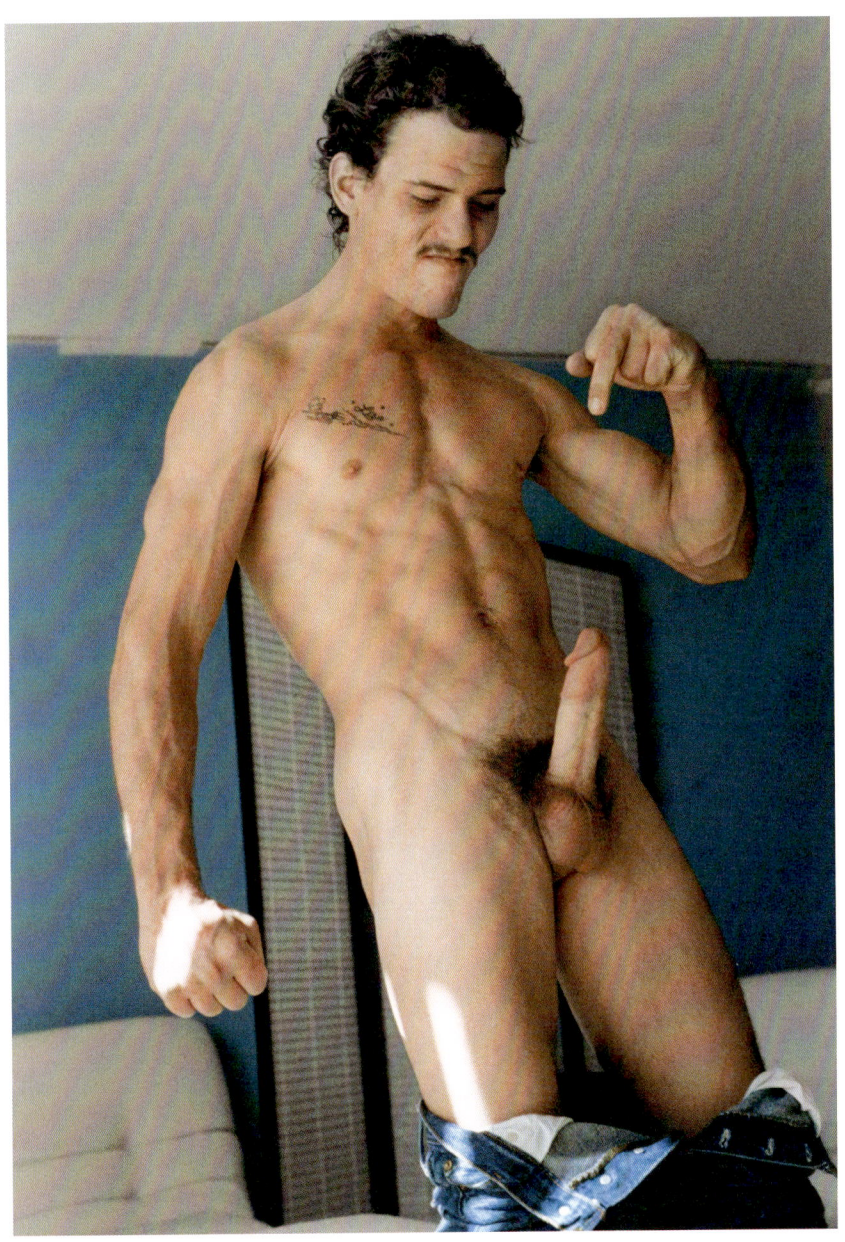

OPPOSITE **Powerful Pierre**   ABOVE **Champ**

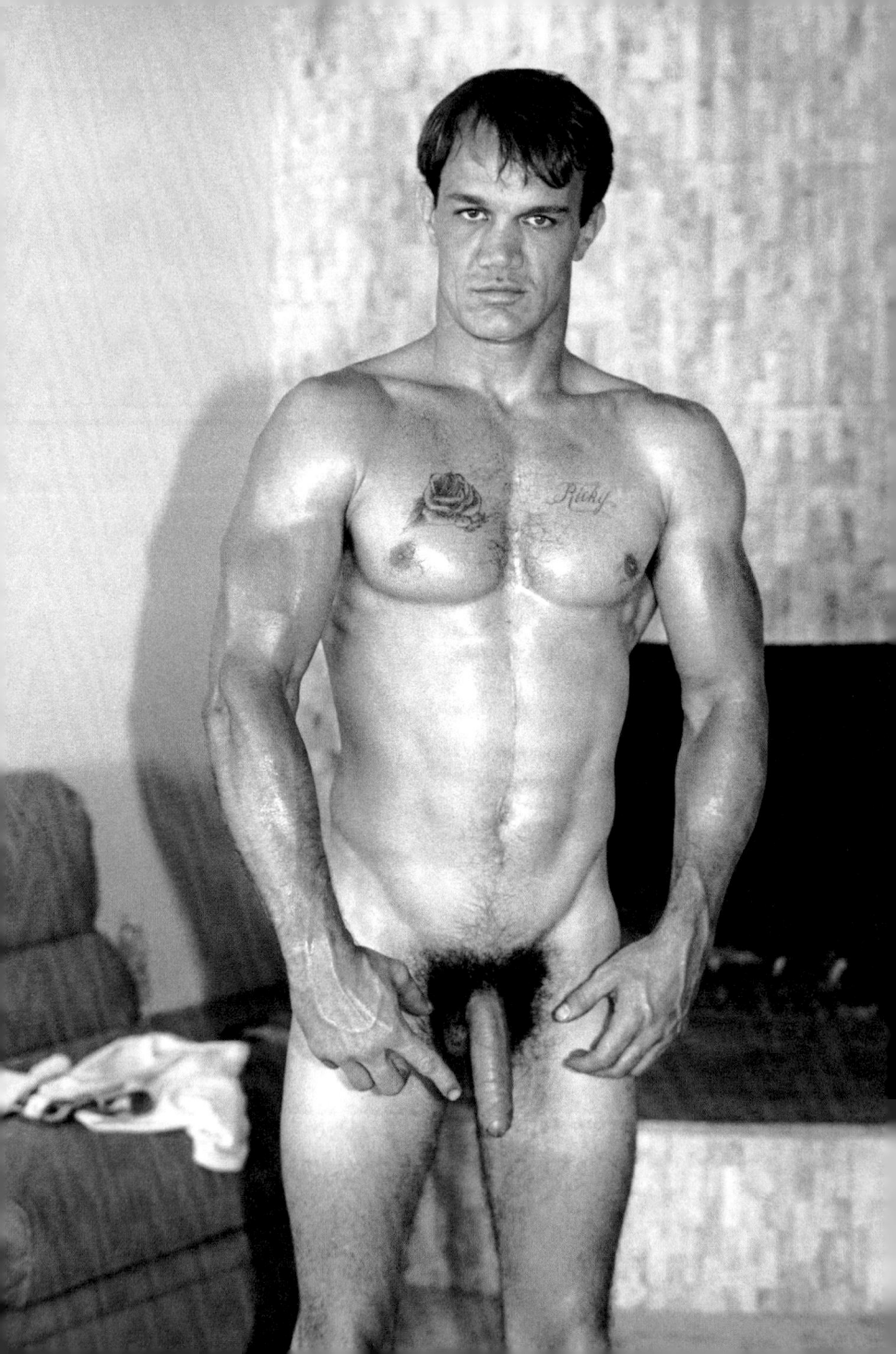

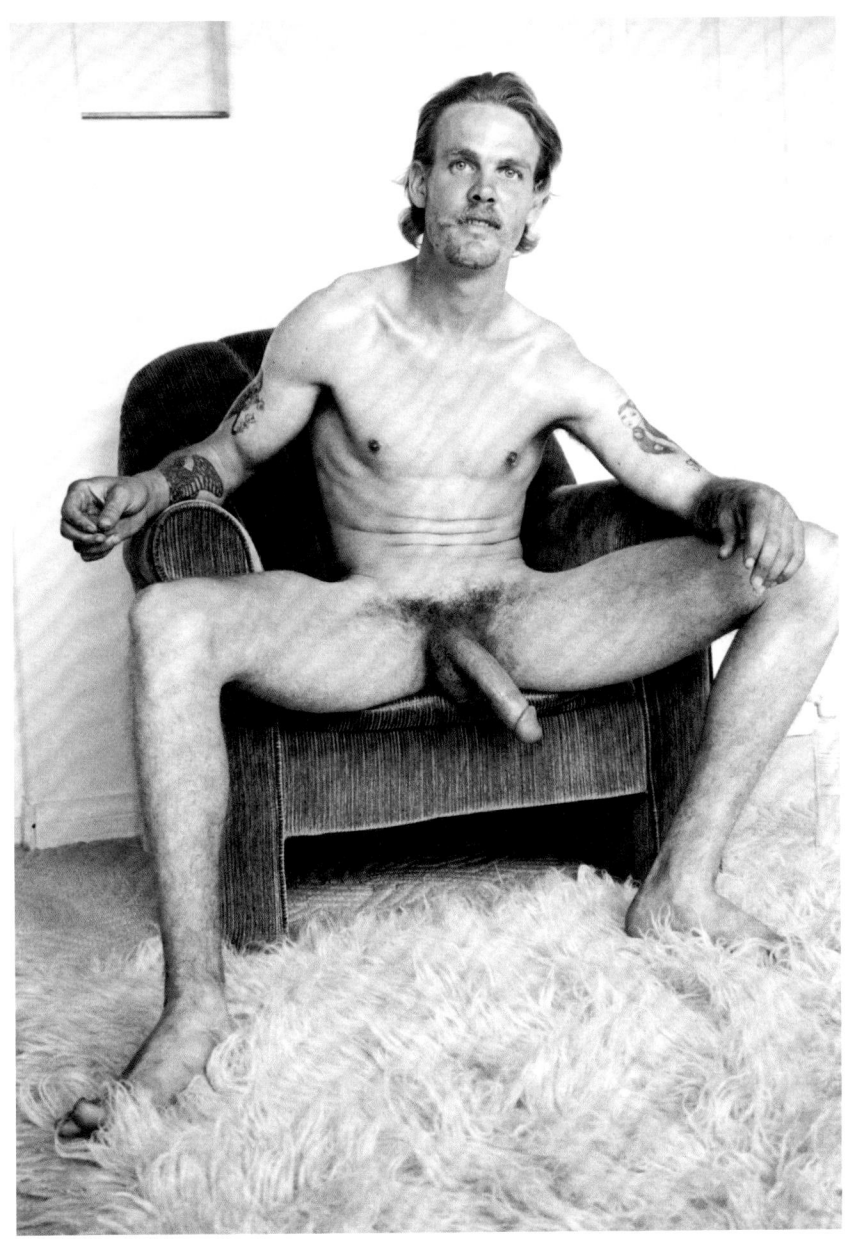

OPPOSITE **Zam** ABOVE **Spider**

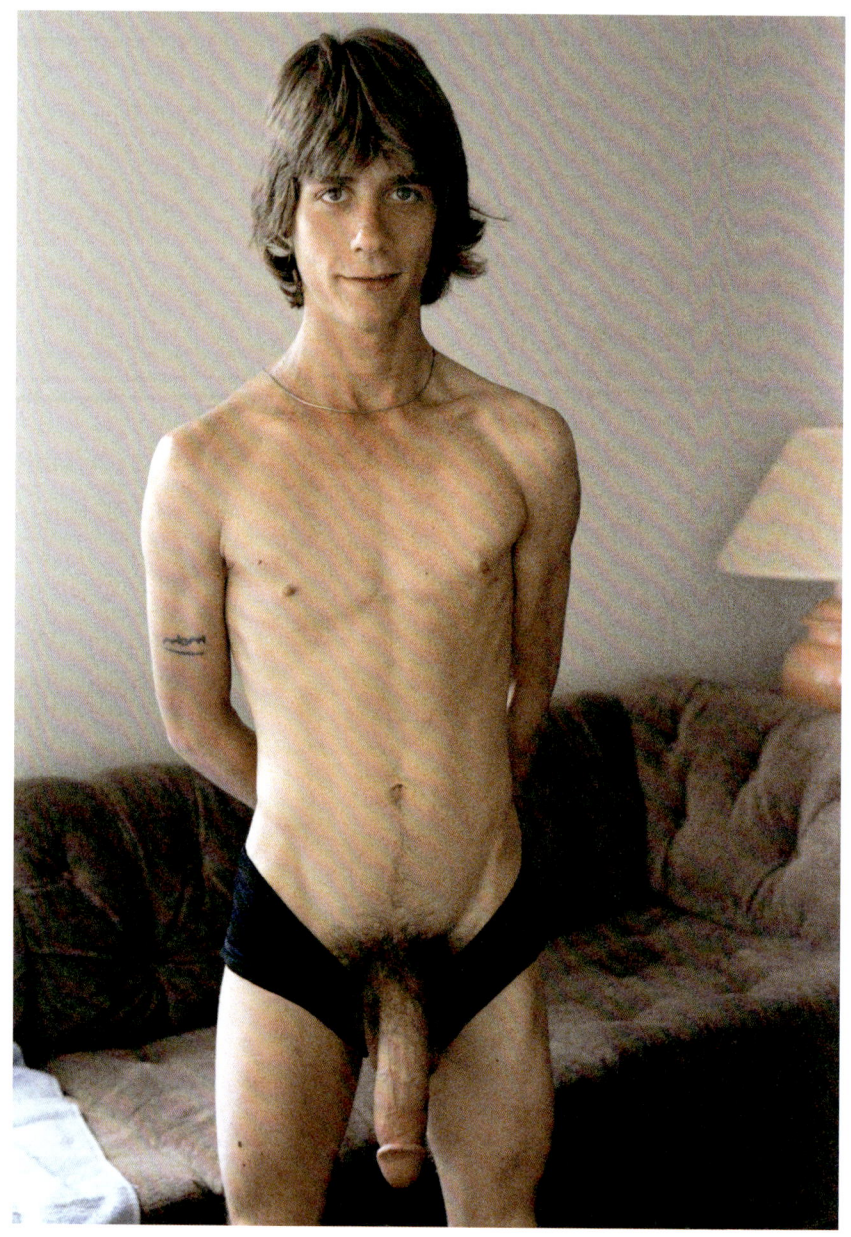

Little Phil

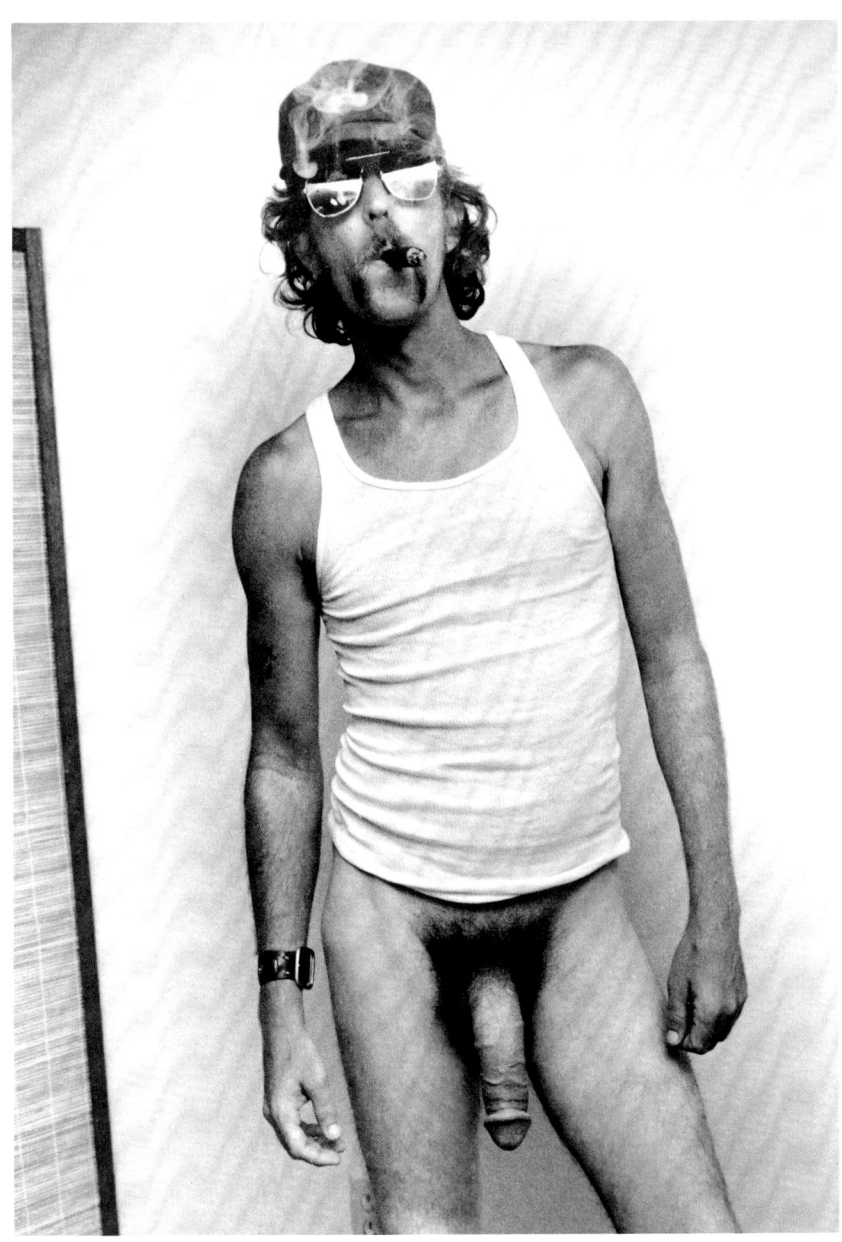

ABOVE AND PAGES 98-99 **Mike "The Spike" Adams**

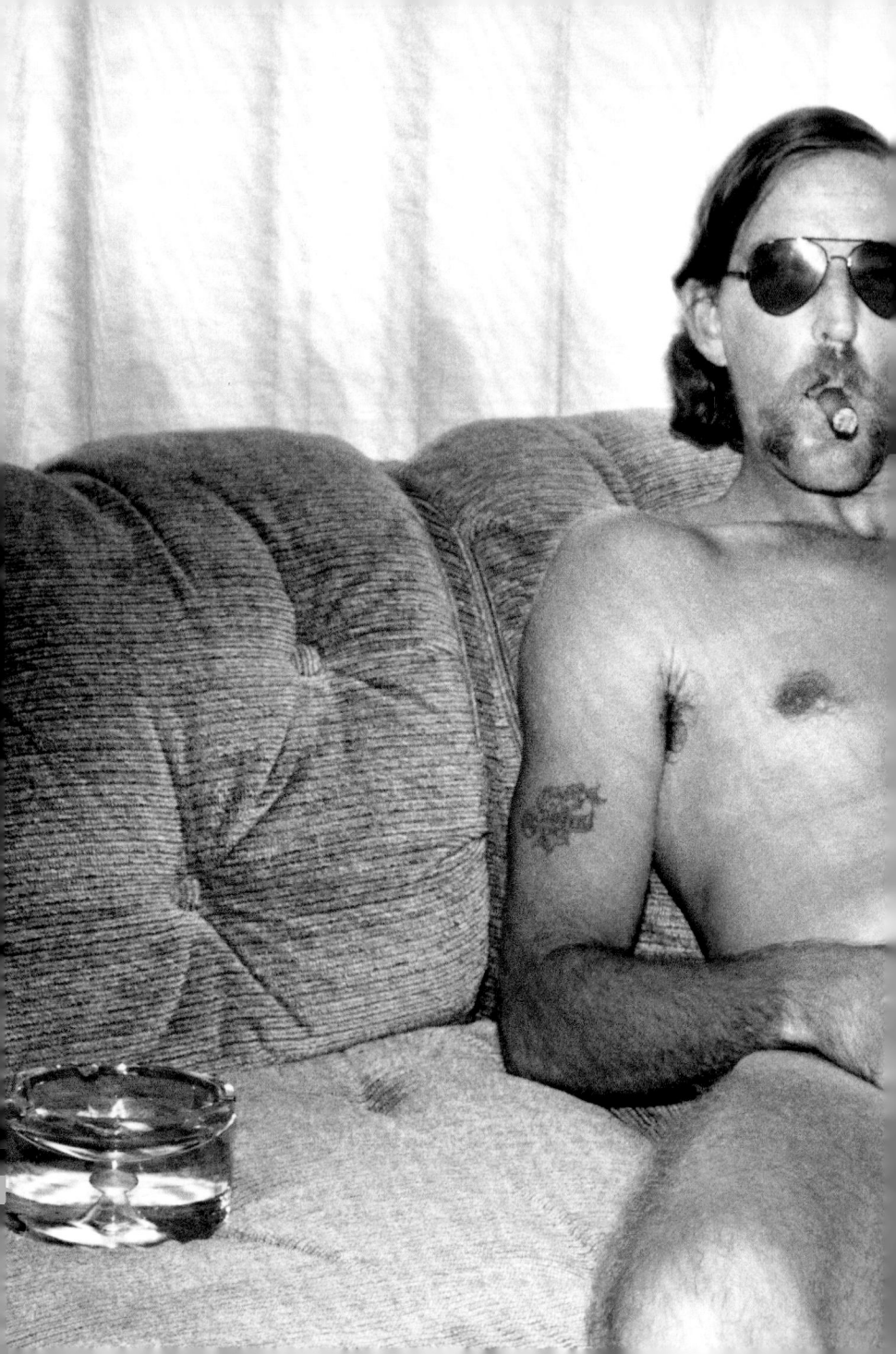

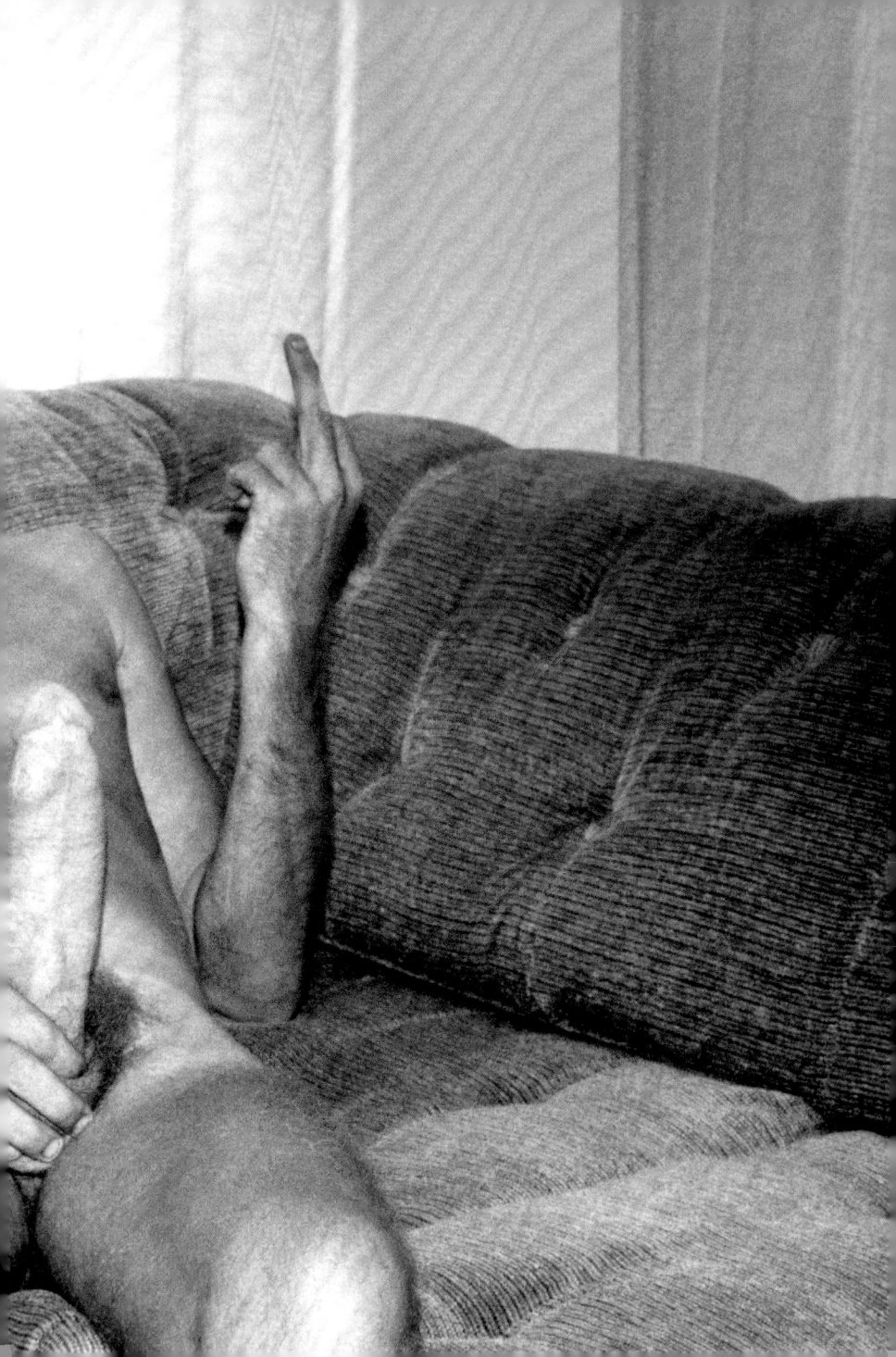

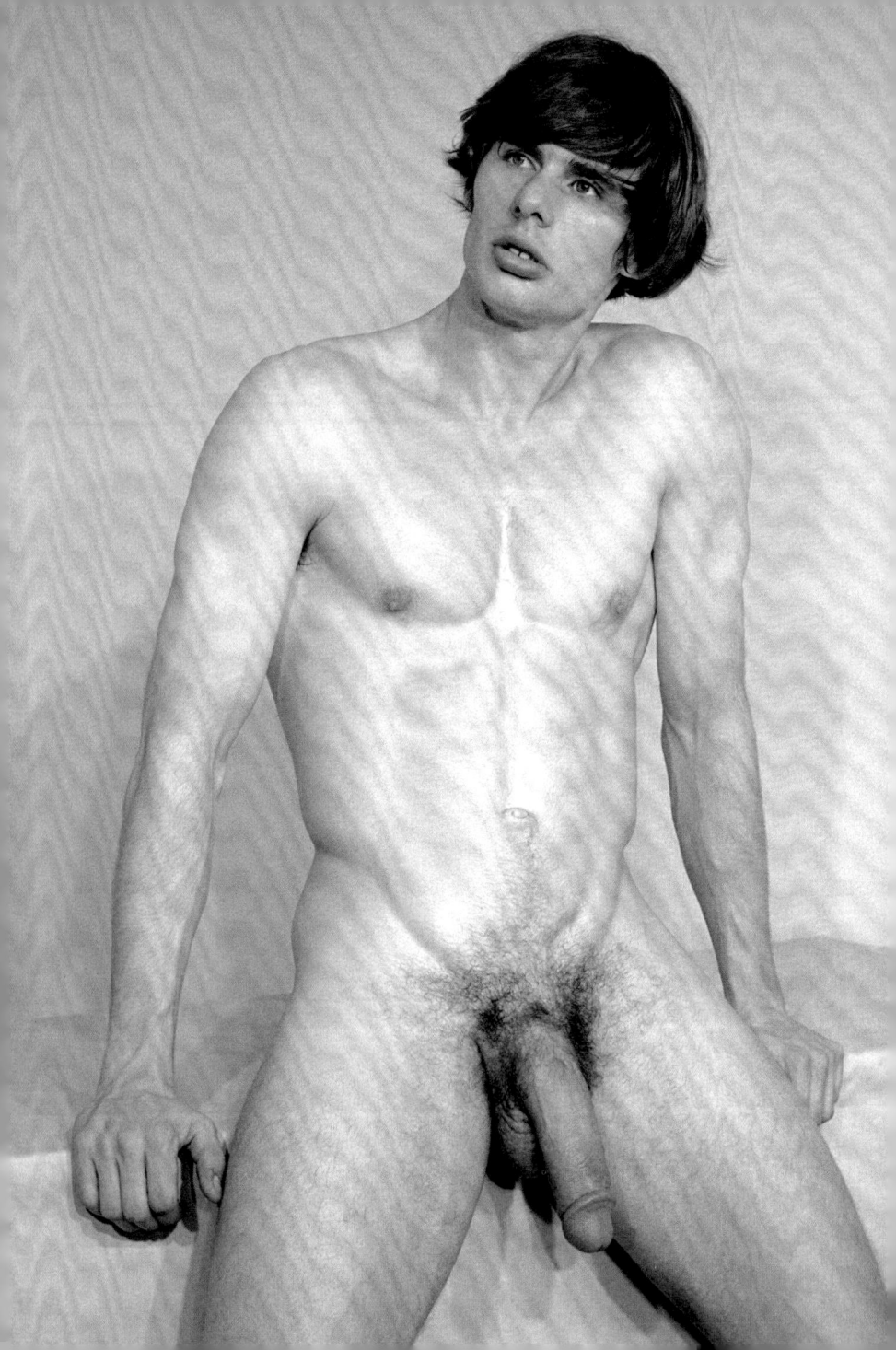

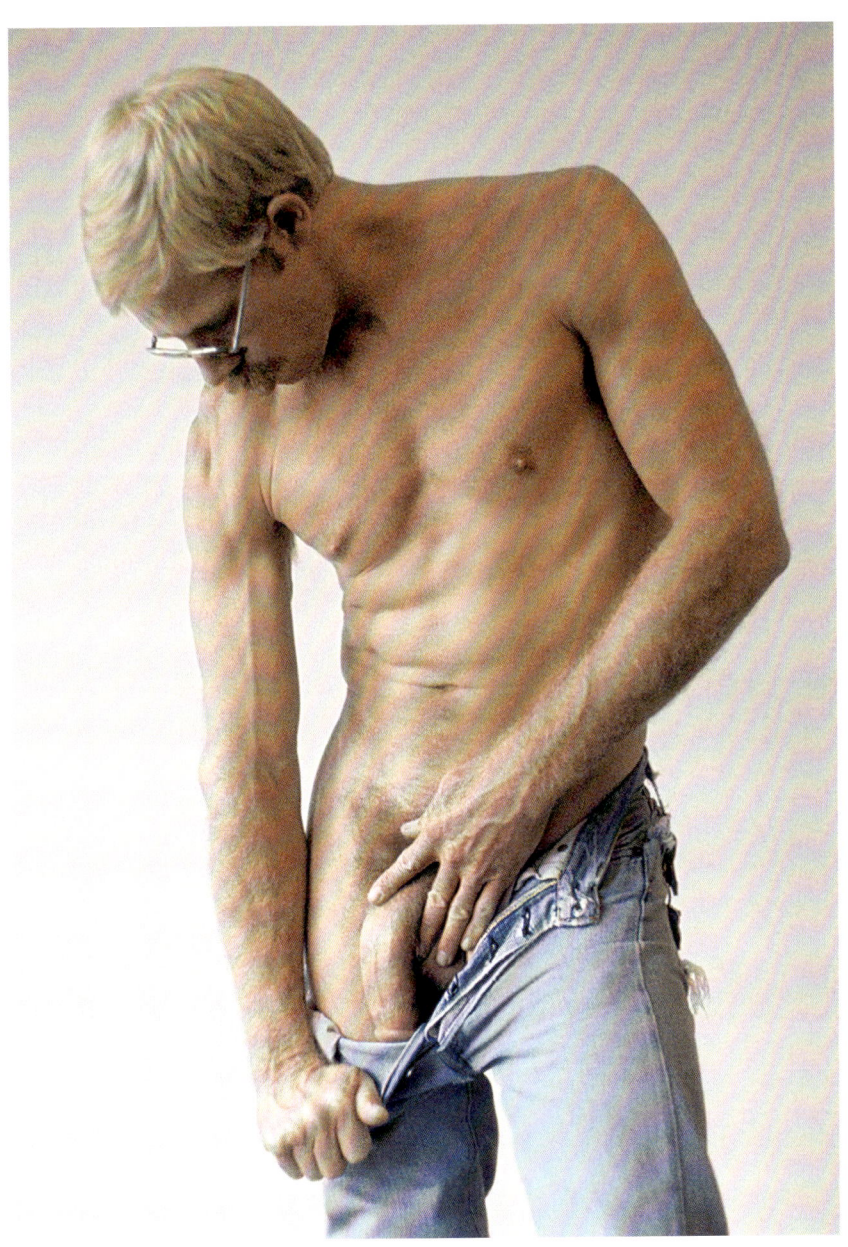

OPPOSITE **Bill Eld**   ABOVE **Holtz**

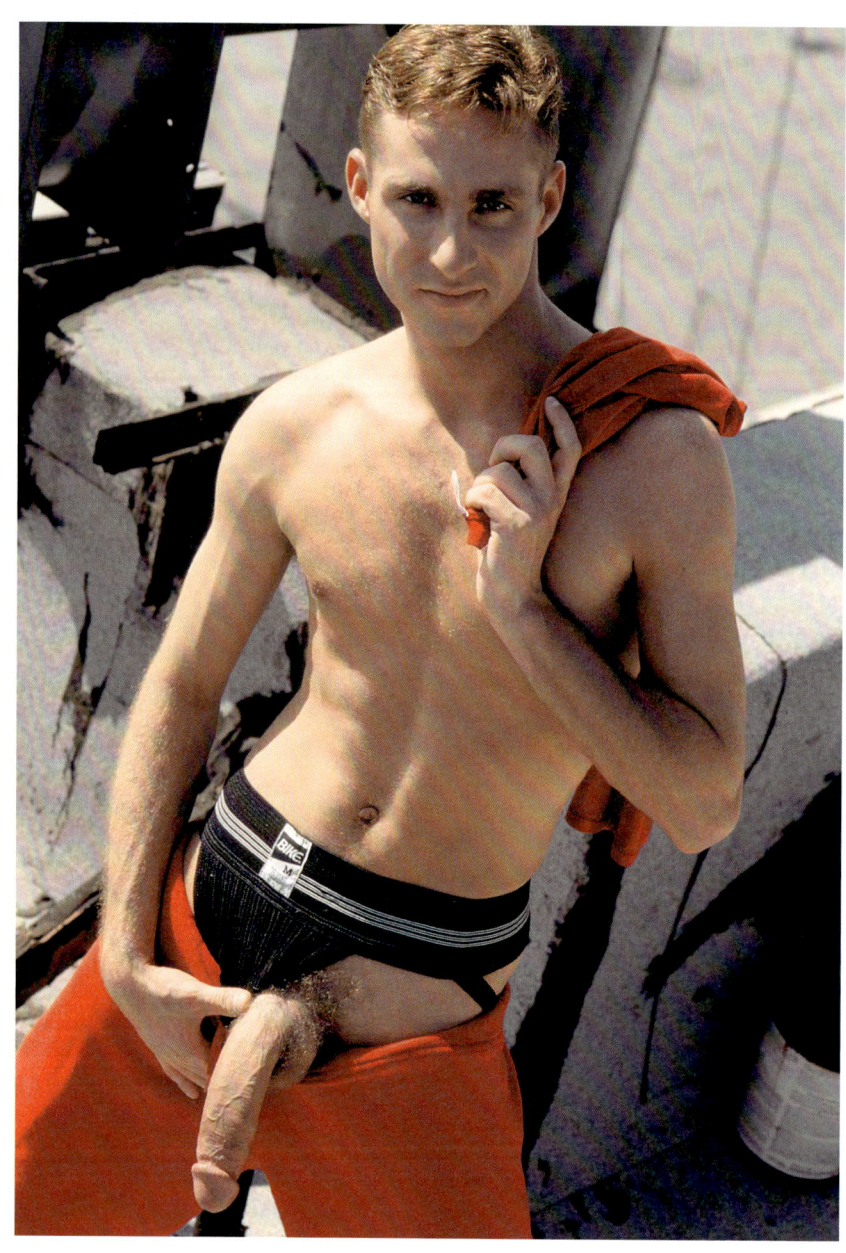

ABOVE **Chad Donovan**   OPPOSITE **Tom Steele**

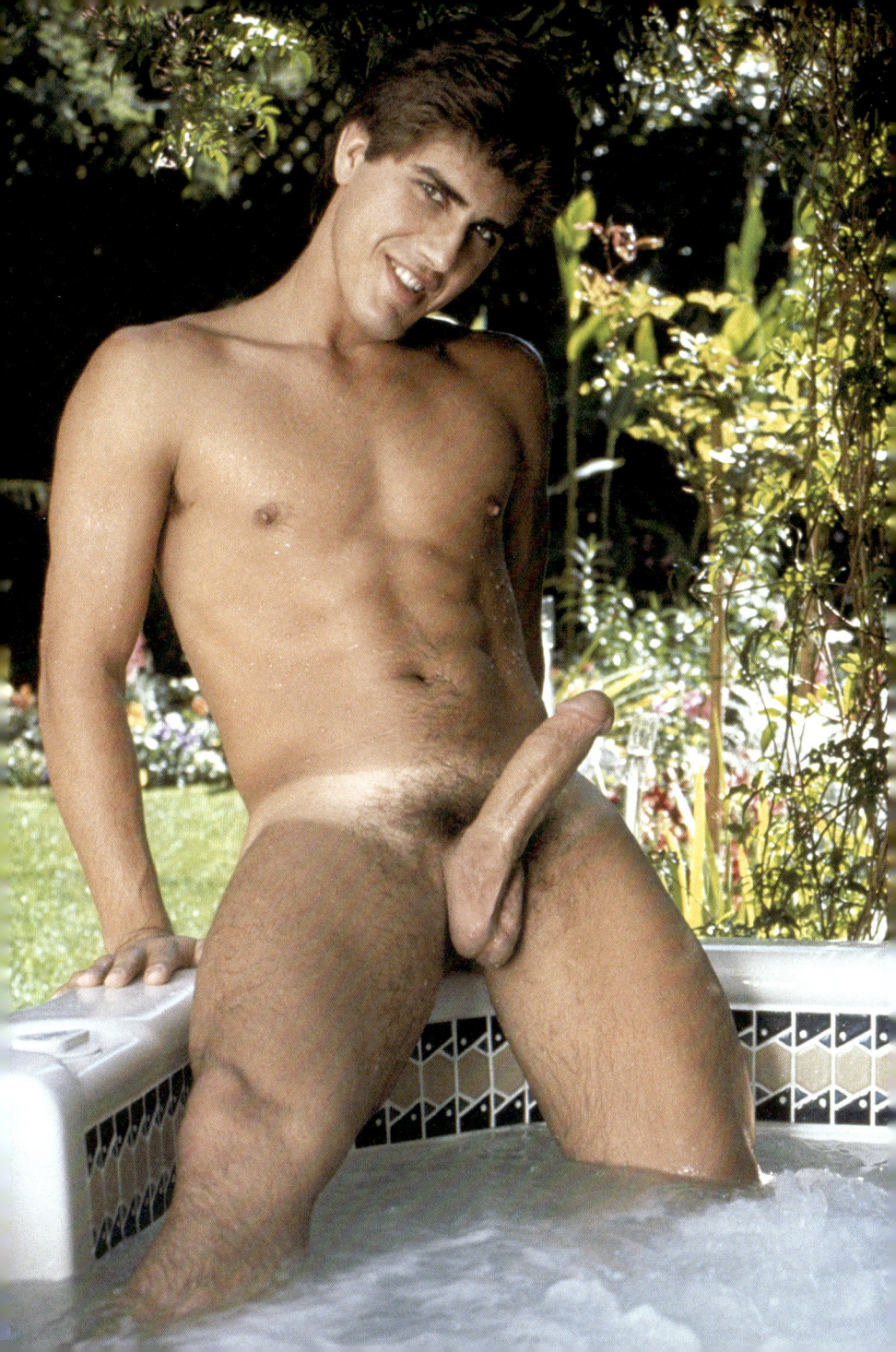

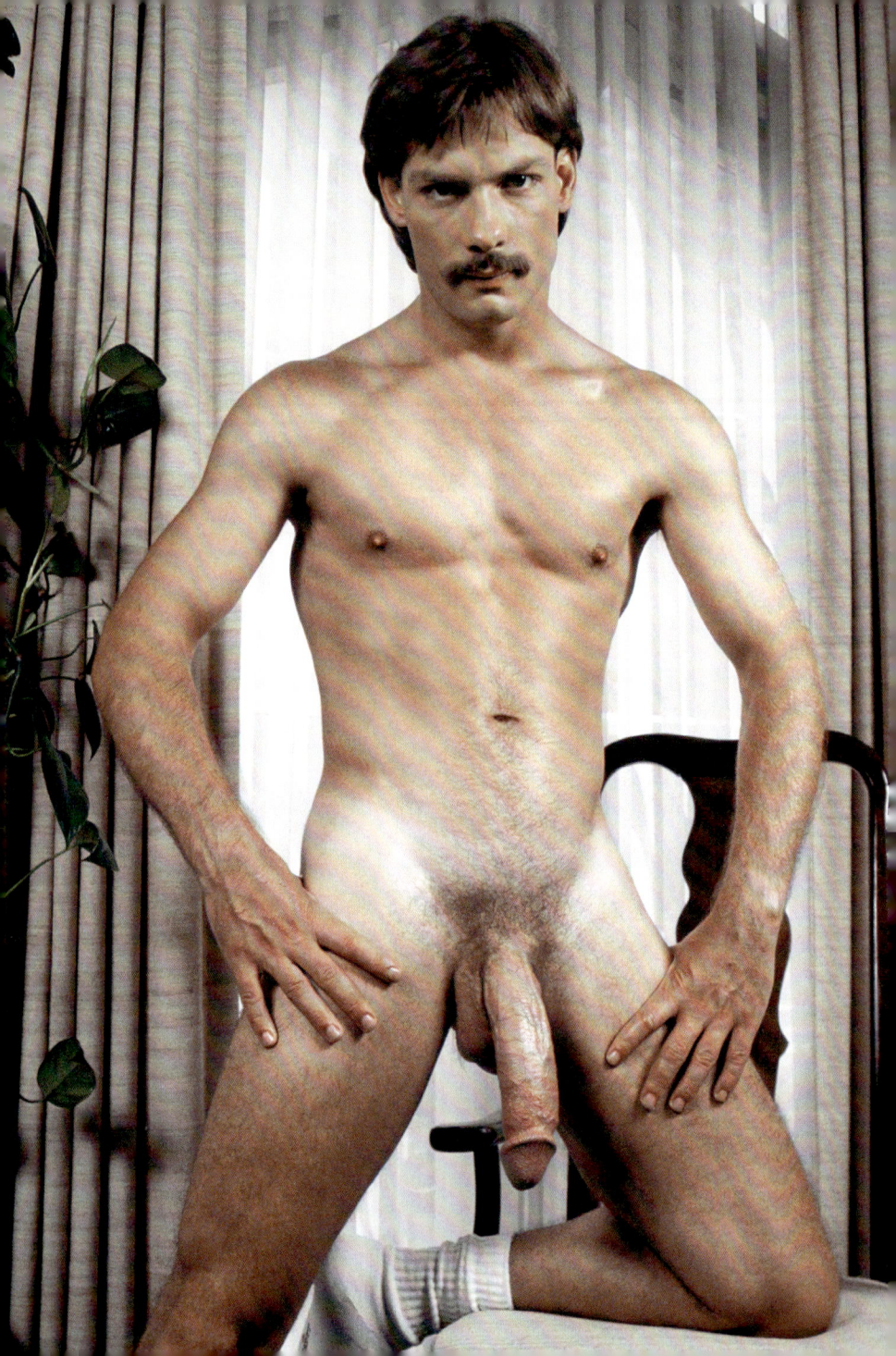

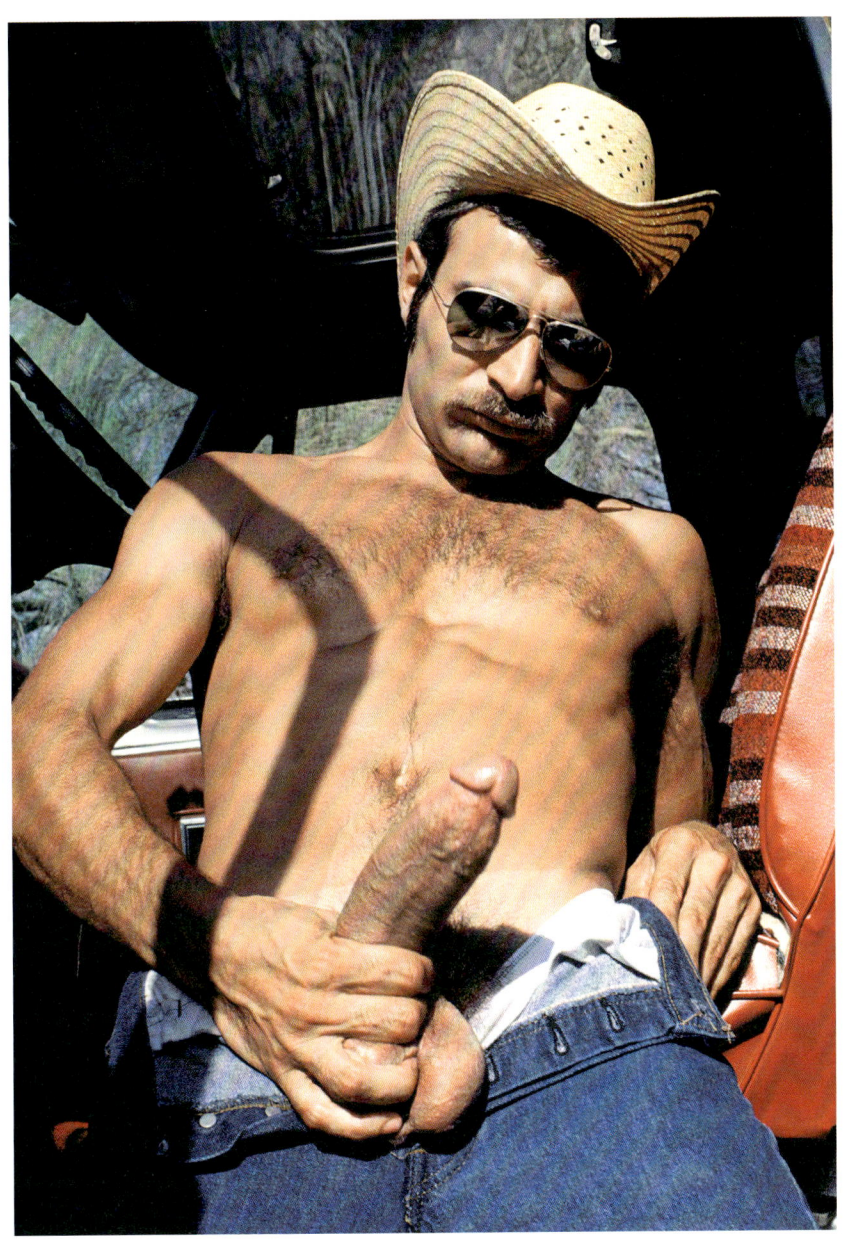

OPPOSITE **Rick Donovan**   ABOVE **Ed Wiley**

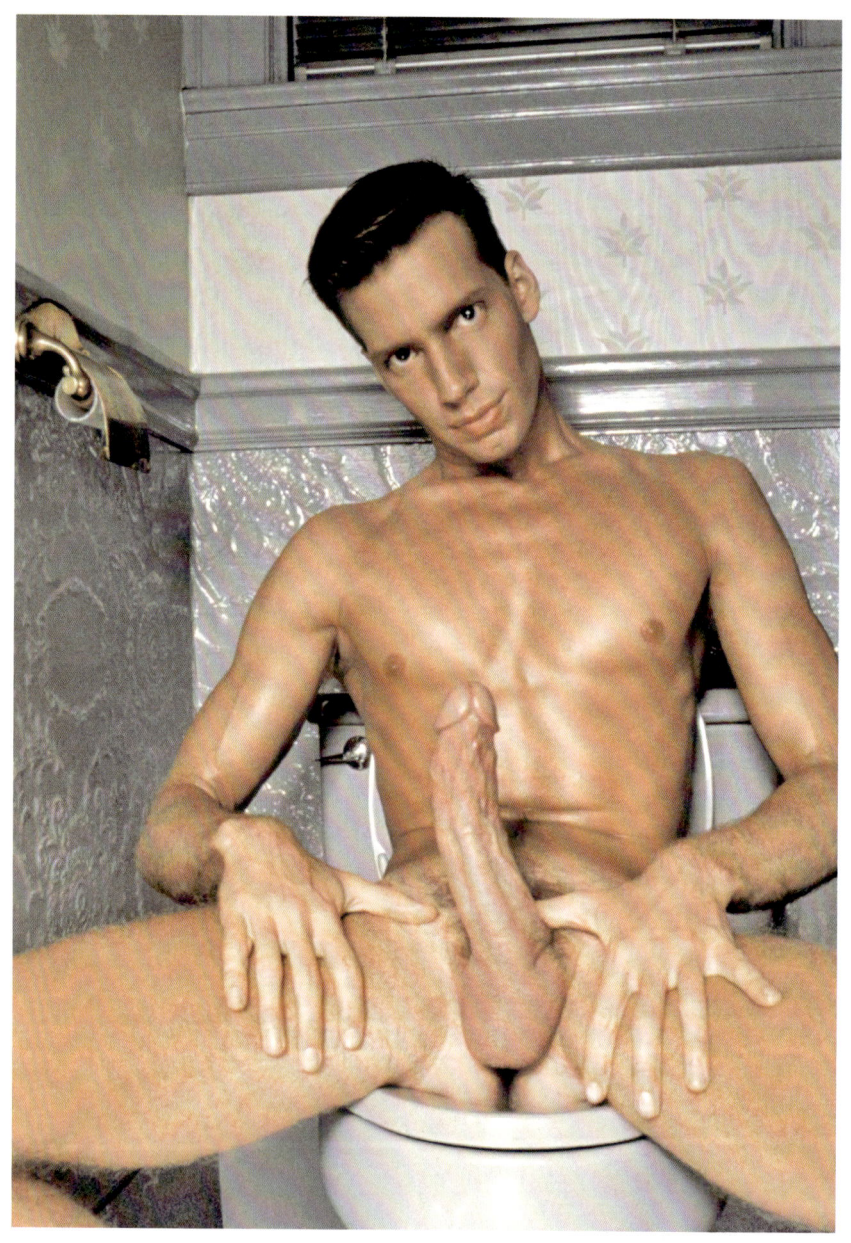

ABOVE **Greg Conrad**   OPPOSITE **Glenn Steers**

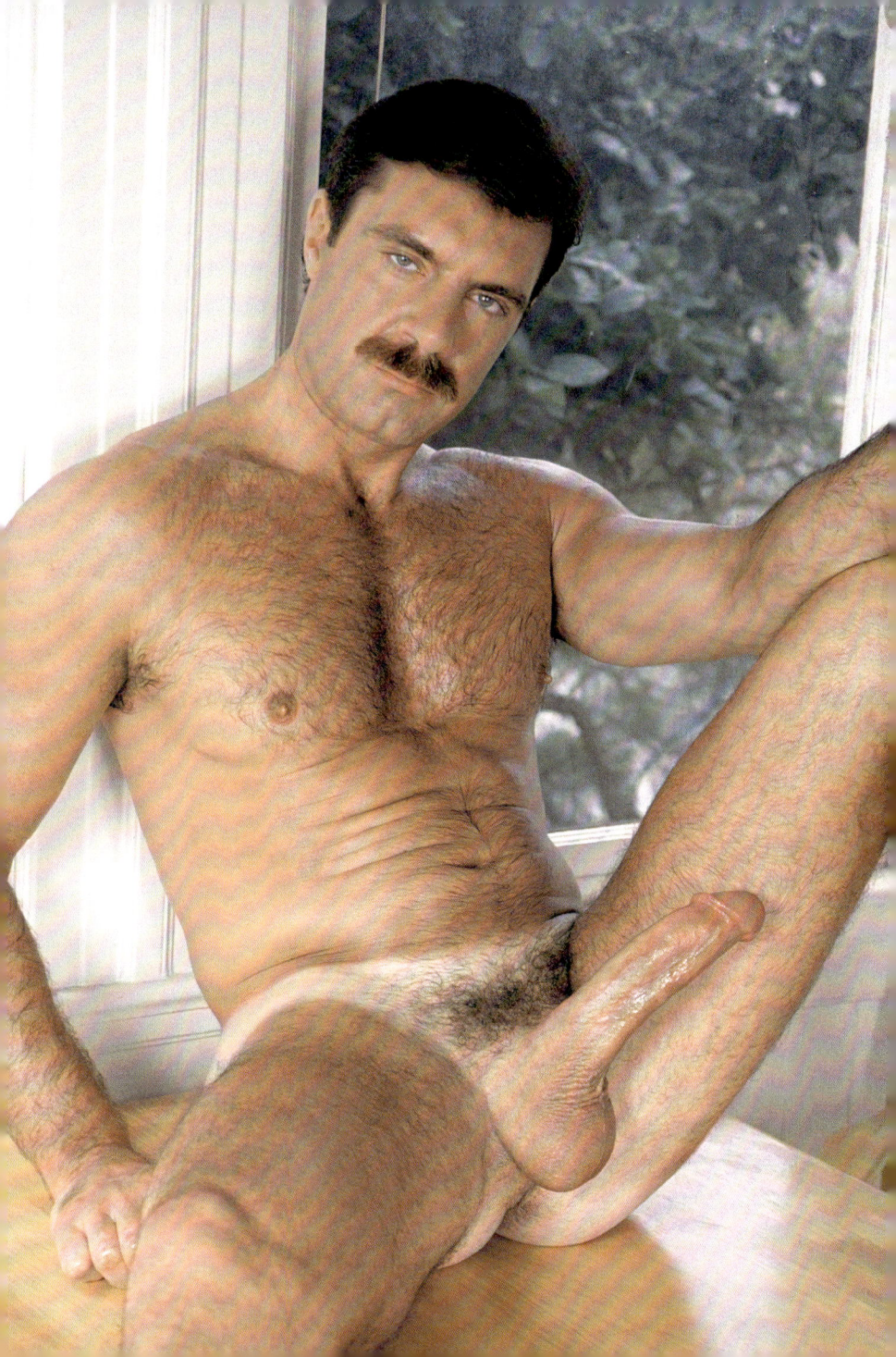

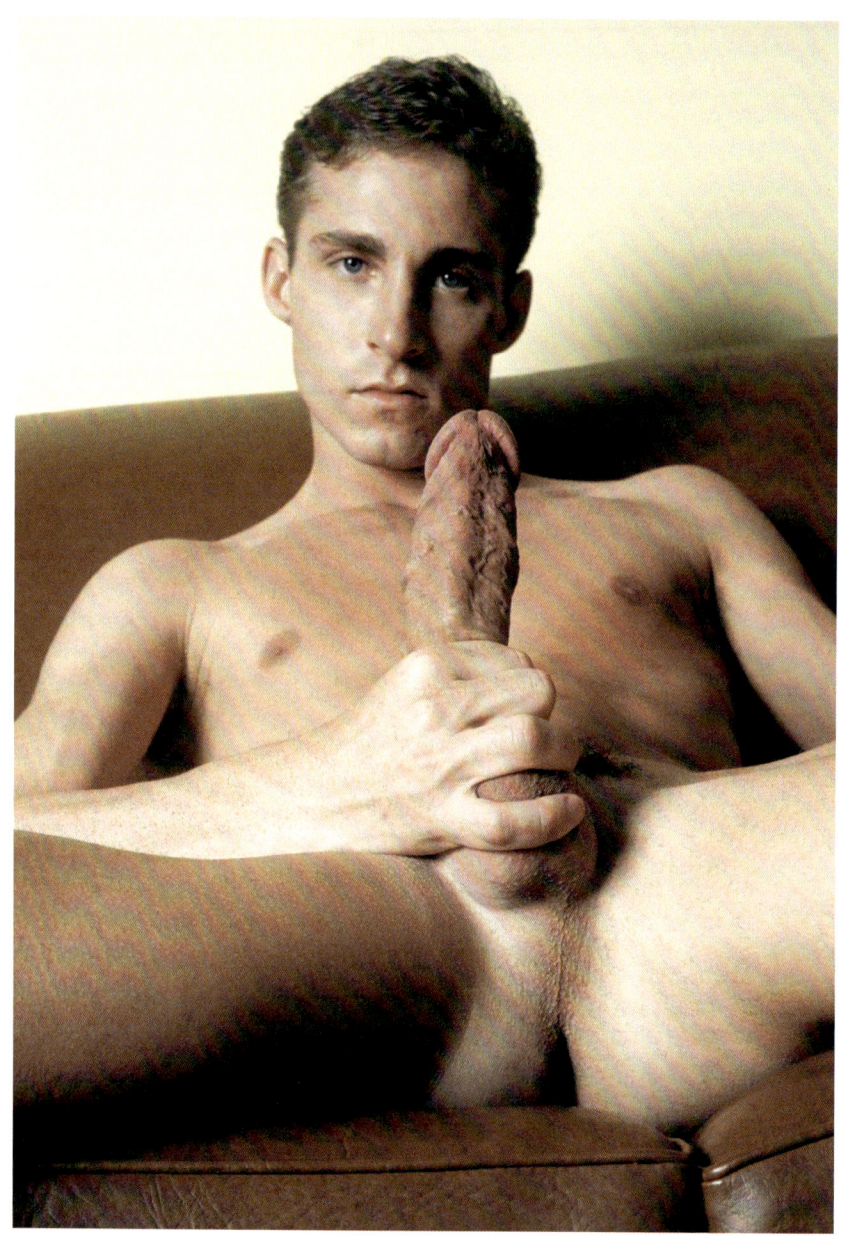

Chad Donovan

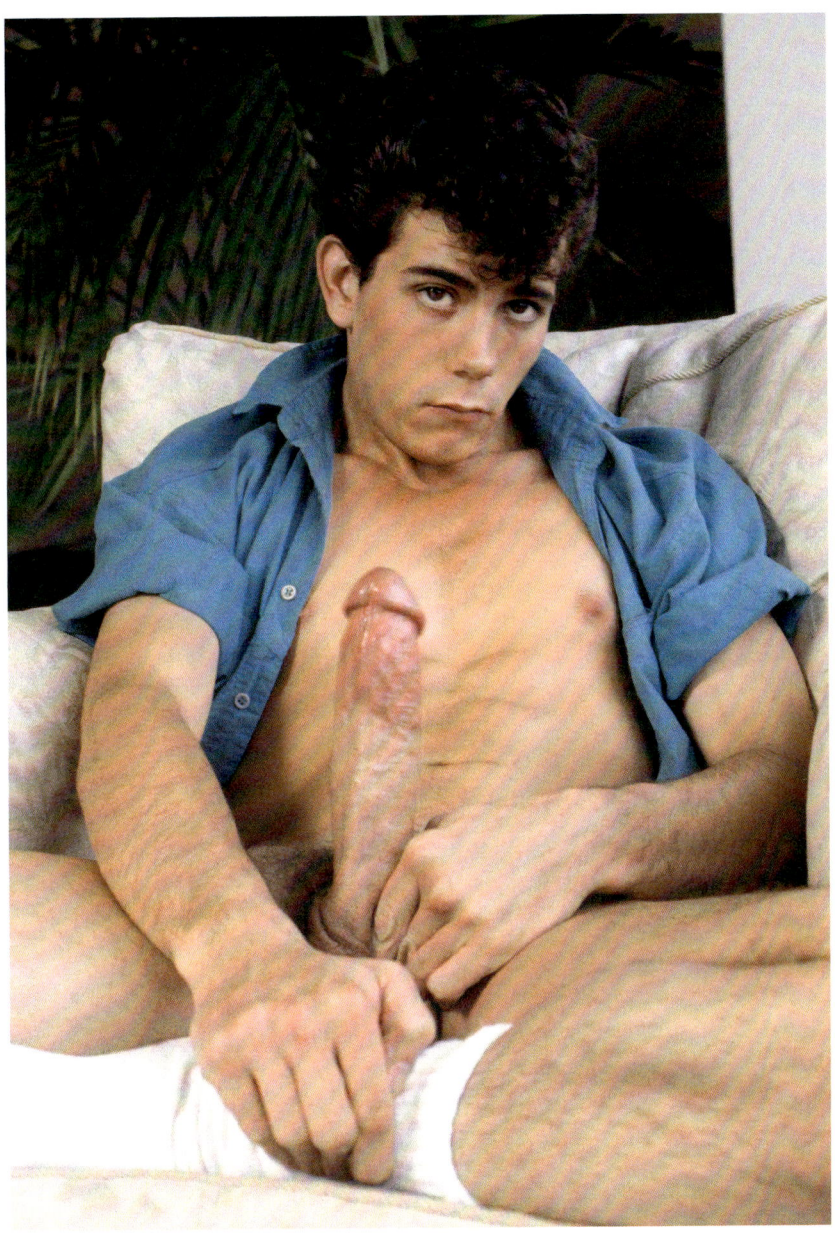

Tony Marino

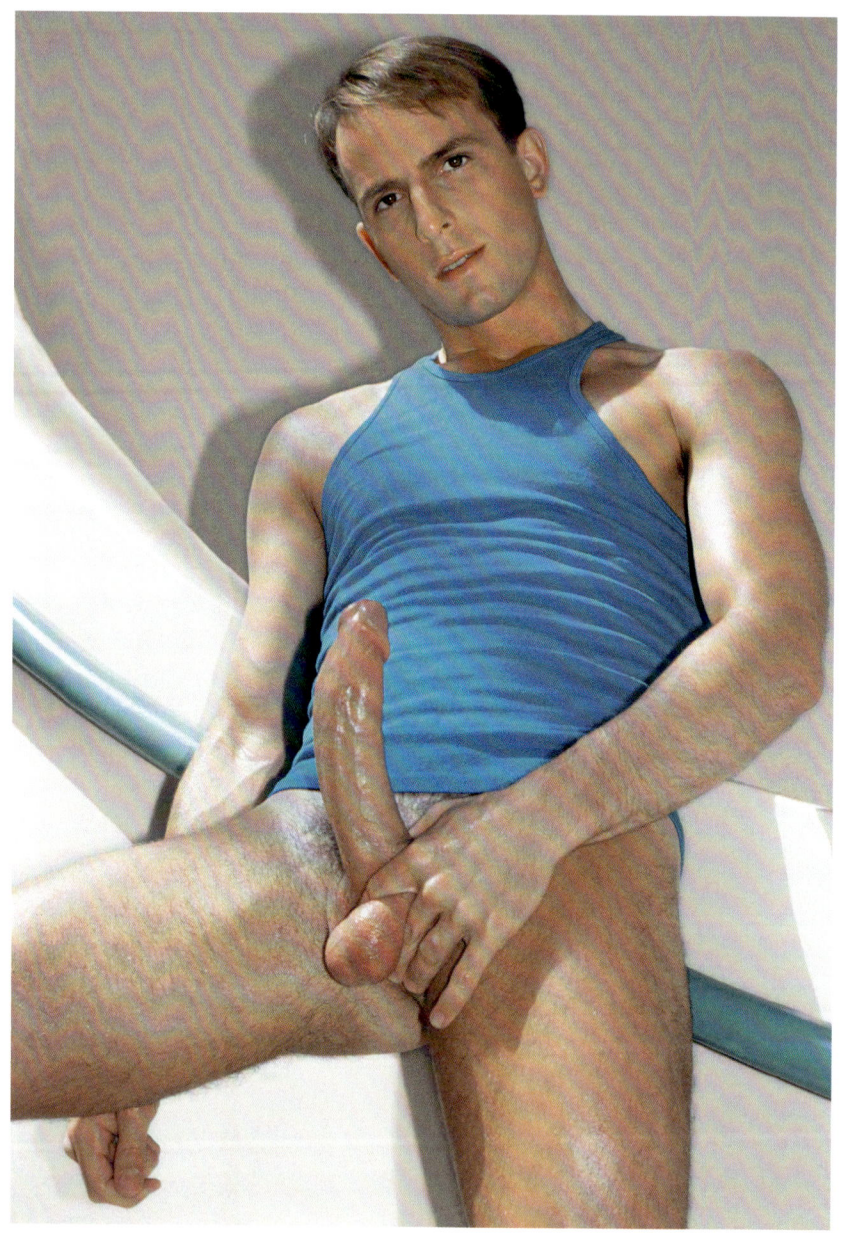

Dick Masters

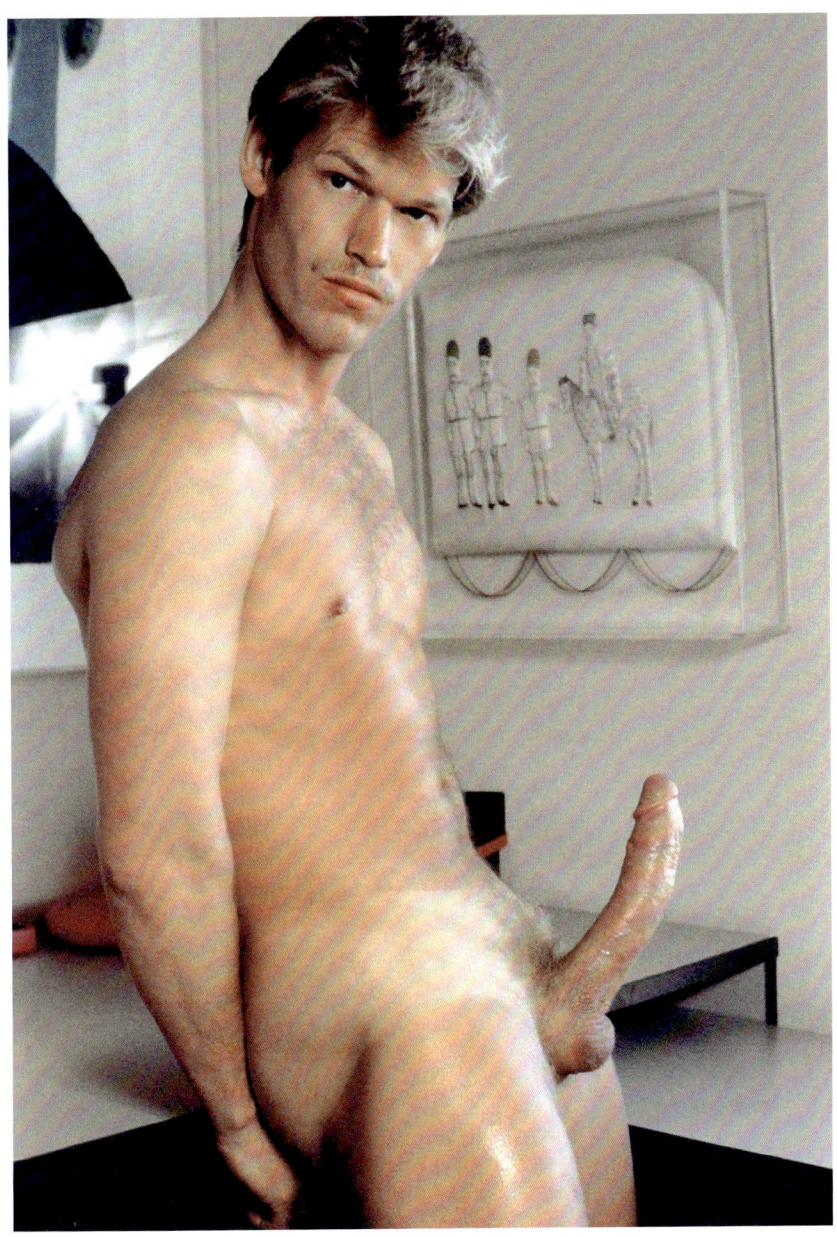

Scott O'Hara

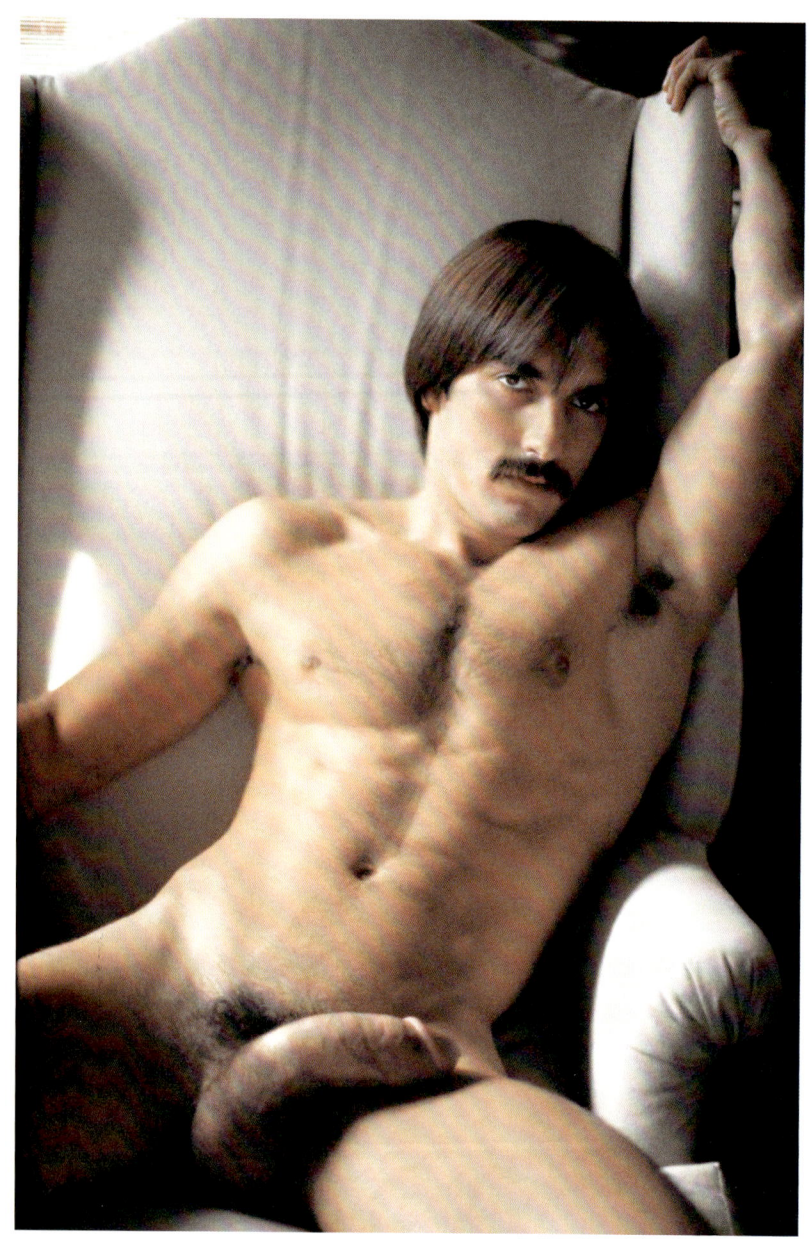

ABOVE **Dick Fisk**   OPPOSITE **Chad Douglas**   PAGES 114-115 **Alain**

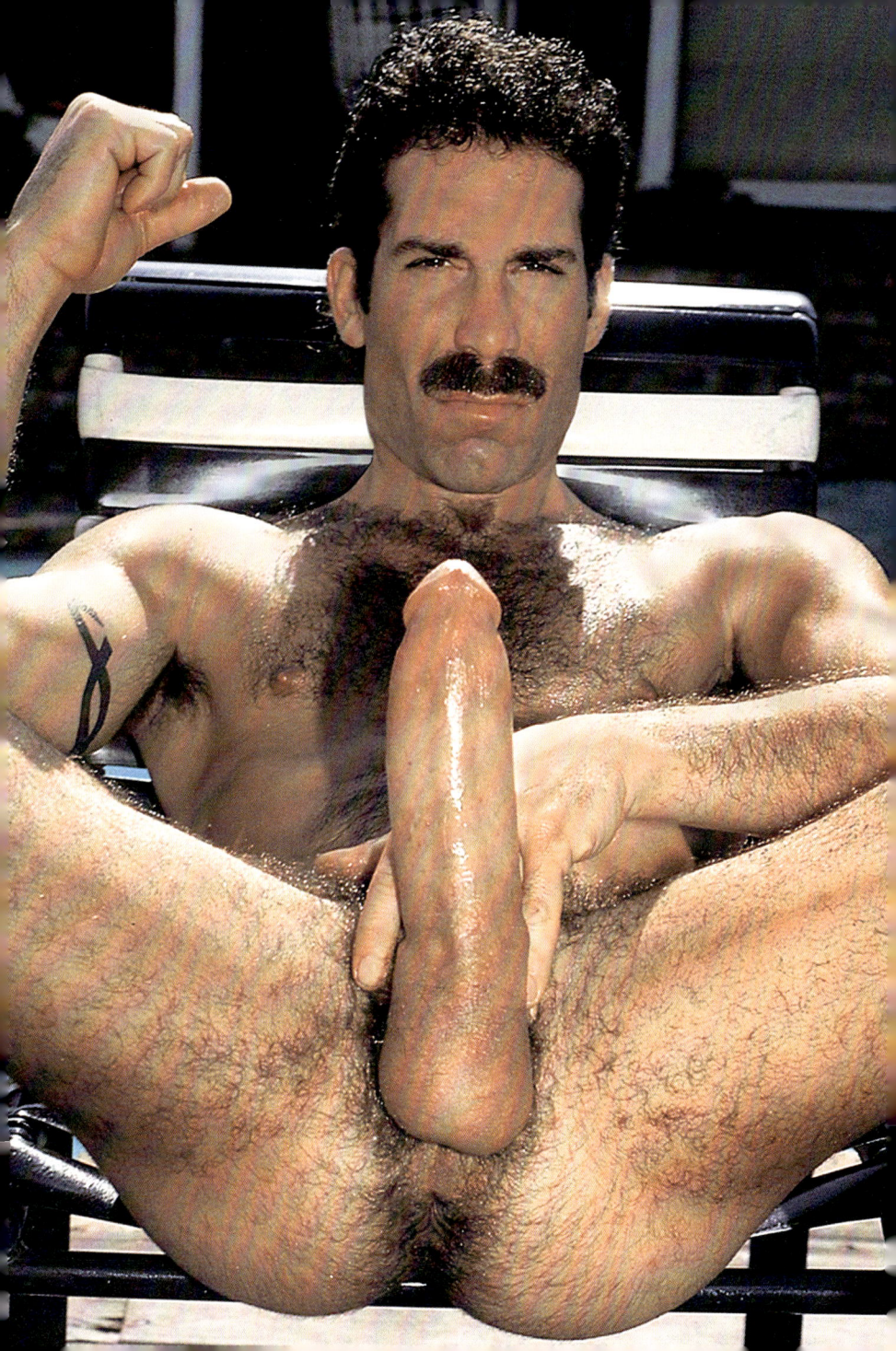

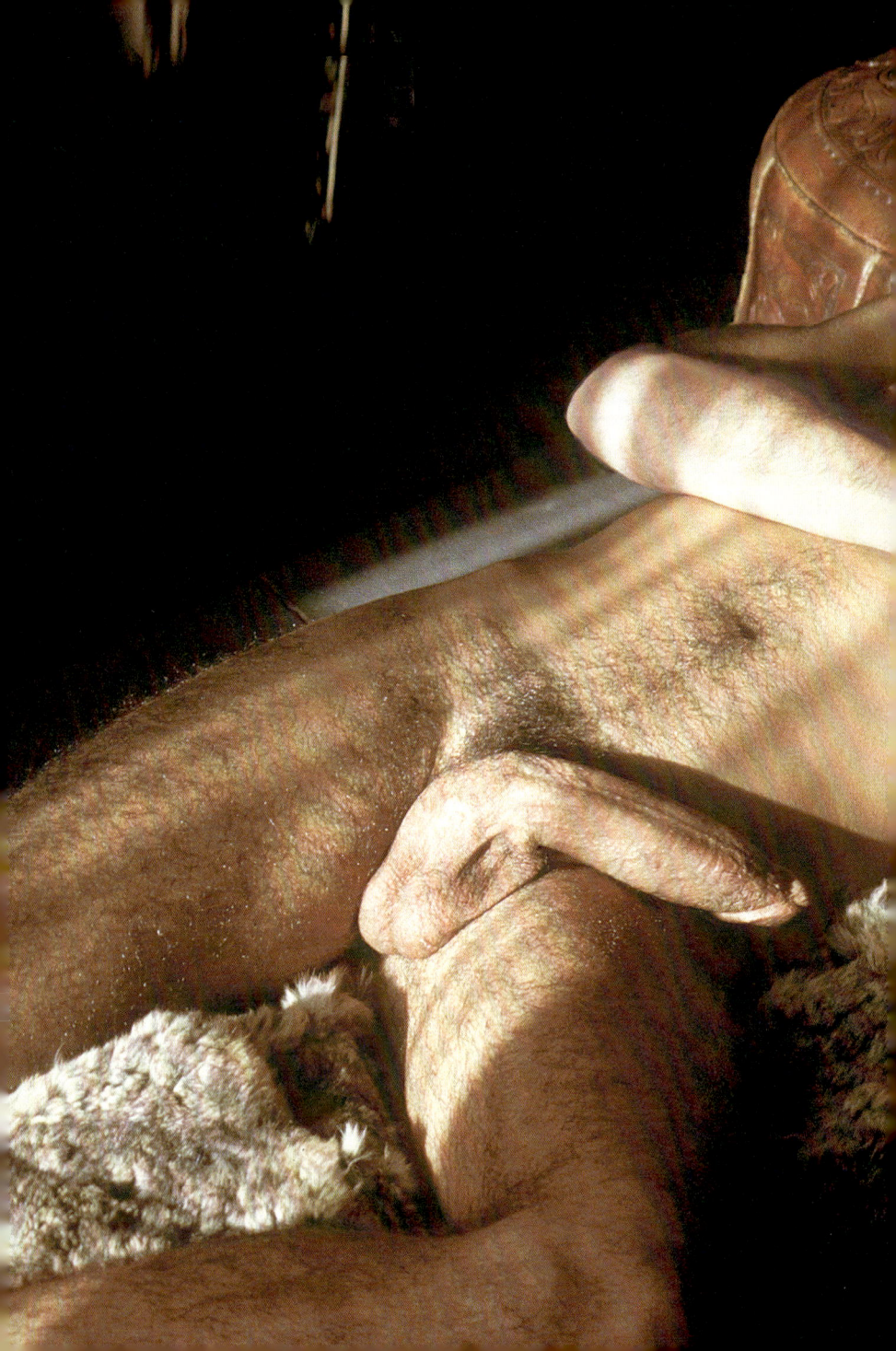

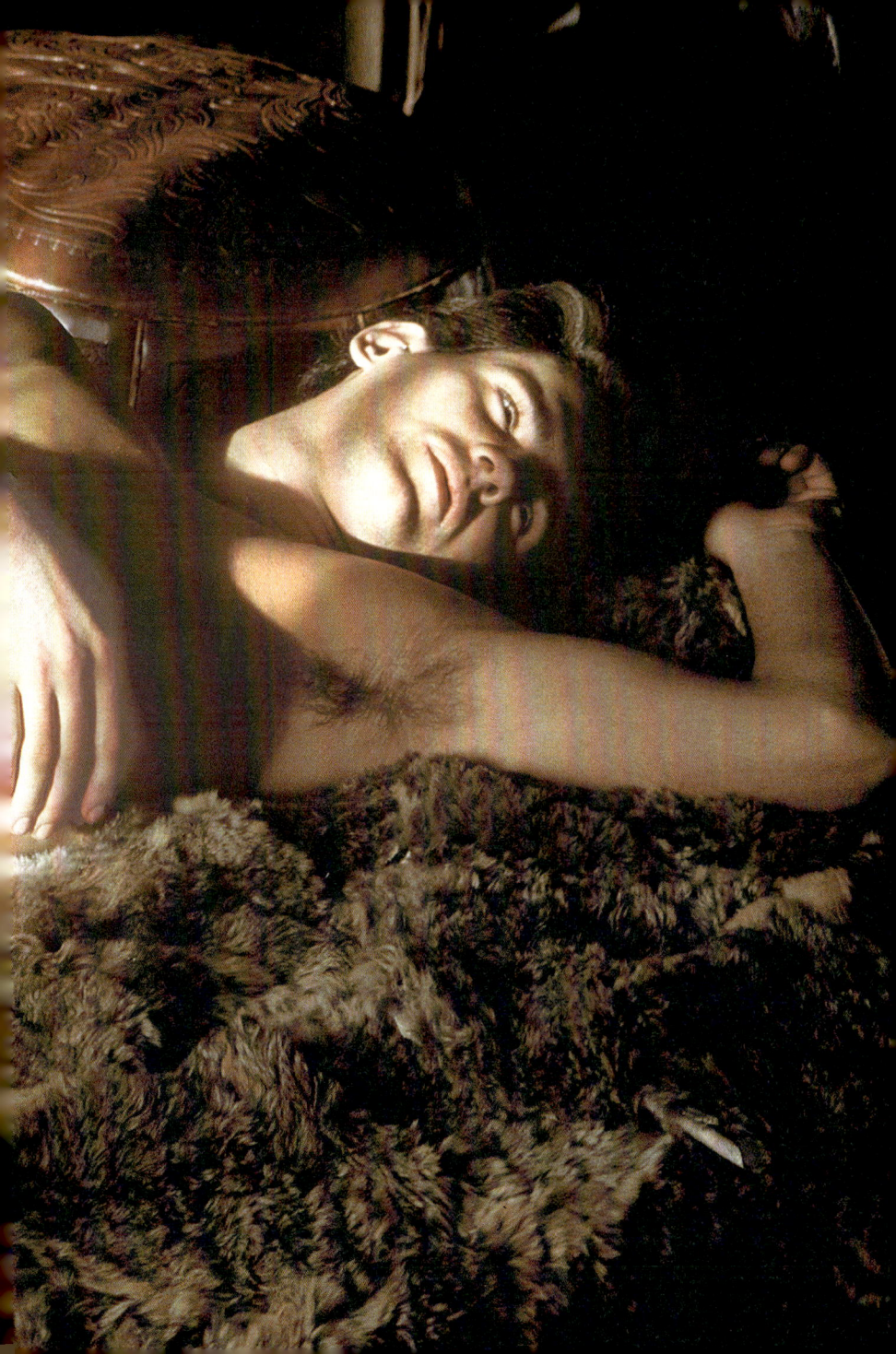

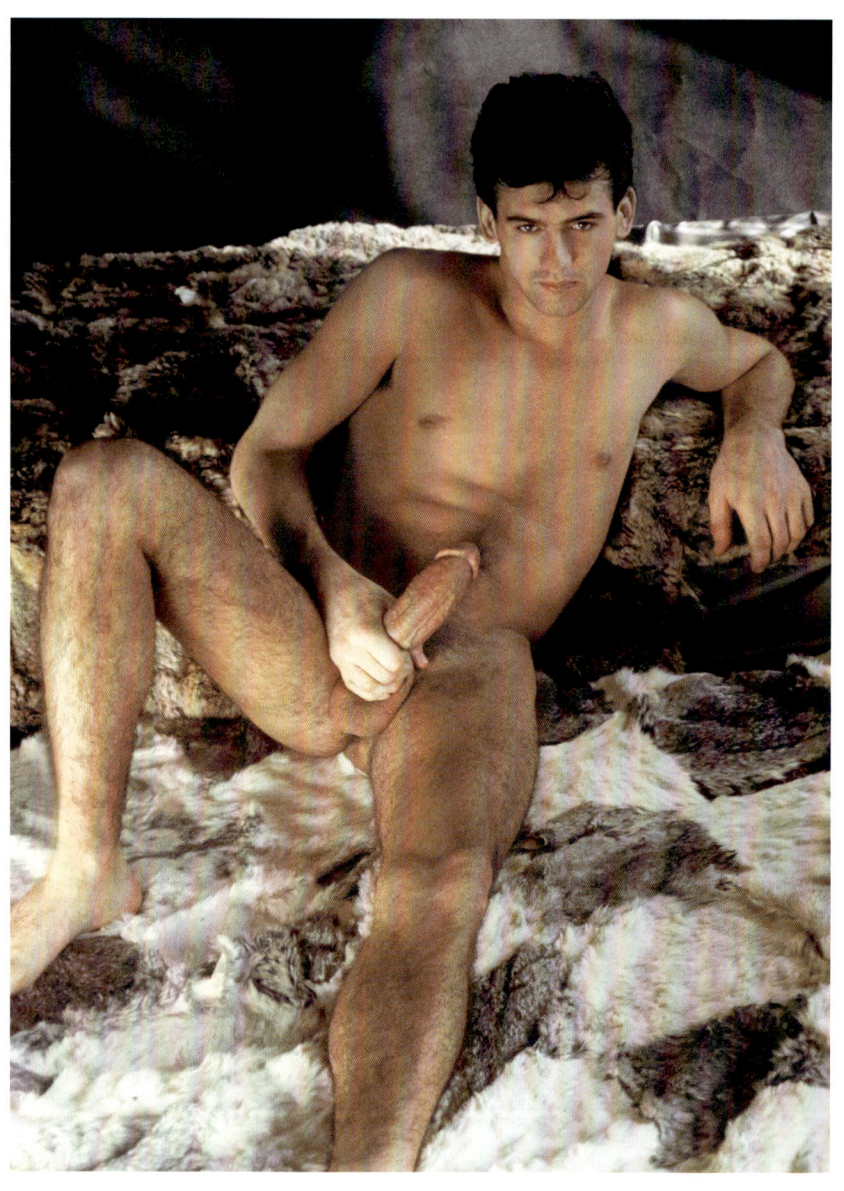

ABOVE **Alain**   OPPOSITE **Ari**   PAGES 118-119 **Vargas**

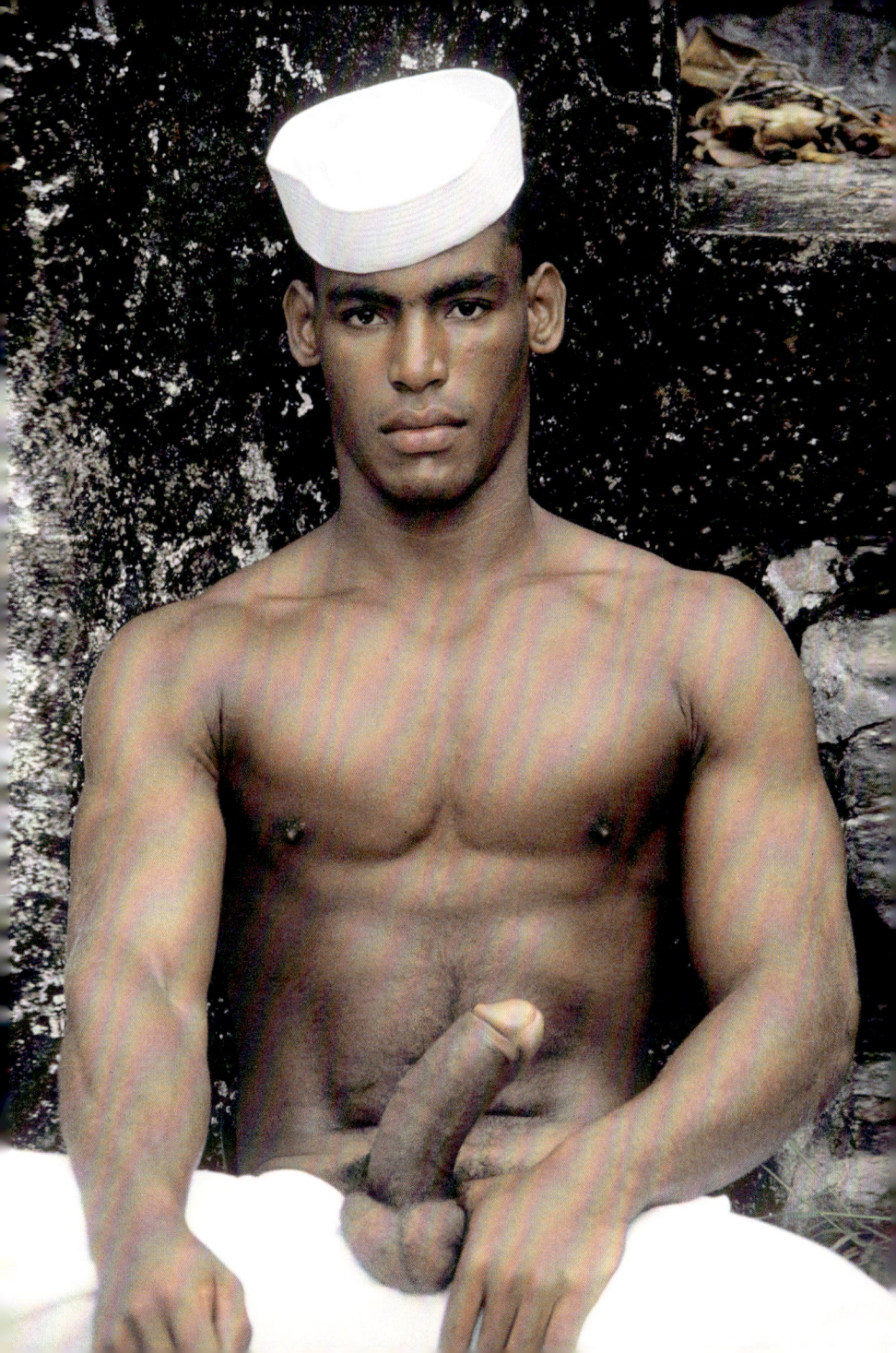

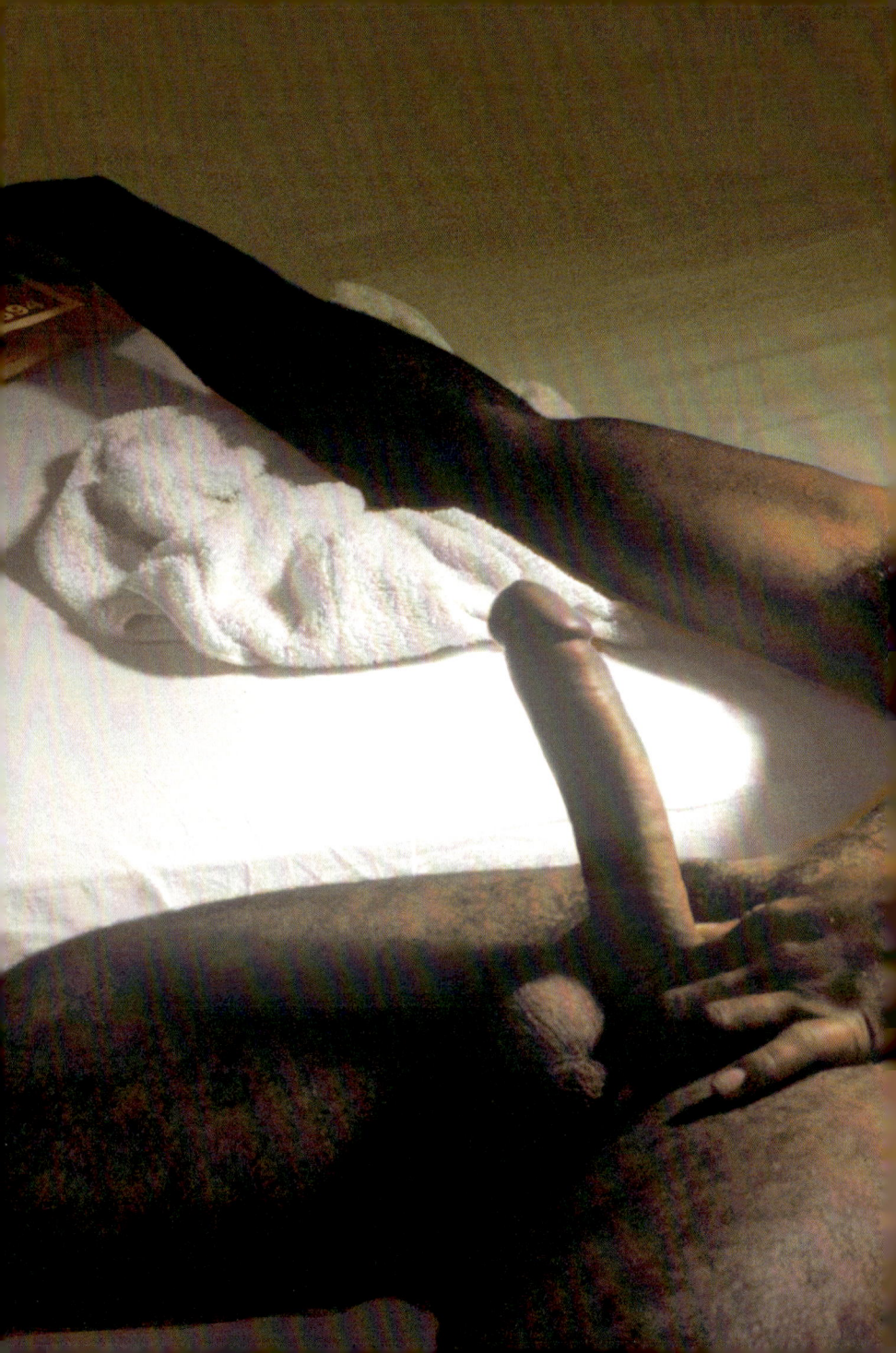

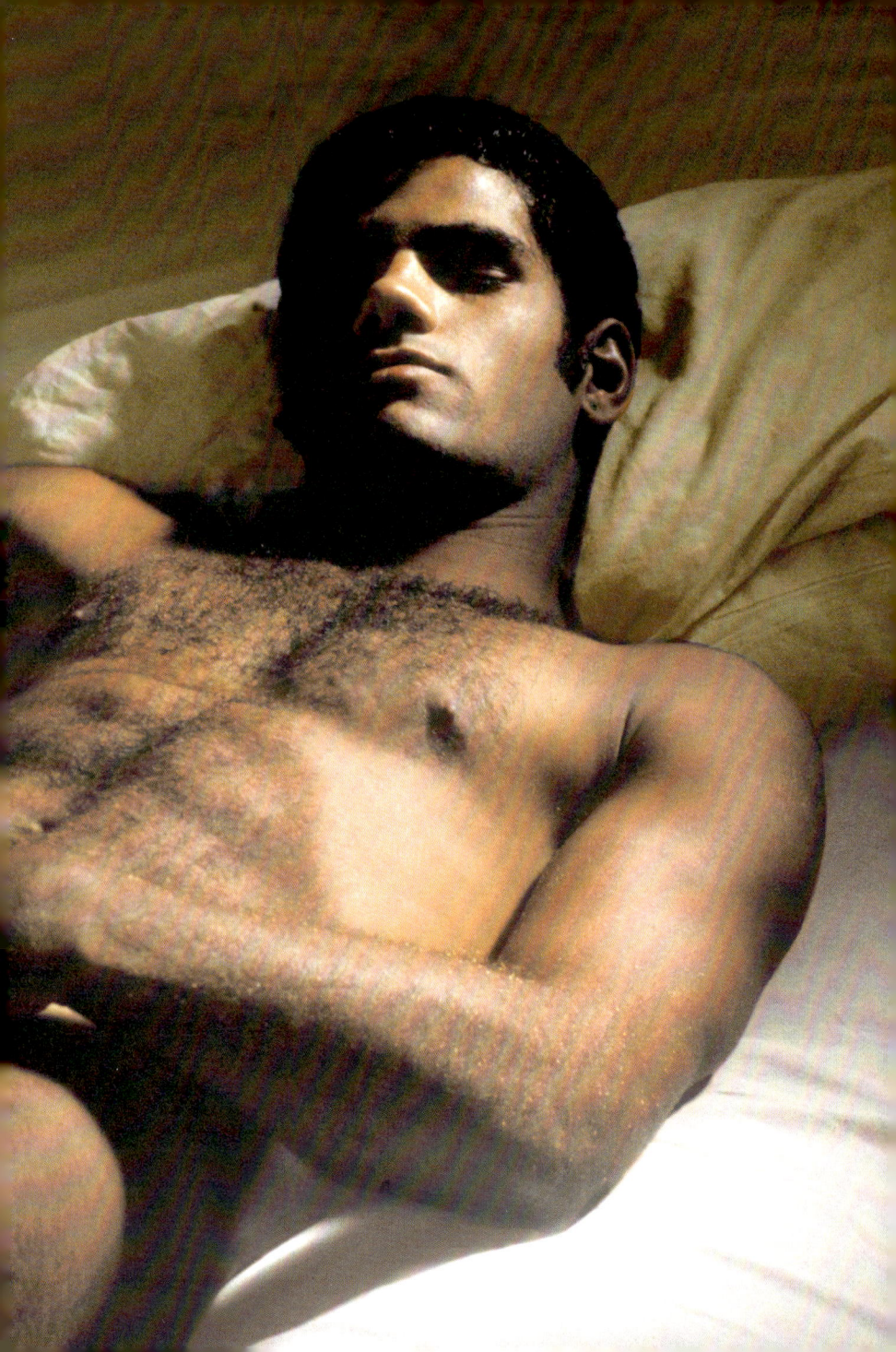

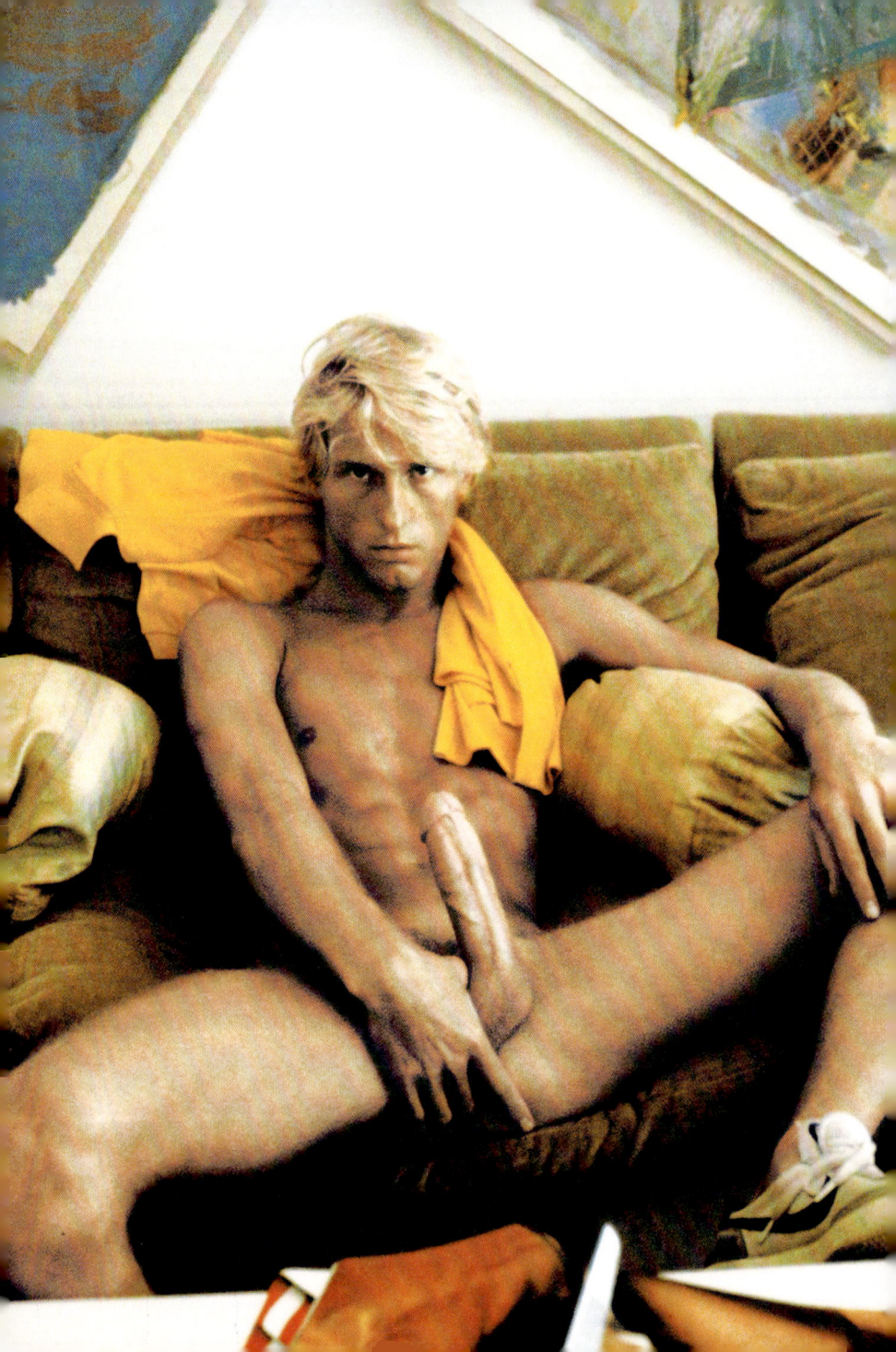

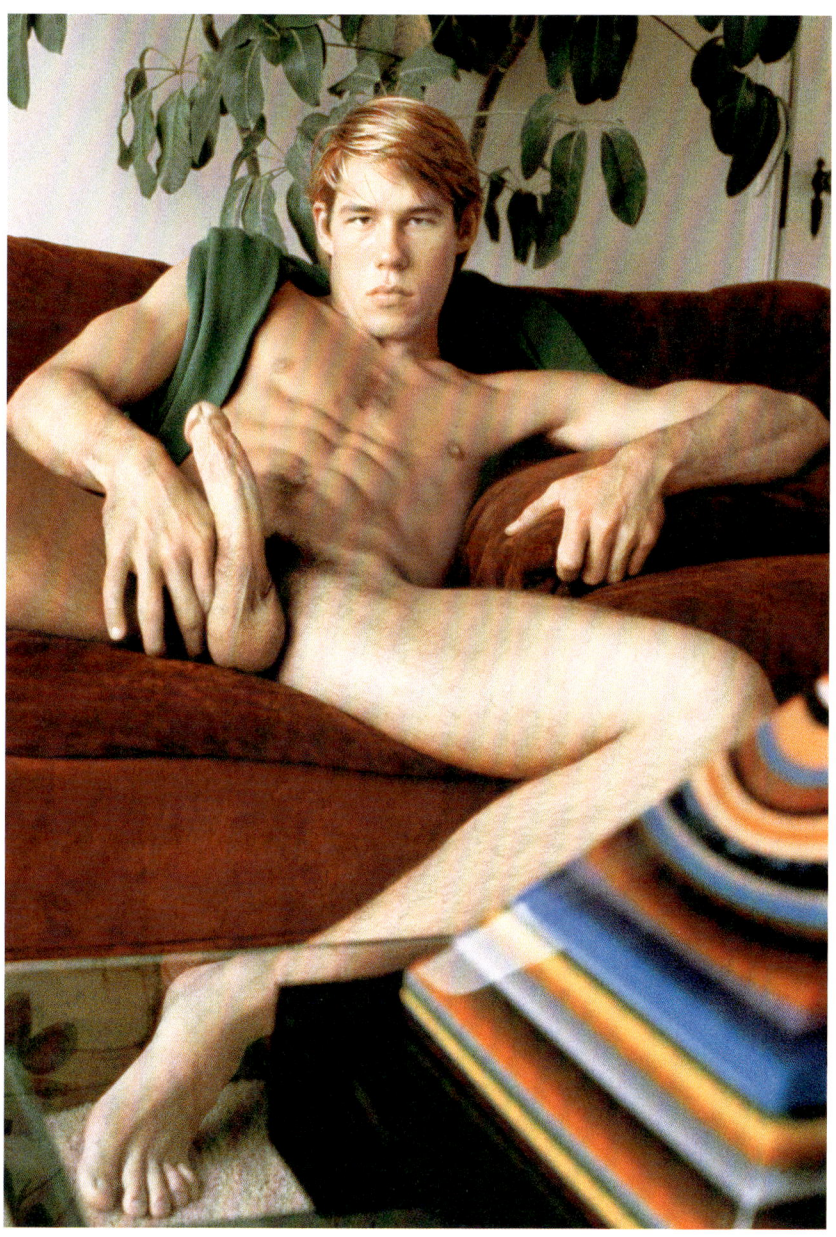

OPPOSITE **Leo Ford** ABOVE **Tim Kramer** PAGES 122-123 **Paul Brandt**

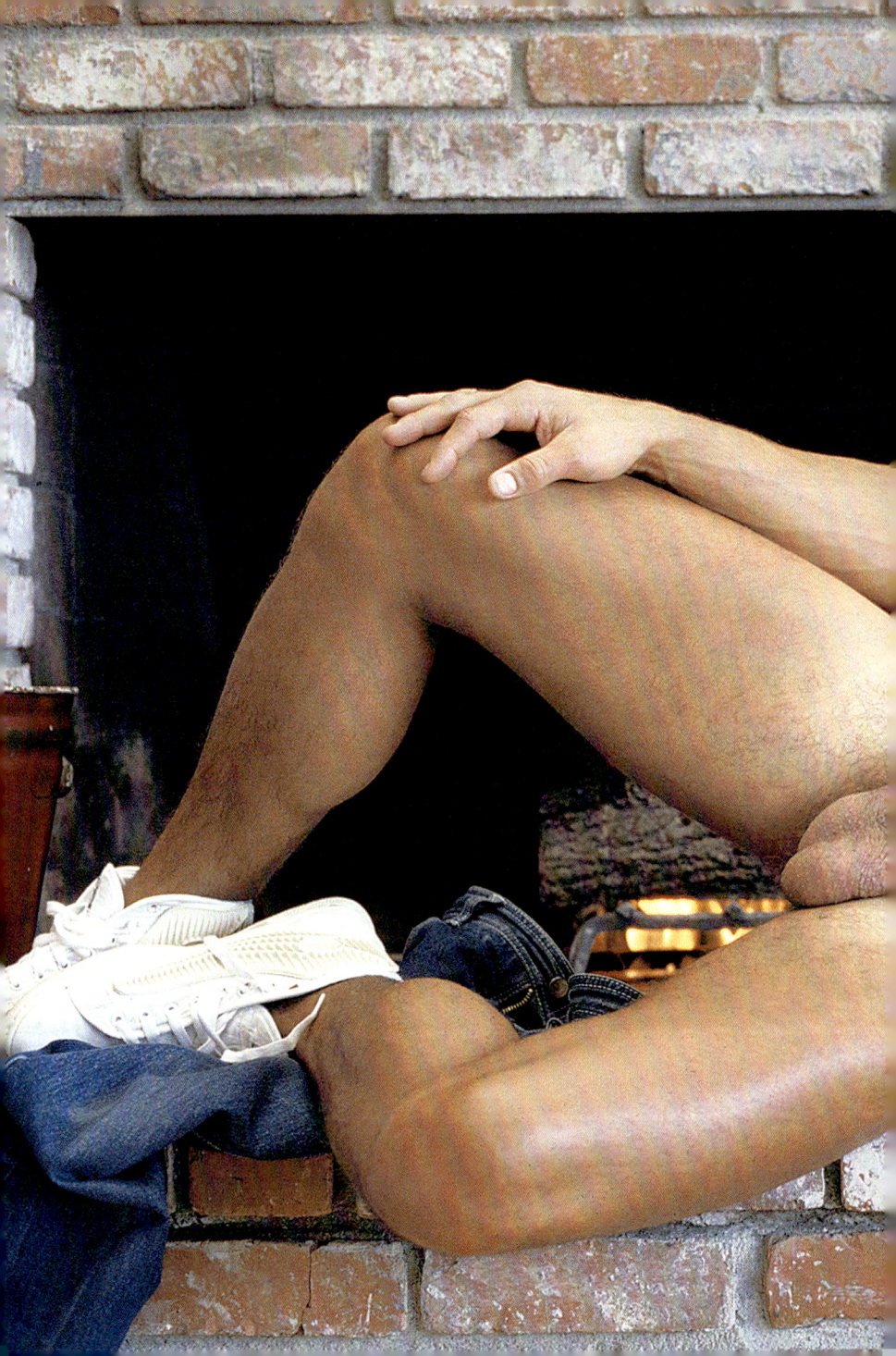

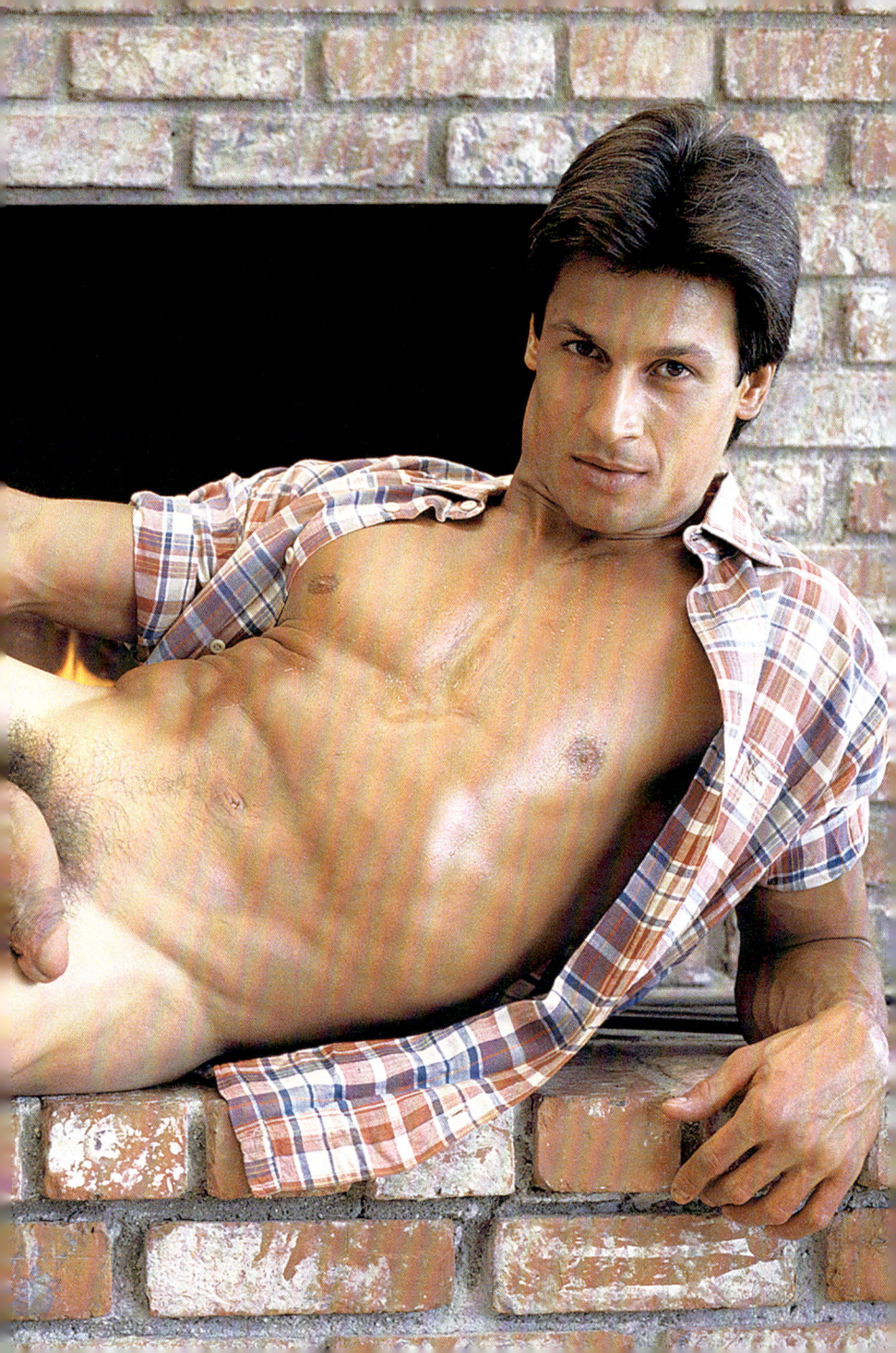

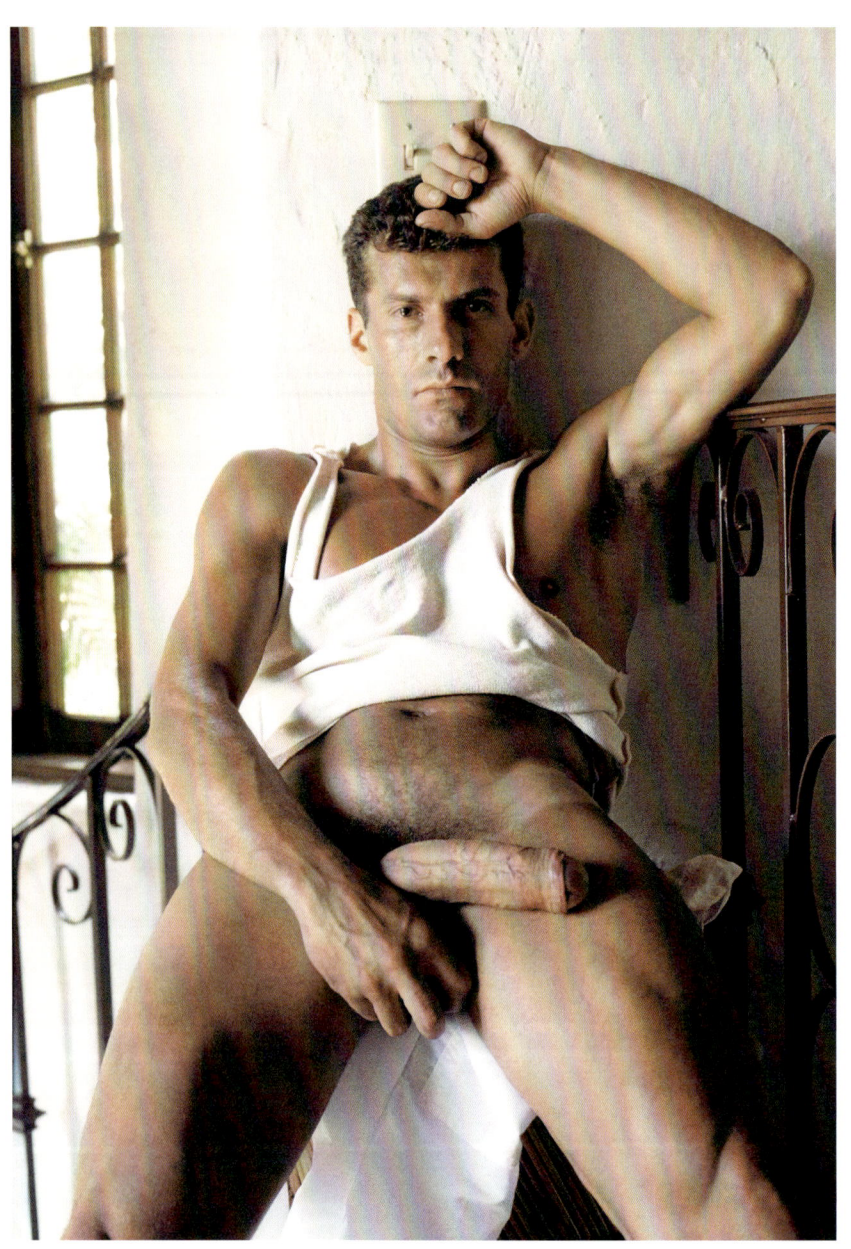

ABOVE **Giorgio Canali** OPPOSITE **Alain Jourdan**

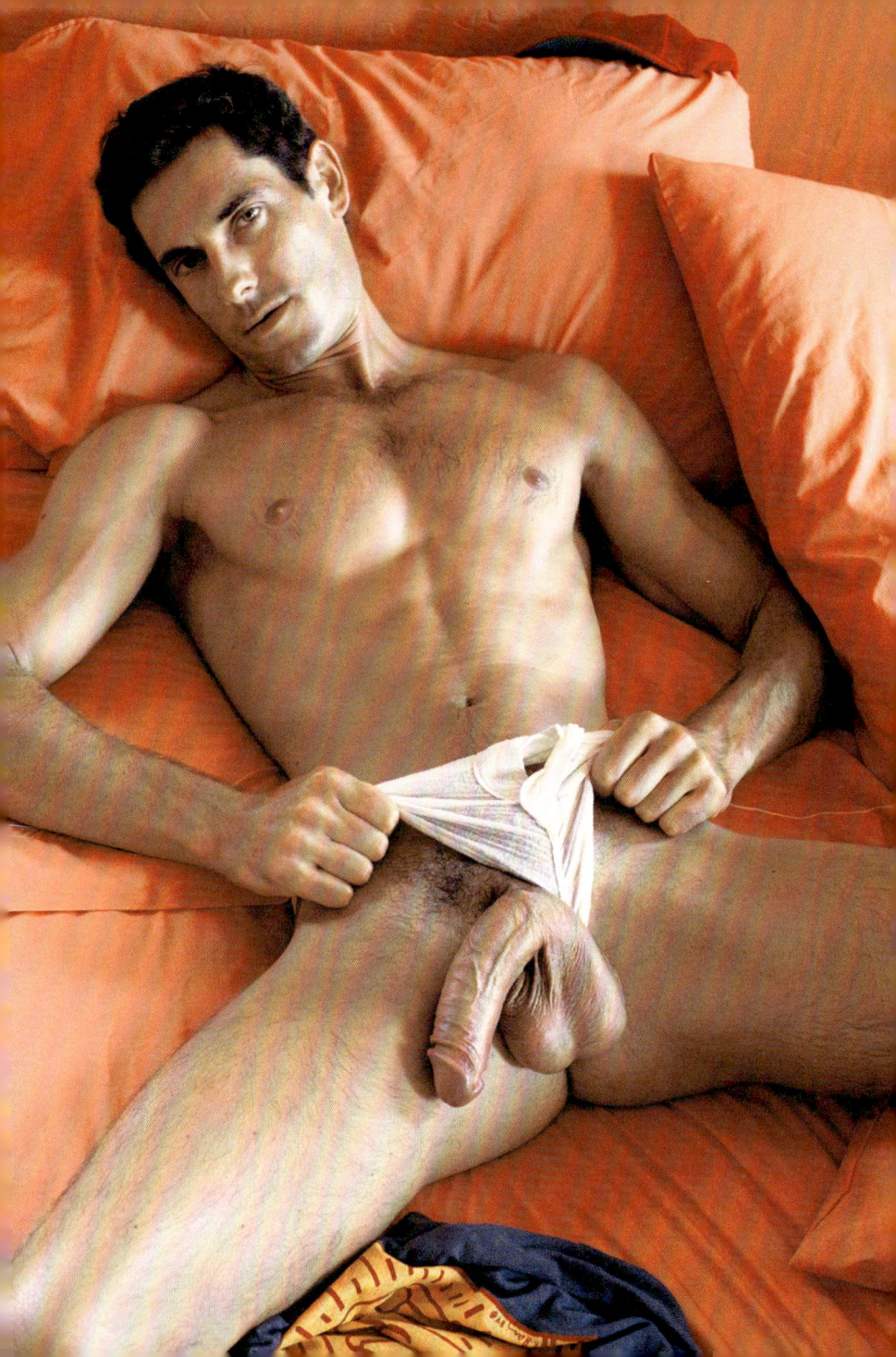

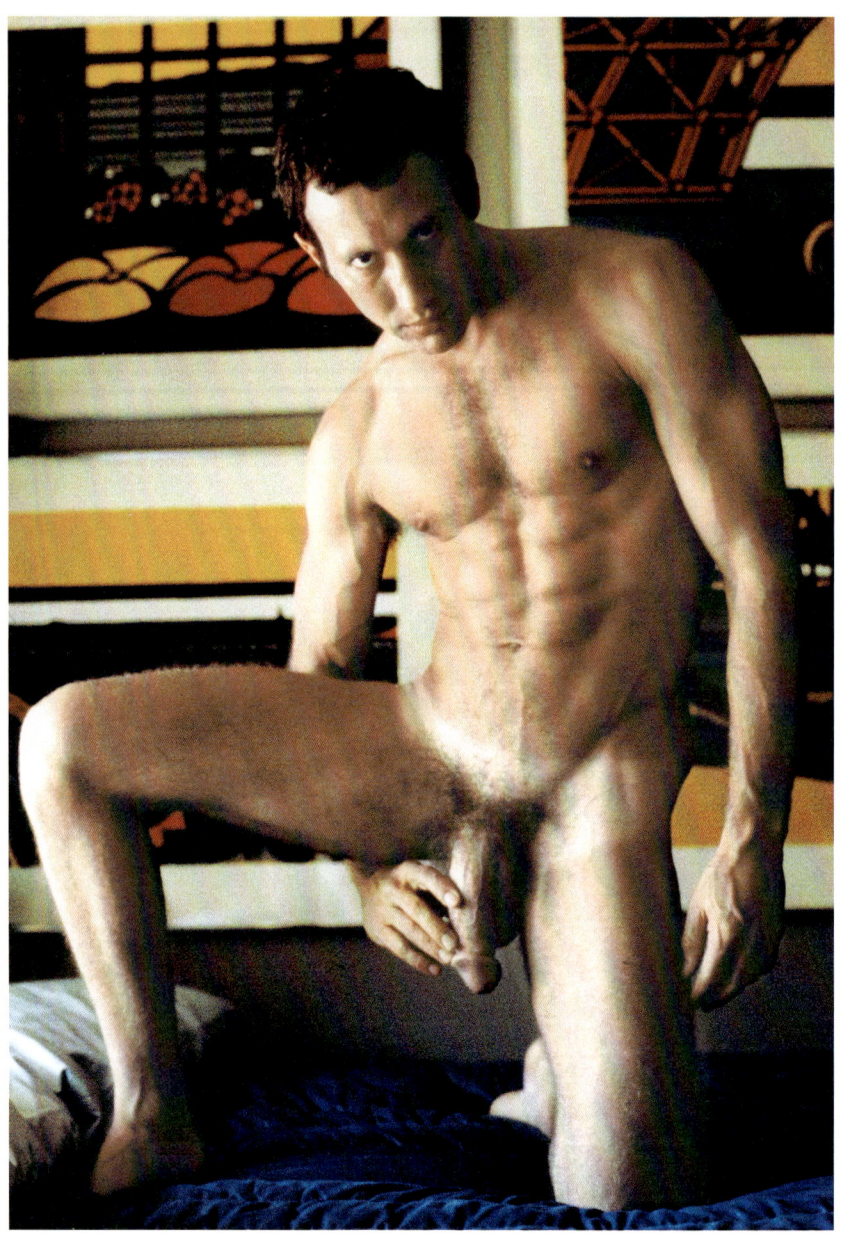

ABOVE **Hal Drake** OPPOSITE **O.J. Johnson**

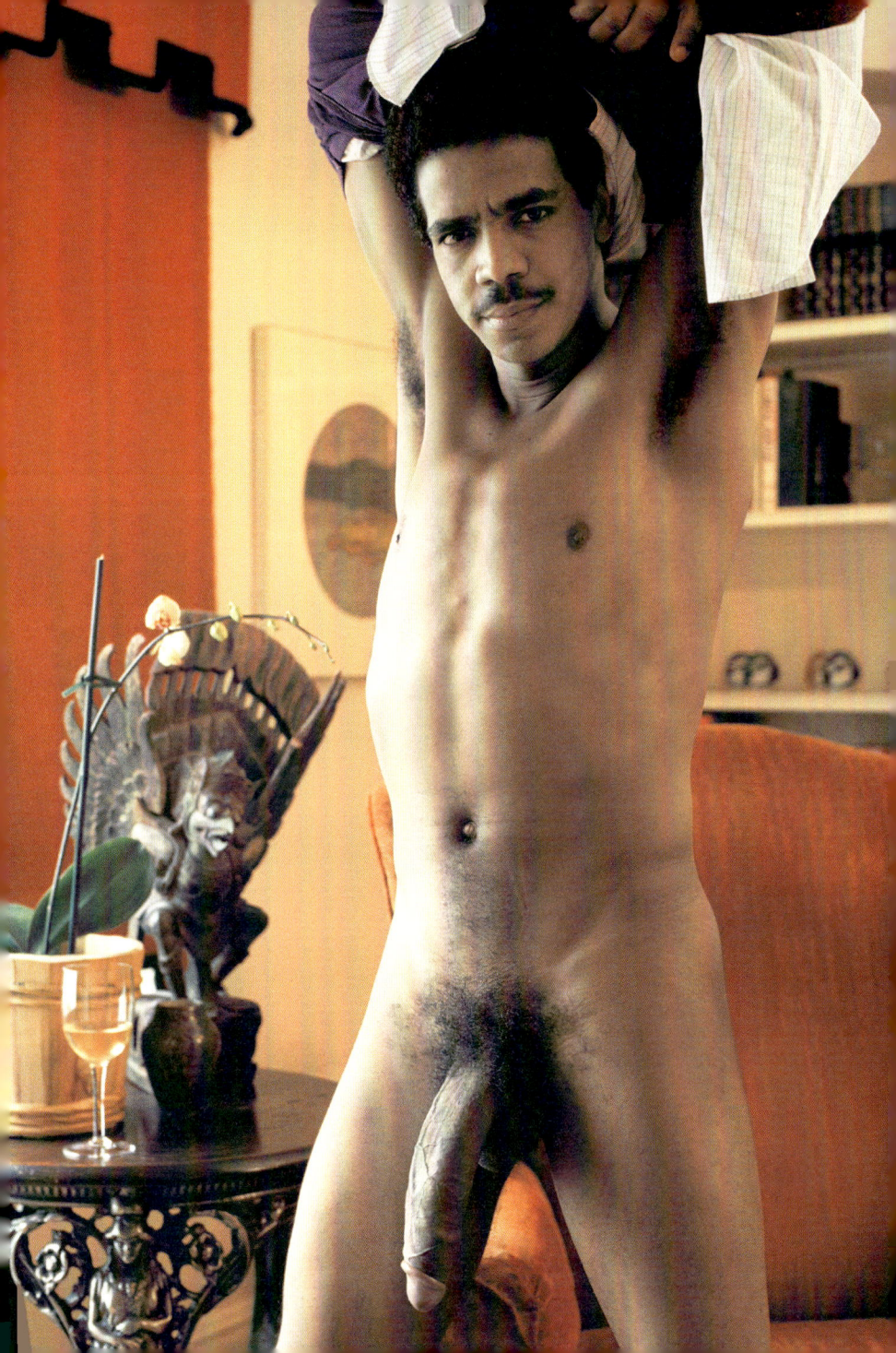

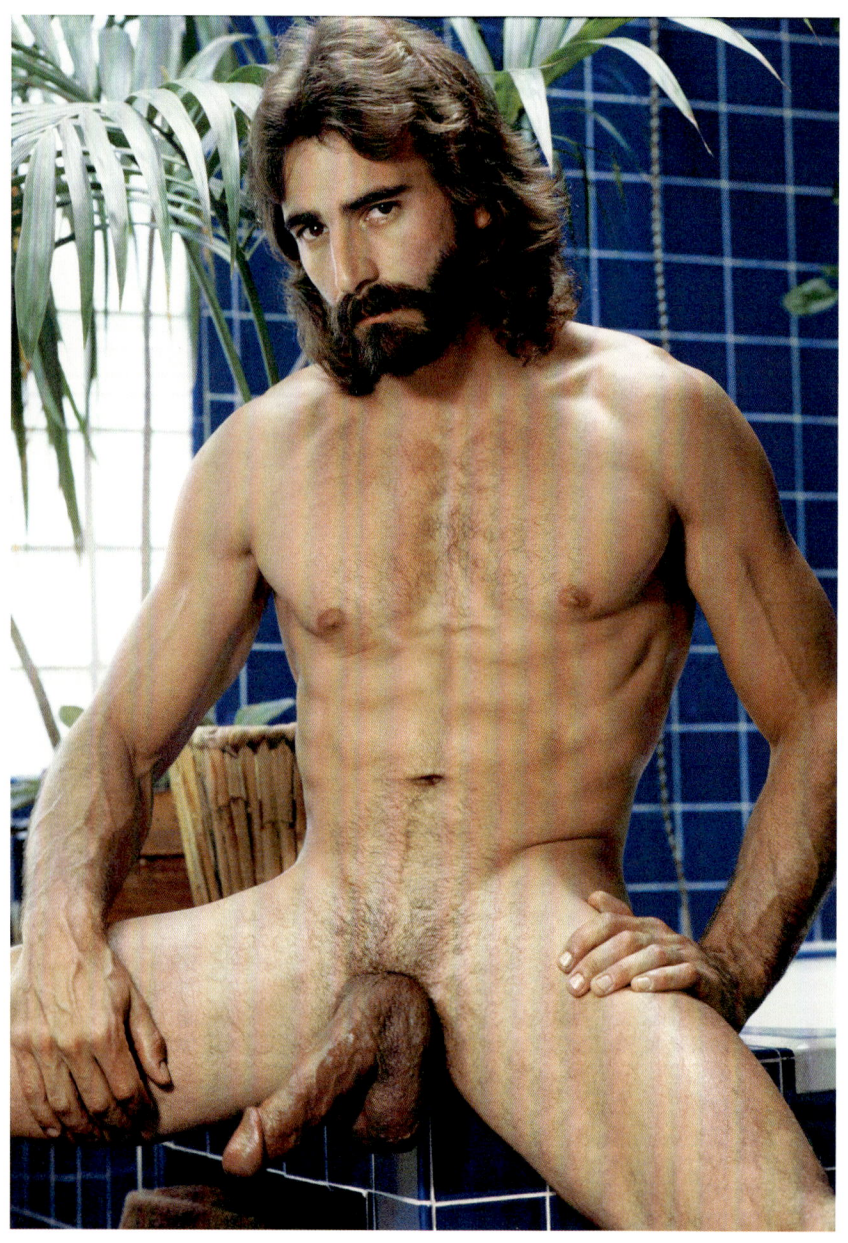

ABOVE **Al Parker** OPPOSITE **Lee Rider**

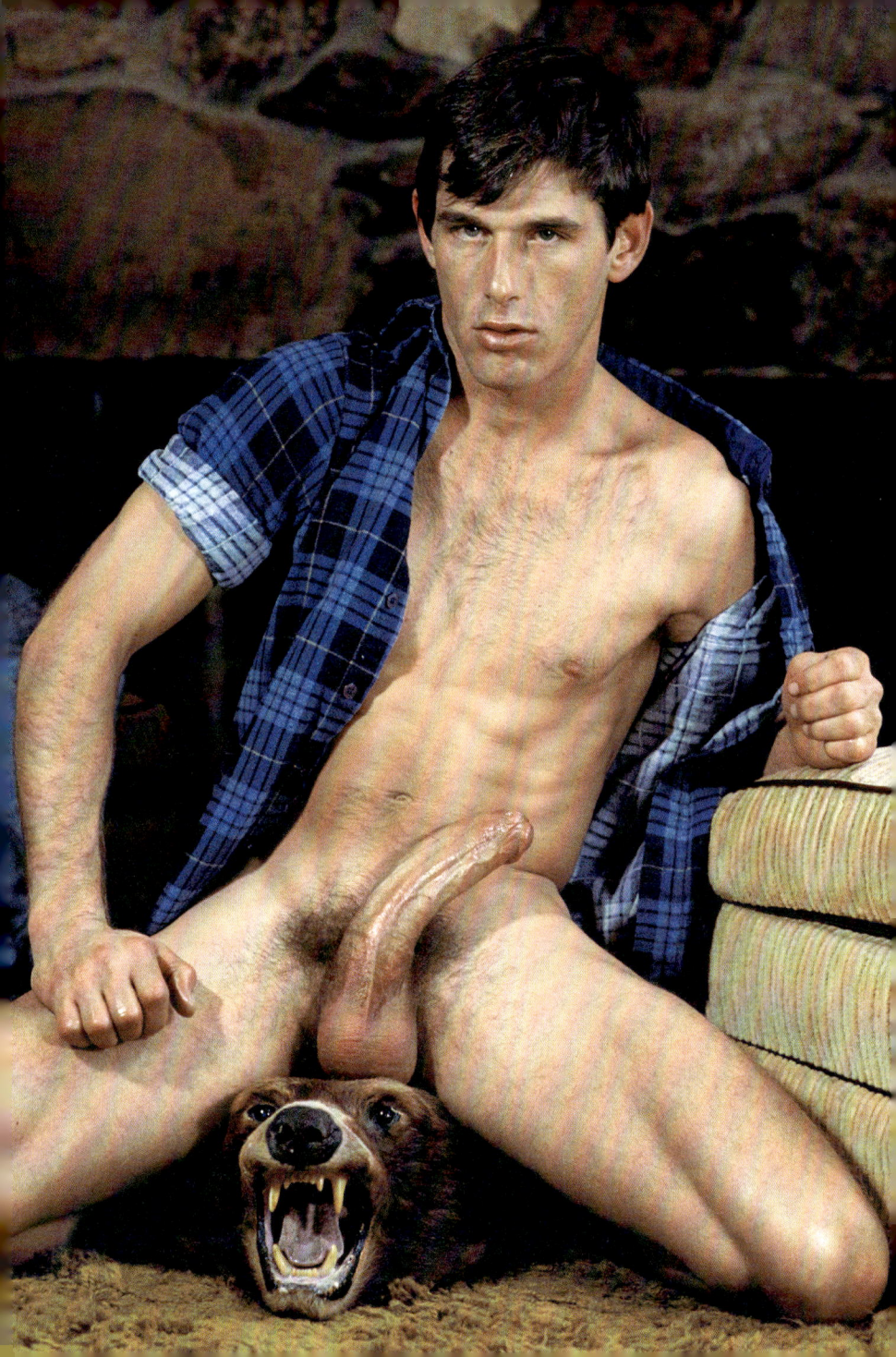

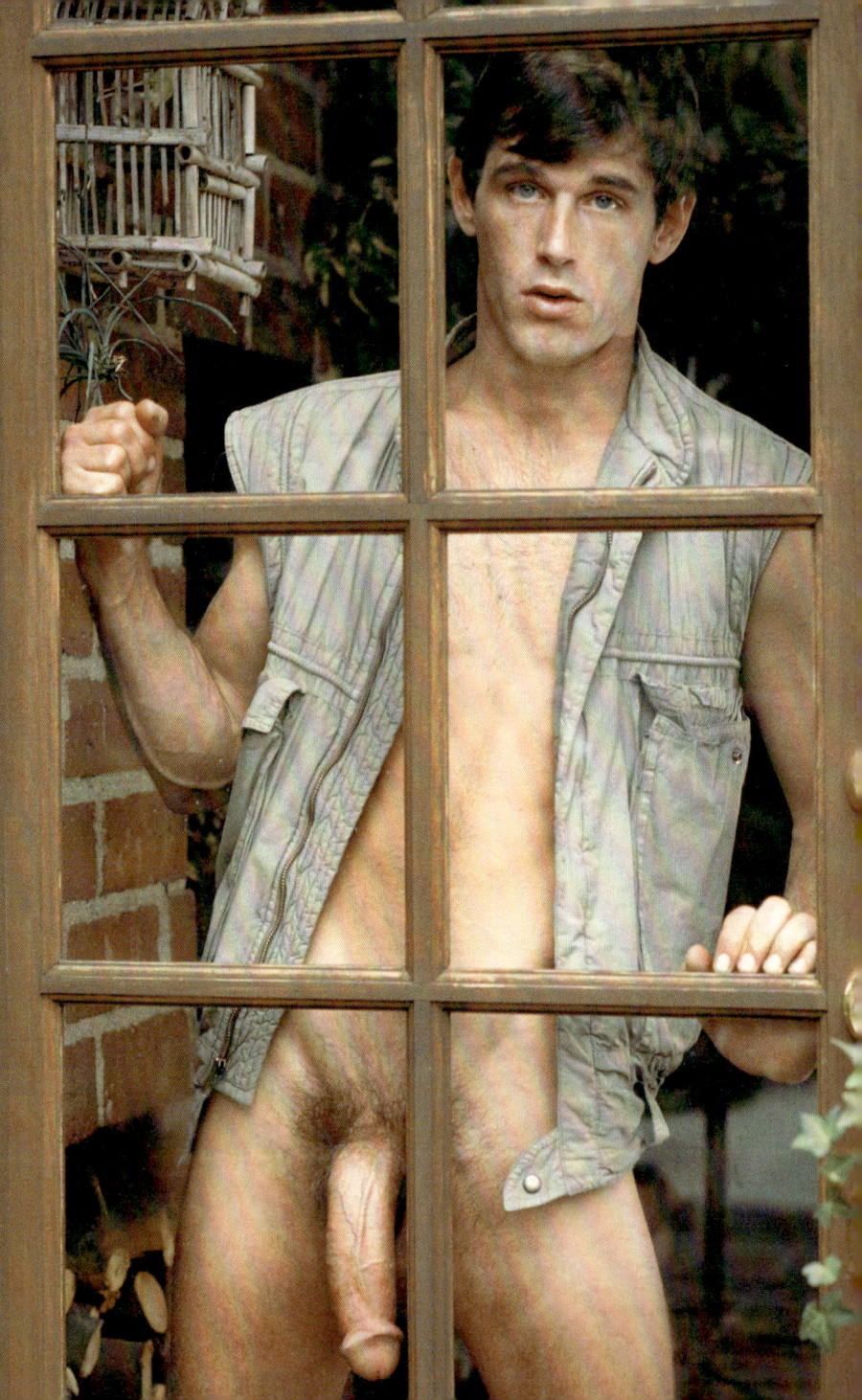

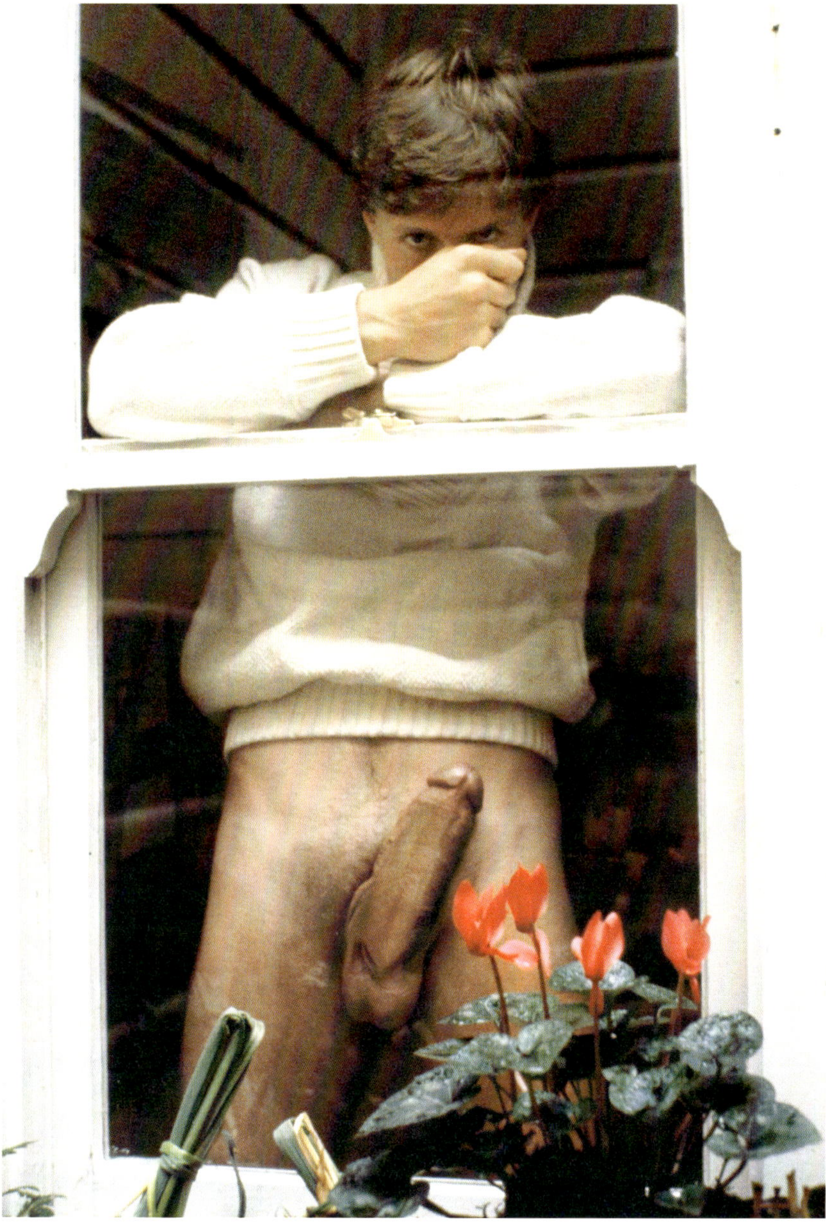

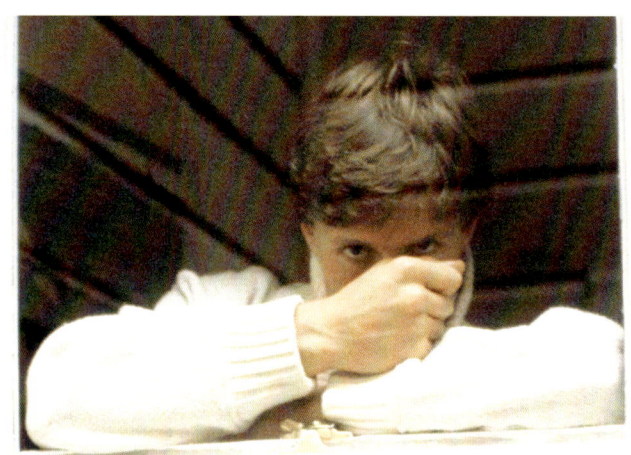

OPPOSITE **Lee Rider**   ABOVE **Kristen Bjorn**

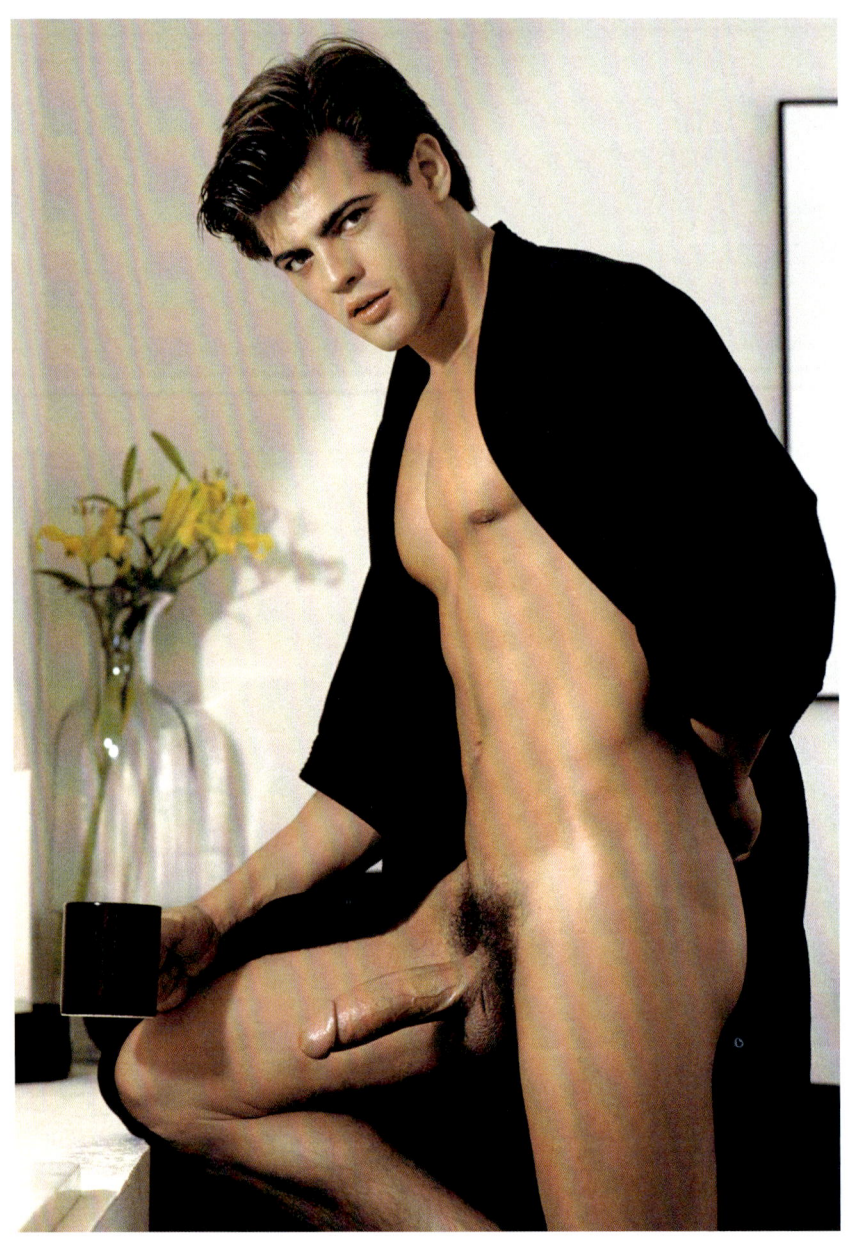

ABOVE **Jeff Stryker**   OPPOSITE **Scott O'Hara**   PAGES 134-135 **Ken Foxx**

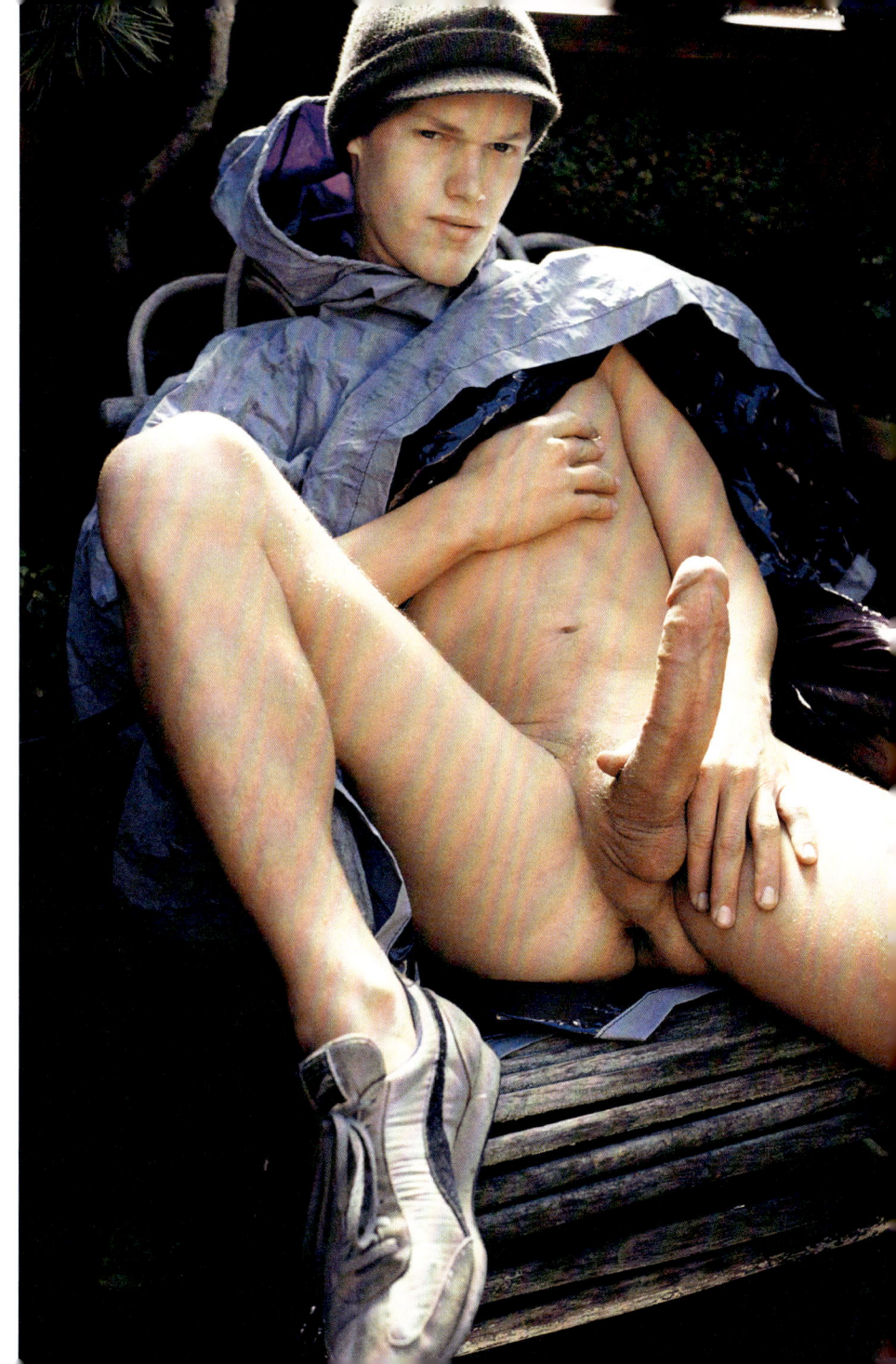

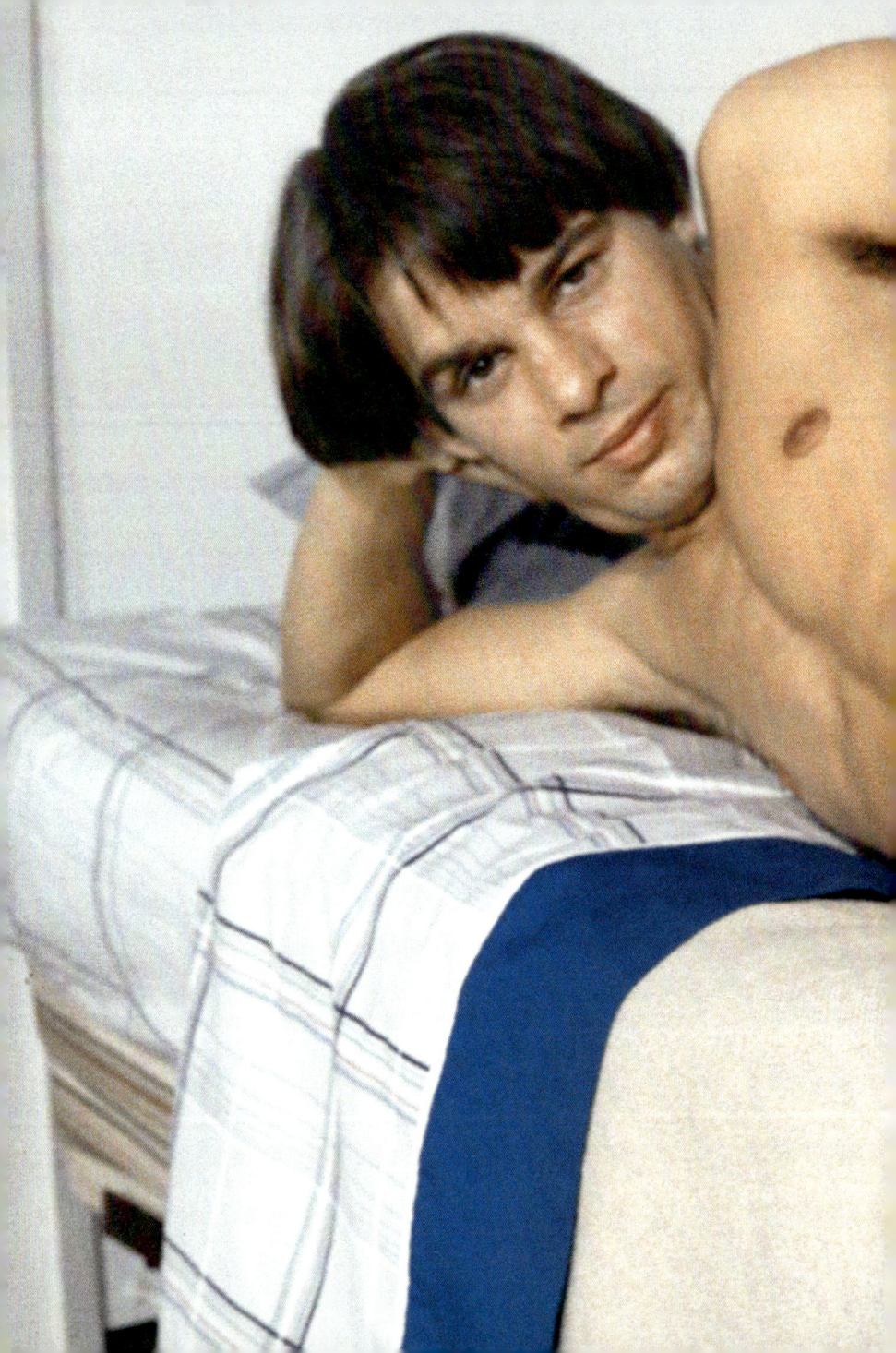

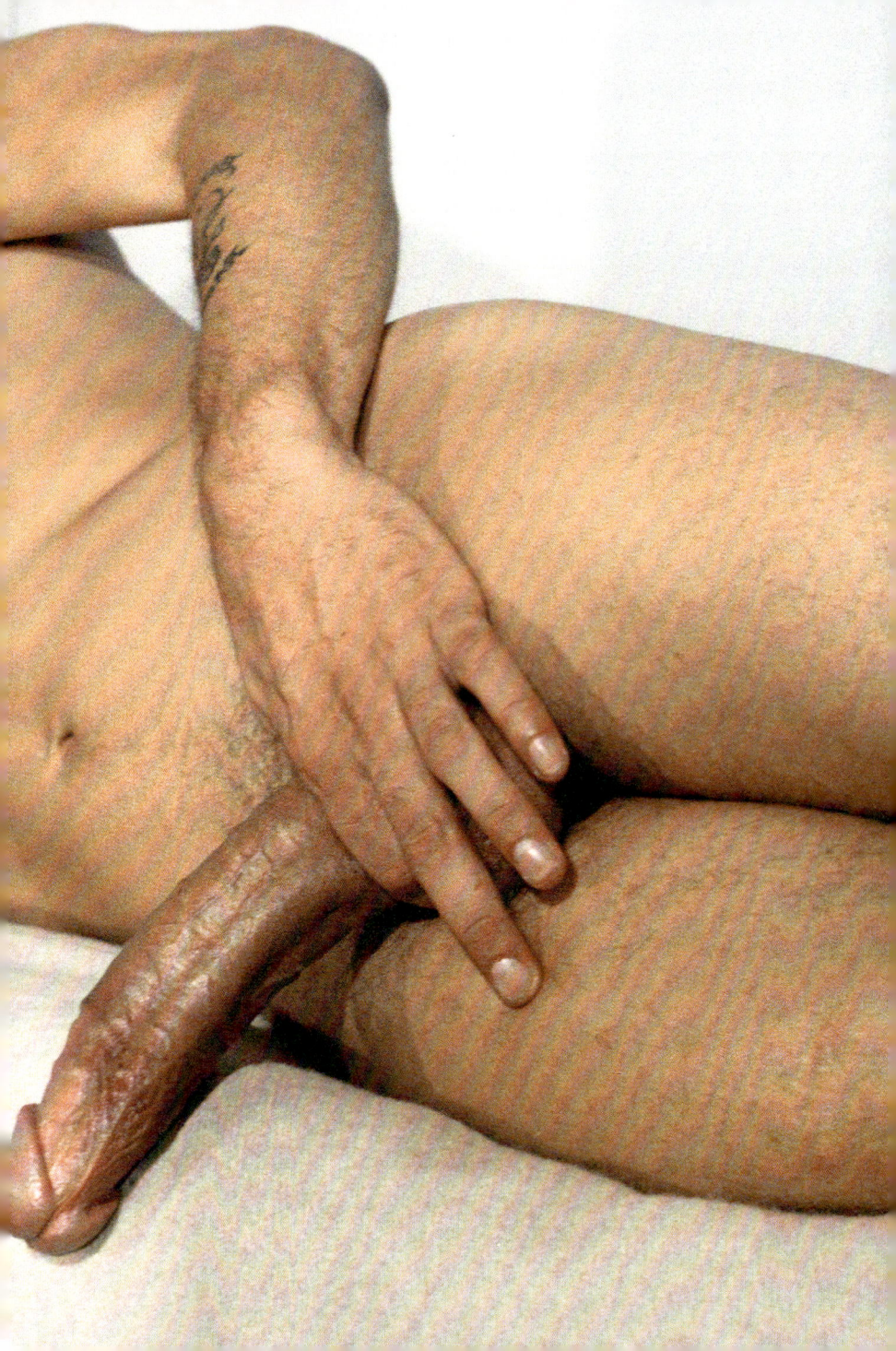

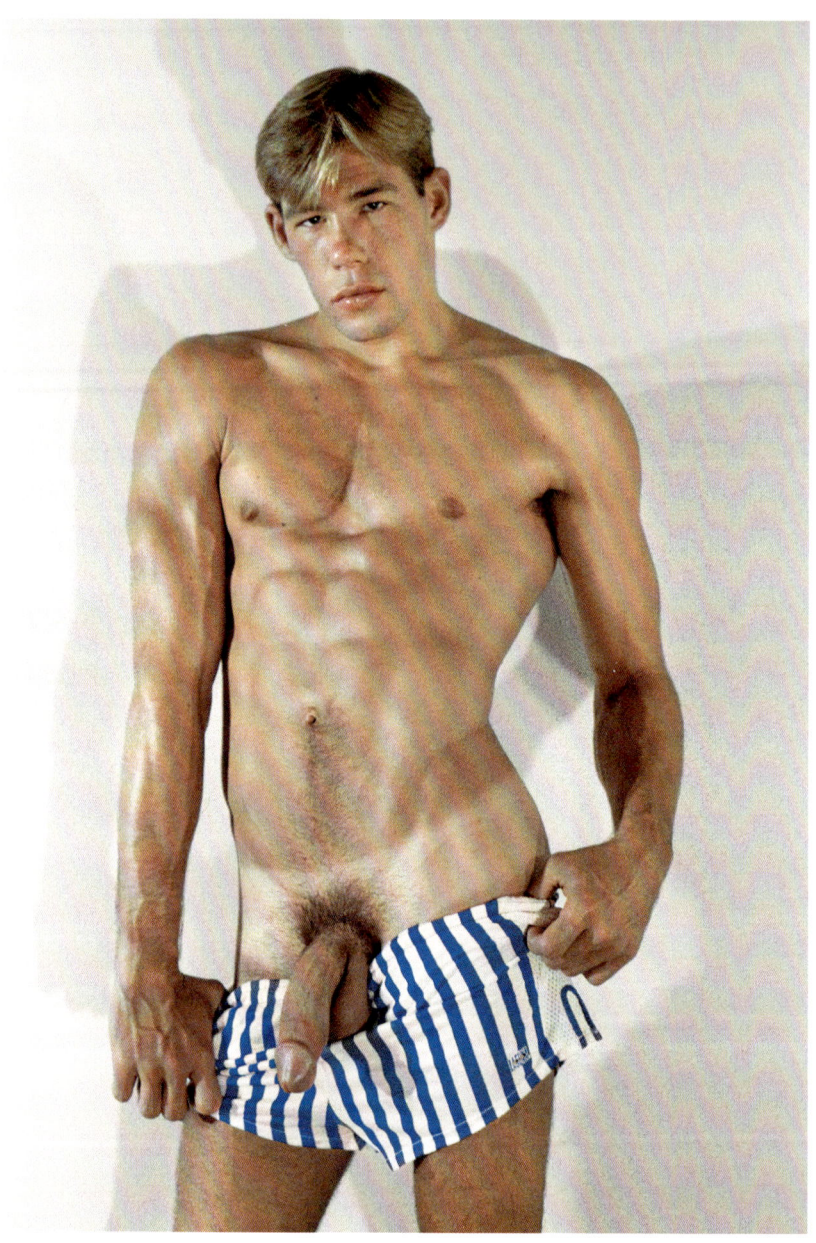

Tim Kramer

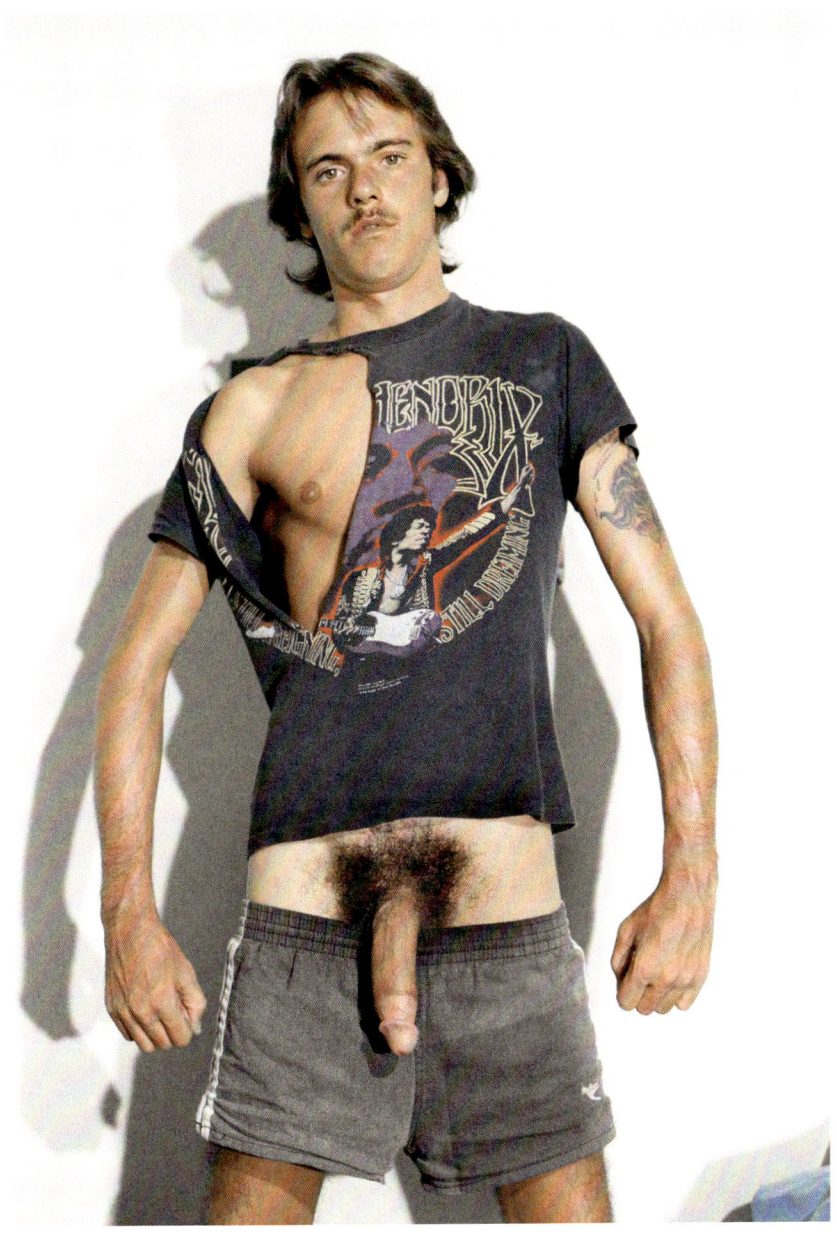

ABOVE **Randy Sutton**   PAGES 138-139 **Bam Johnson**

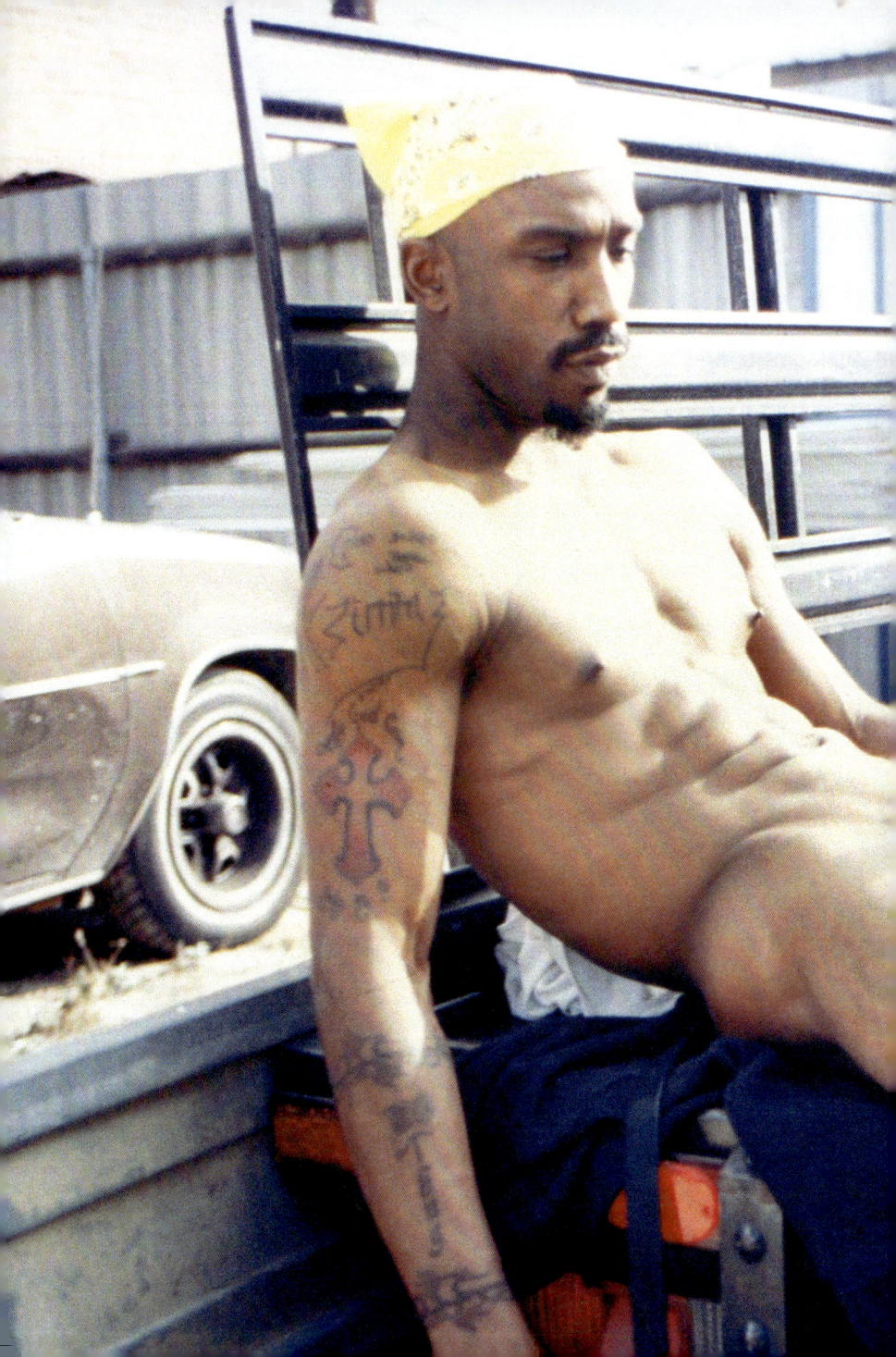

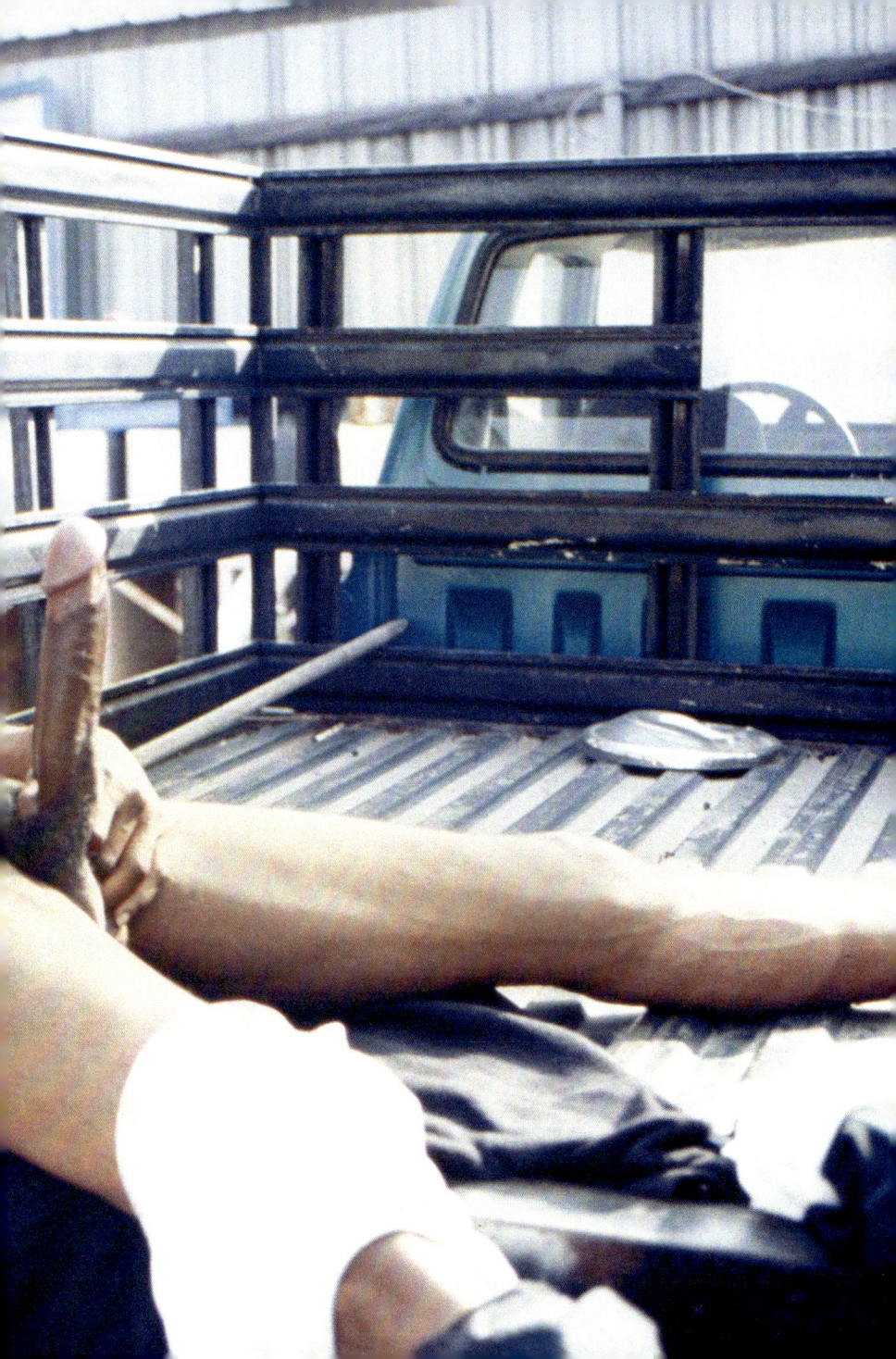

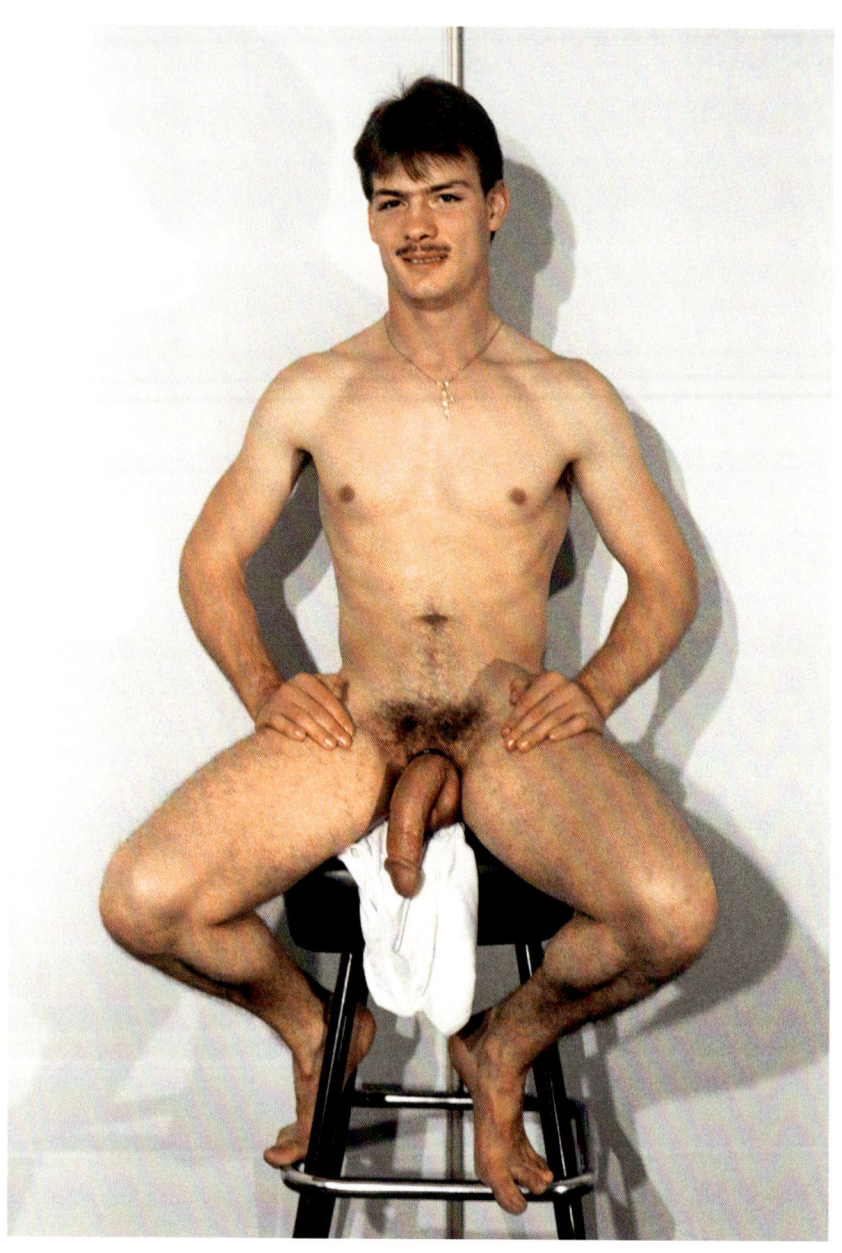

ABOVE **Rick Donovan**   OPPOSITE **Ray Victory**   PAGES 142-143 **Ernie Nava**

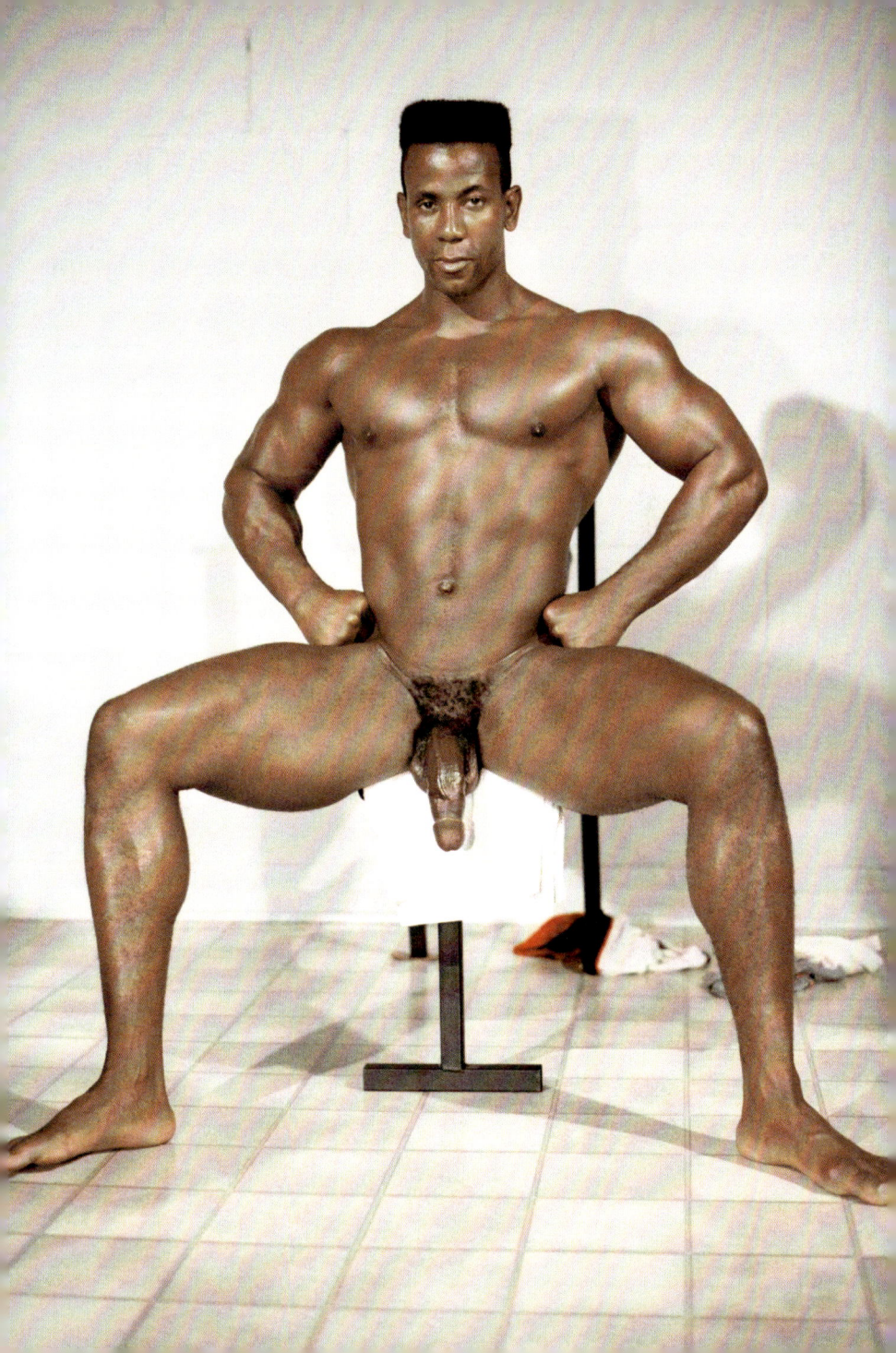

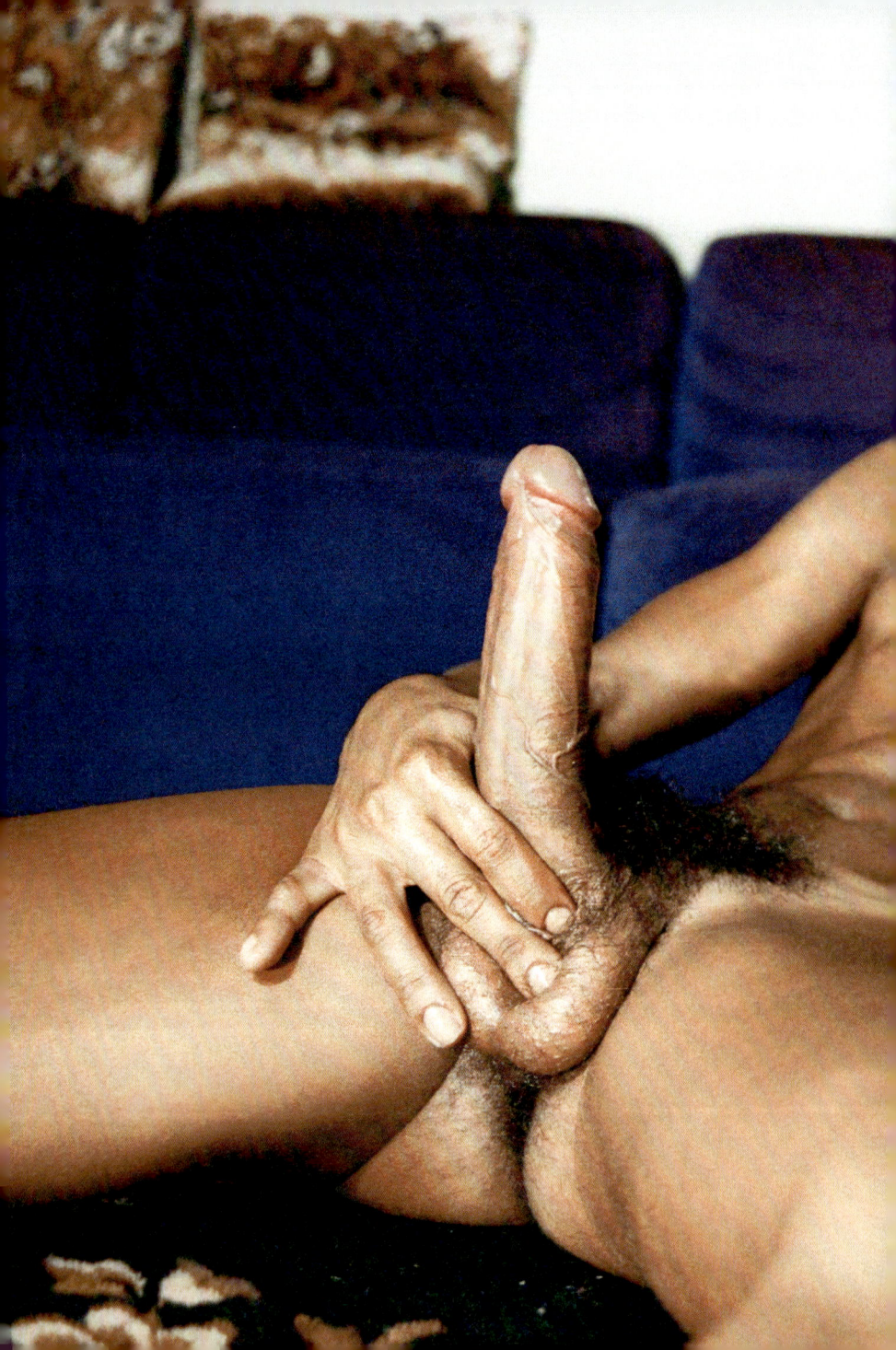

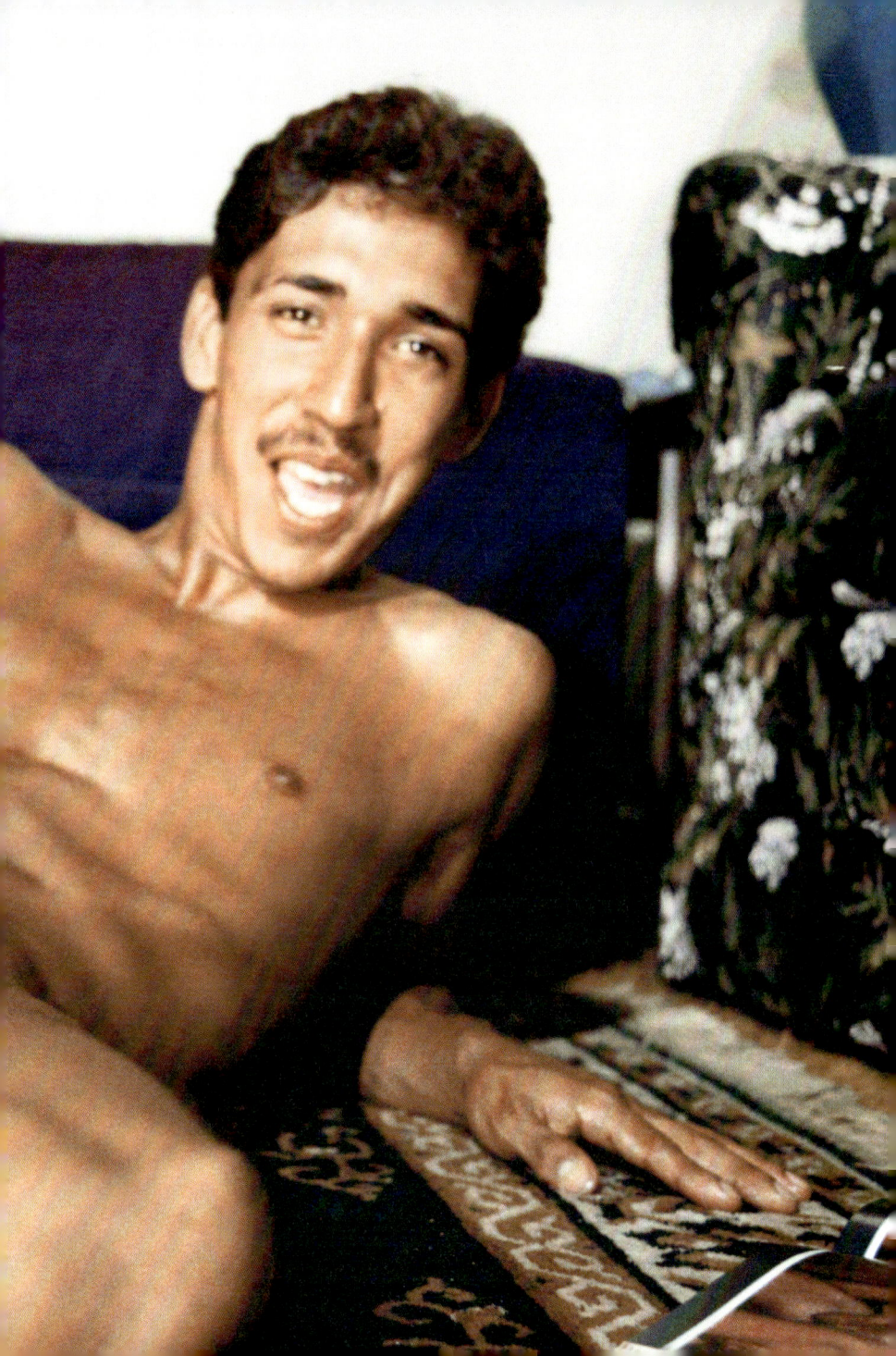

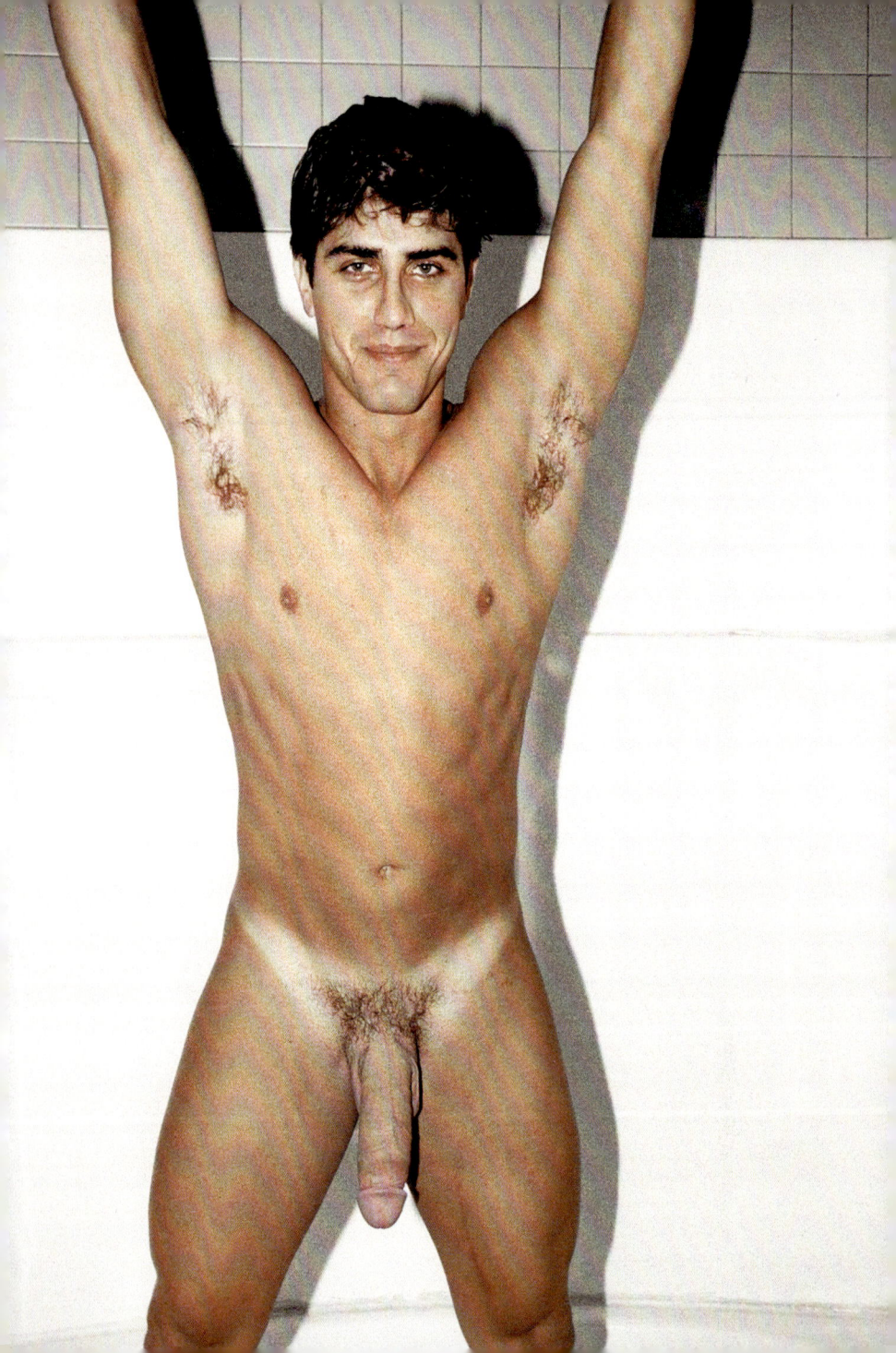

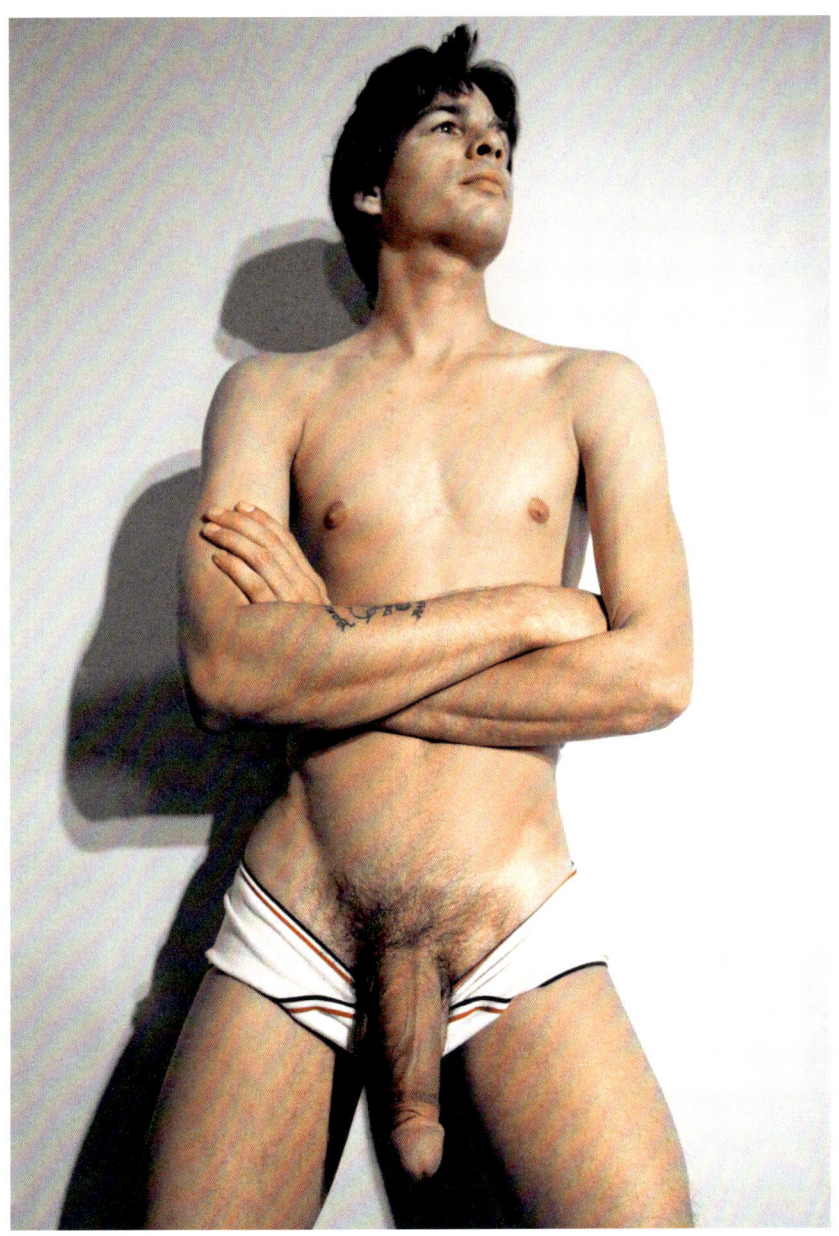

OPPOSITE **Tom Steele**   ABOVE **Ken Foxx**

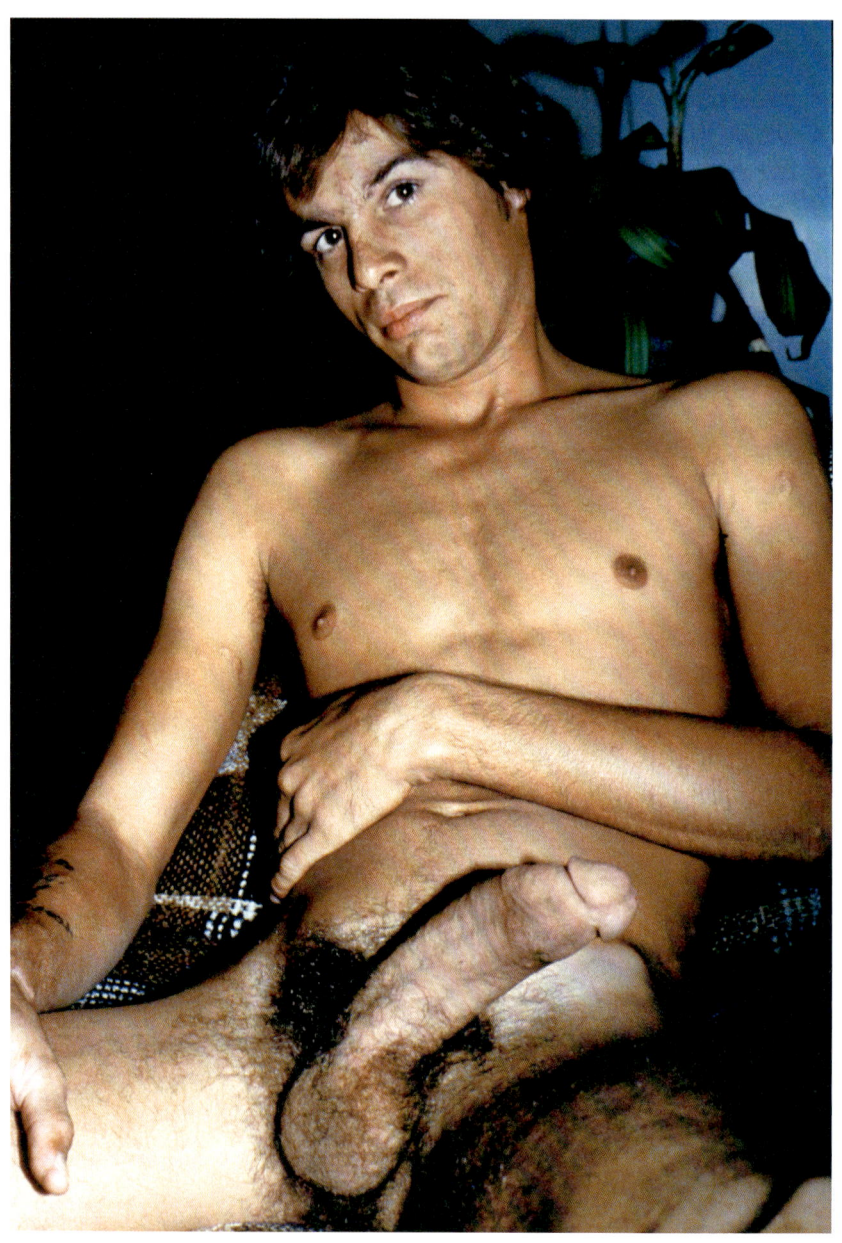

ABOVE **Ken Foxx** OPPOSITE **Bam Johnson**

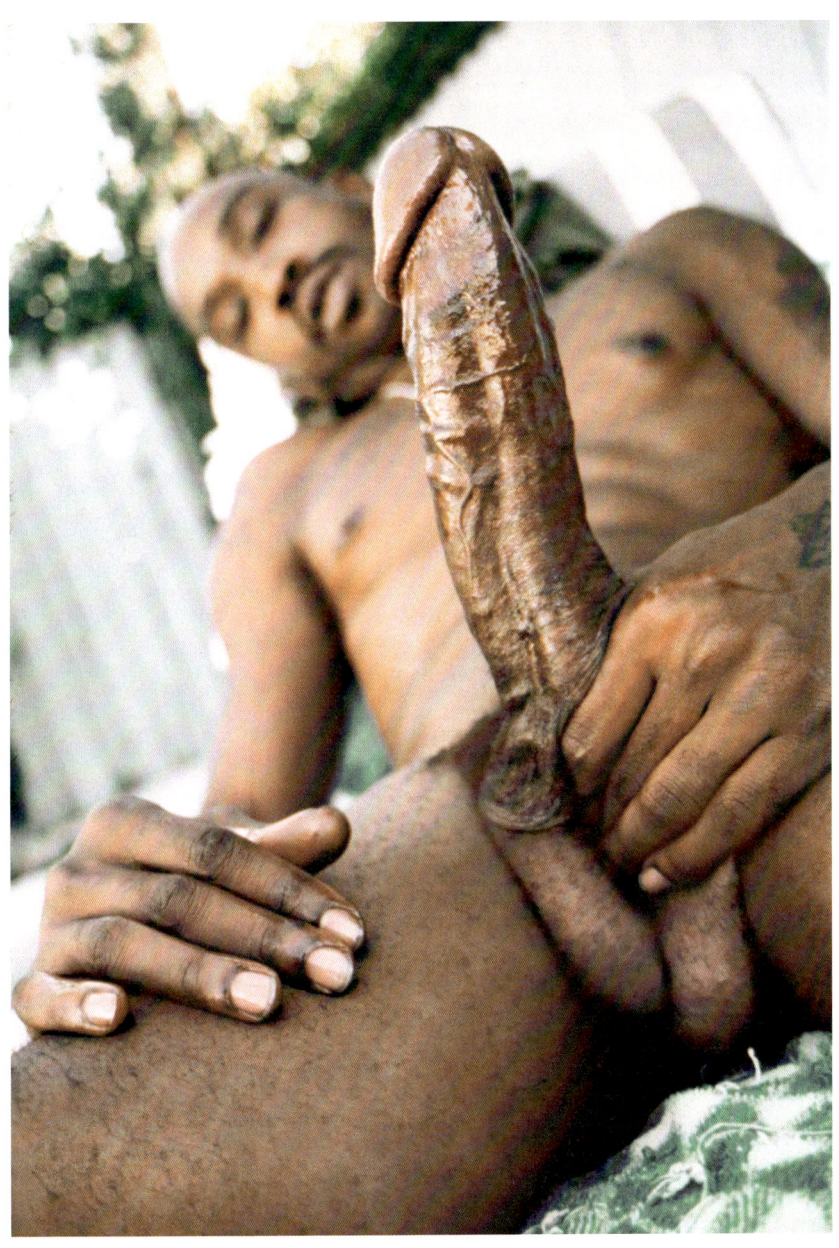

PAGE 148 **Brad Fuller**   PAGE 149 **Leslie Gavin**

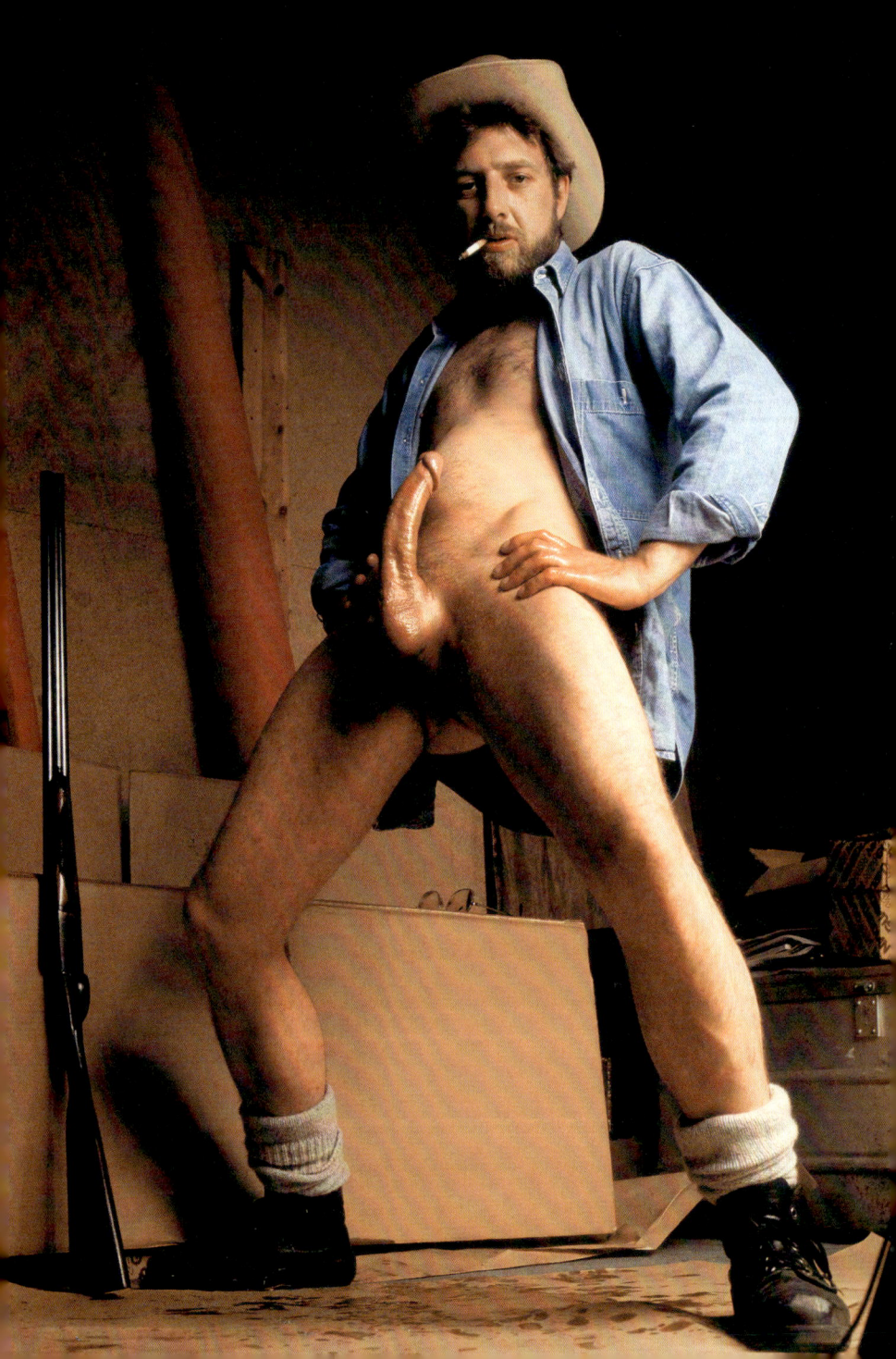

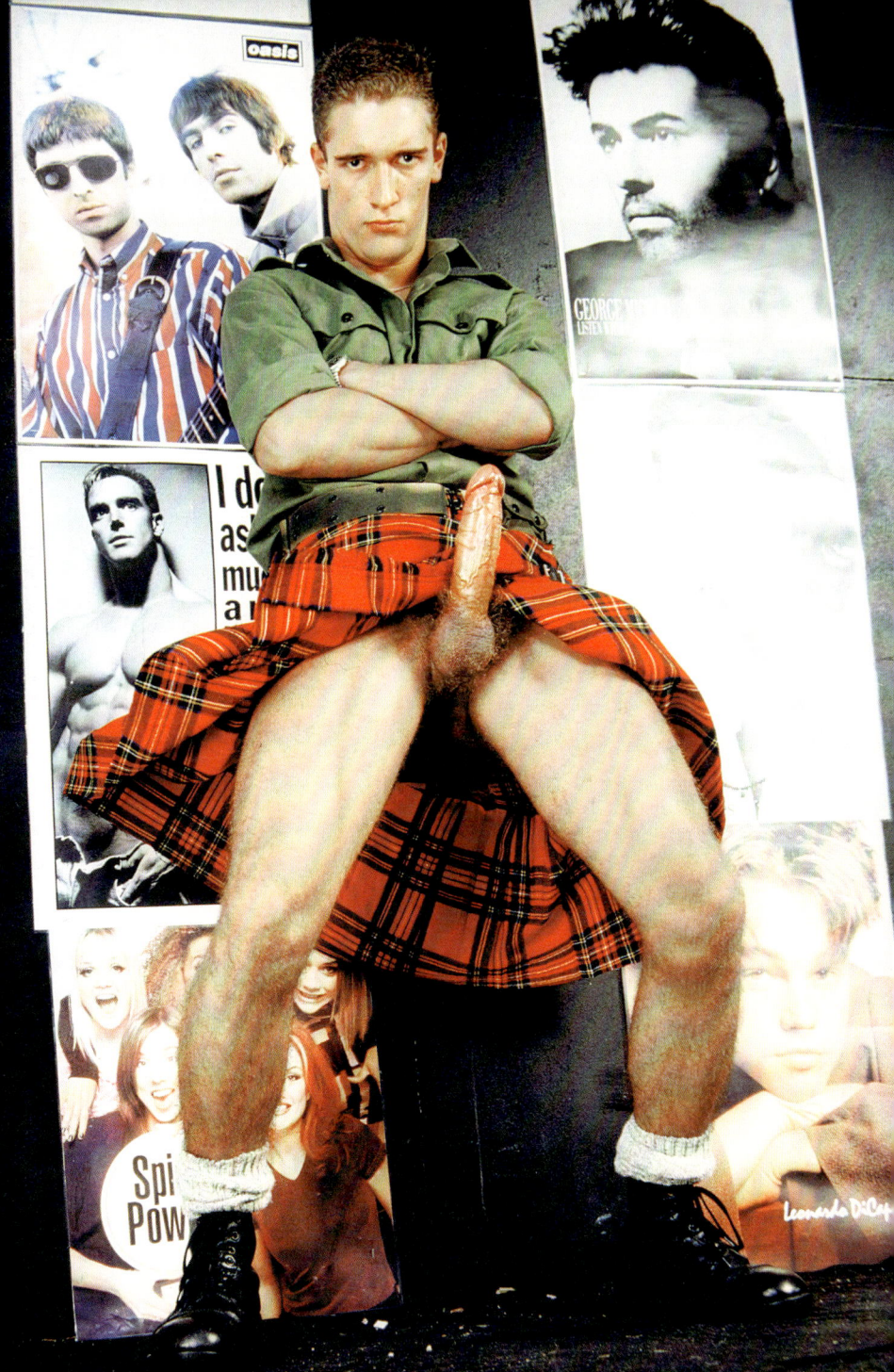

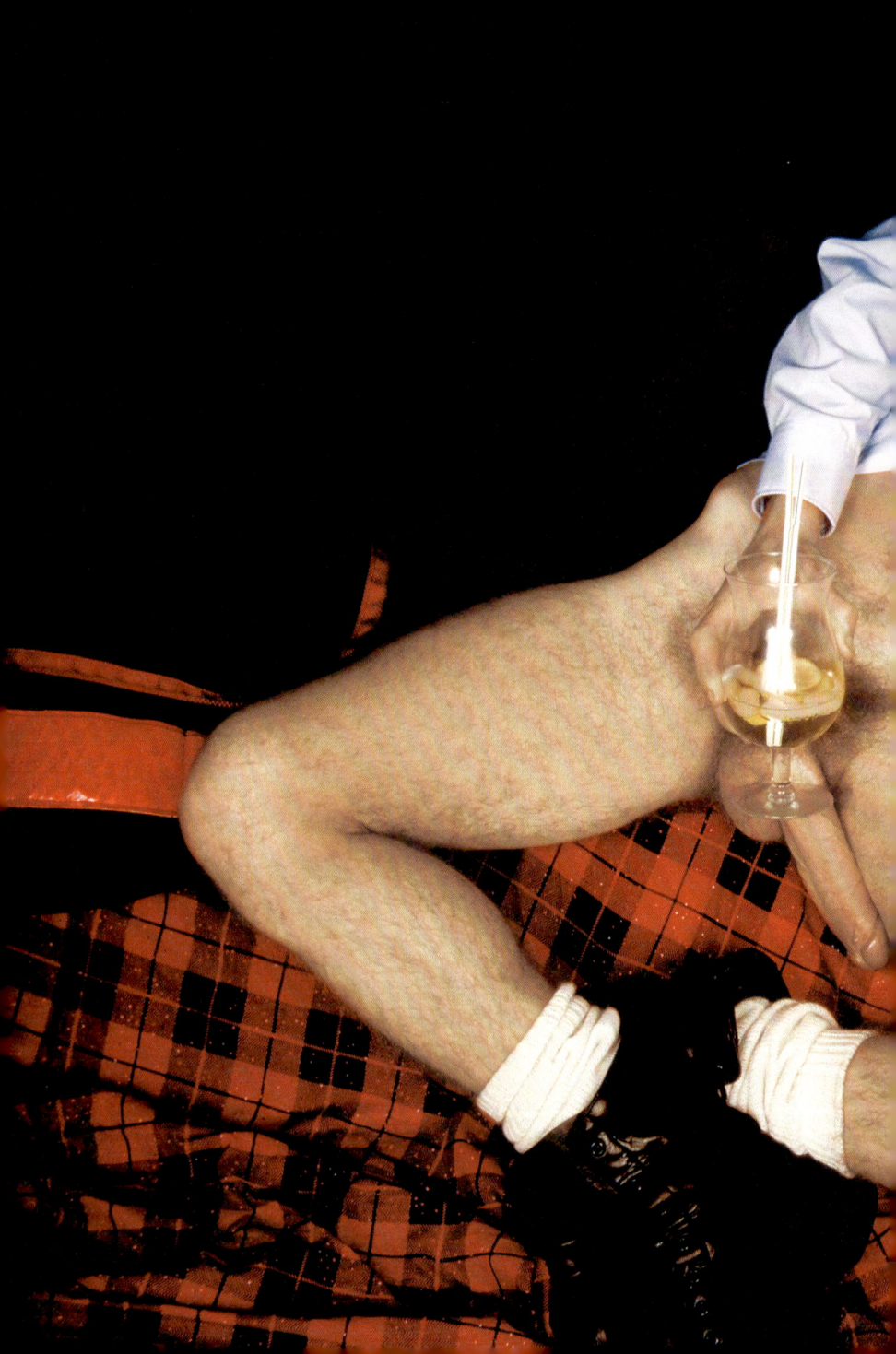

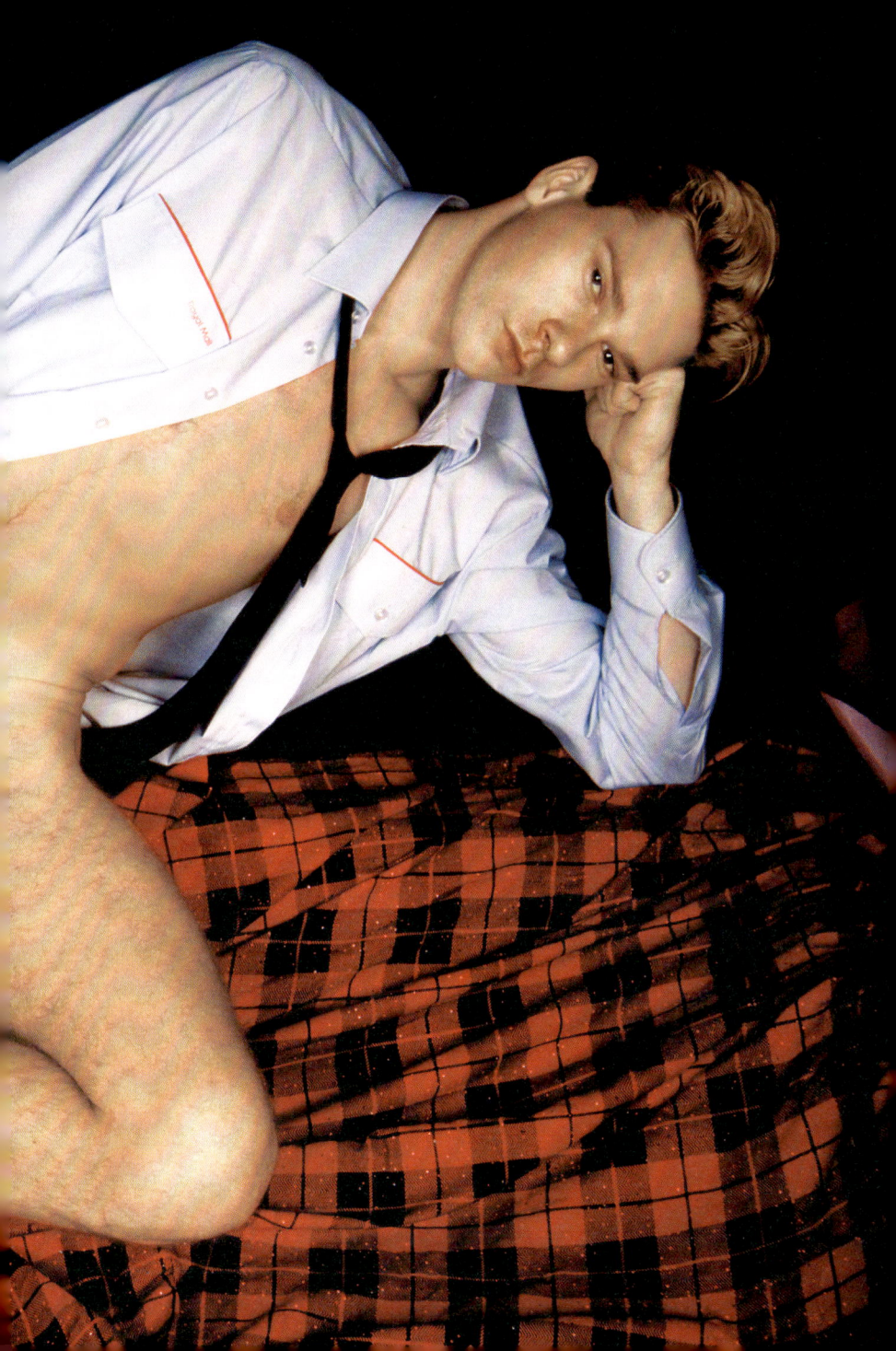

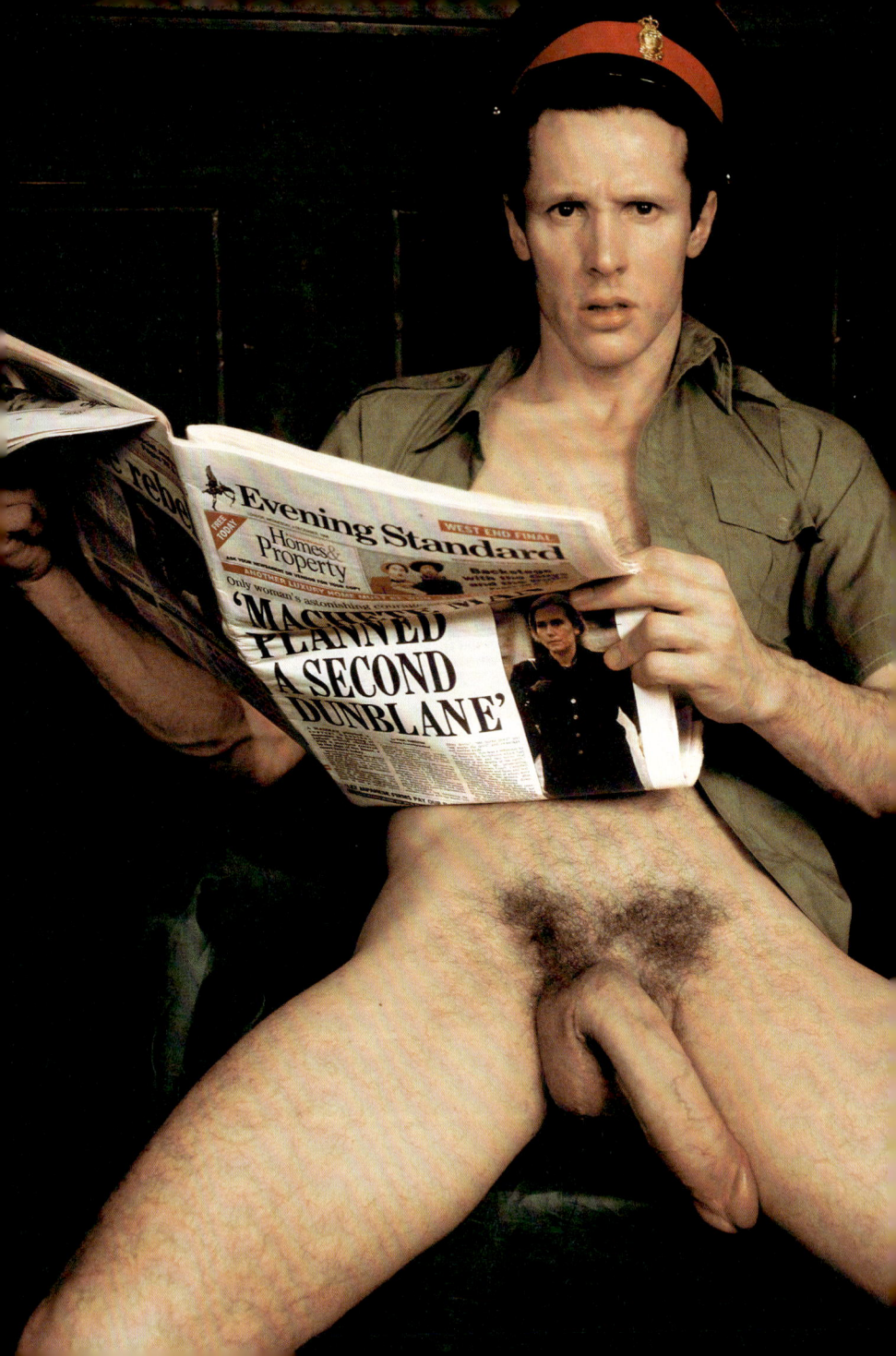

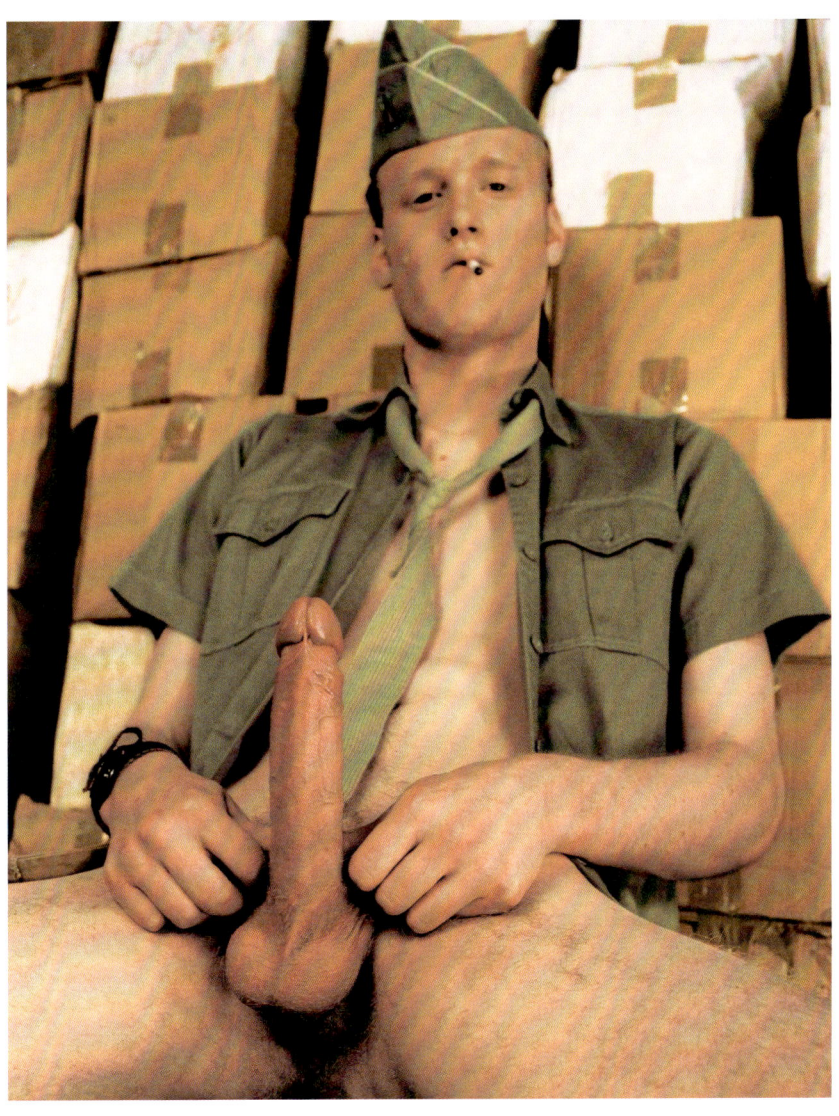

PAGES 150-151 **Chris Donovan**   OPPOSITE **Jan Weiss**   ABOVE **Simon McBryde**

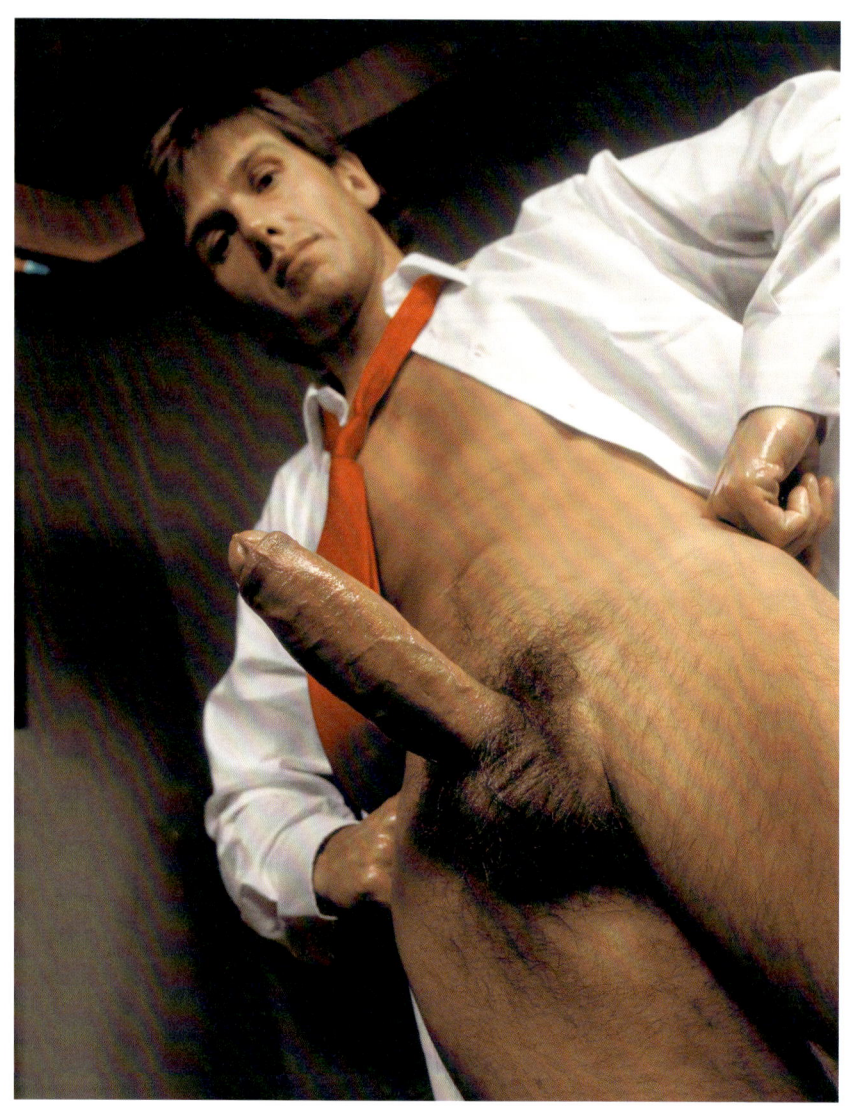

Mick Gillen

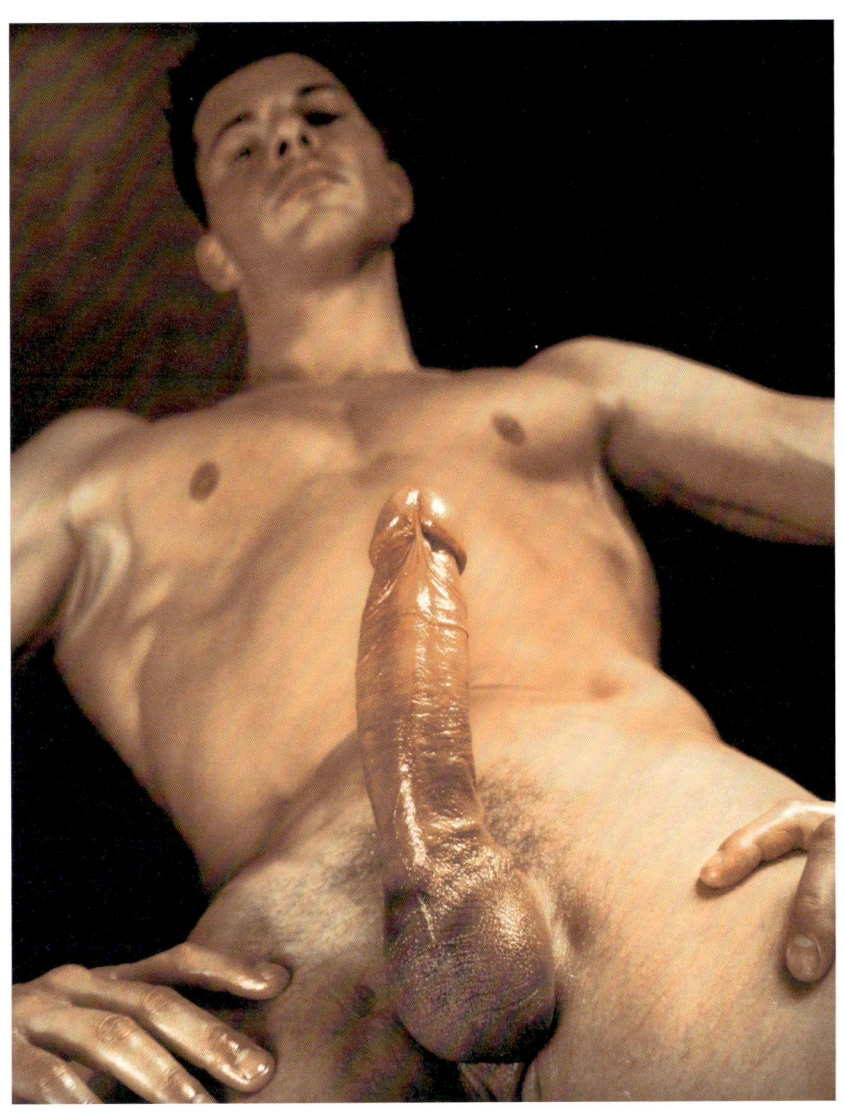

ABOVE **John Bove**   PAGES 156-157 **Jay Alexander**

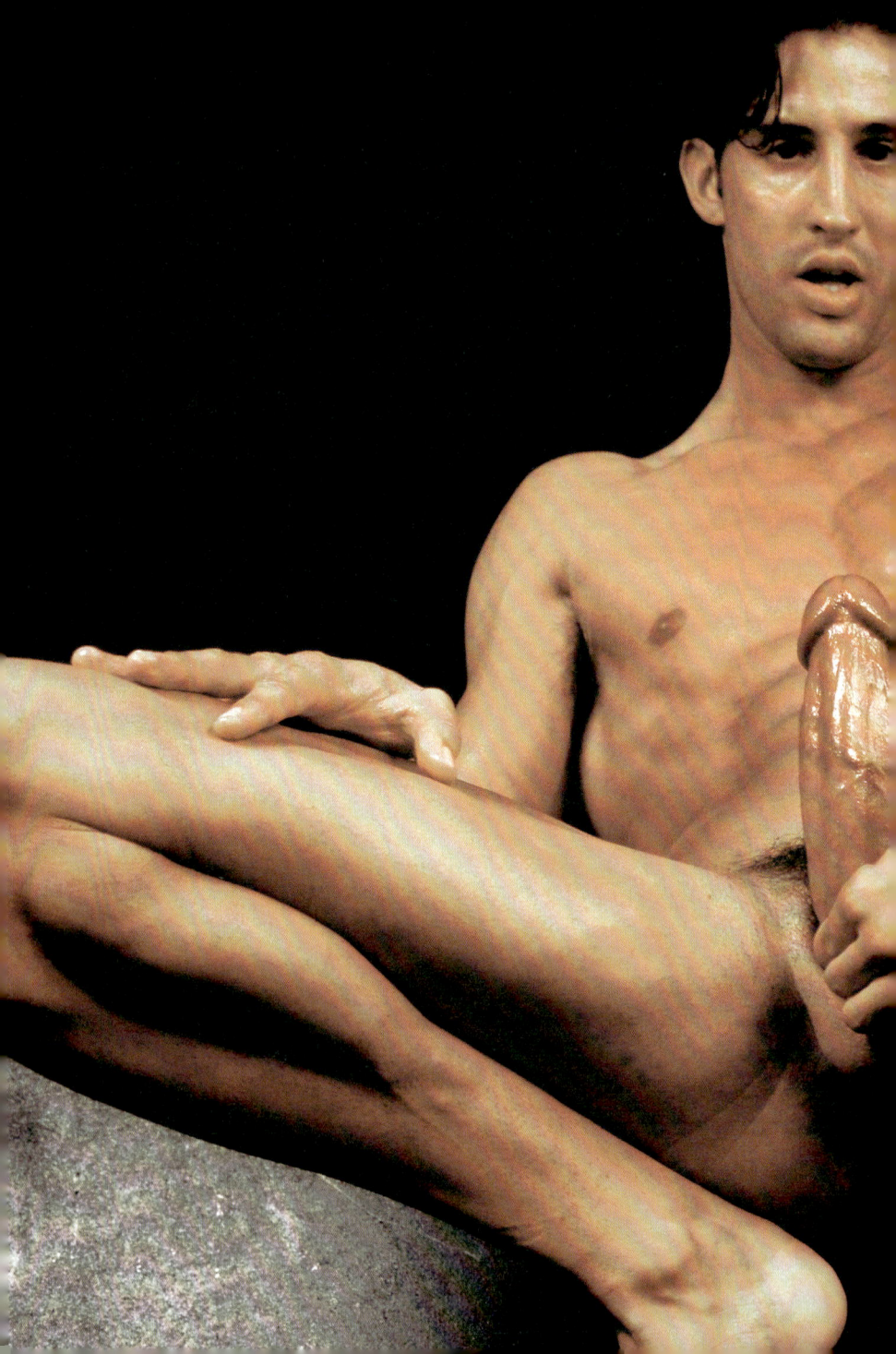

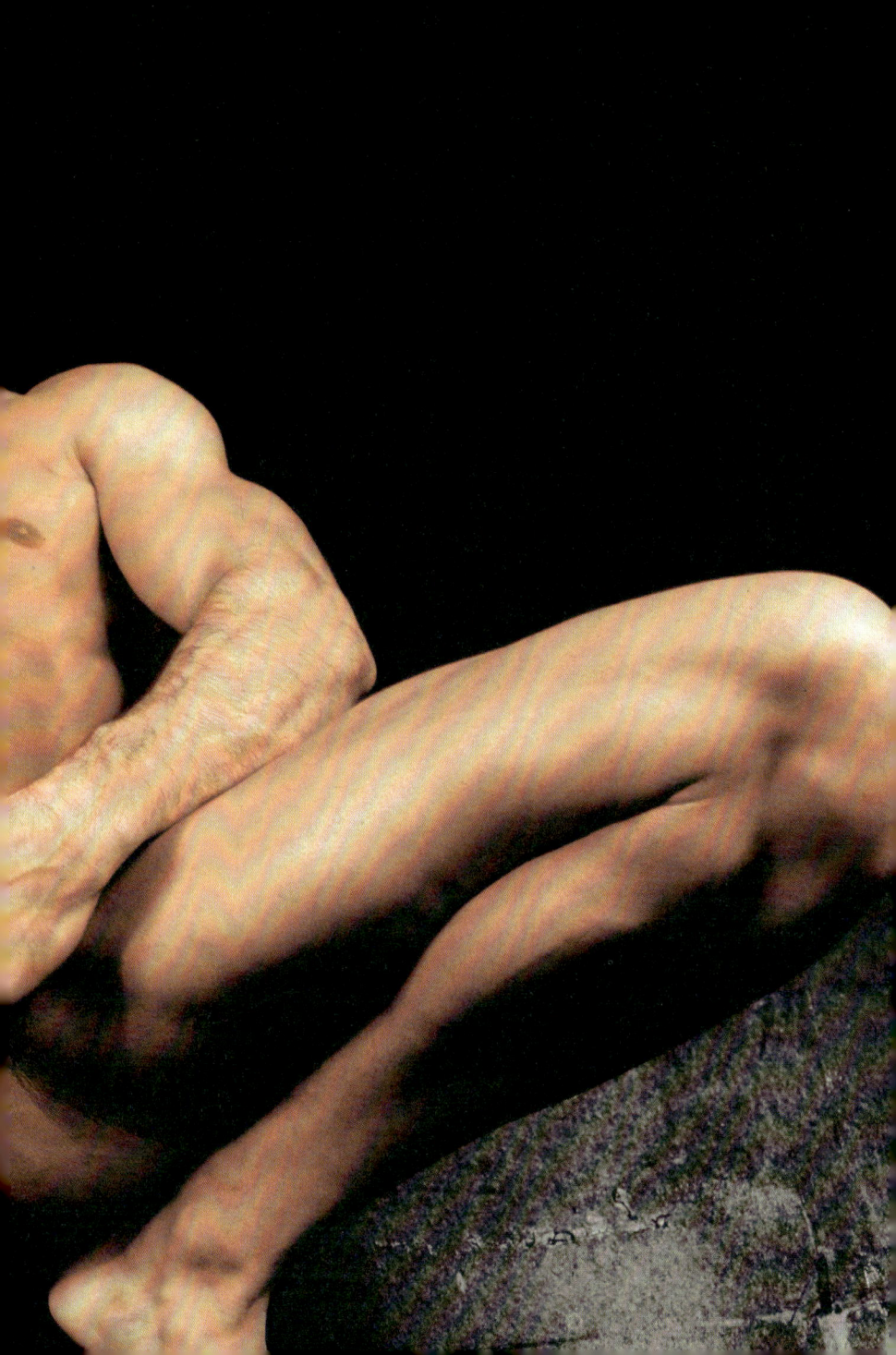

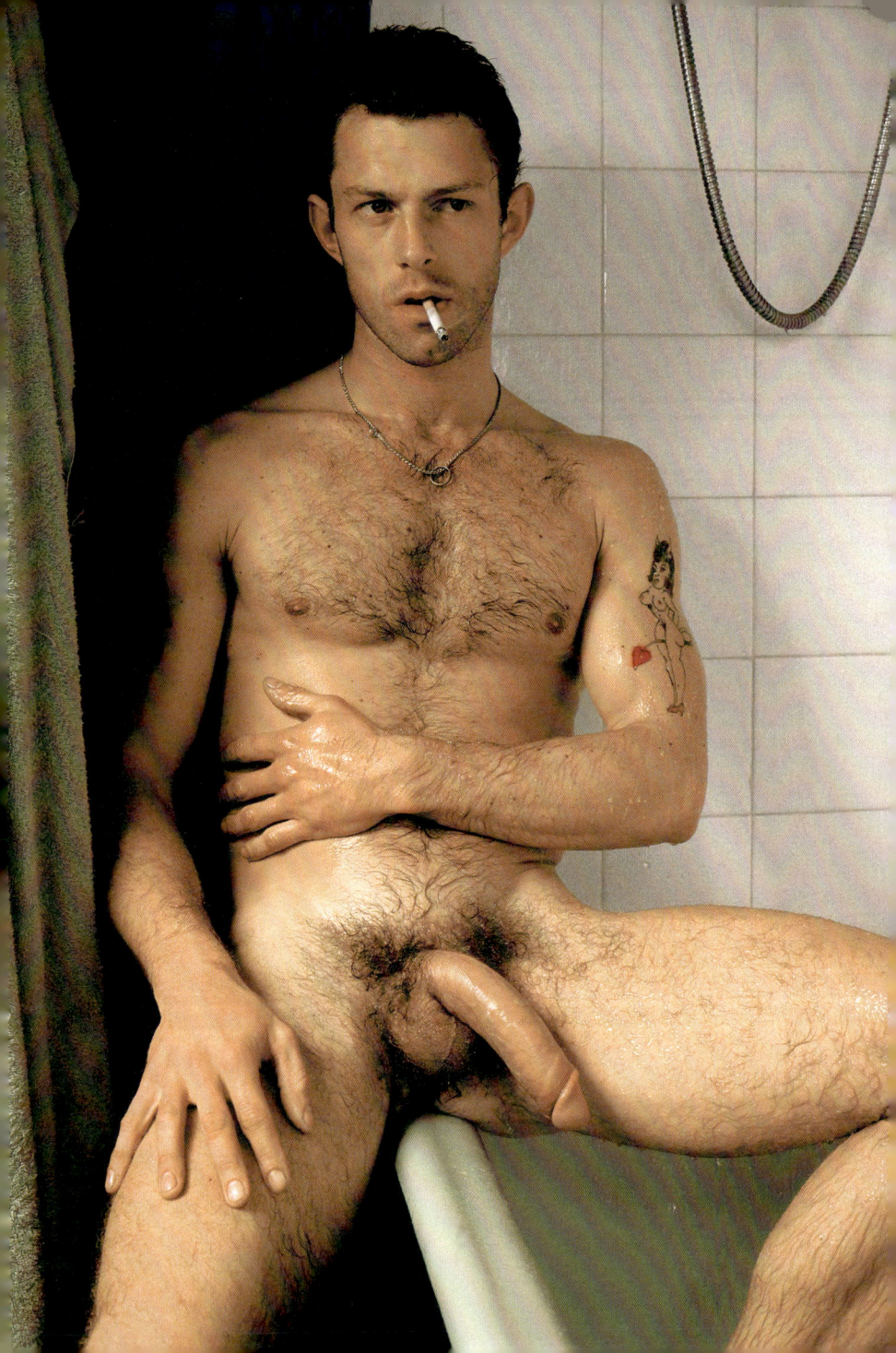

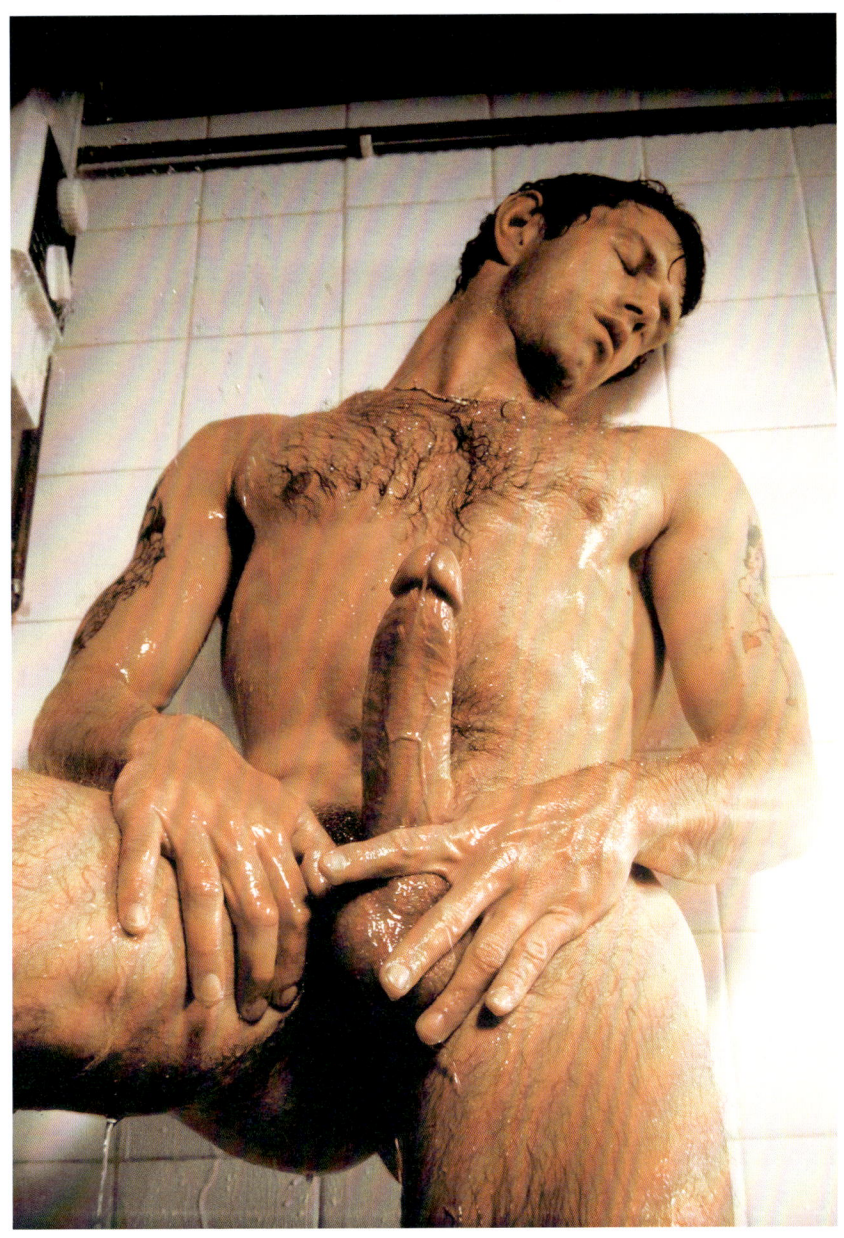

OPPOSITE AND ABOVE **Glen Milbank**

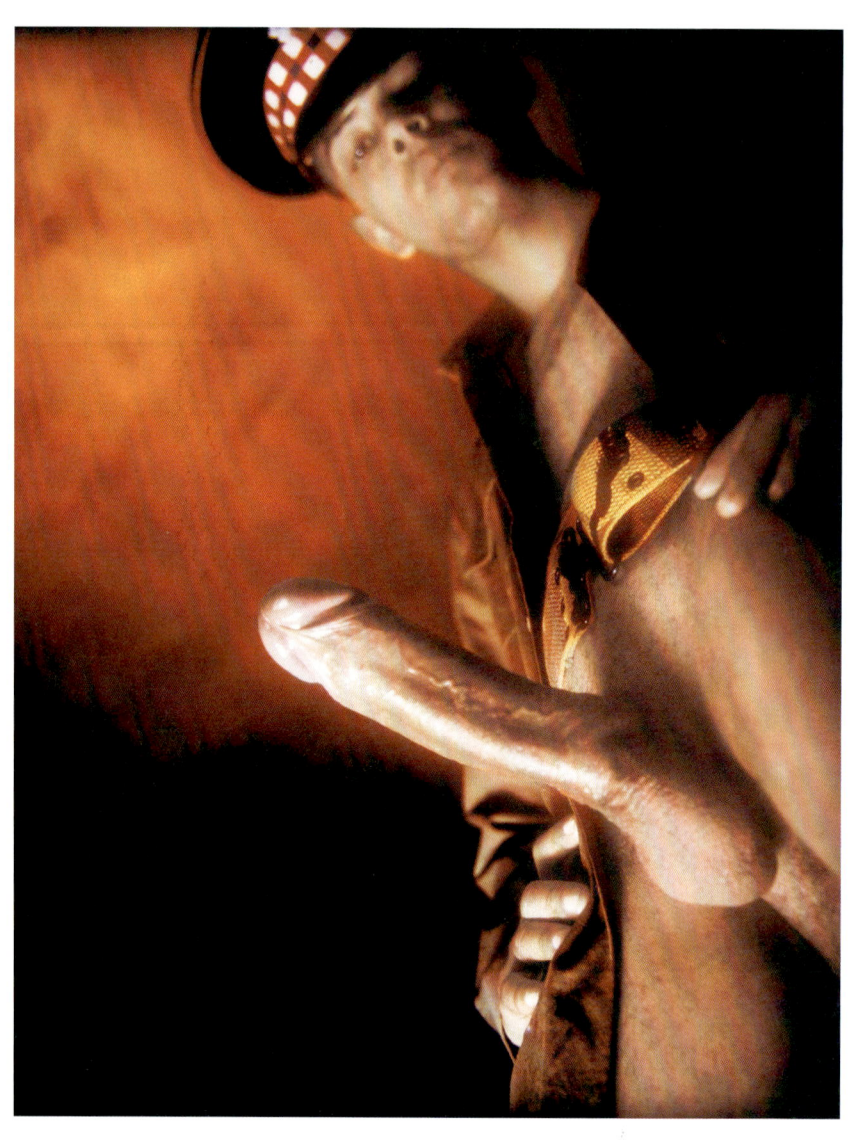

ABOVE **David Doyle**   OPPOSITE **Alf Kolenberg**

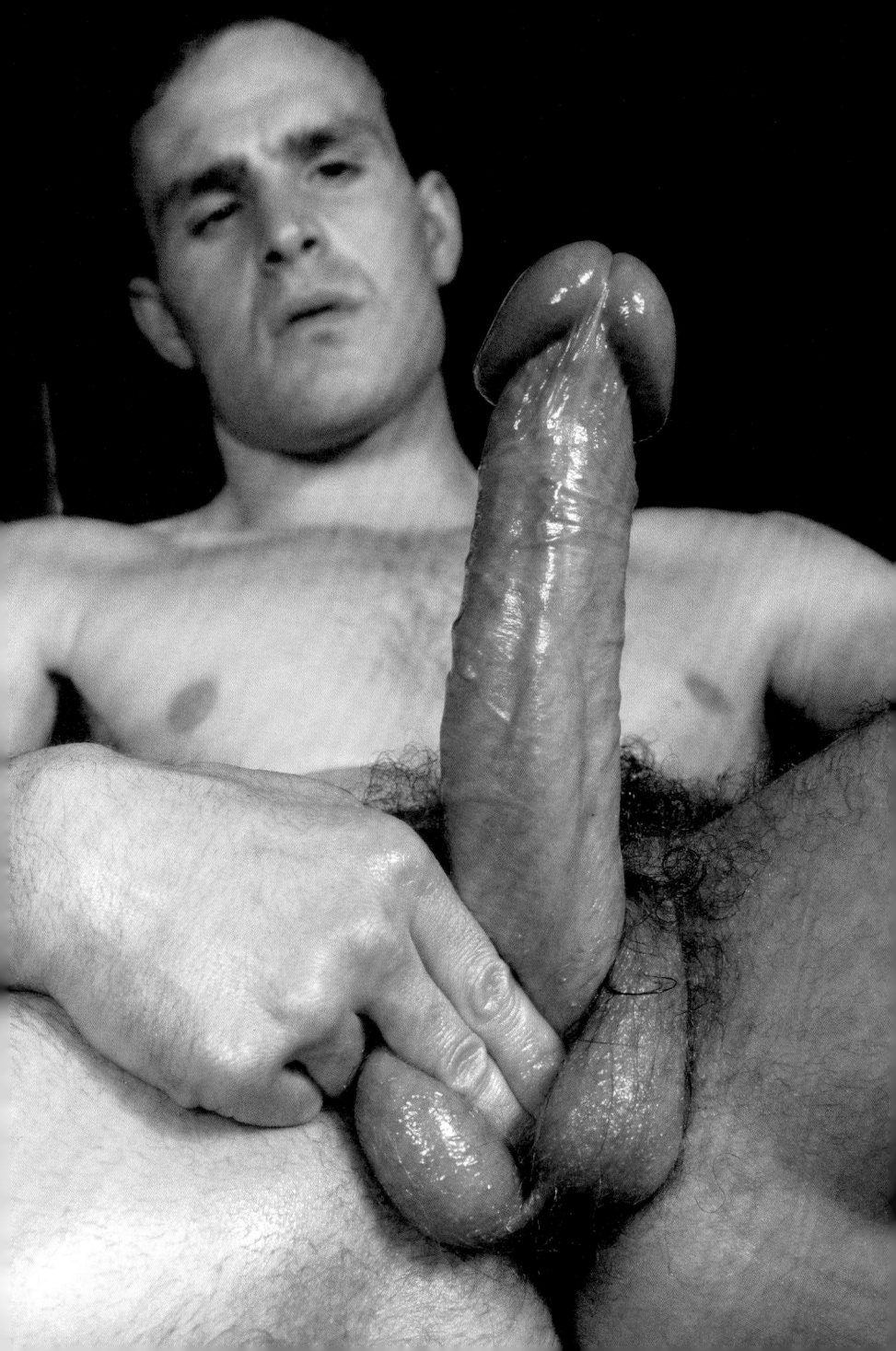

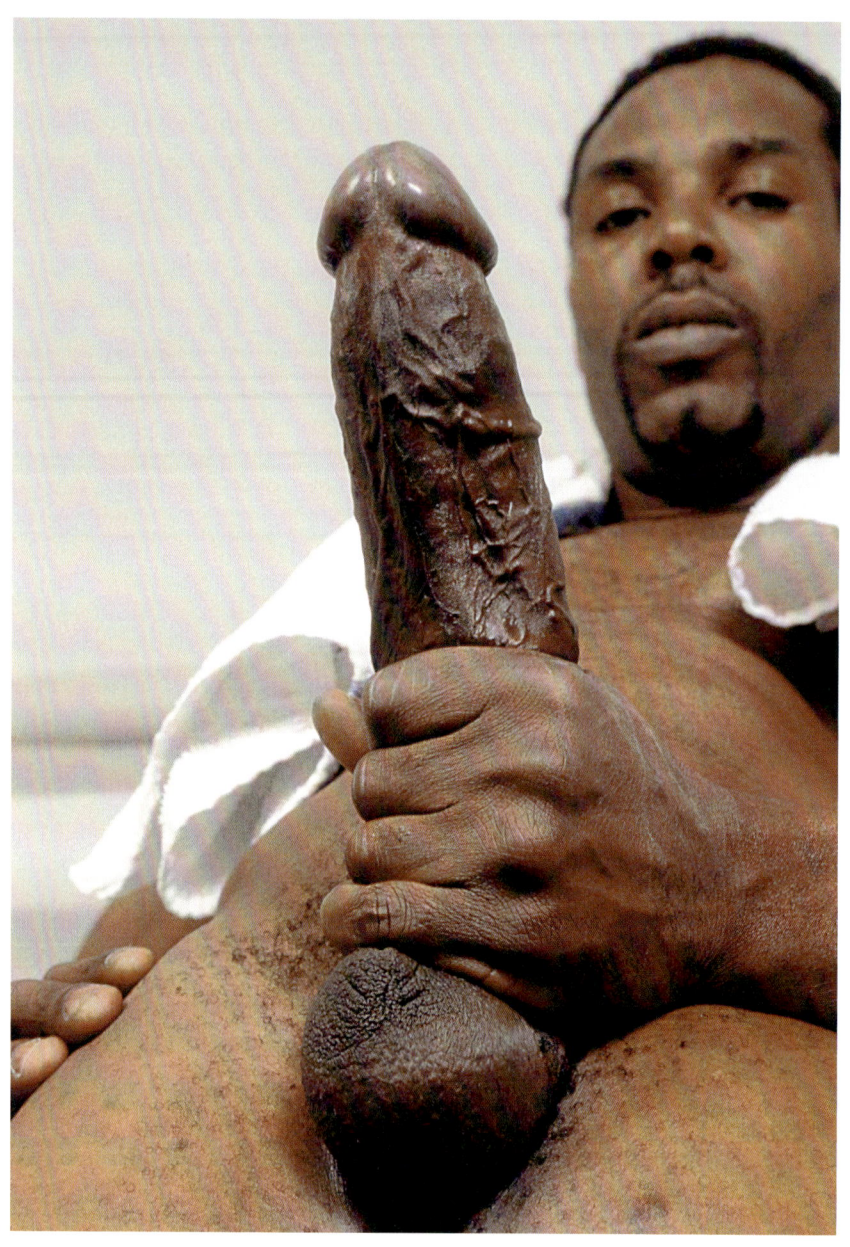

ABOVE **Passion**   OPPOSITE **Ray**   PAGES 164-165 **Babyface**

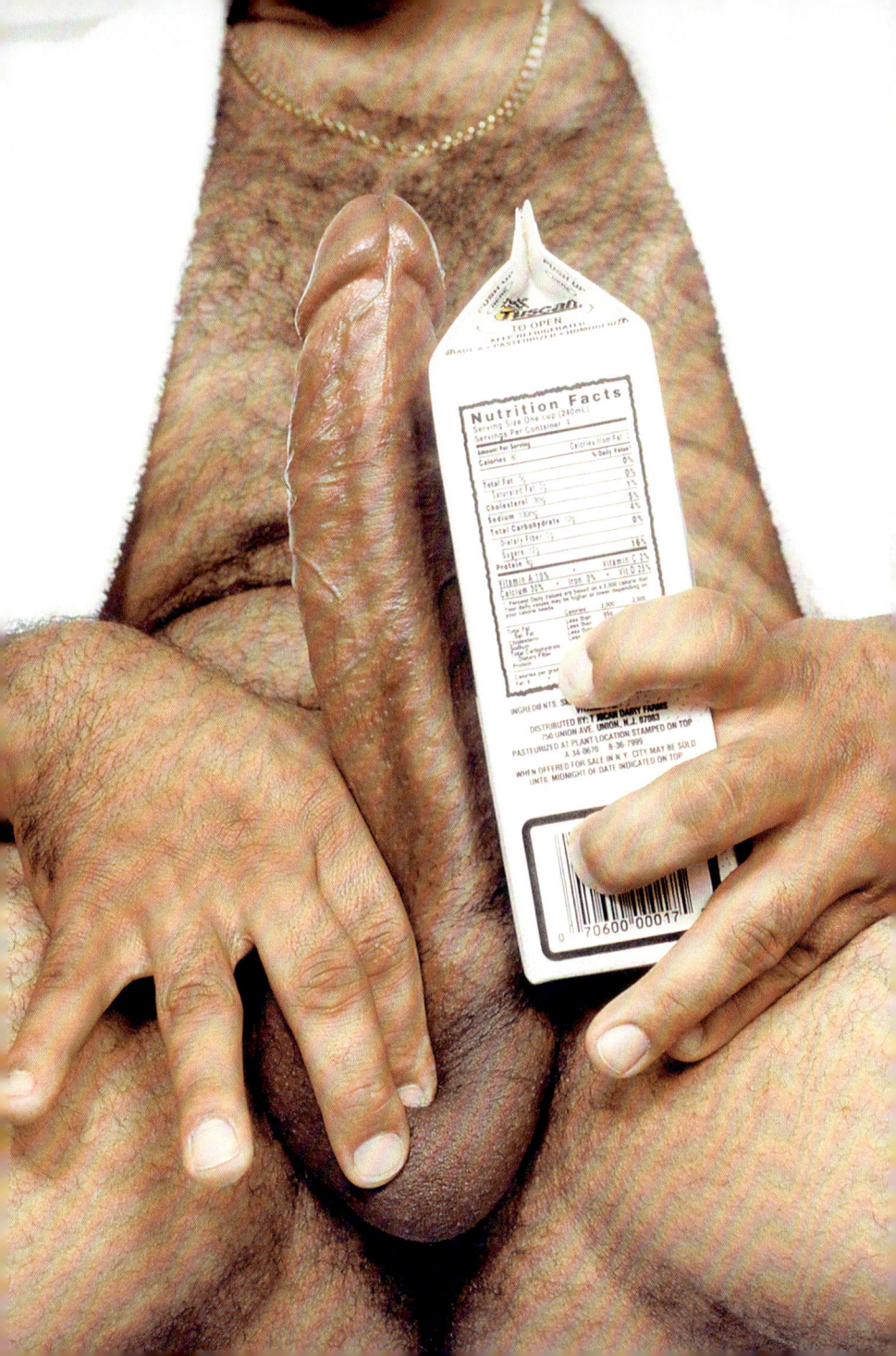

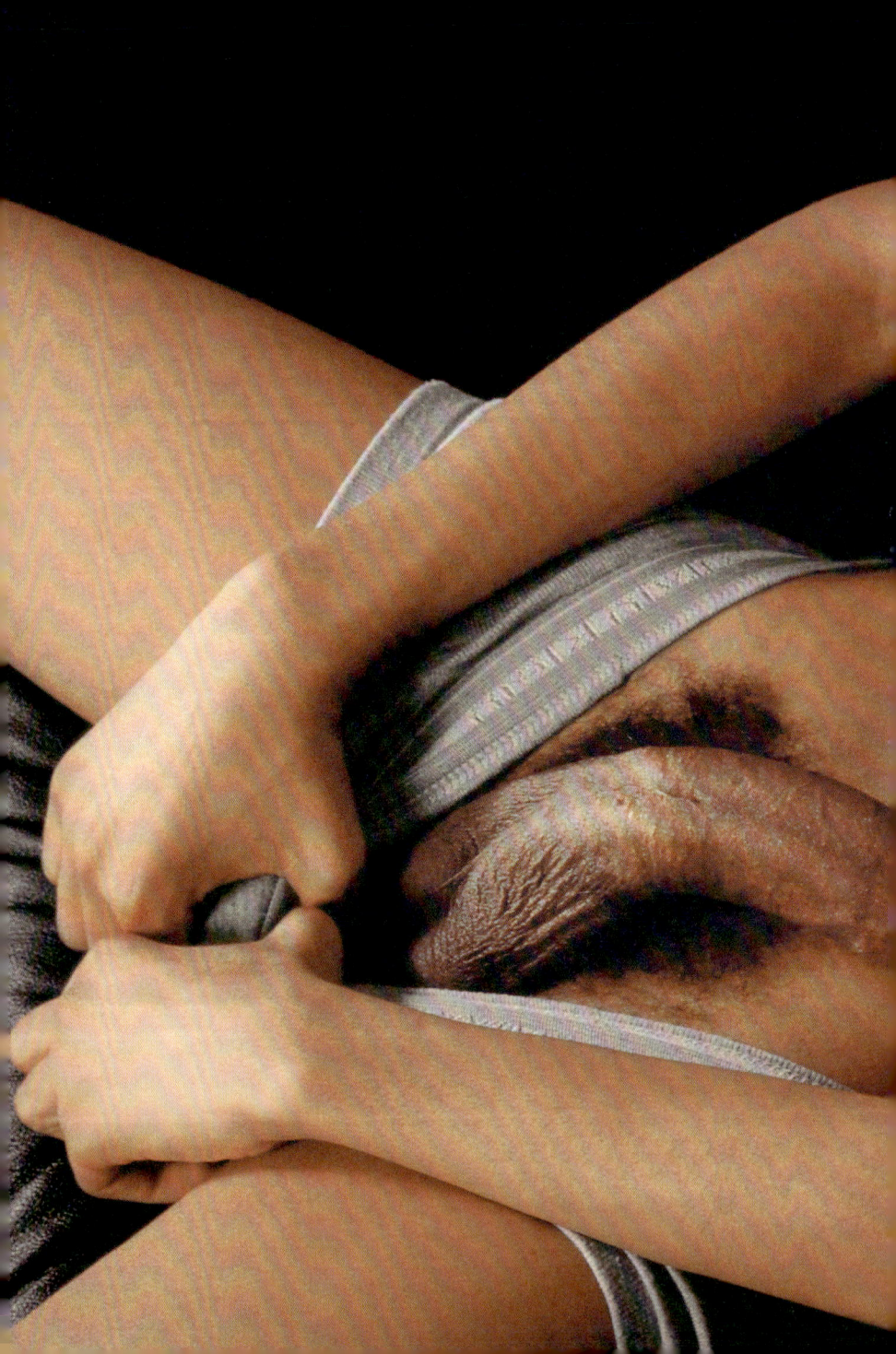

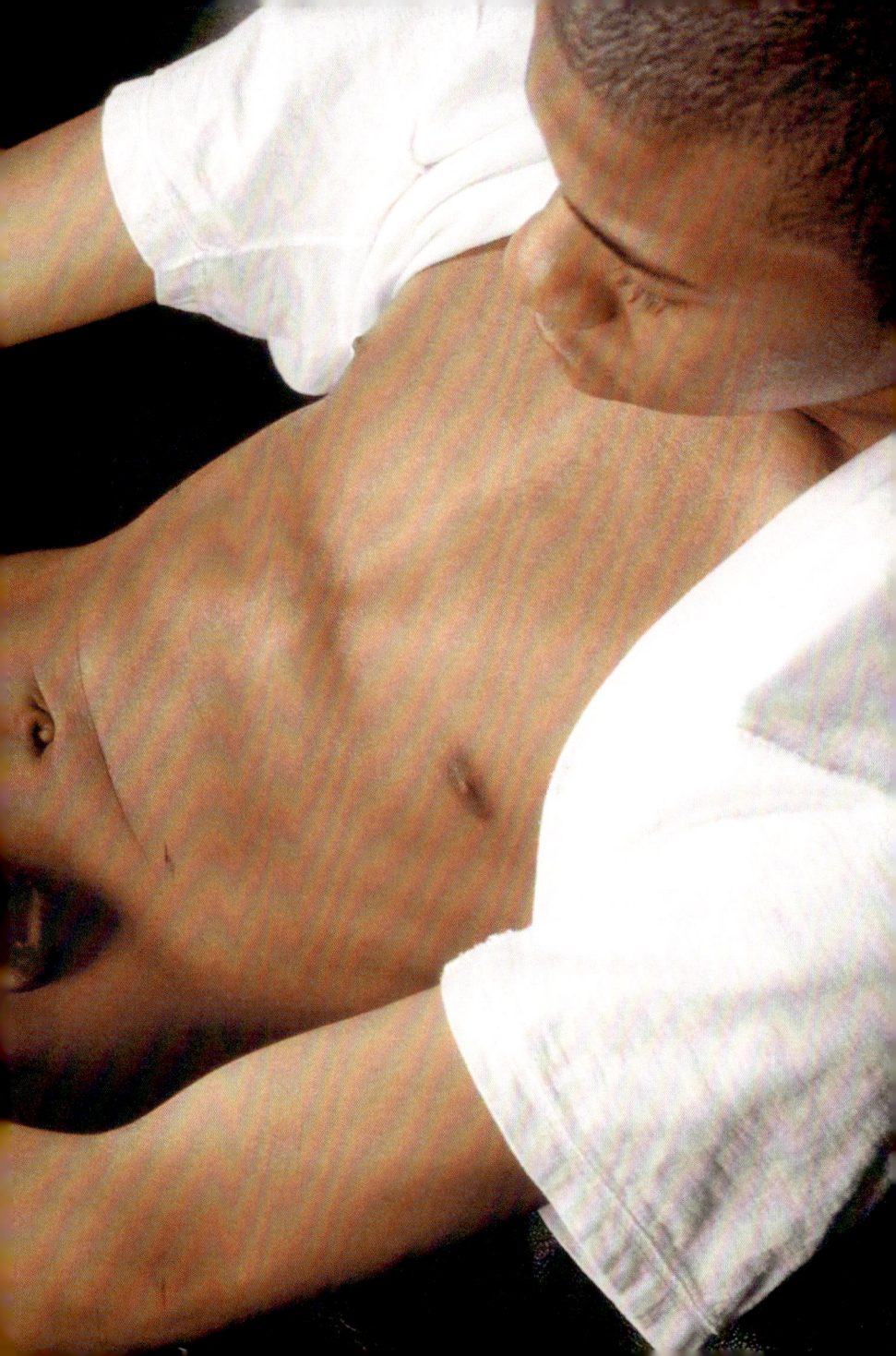

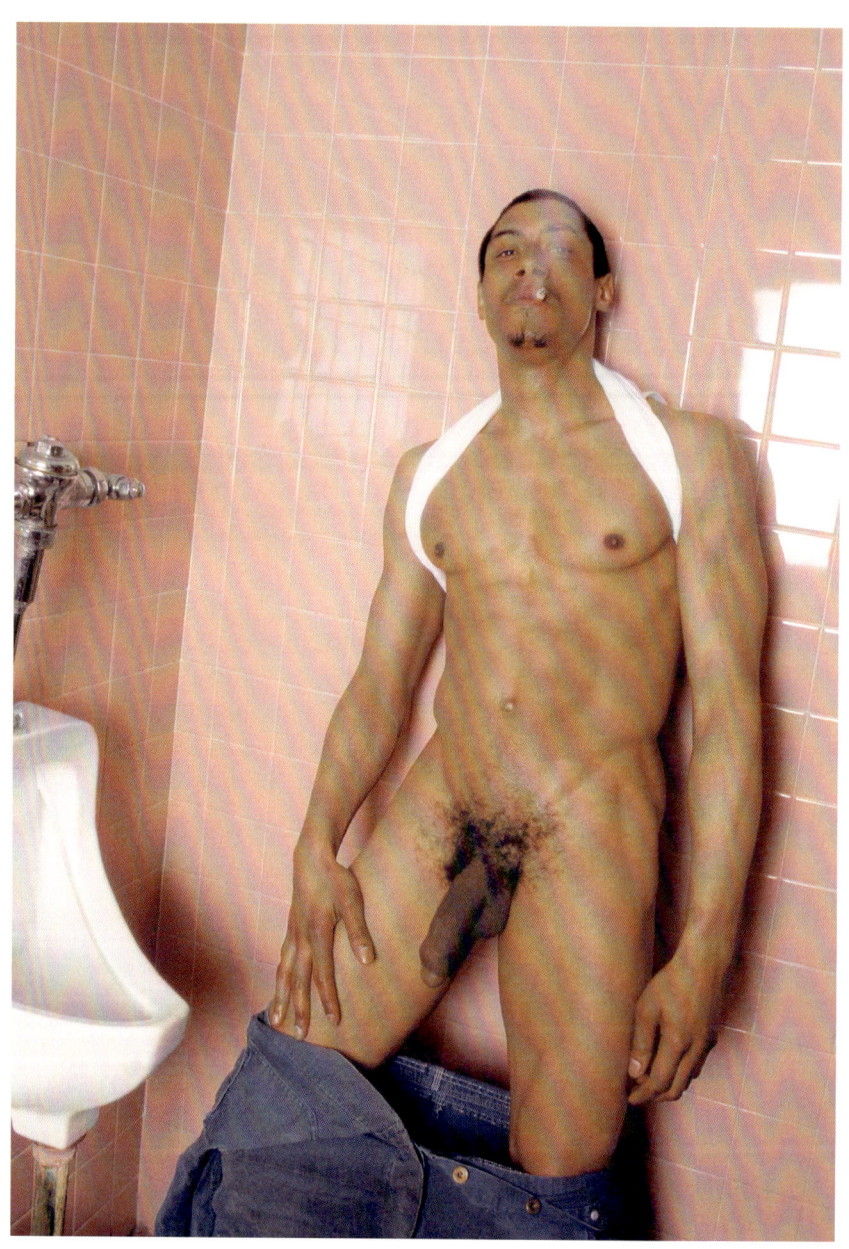

ABOVE **Eduardo**   OPPOSITE **Matt Bradshaw**

166

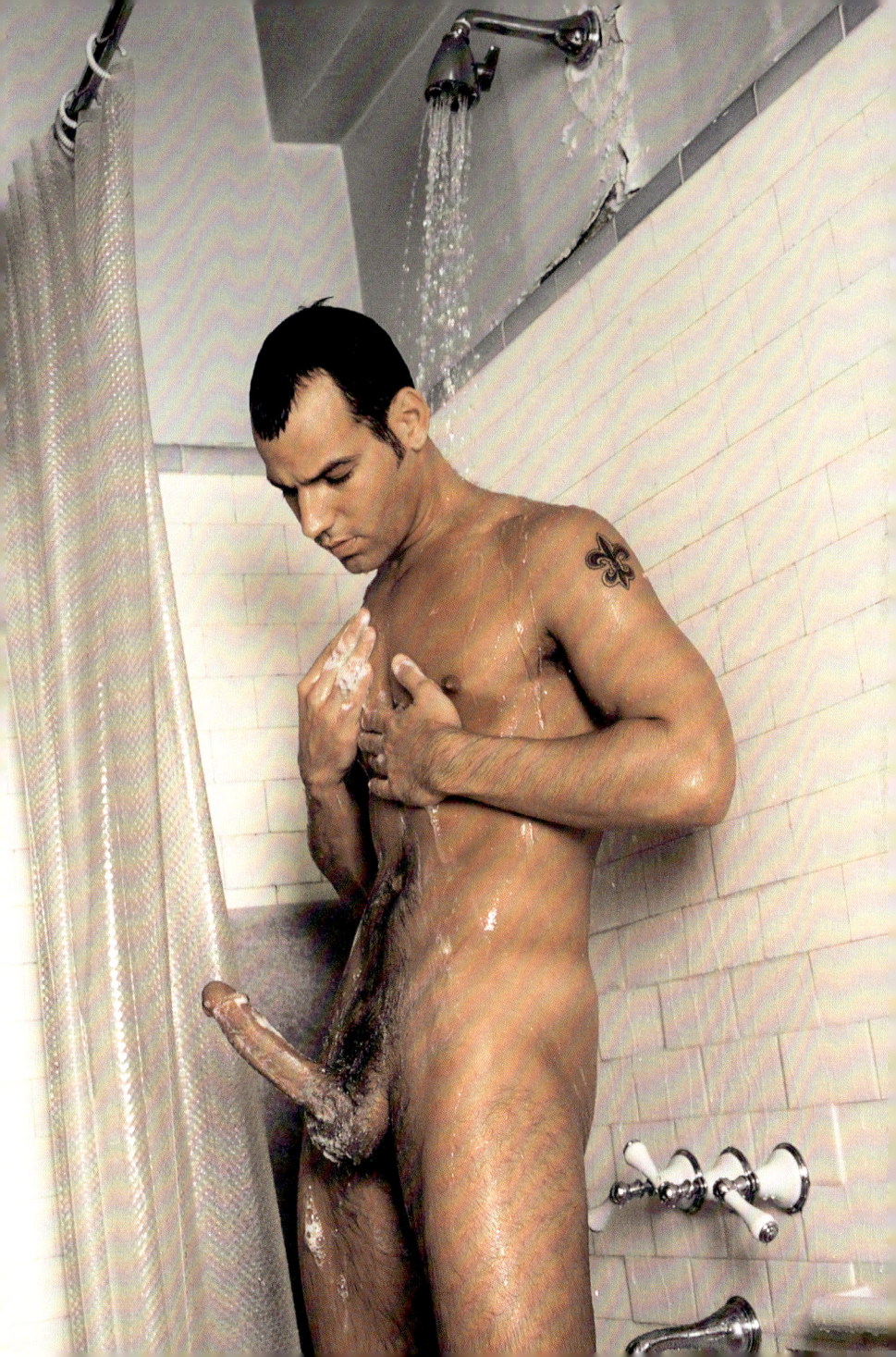

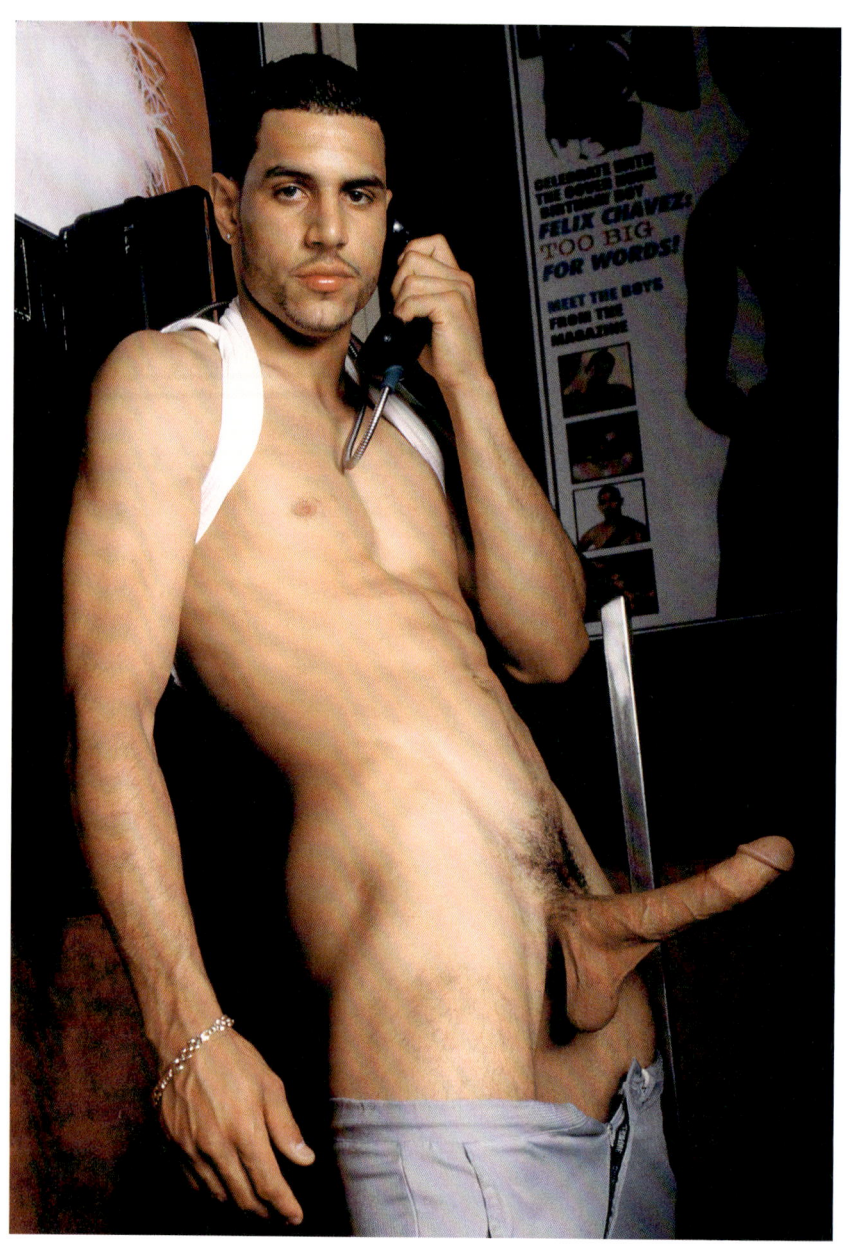

ABOVE **Phoenix**   OPPOSITE **Melshawn**

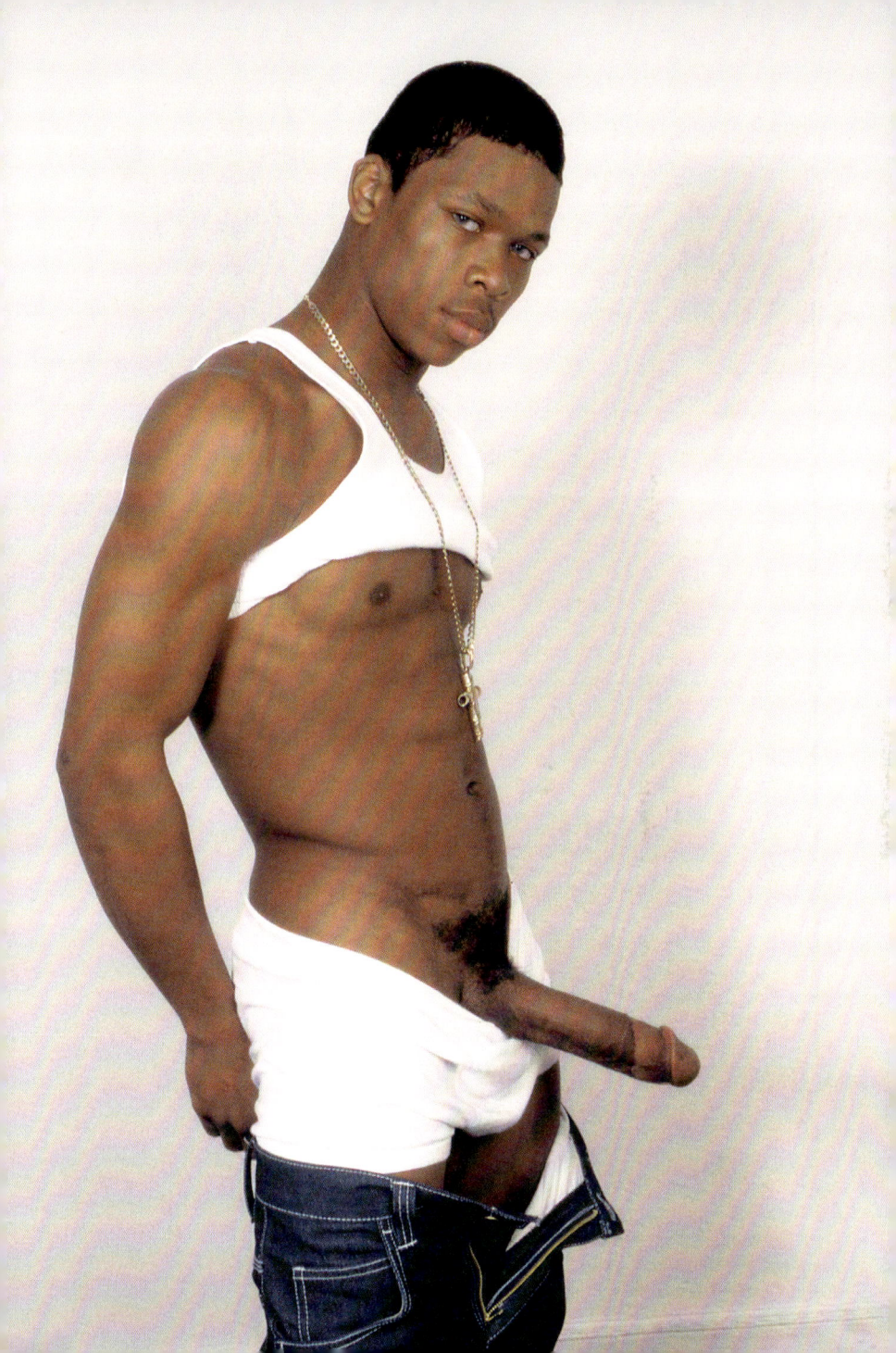

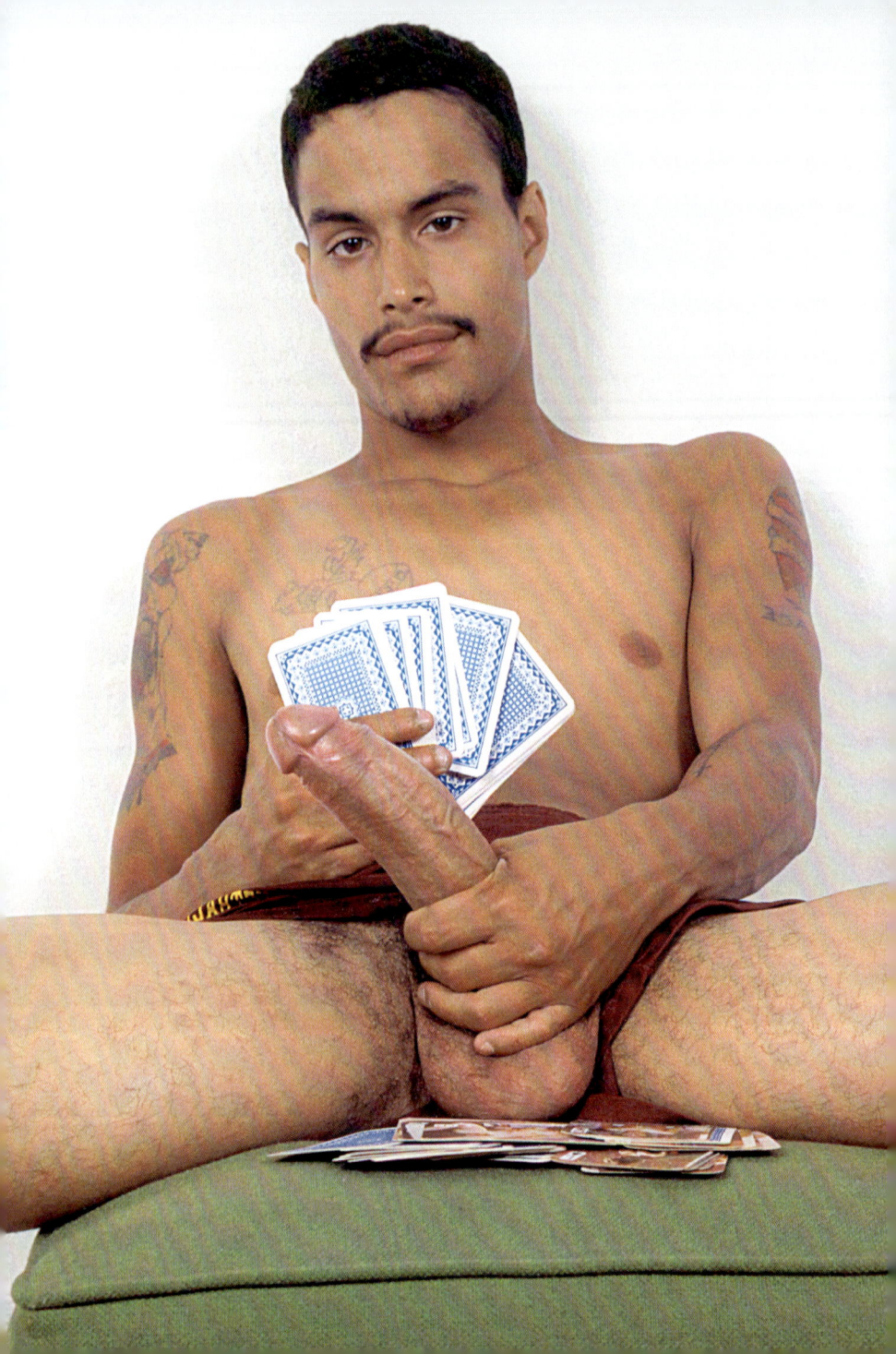

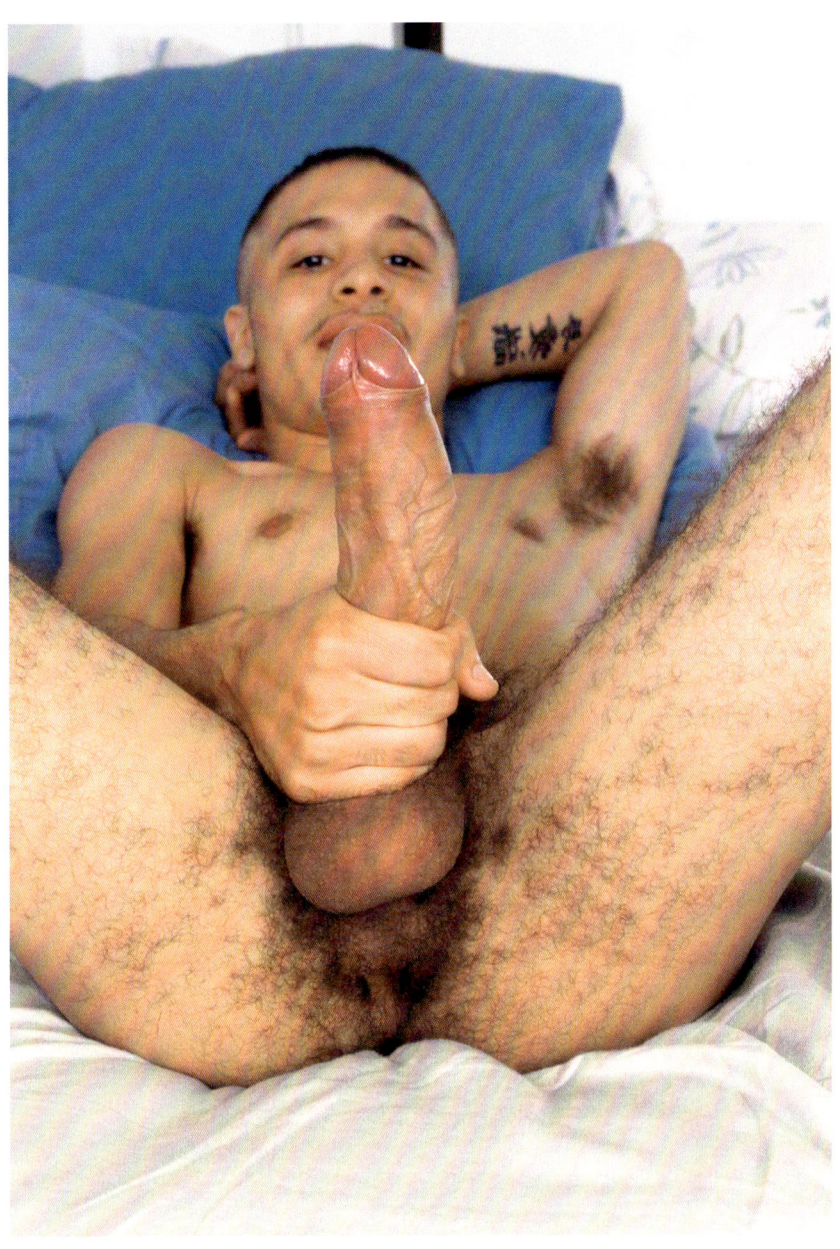

OPPOSITE **Cobra**   ABOVE **Pothead**

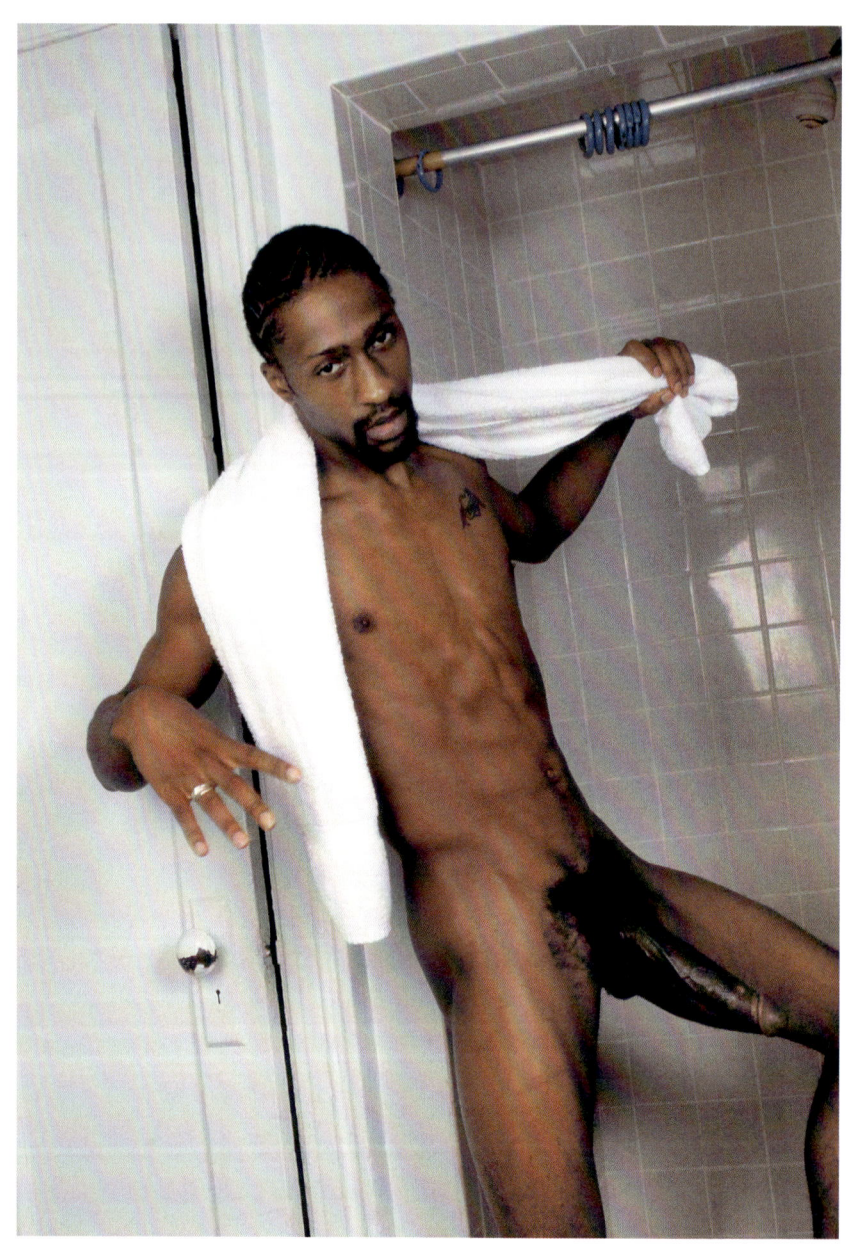

ABOVE AND OPPOSITE **Obsession**   PAGES 174-175 **Unknown**

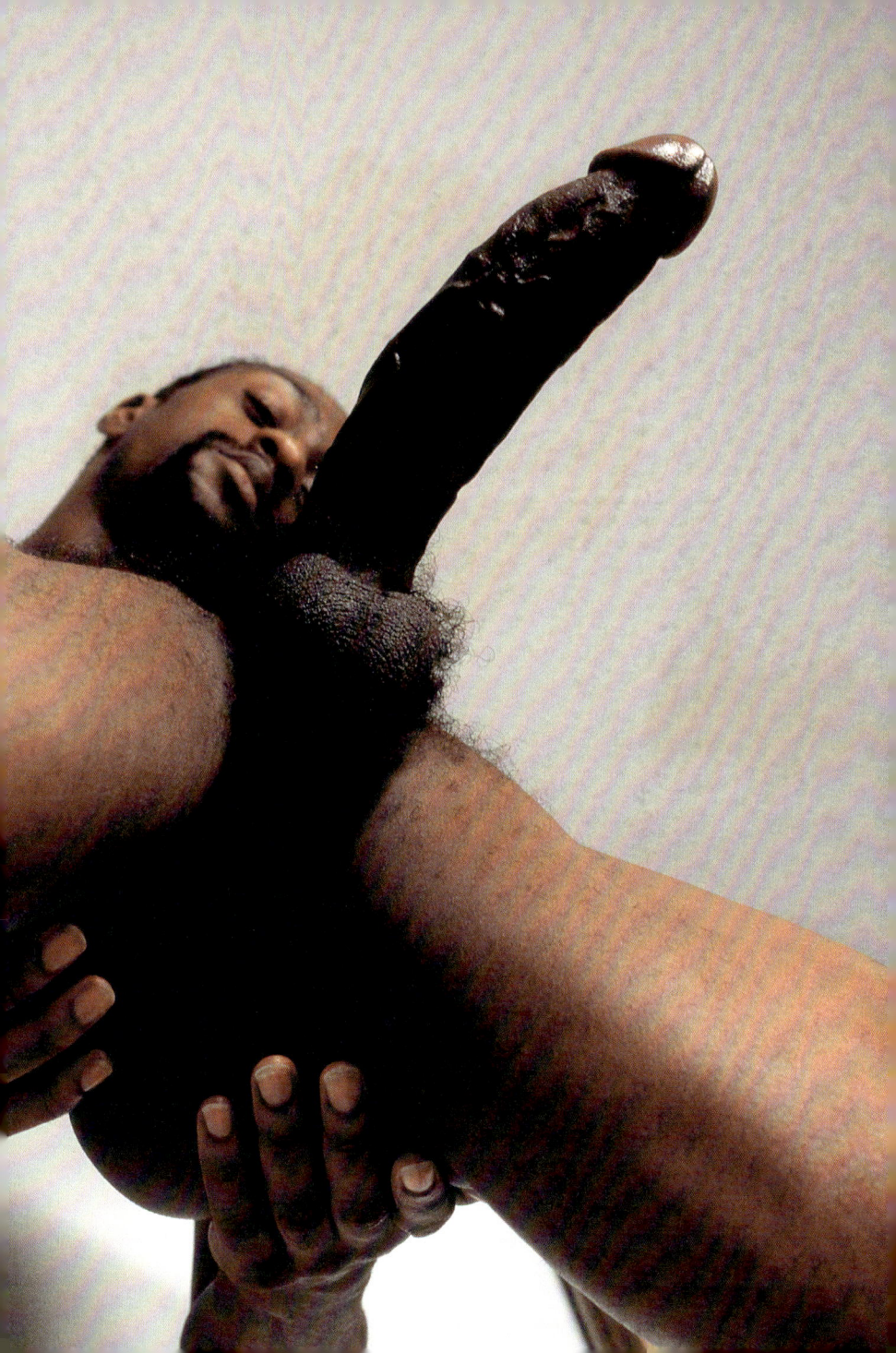

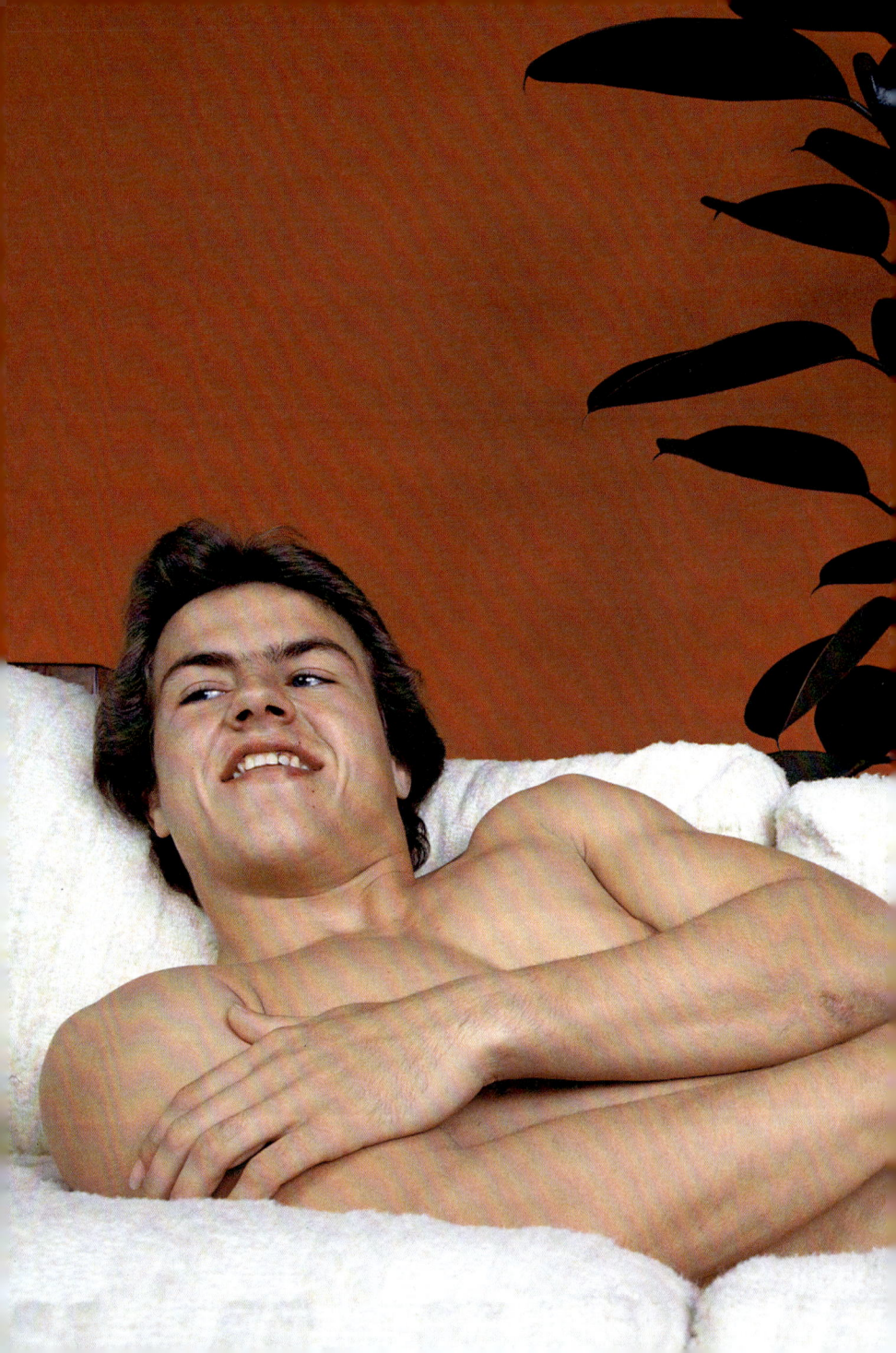

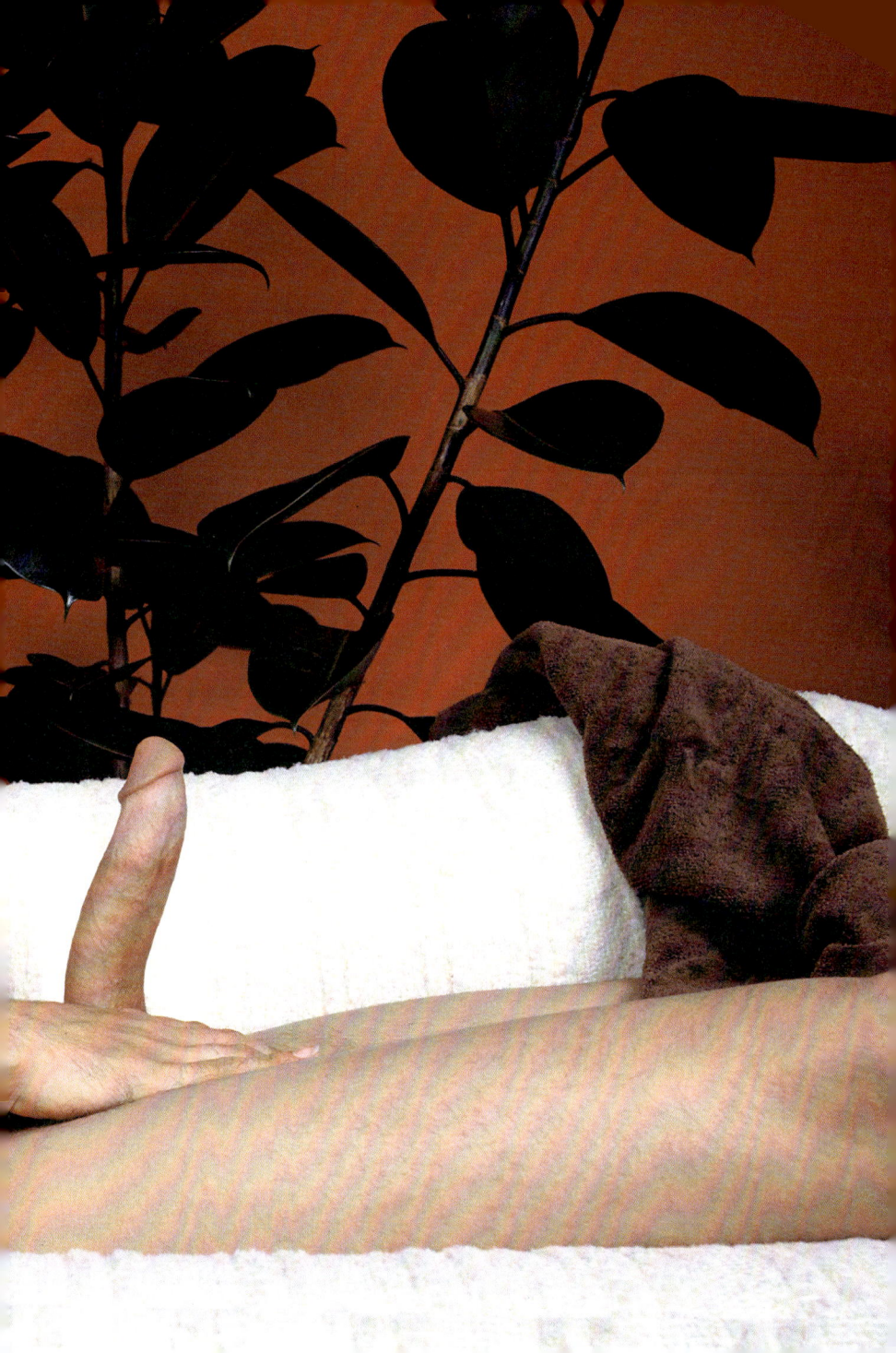

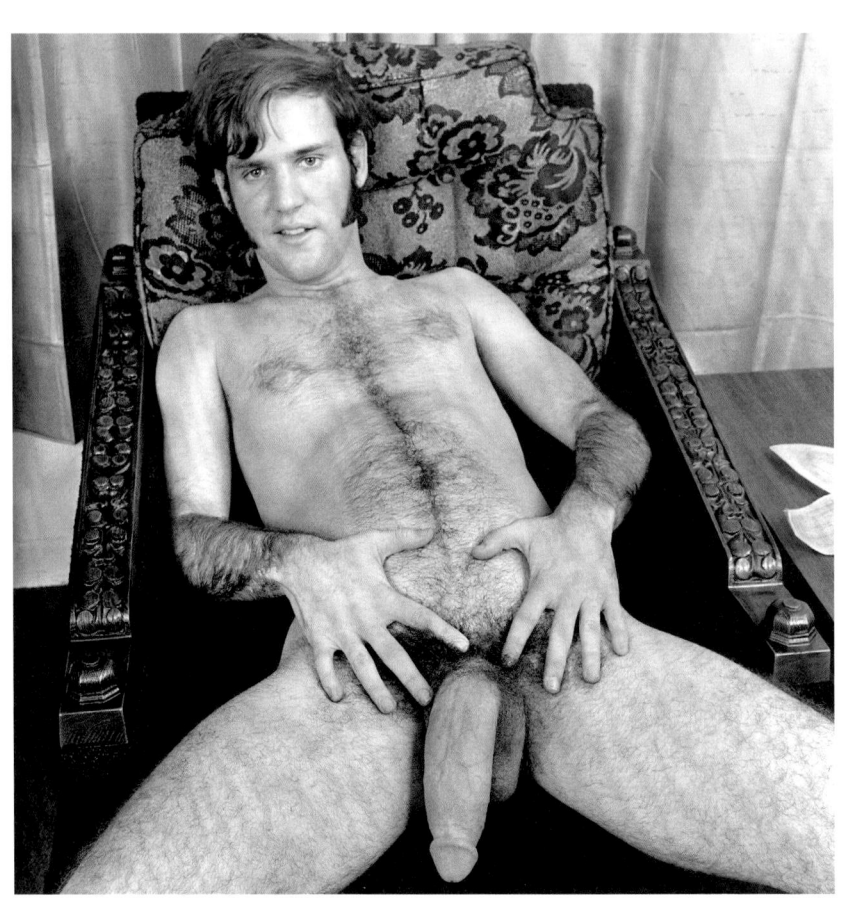

ABOVE AND OPPOSITE **Unknown**

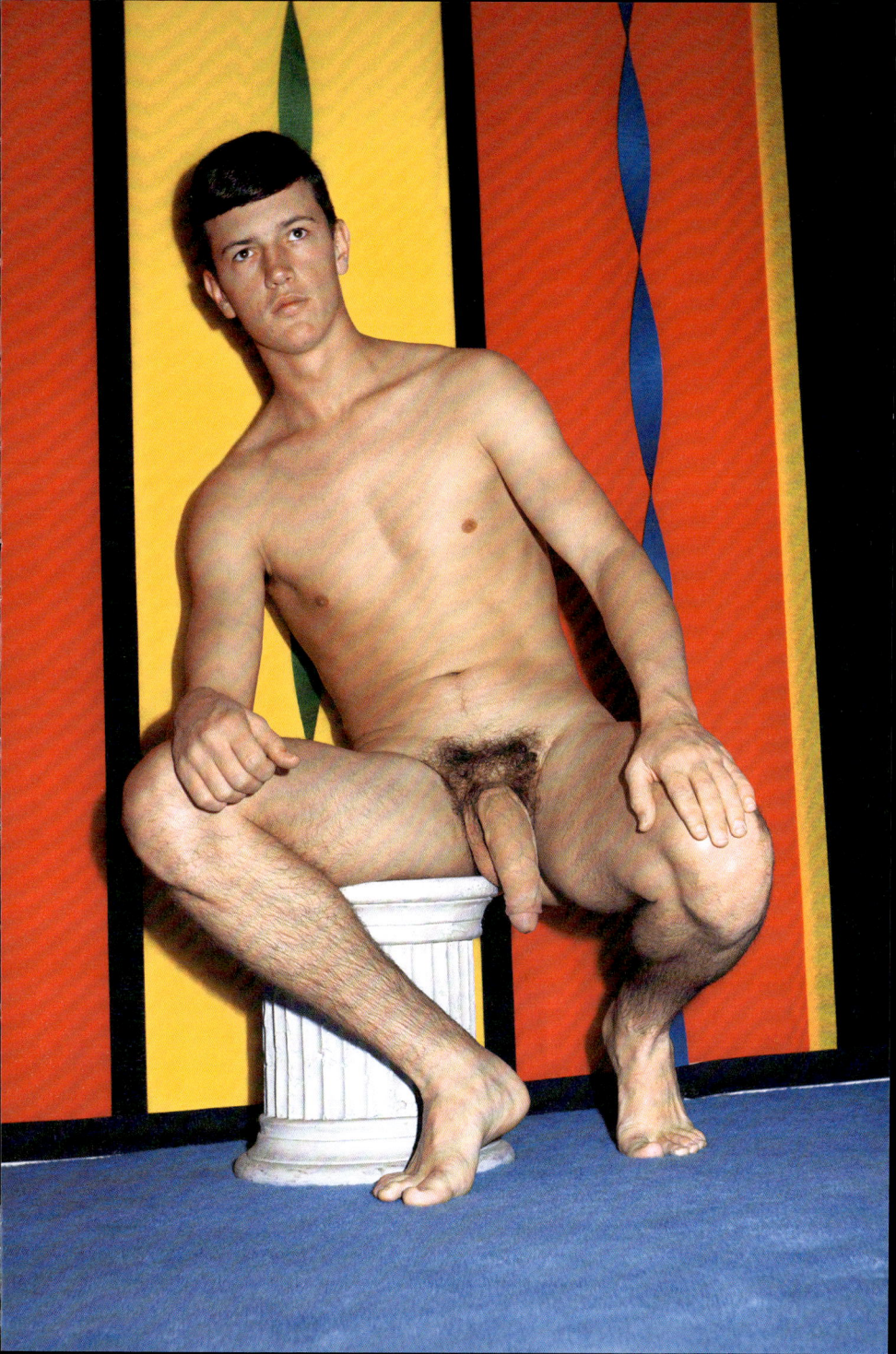

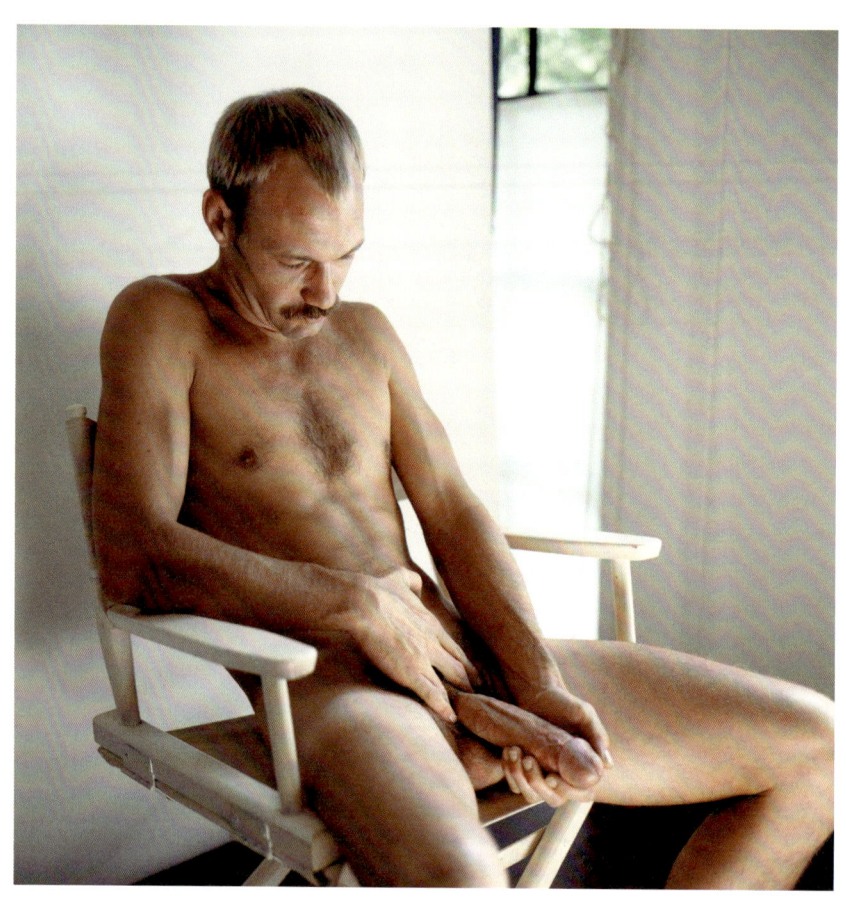

Steve McCormick

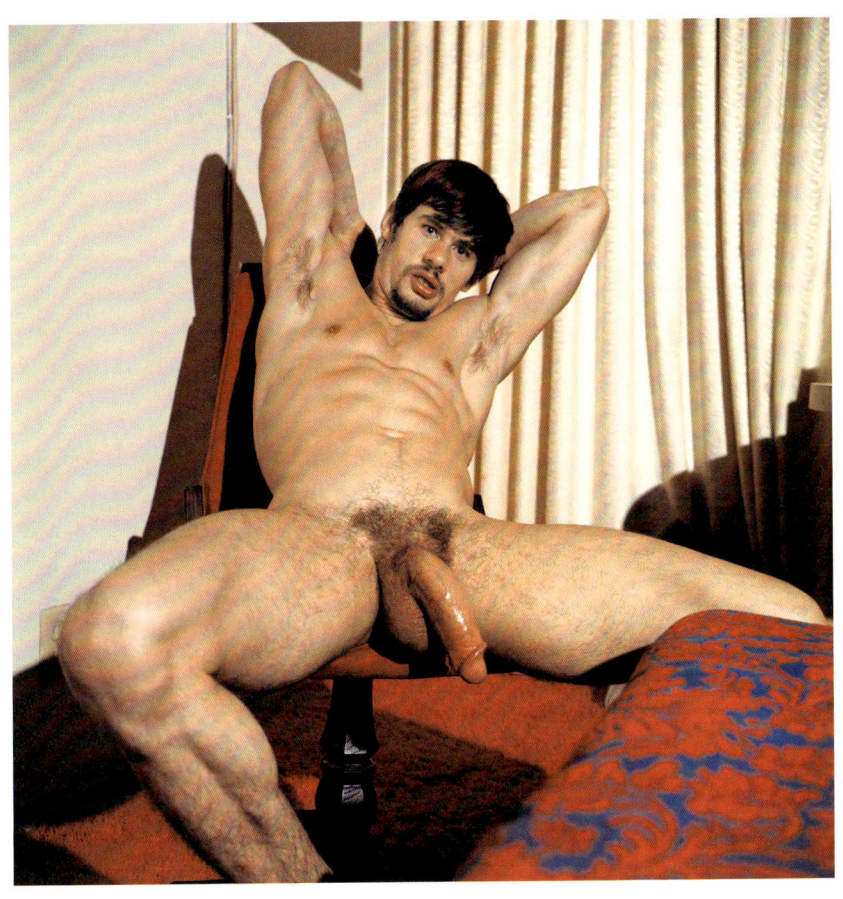

Bill Eld

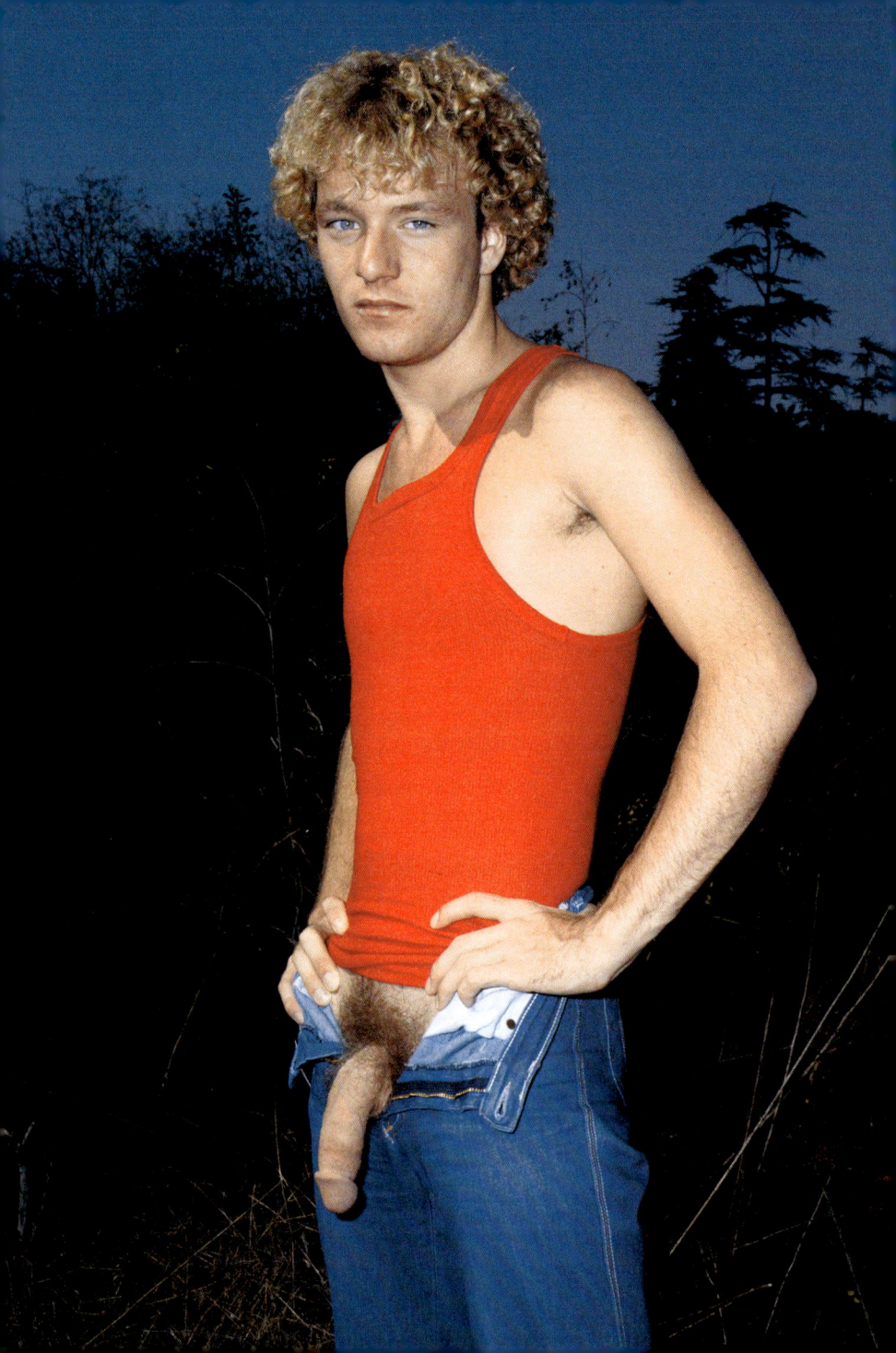

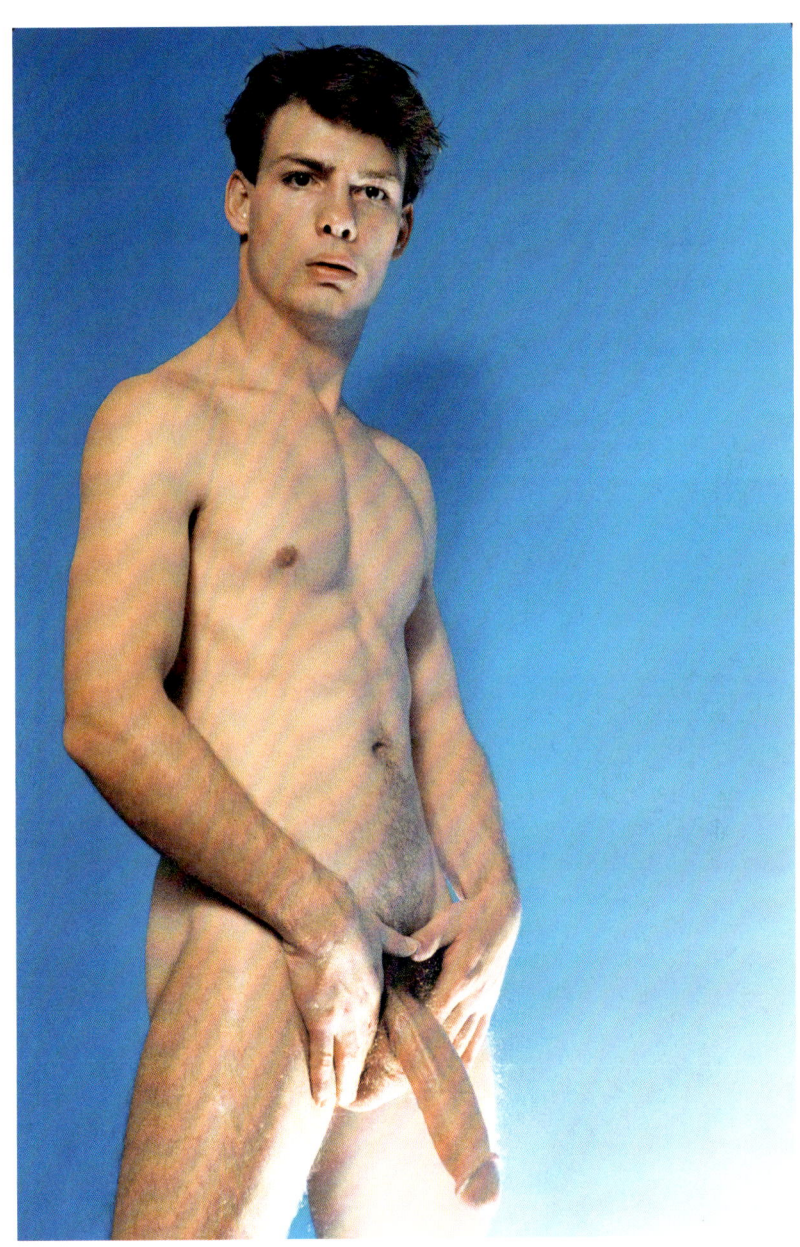

OPPOSITE **Unknown**   ABOVE **Rick Donovan**

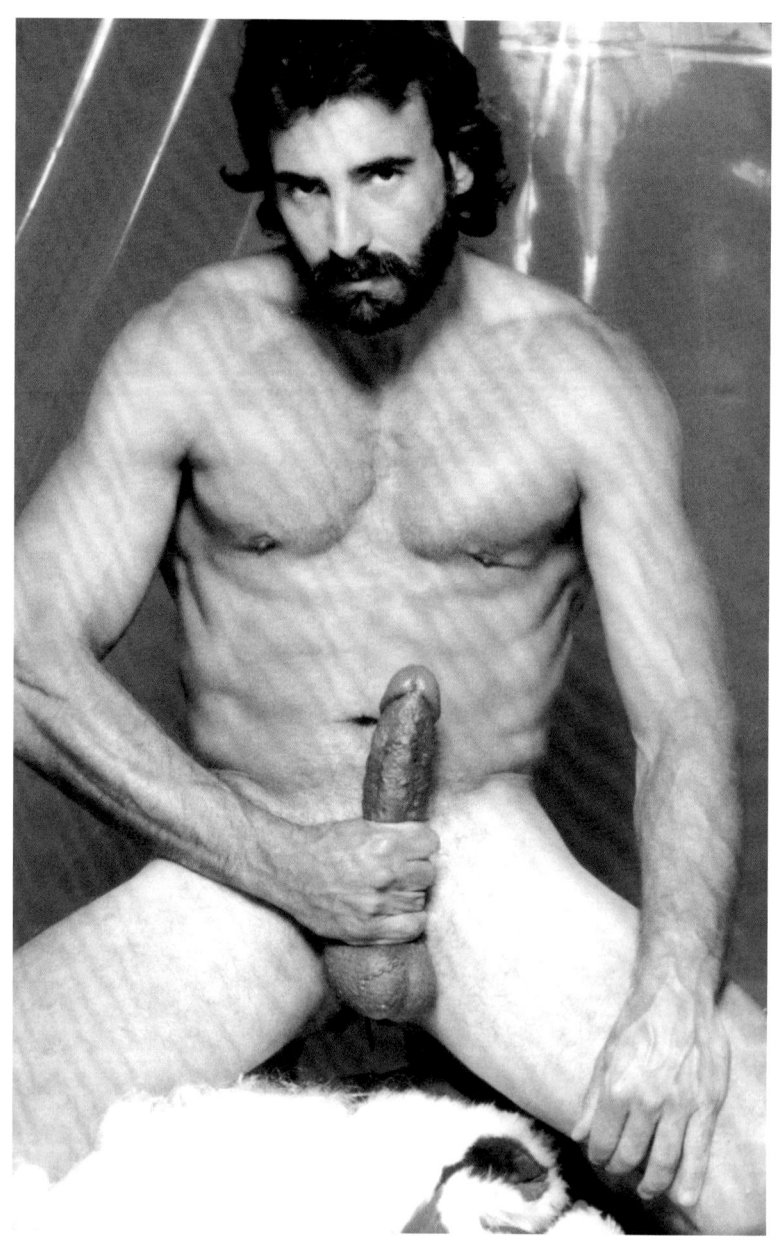

ABOVE **Al Parker**   OPPOSITE **Joe Markum**

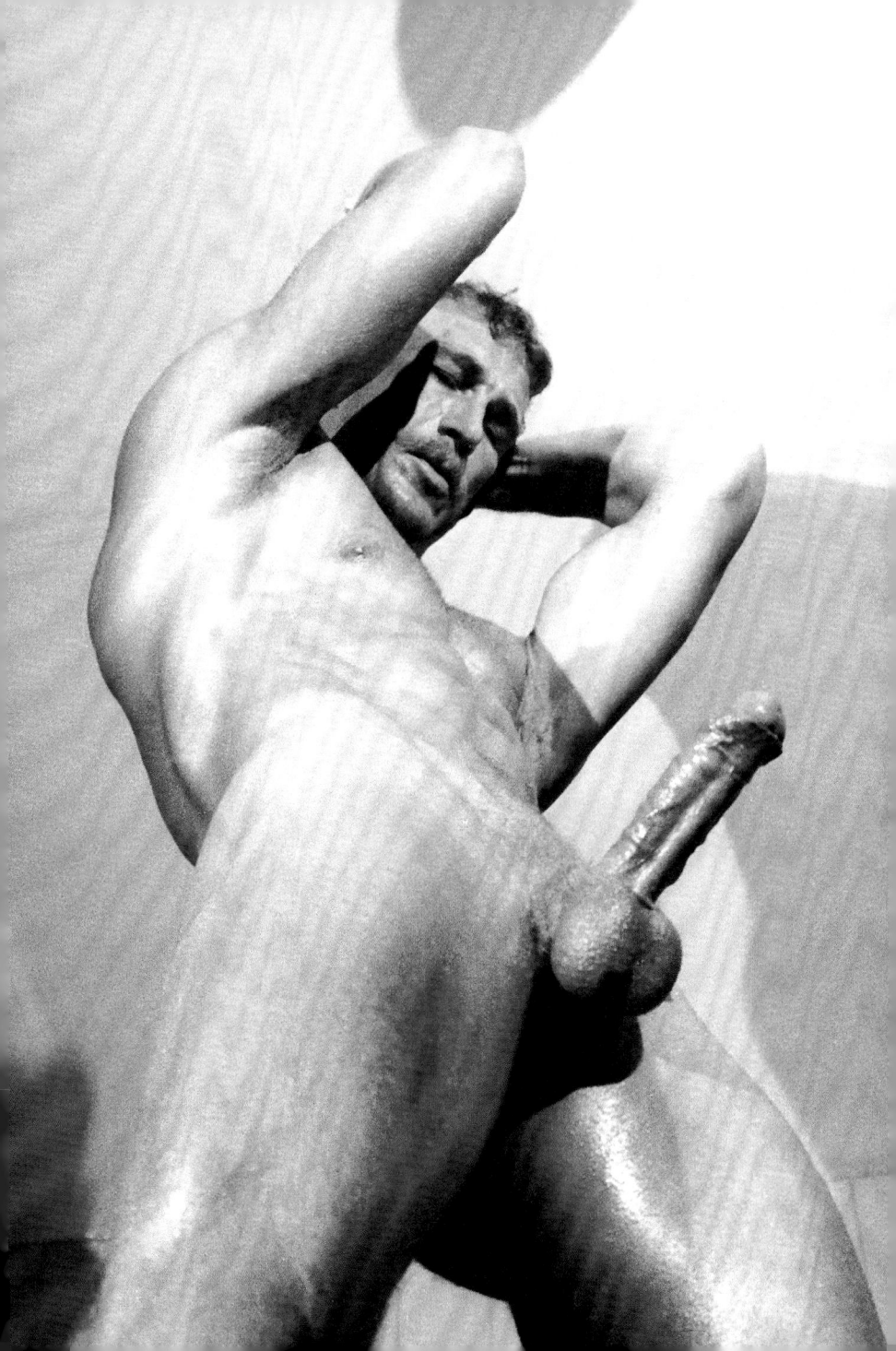

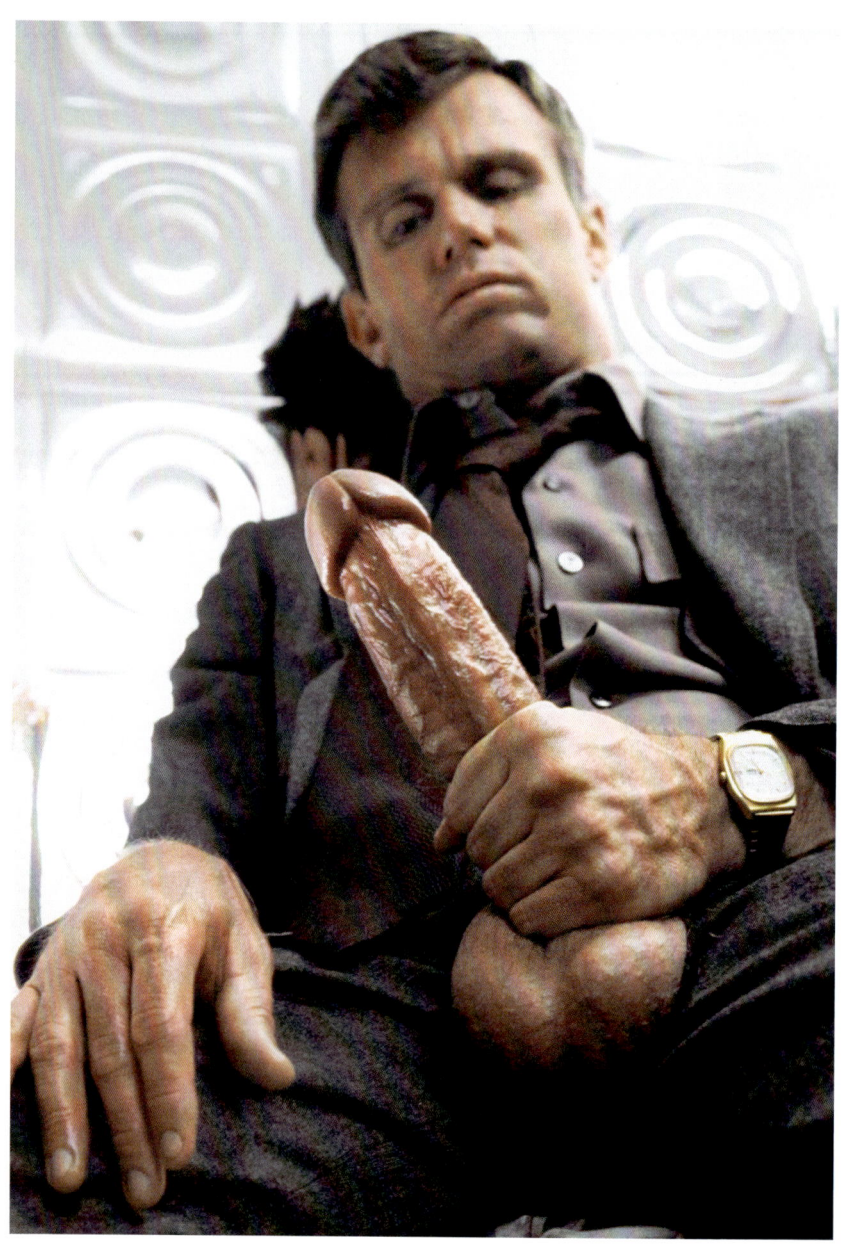

ABOVE AND OPPOSITE **Dave Connors**

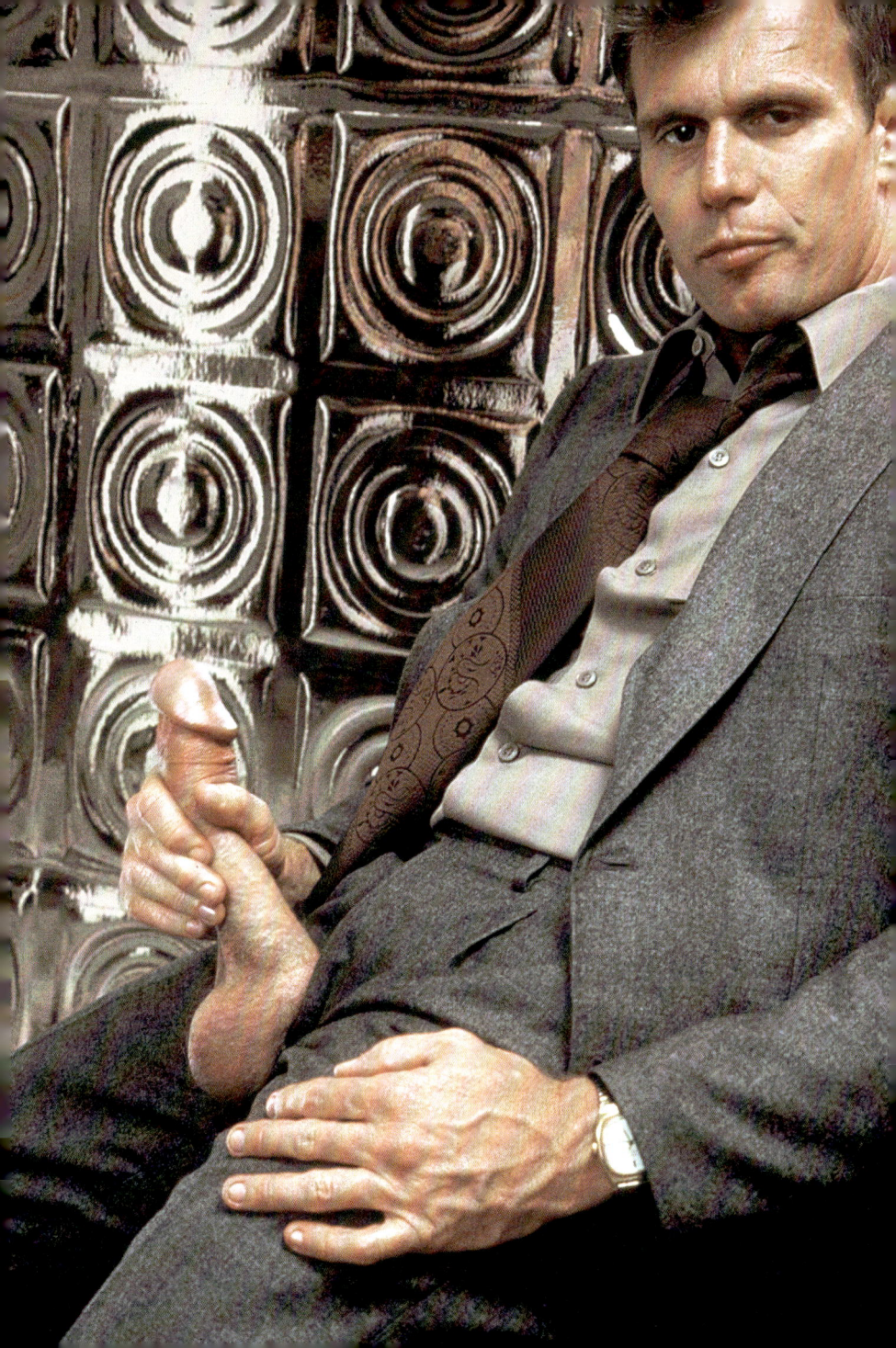

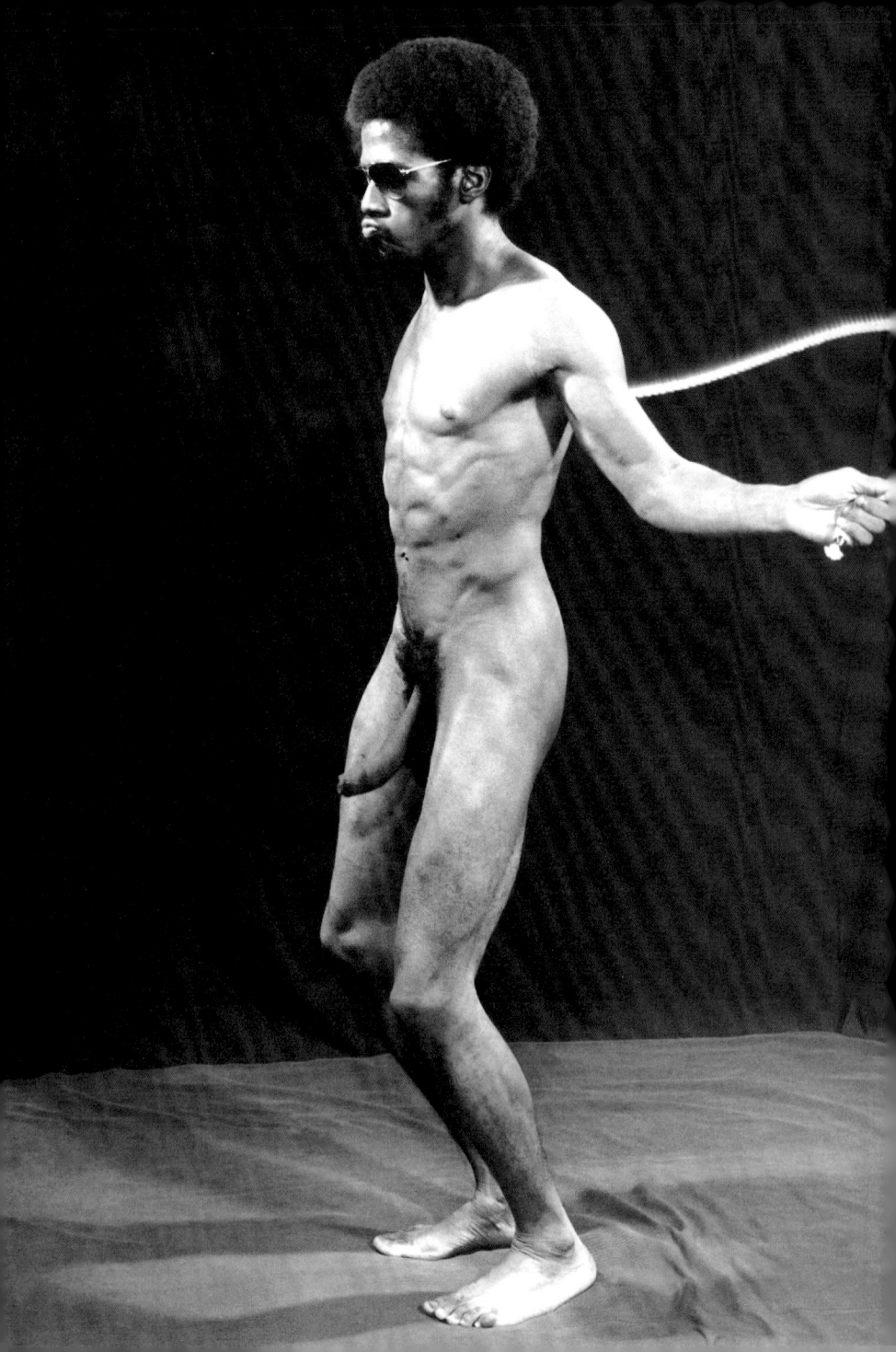

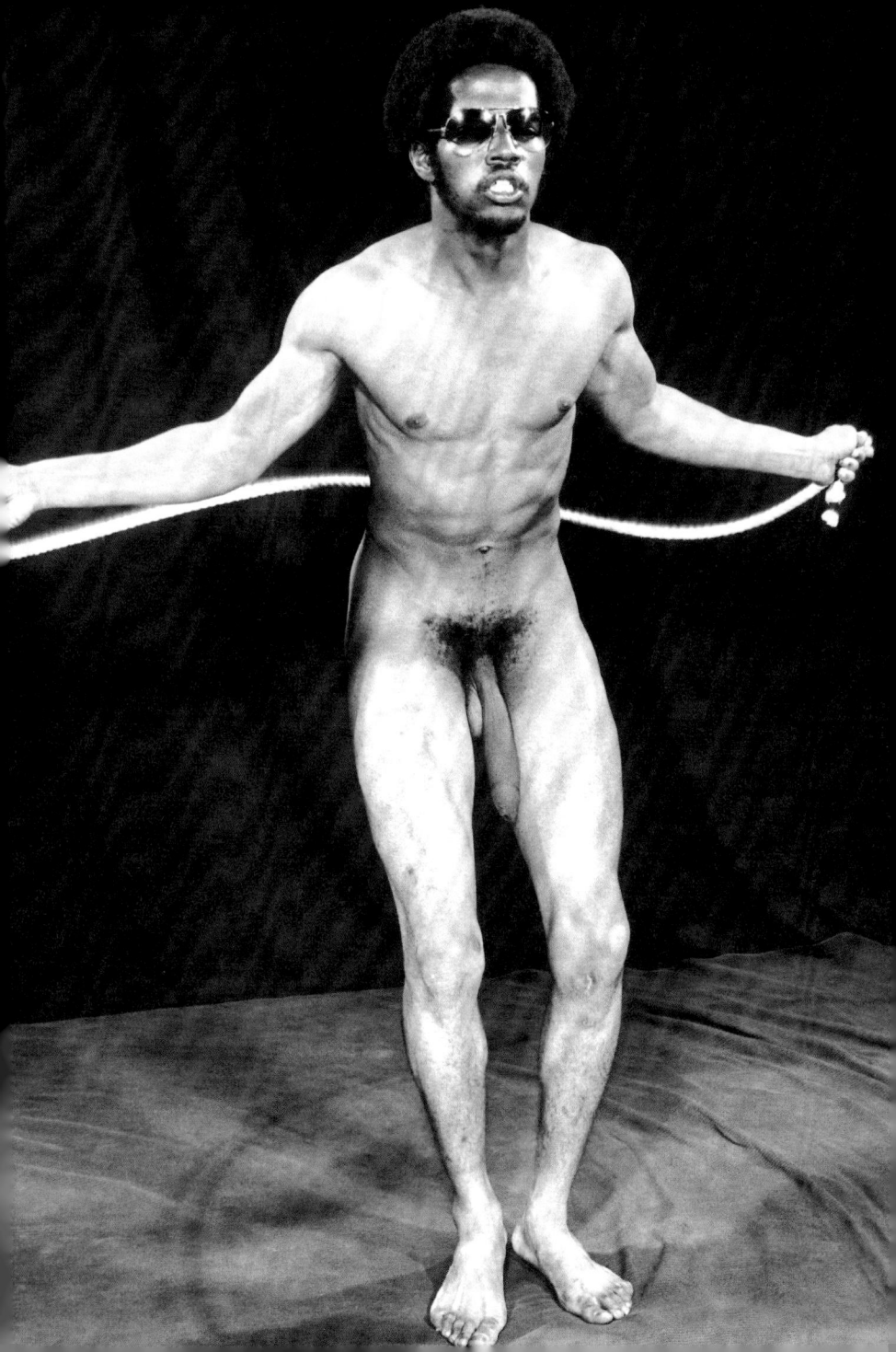

PAGES 186-187 **Unknown**   OPPOSITE **Long Dong Silver**

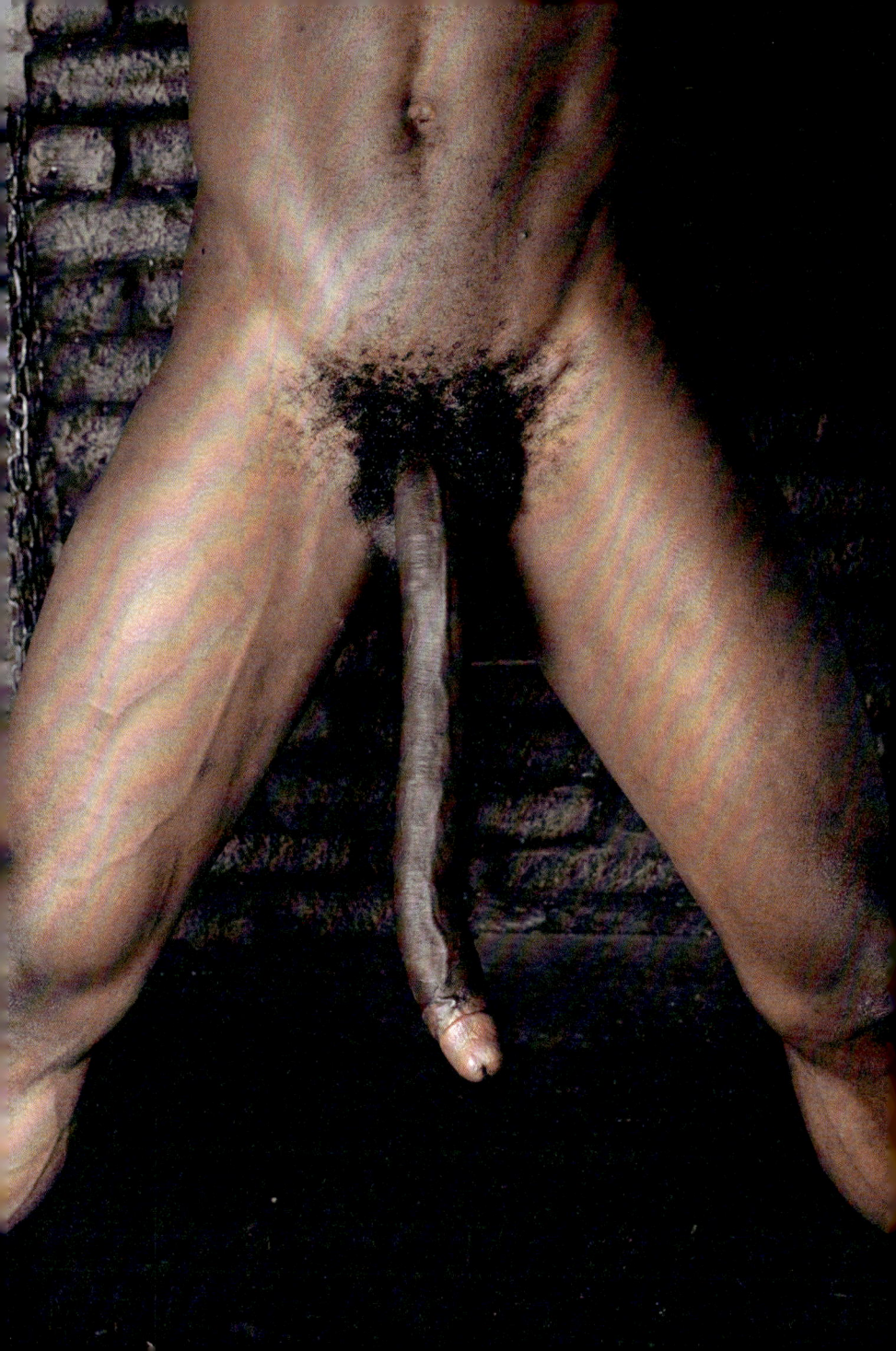

Acknowledgments

I would like to thank all the photographers and their archives for contributing to this book. They are, in alphabetical order: Mike Arlen ©: pages 148–161; Athletic Model Guild © bobmizer.org: pages 34–51; Fred Bisonnes for Advocate Men ©: pages 122/123, 125, 128, 129, 130 and 132; Fred Bisonnes for Falcon Studios © falconstudios.com: pages 120, 121, 124, 126, 127, 131 and 133; Colt Studio © COLTstudiogroup.com: pages 60–68/69; Falcon Studios © falconstudios.com: pages 100–113; Filmco: pages 134/135–147; Jack Fritscher © jackfritscher. com: page 183; Dian Hanson Collection: pages 6, 7, 8, 9 and 14; Charles Hovland © chuckpixxx.com: pages 162–173; Eric Kroll Collection: pages 22 (left) and 176; Lobo Studio ©: pages 114/115–118/119; The Magazine Archives, SF: pages 2, 10, 15, 16, 18, 20, 23, 24, 25, 26, 27, 29, 30, 31 and 32; Jay Myrdal ©: page 189; Old Reliable © David Hurles: pages 82/83–98/99; Private Collections: Endpapers, pages 12, 17, 21, 22 (right), 28, 33, 174/175, 177, 178, 179, 180, 181, 182, 184, 185 and 191; Sierra Domino Studios © Craig Calvin Anderson: pages 4, 52–58/59, 186 and 187; Third World Studios/Jim Jaeger © David Klein, zebrastuds.com: pages 70, 71, 72, 73, 74, 75, 76/77, 79, 80 and 192; David Klein © Zebra Studios Collection: pages 78 and 81.

In addition, special thanks to Ed Fox for his cover photos of the awesome Chad Hunt, to Sven Kirsten for the Tiki god on page 1 and to Josh Baker and Jessica Sappenfield for design.

Any credit omissions are unintentional, and appropriate credit will be given in future editions if such copyright holders contact the publisher.

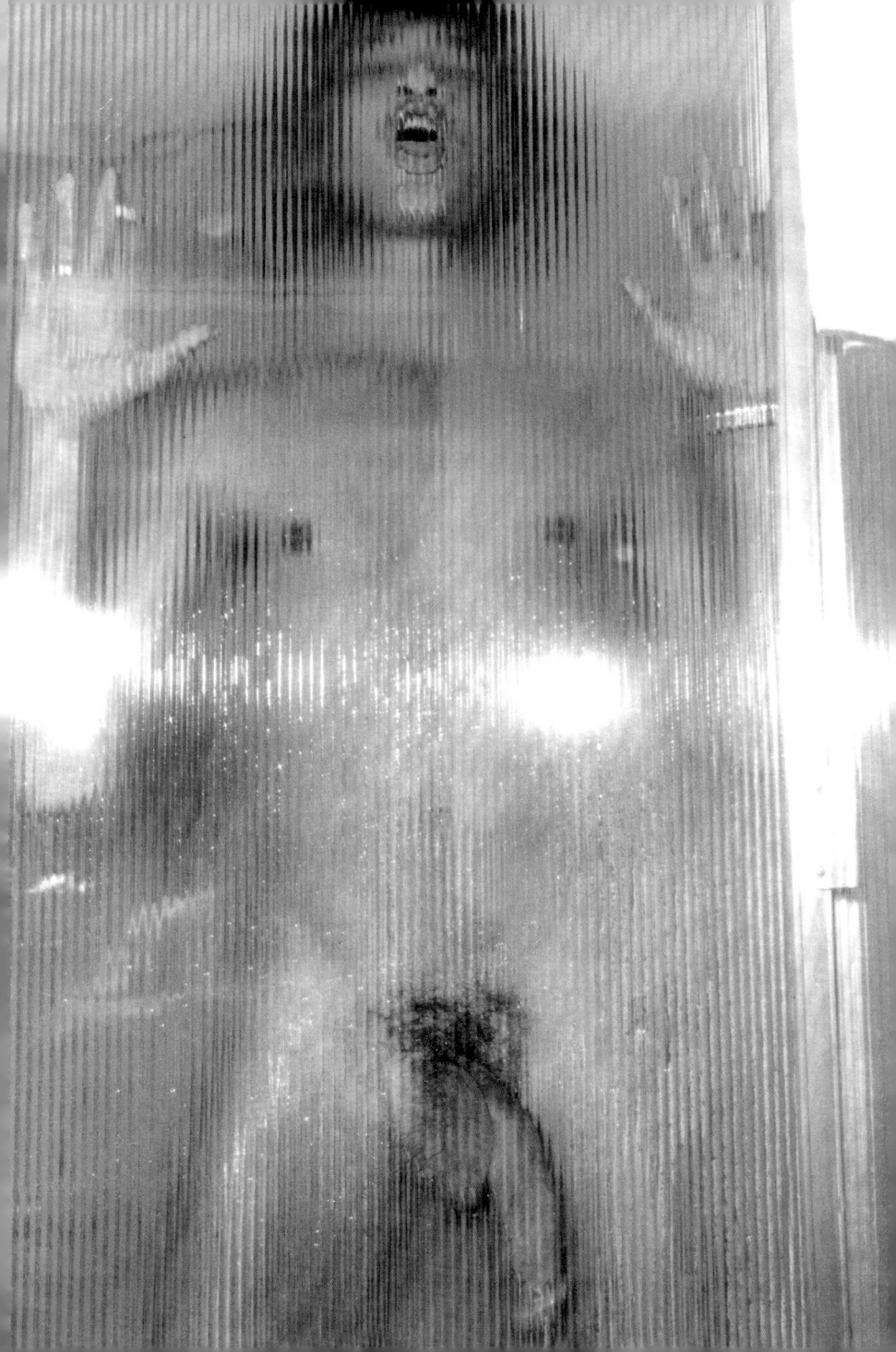

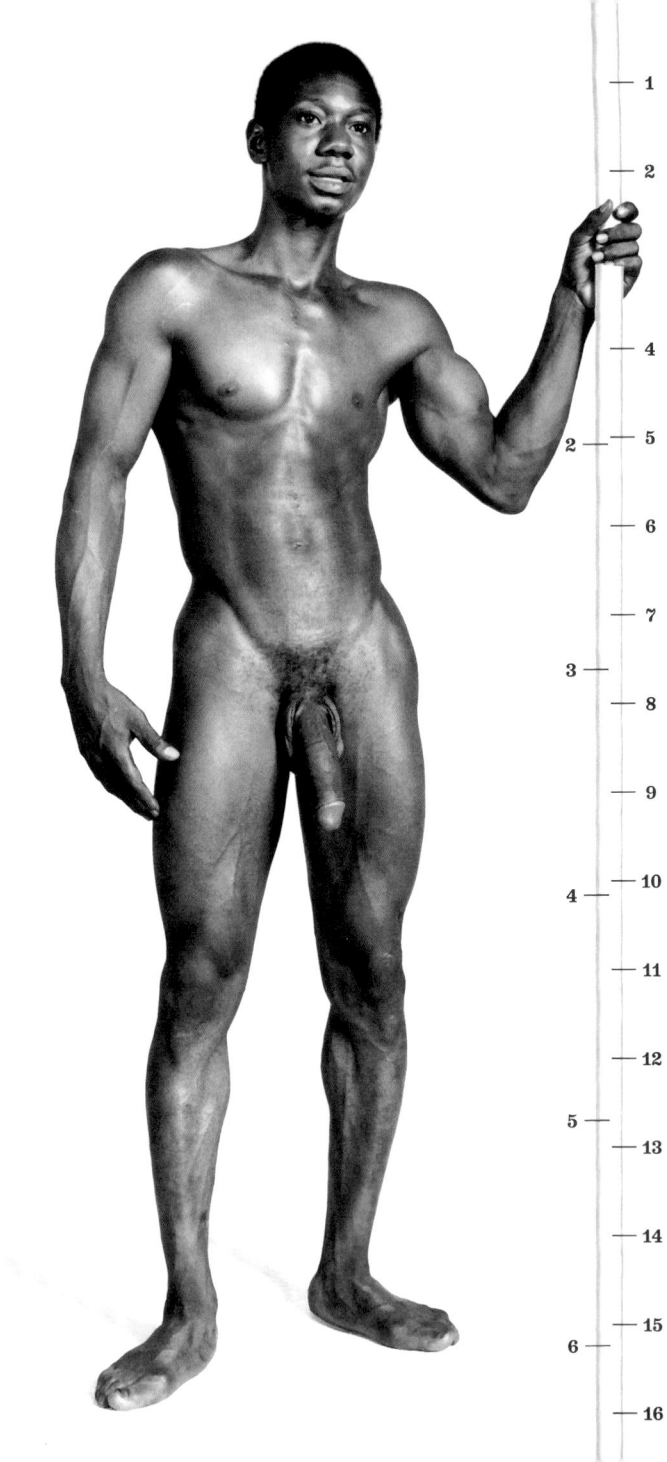

1

2

4

2 — 5

6

7

3 — 8

9

4 — 10

11

12

5 — 13

14

6 — 15

16

FRONT AND BACK COVERS Chad Hunt by Ed Fox
ENDPAPERS John Holmes, circa 1978
PAGE 1 Tiki stud courtesy Sven Kirsten
PAGE 2 Sausage with mustard, circa 1970
PAGE 191 Porn superstar John Holmes in the shower, circa 1978
LEFT Third World Studios model Shark, circa 1978

EACH AND EVERY TASCHEN BOOK PLANTS A SEED!
TASCHEN is a carbon neutral publisher. Each year, we offset our annual carbon emissions with carbon credits at the Instituto Terra, a reforestation program in Minas Gerais, Brazil, founded by Lélia and Sebastião Salgado. To find out more about this ecological partnership, please check: www.taschen.com/zerocarbon
Inspiration: unlimited. Carbon footprint: zero

To stay informed about TASCHEN and our upcoming titles, please subscribe to our free magazine at www.taschen.com/magazine, follow us on Instagram and Facebook, or e-mail your questions to contact@taschen.com.

© 2021 TASCHEN GmbH
Hohenzollernring 53, D-50672 Köln
www.taschen.com

German translation by Harald Hellmann, Cologne
French translation by Alice Pétillot, Bayonne

Printed in Slovakia
ISBN 978-3-8365-7891-2

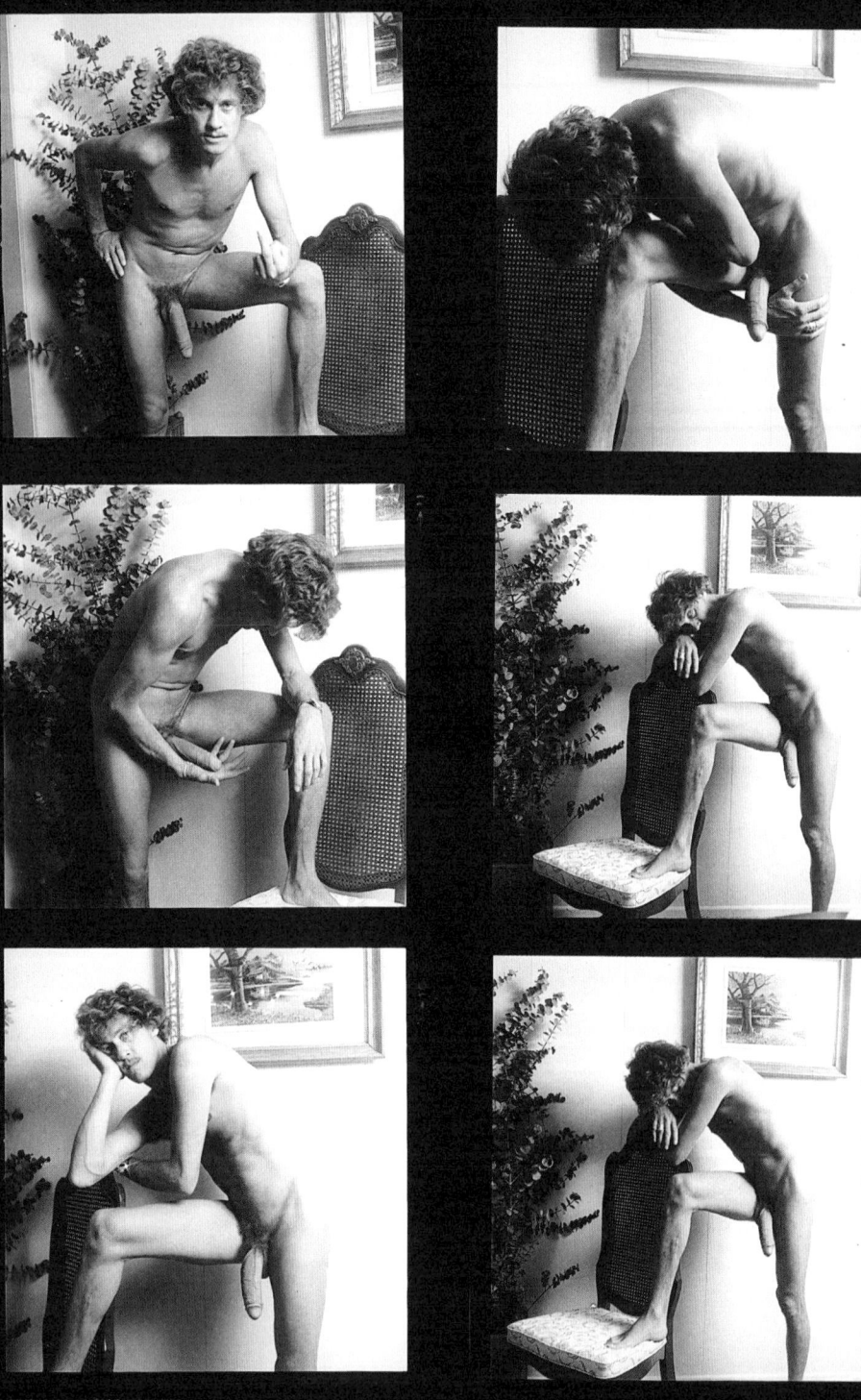